Thackray's 2021 Investor's Guide

THACKRAY'S
2021
INVESTOR'S GUIDE

Brooke Thackray MBA, CIM

Published in 2020 by: MountAlpha Media:

alphamountain.com

Brooke Thackray is a research analyst for Horizons ETFs Management (Canada) Inc. All of the views expressed herein are the personal views of the author and are not necessarily the views of Horizons ETFs Management (Canada) Inc., although any of the strategies/recommendations found herein may be reflected in positions or transactions in the various client portfolios managed by Horizons ETFs Management (Canada) Inc. Securities (if any) discussed in this publication are meant to highlight investment strategies for educational purposes only not investment advice.

Horizons ETFs is a Member of Mirae Asset Global Investments. Commissions, management fees and expenses all may be associated with an investment in exchange traded products managed by Horizons ETFs Management (Canada) Inc. (the "Horizons Exchange Traded Products"). The Horizons Exchange Traded Products are not guaranteed, their values change frequently and past performance may not be repeated. The prospectus contains important detailed information about the Horizons Exchange Traded Products. **Please read the relevant prospectus before investing**.

ISBN13: 978-1-989125-04-5

Printed and Bound in Canada by Marquis.

To my wife Jane

Acknowledgments

This book is the product of many years of research and could not have been written without the help of many people. I would like to thank my wife, Jane Steer-Thackray, and my children Justin, Megan, Carly and Madeleine, for the help they have given me and their patience during the many hours that I have devoted to writing this book.

INTRODUCTION

2021 THACKRAY'S INVESTOR'S GUIDE
Technical Commentary

The seasonal strategies that I have included in my previous books have proven to be very successful. The buy and sell dates are based upon iterative comparisons of different time periods measured by gain and frequency of success. Although the buy and sell dates are the optimal dates on which seasonal investors should focus on making their investment decisions, the markets have different dynamics from year to year, shifting the optimal buy and sell dates. Combining technical analysis with seasonal trends helps to adjust the decision process, allowing seasonal investors to enter and exit trades early or late, depending on market conditions.

The universe of technical indicators and techniques is huge. It is impossible to use all of the indicators. Only a small number of indicators and techniques that suit an investment style should be used. In the case of seasonal investing, a lot of long-term indicators provide little benefit. For example, the standard Moving Average Convergence Divergence (MACD), is too slow to be of use in shorter term seasonal strategies. In this book I have chosen to illustrate three technical indicators that can provide value in fine-tuning the dates for seasonal investing: Full Stochastic Oscillator (FSO), Relative Strength Index (RSI) and Relative Strength. The indicators are used in conjunction with the price pattern and moving averages of the security being considered. Investors must remember that technical analysis is not absolute and there will be exceptions when utilizing indicators and price patterns.

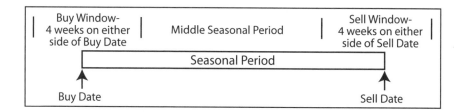

To combine technical indicators with seasonal trends, it is best that the indicators be used within the windows of the buy and sell dates. The indicators should be ignored outside the seasonal buy/sell windows. An exception to this occurs when an indicator gives a signal during its middle seasonal period, which is in the seasonal period, but after the buy window and before the sell window. In this case a technical signal can support selling a full position based upon a fundamental breakdown in the price action of a security. By itself, a FSO or RSI indicator showing weakness in a security during its middle seasonal period, does not necessarily warrant action, it can be used to support a decision being made in conjunction with underperformance relative to the broad market, or a major price action break.

Below are short descriptions of three technical indicators that can be used with seasonal analysis. Full evaluation of the indicators and their uses with seasonal analysis is beyond the scope of this book.

Full Stochastic Oscillator (FSO)

A stochastic oscillator is a range bound momentum indicator that tracks the location of the close price relative to the high-low range, over a set number of periods. It tracks the momentum of price change and helps to indicate the strength and direction of price movement.

I have found that generally the best method to combine the FSO with seasonal trends is to buy an early partial position when the FSO turns up above 20 within four weeks of the seasonal buy date. Additionally, the best time to sell an early partial position occurs when the FSO turns below 80, within four weeks of the seasonal exit date.

Relative Strength Index (RSI)

The RSI is a momentum oscillator that measures the speed and change of price movements. I have found that the best method to combine the RSI with seasonal trends is to buy an early partial position when the RSI turns up above 30 within four weeks of the seasonal buy date. The best time to sell an early partial position occurs when the RSI turns below 70, within four weeks of the seasonal exit date. Compared with the FSO, the RSI is less useful as it is slower and gives too few signals in the buy/sell windows.

Relative Strength

Relative strength calculates the performance of one security versus another security. When the relative strength is increasing, it indicates the seasonal security is outperforming. When the relative strength is declining, the seasonal security is underperforming. When a downward trend line is broken to the upside by the performance of the seasonal security, relative to the benchmark, this is a positive signal. This action carries a lot of weight and can justify a full early entry into a position if other technical evidence is positive. Likewise, if an upward trend line is broken to the downside, a negative technical signal is given and can justify a full early exit from a position if other technical evidence is negative.

THACKRAY'S 2021 INVESTOR'S GUIDE

You can choose great companies to invest in and still underperform the market. Unless you are in the market at the right time and in the best sectors, your investment expertise can be all for naught.

Successful investors know when they should be in the market. Very successful investors know when they should be in the market, and the best sectors in which to invest. *Thackray's 2021 Investor's Guide* is designed to provide investors with the knowledge of when and what to buy, and when to sell.

The goal of this book is to help investors capture extra profits by taking advantage of the seasonal trends in the markets. This book is straightforward. There are no complicated rules and there are no complex algorithms. The strategies put forward are intuitive and easy to understand.

It does not matter if you are a short-term or long-term investor, this book can be used to help establish entry and exit points. For the short-term investor, specific periods are identified that can provide profitable opportunities. For the long-term investor best buy dates are identified to launch new investments on a sound footing.

The stock market has its seasonal rhythms. Historically, the broad markets, such as the S&P 500, have a seasonal trend of outperforming during certain times of the year. Likewise, different sectors of the market have their own seasonal trends of outperformance. When oil stocks tend to do well in the springtime before "driving season," health care stocks tend to underperform the market. When utilities do well in the summertime, industrials do not. With different markets and different sectors having a tendency to outperform at different times of the year, there is always a place to invest.

Until recently, investors did not have access to the information necessary to analyse and create sector strategies. In recent years there have been a great number of sector Exchange Traded Funds (ETFs) and sector indexes introduced into the market. For the first time, investors are now able to easily implement a sector rotation strategy. This book provides a seasonal road map of what sectors tend to do well at different times of the year. It is a first of its kind, revealing new sector-based strategies that have never before been published.

In terms of market timing there are ample strategies in this book to help determine the times when equities should be over or underweight. During a favorable time for the market, investments can be purchased to overweight equities relative to their target weight in a portfolio (staying within risk tolerances). During an unfavorable time, investments can be sold to underweight equities relative to their target.

A large part of the book is devoted to sector seasonality – the underpinnings for a sector rotation strategy. The most practical rotation strategy is to create a core part of a portfolio that represents the broad market and then set aside an allocation to be rotated between favored sectors from one time period to the next.

It does not makes sense to apply any investment strategy only once with a large investment. Seasonal strategies are no exception. The best way to apply an investment strategy is to use a disciplined methodology that allows for diversification and a large enough number of investments to help remove the anomalies of the market. This reduces risk and increases the probability of a long term gain.

Following the specific buy and sell dates put forth in this book would have netted an investor large, above market returns. To "turbo-charge" gains, an investor can combine seasonality with technical analysis. As the seasonal periods are never exactly the same, technical analysis can help investors capture the extra gains when a sector turns up early, or momentum extends the trend.

IMPORTANT: Strategy Buy and Sell Dates

The beginning date of every strategy period in this book represents a full day in the market; therefore, investors should buy at the end of the preceding market day. For example the *Biotech Summer Solstice* seasonal period of strength is from June 23rd to September 13th. To be in the sector for the full seasonal period, an investor would enter the market before the closing bell on June 22nd. If the buy date landed on a weekend or holiday, then the buy would occur at the end of the preceding trading day.

The last day of a trading strategy is the sell date. For example, the Biotech sector investment would be sold at the end of the day on September 13th. If the sell date is a holiday or weekend, then the investment would be sold at the close on the preceding trading day.

What is Seasonal Investing?

In order to properly understand seasonal investing in the stock market, it is important to look briefly at its evolution. It may surprise investors to know that seasonal investing at the broad market level, i.e. Dow Jones or S&P 500, has been around for a long time. The initial seasonal strategies were written by Fields (1931, 1934) and Watchel (1942), who focused on the *January Effect*. Coincidentally, this strategy is still bantered about in the press every year.

Yale Yirsch Senior has been largely responsible for the next stage in the evolution, producing the *Stock Trader's Almanac* for more than forty years. This publication focuses on broad market trends such as the best six months of the year and tendencies of the market to do well depending on the political party in power and holiday trades.

In 2000, Brooke Thackray and Bruce Lindsay wrote, *Time In Time Out: Outsmart the Market Using Calendar Investment Strategies*. This work focused on a comprehensive analysis of the six month seasonal cycle and other shorter seasonal cycles in the broad markets such as the S&P 500.

Seasonal investing has changed over time. The focus has shifted from broad market strategies to taking advantage of sector rotation opportunities – investing in different sectors at different times of the year, depending on their seasonal strength. This has created a whole new set of investment opportunities. Rather than just being "in or out" of the market, investors can now always be invested by shifting between different sectors and asset classes, taking advantage of both up and down markets.

Definition – Seasonal investing is a method of investing in the market at the time of the year when it typically does well, or investing in a sector of the market when it typically outperforms the broad market such as the S&P 500.

The term seasonal investing is somewhat of a misnomer, and it is easy to see why some investors might believe that the discipline relates to investing based upon the seasons of the year – winter, spring, summer and autumn. Other than some agricultural commodities where the price is often correlated to growing seasons, generally seasonal investment strategies use the calendar as a reference for buy and sell dates. It is usually a specific event, i.e. Christmas sales, that occurs on a recurring annual basis that creates the seasonal opportunity.

The discipline of seasonal investing is not restricted to the stock market. It has been used successfully for a number of years in the commodities market. The opportunities in this market tend to be based upon changes in supply and/or demand that occur on a yearly basis. Most commodities, especially the agricultural commodities, tend to have cyclical supply cycles, i.e., crops are harvested only at certain times of the year. The supply bulge that occurs at the same time every year provides seasonal investors with profit opportunities. Recurring increased seasonal demand for commodities also plays a major part in providing opportunities for seasonal investors. This applies to most metals and many other commodities, whether the end-product is industrial or consumer based.

Seasonal investment strategies can be used with a lot of different types of investments. The premise is the same, outperformance during a certain period of the year based upon a repeating event in the markets or economy. In my past writings I have developed seasonal strategies that have been used successfully in the stock, commodity, bond and foreign exchange markets. Seasonal investing is still relatively new for most markets with a lot of new opportunities waiting to be discovered.

How Does Seasonal Investing Work?

Most stock market sector seasonal trends are the result of a recurring annual catalyst: an event that affects the sector positively. These events can range from a seasonal spike in demand, seasonal inventory lows, weather effects, conferences and other events. Mainstream investors very often anticipate a move in a sector and incorrectly try to take a position just before an event takes place that is supposed to drive a sector higher. A good example of this would be investors buying oil just before the cold weather sets in. Unfortunately, their efforts are usually unsuccessful as they are too late to the party and the opportunity has already passed.

By the time the anticipated event occurs, a substantial amount of investors have bought into the sector – fully pricing in the expected benefit. At this time there is little potential left in the short-term. Unless there is a strong positive surprise, the sector's outperformance tends to slowly roll over. If the event produces less than its desired result, the sector can be severely punished.

So how does the seasonal investor take advantage of this opportunity? "Be there" before the mainstream investors, and get out before they do. Seasonal investors usually enter a sector two or three months before an event is anticipated to have a positive effect on a sector and get out before the actual event takes place. In essence, seasonal investors are benefiting from the mainstream investor's tendency to "buy in" too late.

Seasonality in the markets occurs because of three major reasons: money flow, changing market analyst expectations and the *Anticipation-Realization Cycle*. First, money flows vary throughout the year and at different times of the month. Generally, money flows increase at the end of the year and into the start of the next year. This is a result of year end bonuses and tax related investments. In addition, money flows increase at month end from money managers "window dressing" their portfolios. As a result of these money flows, the months around the end of the year and the days around the end of the month, tend to have a stronger performance than the other times of the year.

Second, the analyst expectations cycle tends to push markets up at the end of the year and the beginning of the next year. Stock market analysts tend to be a positive bunch – the large investment houses pay them to be positive. They start the year with aggressive earnings for all of their favorite companies. As the year progresses, they generally back off their earnings forecast, which decreases their support for the market. After a lull in the summer and early autumn months, they start to focus on the next year with another rosy forecast. As a result, the stock market tends to rise once again at the end of the year.

Third, at the sector level, sectors of the market tend to be greatly influenced by the *Anticipation-Realization Cycle*. Although some investors may not be familiar with the term "anticipation-realization," they probably are familiar with the concept of "buy the rumor – sell the fact," or in the famous words of Lord Rothschild "Buy on the sound of the war-cannons; sell on the sound of the victory trumpets."

The *Anticipation-Realization Cycle* as it applies to human behavior has been much studied in psychology journals. In the investment world, the premise of this cycle rests on investors anticipating a positive event in the market to drive prices higher and buying in ahead of the event. When the event takes place, or is realized, upward pressure on prices decreases as there is very little impetus for further outperformance.

A good example of the *Anticipation-Realization Cycle* takes place with the "conference effect." Very often large industries have major conferences that occur at approximately the same time every year. Major companies in the industry often hold back positive announce-

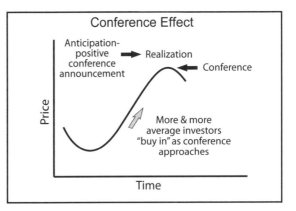

ments and product introductions to be released during the conference.

Two to three months prior to the conference, seasonal investors tend to buy into the sector. Shortly afterwards, the mainstream investors anticipate "good news" from the conference and start to buy in. As a result, prices are pushed up. Just before the conference starts, seasonal investors capture their profits by exiting their positions. As the conference unfolds, company announcements are made (realized), but as the potential good news has already been priced into the sector, there is little to push prices higher and the sector typically starts to rolls over.

The same *Anticipation-Realization Cycle* takes place with increased demand for oil to meet the "summer driving season", increased sales of goods at Christmas time, increased demand for gold jewellery to meet the autumn and winter demand, and many other events that tend to drive the outperformance of different sectors.

Does Seasonal Investing ALWAYS Work?

The simple answer to the above question is "No." There is not any investment system in the world that works all of the time. When following any investment system, it is probability of success that counts. It has often been said that "being correct in the markets 60% of the time will make you rich." Investors tend to forget this and become too emotionally attached to their losses. Just about every investment trading book states that investors typically fail to let their profits run and cut their losses quickly. I concur. In my many years in the investment industry, the biggest mistake that I have found with investors is not being able to cut their losses. Everyone wants to be right, that is how we have been raised. Investors feel that if they sell at a loss they have failed, and as a result, often suffer bigger losses by waiting for their position to trade at profit. With any investment system, investors should let probability work for them. This means that investors should be able to enter and exit positions capturing both gains and losses without becoming emotionally attached to any posi-

XOI vs S&P 500 1984 to 2019			
Feb 25 to May 9	S&P 500	positive XOI	Diff
1984	1.7 %	5.6 %	3.9 %
1985	1.4	4.9	3.5
1986	6.0	7.7	1.7
1987	3.7	25.5	21.8
1988	-3.0	5.6	8.6
1989	6.3	8.1	1.8
1990	5.8	-0.6	-6.3
1991	4.8	6.8	2.0
1992	0.9	5.8	4.9
1993	0.3	6.3	6.0
1994	-4.7	3.2	7.9
1995	7.3	10.3	3.1
1996	-2.1	2.2	4.3
1997	1.8	4.7	2.9
1998	7.5	9.8	2.3
1999	7.3	35.4	28.1
2000	4.3	22.2	17.9
2001	0.8	10.2	9.4
2002	-1.5	5.3	6.9
2003	12.1	5.7	-6.4
2004	-3.5	4.0	7.5
2005	-1.8	-1.0	0.8
2006	2.8	9.4	6.6
2007	4.2	10.1	5.8
2008	2.6	7.6	5.0
2009	20.2	15.8	-4.4
2010	0.5	-2.3	-2.8
2011	3.1	-0.6	-3.7
2012	-0.8	-13.4	-12.5
2013	7.3	3.8	-3.5
2014	1.7	9.1	7.4
2015	0.3	1.2	1.1
2016	6.7	11.1	4.4
2017	1.3	-4.0	-5.2
2018	-1.8	15.4	17.2
2019	2.8	-2.6	-5.4
Avg	2.9 %	6.9 %	4.0 %
Fq > 0	78 %	81 %	75 %

tions. Emotional attachment clouds judgement, which leads to errors. When all of the trades are put together, the goal is for profits to be larger than losses in a way that minimizes risks and beats the market.

If we examine the winter oil stock trade, we can see how probability has worked in an investor's favor. This trade is based upon the premise that at the tail end of winter, the refineries drive up demand for oil in order to produce enough gas for the approaching "driving season" that starts in the spring. As a result, oil stocks tend to increase and outperform the market (from February 25 to May 9). The oil stock sector, represented by the NYSE Arca Oil Index (XOI), has been very successful at this time of year, producing an average return of 6.9% and beating the S&P 500 by 4.0%, from 1984 to 2019. In addition it has been positive 29 out of 36 times. Investors should always evaluate the strength of seasonal trades before applying them to their own portfolios.

If an investor started using the seasonal investment discipline in 1984 and chose to invest in the winter-oil trade, they would have been very happy with the results. If an investor started using the strategy in 2010 a loss would have occurred following the strategy. The fact that the strategy did not produce gains in 2010, 2011 and 2012, does not mean that the seasonal trade no longer works. All seasonal trades go through periods, sometimes multiple years where they do not work. An investor can start any methodology of trading at the "wrong time," and be unsuccessful in a particular trade. In fact, if an investor started the oil-winter trade in 1990 and had given up in the same year, they would have missed the following successful twelve years. Investors have to remember that it is the final score that counts, after all of the gains have been weighed against the losses.

In practical terms, investors should not put all of their investment strategies in one basket. If one or two large investments were made based upon seasonal strategies, it is possible that the seasonal methodology might be inappropriately evaluated and its use discontinued. A much more prudent strategy is to use a larger number of strategic seasonal investments with smaller investments. The end result will be to put the seasonal probability to work with a much greater chance of success.

Measuring Seasonal Performance

How do you determine if a seasonal strategy has been successful? Many people feel that ten years of data is a good sample size, others feel that fifteen years is better, and yet others feel that the more data the better. I tend to fall into the camp that, if possible, it is best to use fifteen or twenty years of data for sectors and more data for the broad markets, such as the S&P 500. Although the most recent data in almost any analytical framework is the most relevant, it is important to get enough data to reflect a sector's performance across different economic conditions. Given that historically the economy has performed on an eight year cycle, four years of expansion and then four years of contraction, using a short data set does not provide for enough exposure to different economic conditions.

A data set that is too long can run into the problem of older data having too much of an influence on the numbers when fundamental factors affecting a sector have changed. It is important to look at trends over time and assess if there has been a change that should be considered in determining the dates for a seasonal cycle. Each sector should be judged on its own merit. The analysis tables in this book illustrate the performance level for each year in order to provide the opportunity for readers to determine any relevant changes.

In order to determine if a seasonal strategy is effective there are two possible benchmarks, absolute and relative performance. Absolute performance measures if a profit is made and relative performance measures the performance of a sector in relationship to a major market. Both measurements have their merits and depending on your investment style, one measurement may be more valuable than another. This book provides both sets of measurement in tables and graphs.

It is not just the average percent gain of a sector over a certain time period that determines success. It is possible that one or two spectacular years of performance skew the results substantially (particularly with a small data set). The frequency of success is also very important: the higher the percentage of success the better. Also, the fewer large drawdowns the better. There is no magic number (percent success rate) per se of what constitutes a successful strategy. The success rate should be above fifty percent, otherwise it would be better to just invest in the broad market. Ideally speaking a strategy should have a high percentage success rate on both an absolute and relative basis. Some strategies are stronger than others, but that does not mean that the weaker strategies should not be used. Prudence should be used in determining the ideal portfolio allocation.

Illustrating the strength of a sector's seasonal performance can be accomplished through either an absolute yearly average performance graph, or a relative yearly average performance graph. The absolute graph shows the average yearly cumulative gain for a set number of years. It lets a reader visually identify the strong periods during the year. The relative graph shows the average yearly cumulative gain for the sector relative to the benchmark index.

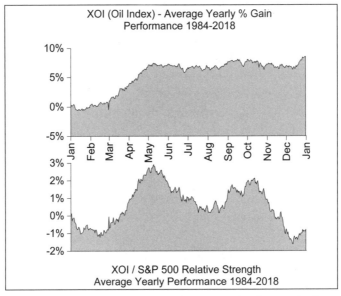

Both graphs are useful in determining the strength of a particular seasonal strategy. In the above diagram, the top graph illustrates the average year for the NYSE Arca Oil Index (XOI) from 1984 to 2018. Essentially it illustrates the cumulative average gain if an investment were made in the index. The steep rising line starting in January/February shows the overall price rise that typically occurs in this sector at this time of year. In May the line flattens out and then rises very modestly starting in July.

The bottom graph is a ratio graph, illustrating the strength of the XOI Index relative to the S&P 500. It is derived by dividing the average year of the XOI by the average year of the S&P 500. When the line in the graph is rising, the XOI is outperforming the S&P 500, and vise versa when it is declining. This is an important graph and should be used in considering seasonal investments because the S&P 500 is a viable alternative to the energy sector. If both markets are increasing, but the S&P 500 is increasing at a faster rate, the S&P 500 represents a more attractive opportunity. This is particularly true when measuring the risk of a volatile sector relative to the broad market. If both investments were expected to produce the same rate of return, generally the broad market is a better investment because of its diversification.

Who Can Use Seasonal Investing?

Any investor from novice to expert, from short-term trader to long-term investor can benefit from using seasonal analysis. Seasonal investing is unique because it is an easy to understand system that can be used by itself or as a complement to another investment discipline. For the novice it provides an easy to follow strategy that makes intuitive sense. For the expert it can be used as a stand-alone system or as a complement to an existing system.

Seasonal investing is easily understood by all levels of investors, which allows investors to make rational decisions. This may seem obvious, but it is very common for investors to listen to a "guru of the market", be impressed and blindly follow his advice. When the advice works there is no problem. When the advice does not work investors wonder why they made the investment in the first place. When investors do not understand their investments it causes stress, bad decisions and a lack of "stick-to-it ness" with any investment discipline. Even expert investors realize the importance of understanding your investments. Peter Lynch of Fidelity Investments used to say "Never invest in any idea that you can't illustrate with a crayon." Investors do not need to go that far, but they should understand their investments.

Novice investors find seasonal strategies very easy to understand because they are intuitive. They do not have to be investing for years to understand why seasonal strategies work. They understand that an increase in demand for gold every year at the same time causes a ripple effect in the stock market pushing up gold stocks at the same time every year.

Most expert investors use information from a variety of sources in making their decisions. Even experts that primarily use fundamental analysis can benefit from using seasonal trends to get an edge in the market. Fundamental analysis is a very crude tool and provides very little in the way of timing an investment. Using seasonal trends can help with the timing of the buy and sell decisions and produce extra profit.

Seasonal investing can be used by both short-term and long-term investors, but in different ways. For short-term investors it provides a complete trade – buy and sell dates. For long-term investors it can provide a buy date for a sector of interest.

Combining Seasonal Analysis with other Investment Disciplines

Seasonal investing used by itself has historically produced above average market returns. Depending on an investor's particular style, it can be combined with one of the other three investment disciplines: fundamental, quantitative and technical analysis. There are two basic ways to combine seasonal analysis with other investment methodologies – as the primary or secondary method. If it is used as a primary method, seasonally strong time periods are established for a number of sectors and then appropriate sectors are chosen based upon fundamental, quantitative or technical screens. If it is used as a secondary method, sector selections are first made based upon one of three methods and then final sectors are chosen based upon which ones are in their seasonally strong period.

Technical analysis is an ideal mate for seasonal analysis. Unlike fundamental and quantitative analysis, which are very blunt timing tools at best, seasonal and technical analysis can provide specific trigger points to buy and sell. The combination can turbo-charge investment strategies, adding extra profits by fine-tuning entry and exit dates.

Seasonal analysis provides both buy and sell dates. Although a sector in the market can sometimes bottom on the exact seasonal buy date, it more often bottoms a bit early or a bit late. After all, the seasonal buy date is based upon an average of historical performance. Depending on the sector, buying opportunities start to develop approximately one month before and after the seasonal buy date. Using technical analysis gives an investor the advantage of buying into a sector when it turns up early or waiting when it turns up late. Likewise, technical analysis can be used to trigger a sell signal when the market turns down before or after the sell date.

The sell decision can be extended with the help of a trailing stop-loss order. If a sector has strong momentum and the technical tools do not provide a sell signal, it is possible to let the sector "run." When a trailing stop-loss is used, a profitable sell point is established. If the price continues to run, then the selling point is raised. If, on the other hand, the price falls through the stop-loss point, the position is sold.

Sectors of the Market

Standard & Poor's has done an excellent job in categorizing the U.S. stock market into its different parts. Although the demand for this service initially came from institutional investors, many individual investors now seek the same information. Knowing the sector breakdown in the market allows investors to see how different their portfolio is relative to the market. As a result, they are able to make conscious decisions on what parts of the stock market to overweight based upon their beliefs of which sectors will outperform. It also helps control the amount of desired risk.

Standard & Poor's uses four levels of detail in its Global Industry Classification Standard (GICS©) to categorize stock markets around the world. From the most specific, it classifies companies into sub-industries, industries, industry groups and finally economic sectors. All companies in the Standard & Poor's global family of indices are classified according to the GICS structure.

This book focuses on the U.S. market, analysing the trends of the venerable S&P 500 index and its economic sectors and industry groups. The following diagram illustrates the index classified according to its economic sectors.

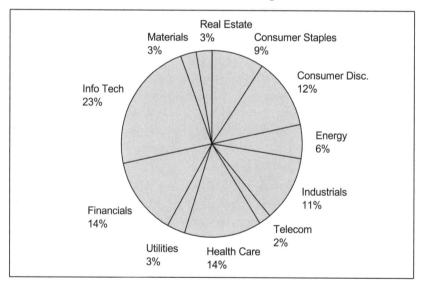

Standard and Poor's, Understanding Sectors, June 30, 2017

For more information on Standard and Poor's Global Industry Classification Standard (GICS©), refer to www.standardandpoors.com

Investment Products –
Which One Is The Right One?

There are many ways to take advantage of the seasonal trends at the broad stock market and sector levels. Regardless of the investment products that you currently use, whether exchange traded funds, mutual funds, stocks or options, all can be used with the strategies in this book. Different investments offer different risk-reward relationships and return potential.

Exchange Traded Funds (ETFs)

Exchange Traded Funds (ETFs) offer the purest method of seasonal investment. The broad market ETFs are designed to track the major indices and the sector ETFs are designed to track specific sectors without using active management. Relatively new, ETFs are a great way to capture both market and sector trends. They were originally introduced into the Canadian market in 1993 to represent the Toronto stock market index. Shortly afterward they were introduced to the U.S. market and there are now hundreds of ETFs to represent almost every market, sector, style of investing and company capitalization. Originally ETFs were mainly of interest to institutional investors, but individual investors have fast realized the merits of ETF investing and have made some of the broad market ETFs the most heavily traded securities in the world.

An ETF is a single security that represents a market, such as the S&P 500; a sector of the market, such as the financial sector; or a commodity, such as gold. In the case of the S&P 500, an investor buying one security is buying all 500 stocks in the index. By investing into a financial ETF, an investor is buying the companies that make up the financial sector of the market. By investing into a gold commodity ETF, an investor is buying a security that represents the price of gold.

ETFs trade on the open market just like stocks. They have a bid and an ask, can be shorted and many are option eligible. They are a very low cost, tax efficient method of targeting specific parts of the market.

Mutual Funds

Mutual funds are a good way to combine market or sector investing with active management. In recent years, many mutual fund companies have added sector funds to accommodate an increasing appetite in this area.

As the seasonal strategies put forward in this book have a short-term nature, it is important to make sure that there are no fees (or a nominal charge) for getting into and out of a position in the market.

Stocks

Stocks provide an opportunity to make better returns than the market or sector. If the market increases during its seasonal period, some stocks will increase dramatically more than the index. Choosing one of the outperforming stocks will greatly enhance returns; choosing one of the underperforming stocks can create substantial loses. Using stocks requires increased attention to diversification and security selection.

Options

Disclaimer: Options involve risk and are not suitable for every investor. Because they are cash-settled, investors should be aware of the special risks associated with index options and should consult a tax advisor. Prior to buying or selling options, a person must receive a copy of Characteristics and Risks of Standardized Options and should thoroughly understand the risks involved in any use of options. Copies may be obtained from The Options Clearing Corporation, 440 S. LaSalle Street, Chicago, IL 60605.

Options, for more sophisticated investors, are a good tool to take advantage of both market and sector opportunities. An option position can be established with either stocks or ETFs. There are many different ways to use options for seasonal trends: establish a long position on the market during its seasonally strong period, establish a short position during its seasonally weak period, or create a spread trade to capture the superior gains of a sector over the market.

THACKRAY'S 2021 INVESTOR'S GUIDE

CONTENTS

JANUARY

MONDAY	TUESDAY	WEDNESDAY
28	29	30
4 27	**5** 26	**6** 25
11 20	**12** 19	**13** 18
18 13 USA Market Closed- Martin Luther King Jr. Day	**19** 12	**20** 11
25 6	**26** 5	**27** 4

WEEK 01   WEEK 02   WEEK 03   WEEK 04

THURSDAY	FRIDAY
31	**1** 30
	CAN Market Closed - New Year's Day
	USA Market Closed - New Year's Day
7 24	**8** 23
14 17	**15** 16
21 10	**22** 9
28 3	**29** 2

FEBRUARY

M	T	W	T	F	S	S
1	2	3	4	5	6	7
8	9	10	11	12	13	14
15	16	17	18	19	20	21
22	23	24	25	26	27	28

MARCH

M	T	W	T	F	S	S
1	2	3	4	5	6	7
8	9	10	11	12	13	14
15	16	17	18	19	20	21
22	23	24	25	26	27	28
29	30	31				

APRIL

M	T	W	T	F	S	S
			1	2	3	4
5	6	7	8	9	10	11
12	13	14	15	16	17	18
19	20	21	22	23	24	25
26	27	28	29	30		

MAY

M	T	W	T	F	S	S
					1	2
3	4	5	6	7	8	9
10	11	12	13	14	15	16
17	18	19	20	21	22	23
24	25	26	27	28	29	30
31						

JANUARY
S U M M A R Y

S&P500 Cumulative Daily Gains for Avg Month 1950 to 2020

	Dow Jones	S&P 500	Nasdaq	TSX Comp
Month Rank	6	5	1	3
# Up	45	43	31	22
# Down	25	27	17	13
% Pos	64	61	65	63
% Avg. Gain	1.0	1.1	2.7	1.2

Dow & S&P 1950-2019, Nasdaq 1972-2019, TSX 1985-2019

♦ Over the last ten years, the stock market in January has had large moves up or down on a number of occasions, and has increased three times by more than 5%. ♦ It has also decreased two times by more than 5%. ♦ In January there is typically a lot of sector rotation. ♦ Small caps tend to perform well. ♦ The technology sector finishes its seasonal period. ♦ The industrials, materials, metals and mining sectors start the second part of their seasonal periods. ♦ The retail sector starts its strongest seasonal period.

BEST / WORST JANUARY BROAD MKTS. 2011-2020

BEST JANUARY MARKETS
- ♦ Russell 2000 (2019) 11.2%
- ♦ Nasdaq (2019) 9.7%
- ♦ TSX Comp. (2019) 8.5%

WORST JANUARY MARKETS
- ♦ Russell 2000 (2016) - 8.8%
- ♦ Nikkei 225 (2016) -8.5%
- ♦ Nikkei 225 (2016) -8.0%

Index Values End of Month

	2011	2012	2013	2014	2015	2016	2017	2018	2019	2020
Dow	11,892	12,633	13,861	15,699	17,165	16,466	19,864	26,149	25,000	28,256
S&P 500	1,286	1,312	1,498	1,783	1,995	1,940	2,279	2,824	2,704	3,226
Nasdaq	2,700	2,814	3,142	4,104	4,635	4,614	5,615	7,411	7,282	9,151
TSX Comp.	13,552	12,452	12,685	13,695	14,674	12,822	15,386	15,952	15,541	17,318
Russell 1000	713	726	832	996	1,112	1,070	1,265	1,562	1,498	1,784
Russell 2000	781	793	902	1,131	1,165	1,035	1,362	1,575	1,499	1,614
FTSE 100	5,863	5,682	6,277	6,510	6,749	6,084	7,099	7,534	6,969	7,286
Nikkei 225	10,238	8,803	11,139	14,915	17,674	17,518	19,041	23,098	20,773	23,205

Percent Gain for January

	2011	2012	2013	2014	2015	2016	2017	2018	2019	2020
Dow	2.7	3.4	5.8	-5.3	-3.7	-5.5	0.5	5.8	7.2	-1.0
S&P 500	2.3	4.4	5.0	-3.6	-3.1	-5.1	1.8	5.6	7.9	-0.2
Nasdaq	1.8	8.0	4.1	-1.7	-2.1	-7.9	4.3	7.4	9.7	2.0
TSX Comp.	0.8	4.2	2.0	0.5	0.3	-1.4	0.6	-1.6	8.5	1.5
Russell 1000	2.3	4.8	5.3	-3.3	-2.8	-5.5	1.9	5.4	8.2	0.0
Russell 2000	-0.3	7.0	6.2	-2.8	-3.3	-8.8	0.3	2.6	11.2	-3.3
FTSE 100	-0.6	2.0	6.4	-3.5	2.8	-2.5	-0.6	-2.0	3.6	-3.4
Nikkei 225	0.1	4.1	7.2	-8.5	1.3	-8.0	-0.4	1.5	3.8	-1.9

January Market Avg. Performance 2011 to 2020[1]

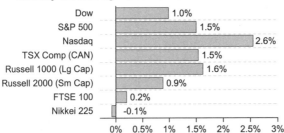

Dow	1.0%
S&P 500	1.5%
Nasdaq	2.6%
TSX Comp (CAN)	1.5%
Russell 1000 (Lg Cap)	1.6%
Russell 2000 (Sm Cap)	0.9%
FTSE 100	0.2%
Nikkei 225	-0.1%

Interest Corner Jan[2]

	Fed Funds % [3]	3 Mo. T-Bill % [4]	10 Yr % [5]	20 Yr % [6]
2020	1.75	1.55	1.51	1.83
2019	2.50	2.41	2.63	2.83
2018	1.50	1.46	2.72	2.83
2017	0.75	0.52	2.45	2.78
2016	0.50	0.33	1.94	2.36

(1) Russell Data provided by Russell (2) Federal Reserve Bank of St. Louis- end of month values (3) Target rate set by FOMC (4)(5)(6) Constant yield maturities.

January 2020 % Sector Performance

S&P GIC	2020	1990-2020[1]	
Sectors	% Gain	GIC[2] % Avg Gain	Fq% Gain >S&P 500
Information Technology	3.9 %	2.8 %	74 %
Consumer Discretionary	0.6	0.9	55
Health Care	-2.9	0.7	58
Industrials	-0.5	0.0	32
Financials	-2.8	-0.1	58
Utilities	6.6	-0.3	35
Energy	-11.2	-0.7	39
Materials	-6.2	-0.7	39
Telecom	0.7	-0.8	45
Consumer Staples	0.2 %	-0.9 %	32 %
S&P 500	-0.2 %	0.3 %	N/A %

Sector Commentary

♦ In January 2020, the S&P 500 had a nominal loss of 0.2%. The small loss does not tell the whole story for the month, as the S&P 500 rallied in the first half of the month and then corrected in the second half. In addition, there was a large dispersion in results between sectors. ♦ Information technology was the top performing sector for the month. For most of the month, the sector was in its seasonal period which finishes in late January. ♦ The energy sector was the worst performing major sector in January, as the price of oil declined as the result of decreasing demand. The materials sector was also negatively impacted in January with a loss of 6.2%.

Sub-Sector Commentary

♦ The top performing sub-sector was homebuilders which benefited from low interest rates. ♦ Gold also performed well as it had just started its seasonal period in late December. ♦ The worst performing sub-sector was steel as slower economic growth expectations increased. ♦ The biotech sub-sector was also down sharply in January, falling 7.2%. Biotech historically has been volatile in January.

SELECTED SUB-SECTORS[3]

SOX (1995-2020)	-3.2 %	3.6 %	58 %
Homebuilders	11.8	3.2	61
Silver	-0.9	3.0	65
Gold	4.6	1.9	58
Biotech (1993-2020)	-7.2	1.6	52
Railroads	3.0	1.5	58
Automotive & Components	-9.0	0.8	48
Retail	2.3	0.7	58
Steel	-15.6	0.5	48
Transportation	-2.1	0.1	48
Pharma	-1.0	-0.1	52
Banks	-7.5	-0.1	48
Agriculture (1994-2020)	-3.4	-0.3	41
Chemicals	-6.9	-0.7	39
Metals & Mining	-6.0	-0.8	42

WALMART – MORE THAN LOW PRICES
① Jan21-Apr12   ② Oct28-Nov29

Walmart, once the darling of the retail industry, leveraging its bricks and mortar big box stores across the retail landscape, suffered when Amazon changed consumer purchasing habits. In recent years, Walmart has tried to adapt with different approaches to its on-line business. Through its different phases of its business cycle, Walmart has managed to perform well in its strong seasonal periods.

13% gain &
positive 77% of the time

Walmart has a strong seasonal period from October 28 to November 29, which mirrors the strong seasonal period for the retail sector approaching the holiday shopping season that starts on American Thanksgiving. In this time period, from 1990 to 2019, Walmart has produced an average gain of 5.7% and has been positive 73% of the time.

Walmart has a strong seasonal period from January 21st to April 12, which closely mirrors the strongest seasonal period for the retail sector.

Covid-19 Performance Update. As the Covid-19 pandemic started to unfold in February, Walmart outperformed the S&P 500. This was largely due to investors favoring defensive consumer staples stocks. Walmart benefited from selling the basic necessities that consumers were buying in large amounts as the pandemic unfolded. At the end of its seasonal period in April, Walmart, like most other consumer staples companies started to underperform the S&P 500, as the broad market rallied. Relative to the S&P 500, Walmart started to stabilize in June.

ⓘ *WMT - stock symbol for Walmart which trades on the NYSE. Stock data adjusted for stock splits.*

Walmart* vs. S&P 500 1990 to 2019   Positive ▭

Year	Jan 21 to Apr 12 S&P 500	WMT	Oct 28 to Nov 29 S&P 500	WMT	Compound Growth S&P 500	WMT
1990	1.5 %	18.1 %	3.8	12.4 %	5.4	32.7 %
1991	14.5	35.3	-2.3	5.7	11.8	43.0
1992	-2.9	-5.2	2.8	3.6	-0.2	-1.7
1993	3.5	0.4	-0.6	14.0	2.9	14.5
1994	-5.8	1.5	-2.3	0.5	-7.9	2.0
1995	9.1	17.1	4.8	11.3	14.4	30.3
1996	4.1	13.8	8.0	-5.6	12.4	7.5
1997	-5.0	20.8	8.9	24.5	3.5	50.3
1998	13.5	21.7	11.9	21.1	27.0	47.3
1999	8.1	30.7	8.6	11.3	17.4	45.5
2000	1.5	-1.5	-2.7	19.9	-1.3	18.2
2001	-11.9	-2.2	3.2	2.3	-9.0	0.1
2002	-1.5	8.7	4.3	-6.0	2.8	2.2
2003	-3.7	6.0	2.6	-3.7	-1.2	2.1
2004	0.6	8.3	4.7	-1.1	5.3	7.1
2005	1.1	-8.9	6.7	9.5	7.8	-0.2
2006	2.1	2.0	1.6	-7.6	3.8	-5.7
2007	1.2	-2.2	-4.3	6.5	-3.1	4.2
2008	0.6	15.2	5.6	12.5	6.2	29.6
2009	6.4	0.2	2.6	9.5	9.2	9.8
2010	5.1	2.2	0.5	0.0	5.6	2.1
2011	2.7	-4.4	-7.0	0.6	-4.5	-3.8
2012	5.5	-1.4	0.3	-5.7	5.8	-7.0
2013	6.9	13.5	2.6	6.5	9.7	20.9
2014	-1.3	0.4	5.4	14.3	4.1	14.8
2015	3.9	-7.0	1.2	4.2	5.2	-3.1
2016	10.9	13.1	3.4	2.2	14.6	15.6
2017	3.2	9.3	1.7	10.7	5.0	21.0
2018	-5.2	-18.3	3.0	-1.7	-2.4	-19.7
2019	8.9	3.9	3.9	0.0	13.1	4.0
Avg.	2.6 %	6.4 %	2.8 %	5.7 %	5.4 %	12.8 %
Fq>0	73 %	70 %	80 %	73 %	73 %	77 %

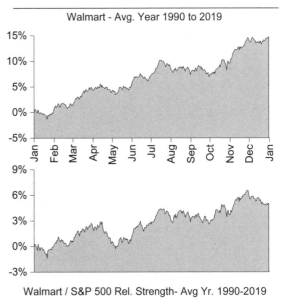

Walmart - Avg. Year 1990 to 2019

Walmart / S&P 500 Rel. Strength- Avg Yr. 1990-2019

WalMart Performance

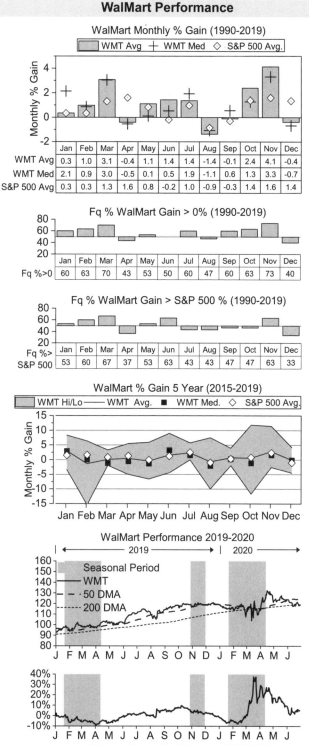

WalMart Monthly % Gain (1990-2019)

Legend: WMT Avg + WMT Med ◇ S&P 500 Avg.

	Jan	Feb	Mar	Apr	May	Jun	Jul	Aug	Sep	Oct	Nov	Dec
WMT Avg	0.3	1.0	3.1	-0.4	1.1	1.4	1.4	-1.4	-0.1	2.4	4.1	-0.4
WMT Med	2.1	0.9	3.0	-0.5	0.1	0.5	1.9	-1.1	0.6	1.3	3.3	-0.7
S&P 500 Avg	0.3	0.3	1.3	1.6	0.8	-0.2	1.0	-0.9	-0.3	1.4	1.6	1.4

Fq % WalMart Gain > 0% (1990-2019)

	Jan	Feb	Mar	Apr	May	Jun	Jul	Aug	Sep	Oct	Nov	Dec
Fq %>0	60	63	70	43	53	50	60	47	60	63	73	40

Fq % WalMart Gain > S&P 500 % (1990-2019)

	Jan	Feb	Mar	Apr	May	Jun	Jul	Aug	Sep	Oct	Nov	Dec
Fq %> S&P 500	53	60	67	37	53	63	43	43	47	47	63	33

WalMart % Gain 5 Year (2015-2019)

Legend: WMT Hi/Lo — WMT Avg. ■ WMT Med. ◇ S&P 500 Avg.

WalMart Performance 2019-2020

Seasonal Period, WMT, 50 DMA, 200 DMA

Relative Strength, % Gain vs. S&P 500

WEEK 01

Market Indices & Rates
Weekly Values**

Stock Markets	2019	2020
Dow	23,433	28,635
S&P500	2,532	3,235
Nasdaq	6,739	9,021
TSX	14,427	17,066
FTSE	6,837	7,622
DAX	10,768	13,219
Nikkei	19,562	23,657
Hang Seng	25,626	28,452

Commodities	2019	2020
Oil	47.96	63.05
Gold	1279.9	1548.8

Bond Yields	2019	2020
USA 5 Yr Treasury	2.49	1.59
USA 10 Yr T	2.67	1.80
USA 20 Yr T	2.83	2.11
Moody's Aaa	3.98	2.94
Moody's Baa	5.12	3.79
CAN 5 Yr T	1.85	1.55
CAN 10 Yr T	1.93	1.54

Money Market	2019	2020
USA Fed Funds	2.50	1.75
USA 3 Mo T-B	2.37	1.49
CAN tgt overnight rate	1.75	1.75
CAN 3 Mo T-B	1.62	1.65

Foreign Exchange	2019	2020
EUR/USD	1.14	1.12
GBP/USD	1.27	1.31
USD/CAD	1.34	1.30
USD/JPY	108.51	108.09

JANUARY

M	T	W	T	F	S	S
				1	2	3
4	5	6	7	8	9	10
11	12	13	14	15	16	17
18	19	20	21	22	23	24
25	26	27	28	29	30	31

FEBRUARY

M	T	W	T	F	S	S
1	2	3	4	5	6	7
8	9	10	11	12	13	14
15	16	17	18	19	20	21
22	23	24	25	26	27	28

MARCH

M	T	W	T	F	S	S
1	2	3	4	5	6	7
8	9	10	11	12	13	14
15	16	17	18	19	20	21
22	23	24	25	26	27	28
29	30	31				

CP RAILWAY – ON TRACK FOR STRONG GAINS
①LONG (Jan22-May10) ②SHORT (Aug5-Oct2)
③LONG (Oct3-Nov10)

CP Railway (CP on NYSE) has three seasonal periods, two positive and one negative. The strongest seasonal period for CP is the period from January 22 to May 10. From 1990 to 2019, in this time period, CP has produced an average gain of 11.4% and has been positive 83% of the time. This seasonal period is largely driven by an increasing active North American economy at this time of the year.

23% gain

CP in its negative seasonal period, from August 5 to October 2 has produced an average loss of 3.7% and has only been positive 57% of the time. Most of the losses occurred in the late 1990's and early 2000's. Nevertheless, it is still an important period to monitor for weak seasonal performance.

CP has a brief period of positive seasonal performance from October 3 to November 10. In this time period, from 1990 to 2019, CP has produced an average gain of 5.9% and has been positive 67% of the time.

Covid-19 Performance Update. CP Rail started to outperform the S&P 500 in March 2020 and continued its strong uptrend into the summer as the transportation sector performed well.

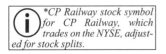
CP Railway stock symbol for CP Railway, which trades on the NYSE, adjusted for stock splits.

CP Railway* vs. S&P 500 1990 to 2019

Negative Short ☐   Positive Long ☐

	Jan 22 to May 10		Aug 5 to Oct 2		Oct 3 to Nov 10		Compound Growth	
Year	S&P 500	CP	S&P 500	CP	S&P 500	CP	S&P 500	CP
1990	1.4 %	-16.5 %	-8.6 %	-8.0 %	-0.5 %	0.0 %	-7.8 %	-9.8 %
1991	13.5	1.5	0.3	-6.0	1.2	9.5	15.2	17.8
1992	0.8	-5.5	-3.3	-15.4	2.0	-6.1	-0.5	2.5
1993	1.7	24.5	2.8	-2.3	0.5	12.0	5.1	42.7
1994	-6.1	-12.9	0.9	2.3	0.4	-9.7	-4.8	-23.1
1995	12.8	18.9	4.1	-9.2	1.9	3.1	19.6	33.9
1996	6.6	10.8	4.8	4.5	5.3	15.7	17.6	22.4
1997	5.4	0.5	1.1	-1.3	-4.1	1.3	2.1	3.0
1998	14.2	20.0	-6.5	-11.6	12.5	12.5	20.1	50.6
1999	8.5	18.4	-1.7	-10.2	7.1	5.4	14.2	37.6
2000	-4.1	18.6	-1.8	2.7	-4.9	6.4	-10.4	22.9
2001	-6.5	44.3	-13.4	-25.2	6.6	20.7	-13.8	118.0
2002	-6.4	20.3	-4.2	-19.1	8.1	22.5	-3.1	75.5
2003	5.2	18.6	3.8	1.1	2.6	18.4	12.0	38.8
2004	-5.3	-21.3	3.0	0.1	2.8	12.2	0.3	-11.8
2005	-0.1	8.8	-0.6	11.4	0.2	-4.1	-0.5	-7.6
2006	4.9	30.3	4.1	3.7	3.7	13.1	13.2	41.8
2007	4.3	21.0	7.9	-0.8	-6.0	-7.3	5.8	13.0
2008	4.8	25.5	-10.8	-20.6	-17.5	-13.0	-22.9	31.7
2009	10.6	29.6	2.0	-5.8	6.6	8.4	20.2	48.7
2010	3.9	13.1	1.7	-0.4	6.3	7.1	12.3	21.6
2011	5.8	-3.3	-5.7	-20.2	9.6	27.2	9.2	47.9
2012	3.2	3.1	3.9	4.1	-4.6	5.0	2.4	3.9
2013	9.9	16.7	-0.9	0.2	4.5	15.6	13.9	34.6
2014	1.9	6.7	0.4	9.5	4.7	-0.6	7.1	-4.1
2015	4.1	2.7	-6.8	-5.9	6.7	-6.4	3.6	1.8
2016	11.5	31.8	0.2	6.7	0.0	-4.3	11.7	17.7
2017	5.7	4.1	2.1	7.6	2.1	4.7	10.2	0.7
2018	-3.1	0.4	2.9	5.8	-4.9	-2.2	-5.1	-7.6
2019	7.9	11.1	-1.5	-8.6	7.1	10.7	13.8	33.7
Avg.	3.9 %	11.4 %	-0.7 %	-3.7 %	2.0 %	5.9 %	5.4 %	23.3 %
Fq>0	77 %	83 %	57	57 %	73 %	67 %	70 %	80 %

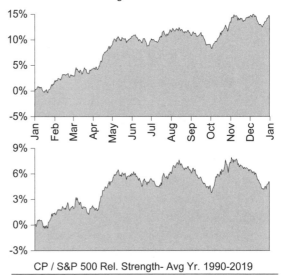

CP - Avg. Year 1992-2019

CP / S&P 500 Rel. Strength- Avg Yr. 1990-2019

CP Railway Performance

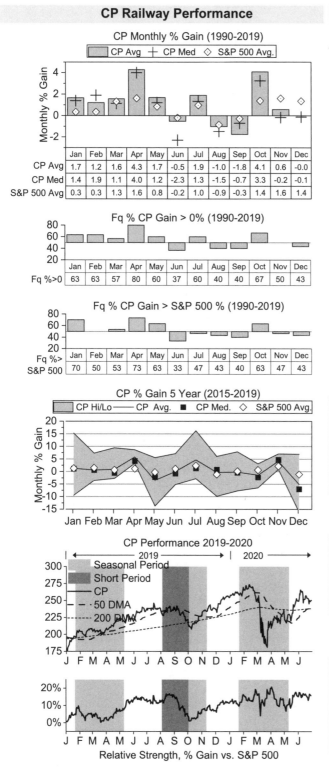

CP Monthly % Gain (1990-2019)

Legend: CP Avg | CP Med | S&P 500 Avg.

	Jan	Feb	Mar	Apr	May	Jun	Jul	Aug	Sep	Oct	Nov	Dec
CP Avg	1.7	1.2	1.6	4.3	1.7	-0.5	1.9	-1.0	-1.8	4.1	0.6	-0.0
CP Med	1.4	1.9	1.1	4.0	1.2	-2.3	1.3	-1.5	-0.7	3.3	-0.2	-0.1
S&P 500 Avg	0.3	0.3	1.3	1.6	0.8	-0.2	1.0	-0.9	-0.3	1.4	1.6	1.4

Fq % CP Gain > 0% (1990-2019)

	Jan	Feb	Mar	Apr	May	Jun	Jul	Aug	Sep	Oct	Nov	Dec
Fq %>0	63	63	57	80	60	37	60	40	40	67	50	43

Fq % CP Gain > S&P 500 % (1990-2019)

	Jan	Feb	Mar	Apr	May	Jun	Jul	Aug	Sep	Oct	Nov	Dec
Fq %> S&P 500	70	50	53	73	63	33	47	43	40	63	47	43

CP % Gain 5 Year (2015-2019)

Legend: CP Hi/Lo | CP Avg. | CP Med. | S&P 500 Avg.

CP Performance 2019-2020

Legend: Seasonal Period | Short Period | CP | 50 DMA | 200 DMA

Relative Strength, % Gain vs. S&P 500

WEEK 02

Market Indices & Rates
Weekly Values**

Stock Markets	2019	2020
Dow	23,996	28,824
S&P500	2,596	3,265
Nasdaq	6,971	9,179
TSX	14,939	17,234
FTSE	6,918	7,588
DAX	10,887	13,483
Nikkei	20,360	23,851
Hang Seng	26,667	28,638

Commodities	2019	2020
Oil	51.59	59.04
Gold	1289.0	1553.6

Bond Yields	2019	2020
USA 5 Yr Treasury	2.52	1.63
USA 10 Yr T	2.71	1.83
USA 20 Yr T	2.90	2.14
Moody's Aaa	3.96	2.99
Moody's Baa	5.13	3.82
CAN 5 Yr T	1.90	1.60
CAN 10 Yr T	1.96	1.59

Money Market	2019	2020
USA Fed Funds	2.50	1.75
USA 3 Mo T-B	2.38	1.51
CAN tgt overnight rate	1.75	1.75
CAN 3 Mo T-B	1.62	1.64

Foreign Exchange	2019	2020
EUR/USD	1.15	1.11
GBP/USD	1.28	1.31
USD/CAD	1.33	1.31
USD/JPY	108.48	109.45

JANUARY

M	T	W	T	F	S	S
				1	2	3
4	5	6	7	8	9	10
11	12	13	14	15	16	17
18	19	20	21	22	23	24
25	26	27	28	29	30	31

FEBRUARY

M	T	W	T	F	S	S
1	2	3	4	5	6	7
8	9	10	11	12	13	14
15	16	17	18	19	20	21
22	23	24	25	26	27	28

MARCH

M	T	W	T	F	S	S
1	2	3	4	5	6	7
8	9	10	11	12	13	14
15	16	17	18	19	20	21
22	23	24	25	26	27	28
29	30	31				

SILVER – SHINES IN LATE DECEMBER
December 27- February 22

Silver is often thought to be poor man's gold. Silver has a lot of similar properties to gold as it is a store of value and is used for jewelery and industrial purposes.

4% gain and
positive 68% of the time

Gold and silver have a high degree of price correlation, with silver typically mirroring the direction of gold's price changes. When gold increases in price, silver typically increases in price and vice versa. Despite this relationship, the seasonal profiles for gold and silver are different because of silver's use in industrial products.

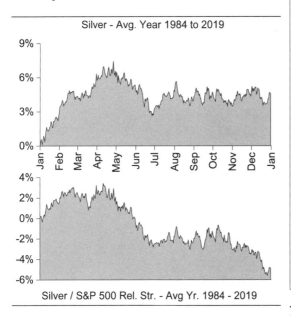

Silver - Avg. Year 1984 to 2019

Silver / S&P 500 Rel. Str. - Avg Yr. 1984 - 2019

Silver* vs. S&P 500
1983/84 to 2019/20

Dec 27 to Feb 22	S&P 500	Silver	Positive Diff
1983/84	-5.5%	6.6%	12.1%
1984/85	7.7	-6.4	-14.1
1985/86	8.4	1.7	-6.7
1986/87	15.6	2.6	-13.0
1987/88	5.4	-5.1	-10.5
1988/89	4.7	-2.9	-7.6
1989/90	-6.1	-5.6	0.5
1990/91	10.5	-10.4	-21.0
1991/92	1.6	5.2	3.6
1992/93	-1.0	-2.8	-1.8
1993/94	0.9	2.7	1.8
1994/95	5.5	0.1	-5.4
1995/96	7.3	9.2	1.9
1996/97	6.1	8.2	2.1
1997/98	10.4	7.9	-2.5
1998/99	3.7	13.7	9.9
1999/00	-7.3	1.0	8.2
2000/01	-4.7	-3.8	0.9
2001/02	-5.2	-2.1	3.1
2002/03	-4.7	0.5	5.2
2003/04	4.4	15.5	11.1
2004/05	-2.2	9.7	11.8
2005/06	1.9	12.1	10.2
2006/07	2.8	14.0	11.2
2007/08	-9.7	25.0	34.7
2008/09	-11.8	38.8	50.6
2009/10	-1.6	-5.1	-3.4
2010/11	4.7	13.1	8.5
2011/12	7.3	16.6	9.3
2012/13	6.8	-4.6	-11.4
2013/14	-0.3	12.1	12.4
2014/15	1.0	3.6	2.6
2015/16	-5.6	5.6	11.2
2016/17	4.4	14.4	10.0
2017/18	0.9	1.8	0.9
2018/19	13.2	8.1	-5.0
2019/20	3.0	5.5	2.5
Avg	2.0%	5.6%	3.6%
Fq > 0	65%	73%	68%

Although the period of seasonal strength for silver finishes in late February, under favorable conditions of rising base metal prices, silver can perform well into late March.

Historically, when silver has corrected sharply in December, it has often rallied strongly at the beginning of its seasonal period. This phenomenon has taken place a few times over the last few years.

Covid-19 Performance Update: Silver was positive in its seasonal period from December 27 to February 22. Silver was able to escape the Covid-19 pandemic carnage in the markets that started in late February. It was volatile in the initial stages of the pandemic and then managed to start rallying on an absolute basis in June.

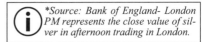

*Source: Bank of England- London PM represents the close value of silver in afternoon trading in London.

Silver Performance

Silver Monthly % Gain (1984-2019)

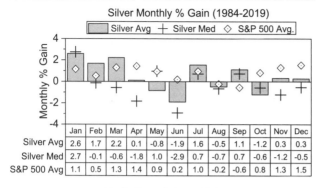

	Jan	Feb	Mar	Apr	May	Jun	Jul	Aug	Sep	Oct	Nov	Dec
Silver Avg	2.6	1.7	2.2	0.1	-0.8	-1.9	1.6	-0.5	1.1	-1.2	0.3	0.3
Silver Med	2.7	-0.1	-0.6	-1.8	1.0	-2.9	0.7	-0.7	0.7	-0.6	-1.2	-0.5
S&P 500 Avg.	1.1	0.5	1.3	1.4	0.9	0.2	1.0	-0.2	-0.6	0.8	1.3	1.5

Fq % Silver Gain > 0% (1984-2019)

	Jan	Feb	Mar	Apr	May	Jun	Jul	Aug	Sep	Oct	Nov	Dec
Fq %>0	64	50	44	39	53	33	56	44	53	44	36	44

Fq % Silver Gain > S&P 500 % (1984-2019)

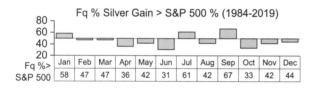

	Jan	Feb	Mar	Apr	May	Jun	Jul	Aug	Sep	Oct	Nov	Dec
Fq %> S&P 500	58	47	47	36	42	31	61	42	67	33	42	44

Silver % Gain 5 Year (2015-2019)

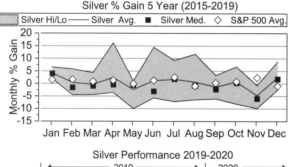

Silver Performance 2019-2020

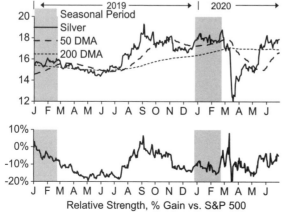

Relative Strength, % Gain vs. S&P 500

Market Indices & Rates
Weekly Values**

Stock Markets	2019	2020
Dow	24,706	29,348
S&P500	2,671	3,330
Nasdaq	7,157	9,389
TSX	15,304	17,559
FTSE	6,968	7,675
DAX	11,206	13,526
Nikkei	20,666	24,041
Hang Seng	27,091	29,056

Commodities	2019	2020
Oil	53.80	58.54
Gold	1284.2	1557.6

Bond Yields	2019	2020
USA 5 Yr Treasury	2.62	1.63
USA 10 Yr T	2.79	1.84
USA 20 Yr T	2.95	2.16
Moody's Aaa	3.96	3.01
Moody's Baa	5.17	3.82
CAN 5 Yr T	1.97	1.58
CAN 10 Yr T	2.04	1.56

Money Market	2019	
USA Fed Funds	2.50	1.2020
		75
USA 3 Mo T-B	2.36	1.53
CAN tgt overnight rate	1.75	1.75
CAN 3 Mo T-B	1.62	1.64

Foreign Exchange	2019	2020
EUR/USD	1.14	1.11
GBP/USD	1.29	1.30
USD/CAD	1.33	1.31
USD/JPY	109.78	110.14

JANUARY

M	T	W	T	F	S	S
				1	2	3
4	5	6	7	8	9	10
11	12	13	14	15	16	17
18	19	20	21	22	23	24
25	26	27	28	29	30	31

FEBRUARY

M	T	W	T	F	S	S
1	2	3	4	5	6	7
8	9	10	11	12	13	14
15	16	17	18	19	20	21
22	23	24	25	26	27	28

MARCH

M	T	W	T	F	S	S
1	2	3	4	5	6	7
8	9	10	11	12	13	14
15	16	17	18	19	20	21
22	23	24	25	26	27	28
29	30	31				

TJX COMPANIES INC.
January 22 to March 30

TJX is an off-price apparel and home fashion retailer that typically reports its fourth quarter earnings in approximately the third week of February. The company, like the retail sector, benefits from investors expecting positive results from the Christmas season.

In 2020, TJX during its seasonally strong period, outperformed the retail sector and outperformed the S&P 500. Over the long-term, TJX has typically outperformed the retail sector when the sector has been positive, making it an excellent complement to a retail sector investment during retail's strong seasonal period that also starts in January.

TJX's period of seasonal strength is similar to the seasonal period for the retail sector. The best time to invest in TJX has been from January 22 to March 30. In this time period, positive economic forecasts by investment analysts tend to increase expected consumption forecasts in the economy helping to drive the retail sector and TJX higher.

11% gain & positive 77% of the time

Since 1990, TJX has produced large gains in its seasonal period, and very few large losses. In the last thirty-one years, TJX has only had two losses of 10% or greater. In the same time period, TJX has had thirteen gains of 10% or greater.

Jan 22 to Mar 30	S&P 500	Retail	TJX
			Positive
1990	0.2%	6.3%	6.7%
1991	13.3	21.7	61.9
1992	-2.3	1.7	16.2
1993	3.8	3.0	21.7
1994	-6.1	-0.1	-2.8
1995	8.1	9.7	-6.9
1996	5.5	19.7	43.6
1997	-1.1	10.4	-0.3
1998	12.6	19.7	25.4
1999	5.3	16.5	18.9
2000	3.2	5.1	35.4
2001	-13.6	1.7	16.4
2002	1.8	4.7	2.9
2003	-2.7	6.6	-6.7
2004	-1.8	5.4	3.5
2005	1.2	-0.6	-1.6
2006	3.1	4.5	3.8
2007	-0.7	-2.7	-10.2
2008	-0.8	1.4	13.1
2009	-6.3	8.1	29.0
2010	5.1	12.5	17.2
2011	3.5	3.5	6.1
2012	7.1	12.9	19.3
2013	5.6	6.2	4.5
2014	0.8	-2.7	-0.2
2015	2.7	12.5	6.8
2016	10.4	10.2	16.0
2017	4.3	5.4	5.7
2018	-6.0	1.6	3.4
2019	6.1	6.7	8.2
2020	-20.9	-10.8	-23.7
Avg	1.3%	6.5%	10.7%
Fq > 0	65%	84%	77%

TJX vs. Retail vs. S&P 500 1990 to 2020

Covid-19 Performance Update. In its seasonal period, TJX was strongly outperforming the S&P 500 until the reality of the Covid-19 pandemic took hold. Once the stock market started to correct in late February, the retail sector and TJX started to perform poorly.

TJX underperformed the S&P 500 in its seasonal period as economies were in lock-down mode. The retail sector was negative in TJX's seasonal period, but managed to outperform the S&P 500, largely as the result of on-line retailers such as Amazon being included in the retail sector index.

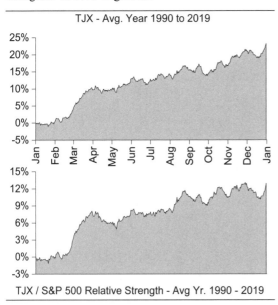

TJX - Avg. Year 1990 to 2019

TJX / S&P 500 Relative Strength - Avg Yr. 1990 - 2019

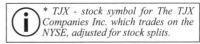

* *TJX - stock symbol for The TJX Companies Inc. which trades on the NYSE, adjusted for stock splits.*

TJX Performance

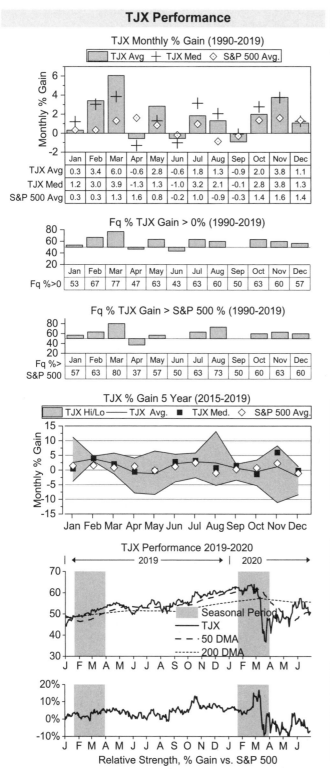

TJX Monthly % Gain (1990-2019)

Legend: TJX Avg | + TJX Med | ◇ S&P 500 Avg.

	Jan	Feb	Mar	Apr	May	Jun	Jul	Aug	Sep	Oct	Nov	Dec
TJX Avg	0.3	3.4	6.0	-0.6	2.8	-0.6	1.8	1.3	-0.9	2.0	3.8	1.1
TJX Med	1.2	3.0	3.9	-1.3	1.3	-1.0	3.2	2.1	-0.1	2.8	3.8	1.3
S&P 500 Avg	0.3	0.3	1.3	1.6	0.8	-0.2	1.0	-0.9	-0.3	1.4	1.6	1.4

Fq % TJX Gain > 0% (1990-2019)

	Jan	Feb	Mar	Apr	May	Jun	Jul	Aug	Sep	Oct	Nov	Dec
Fq %>0	53	67	77	47	63	43	63	60	50	63	60	57

Fq % TJX Gain > S&P 500 % (1990-2019)

	Jan	Feb	Mar	Apr	May	Jun	Jul	Aug	Sep	Oct	Nov	Dec
Fq %> S&P 500	57	63	80	37	57	50	63	73	50	60	63	60

TJX % Gain 5 Year (2015-2019)

Legend: TJX Hi/Lo | TJX Avg. | ■ TJX Med. | ◇ S&P 500 Avg.

TJX Performance 2019-2020

2019 | 2020

Seasonal Period — TJX — · 50 DMA ···· 200 DMA

Relative Strength, % Gain vs. S&P 500

Market Indices & Rates
Weekly Values**

Stock Markets	2019	2020
Dow	24,737	28,990
S&P500	2,665	3,295
Nasdaq	7,165	9,315
TSX	15,366	17,565
FTSE	6,809	7,586
DAX	11,282	13,577
Nikkei	20,774	23,827
Hang Seng	27,569	27,950

Commodities	2019	2020
Oil	53.49	54.12
Gold	1293.9	1564.3

Bond Yields	2019	2020
USA 5 Yr Treasury	2.59	1.51
USA 10 Yr T	2.76	1.70
USA 20 Yr T	2.92	2.00
Moody's Aaa	3.86	2.82
Moody's Baa	5.10	3.68
CAN 5 Yr T	1.90	1.38
CAN 10 Yr T	1.98	1.36

Money Market	2019	2020
USA Fed Funds	2.50	1.75
USA 3 Mo T-B	2.34	1.51
CAN tgt overnight rate	1.75	1.75
CAN 3 Mo T-B	1.63	1.64

Foreign Exchange	2019	2020
EUR/USD	1.14	1.10
GBP/USD	1.32	1.31
USD/CAD	1.32	1.31
USD/JPY	109.55	109.28

JANUARY

M	T	W	T	F	S	S
				1	2	3
4	5	6	7	8	9	10
11	12	13	14	15	16	17
18	19	20	21	22	23	24
25	26	27	28	29	30	31

FEBRUARY

M	T	W	T	F	S	S
1	2	3	4	5	6	7
8	9	10	11	12	13	14
15	16	17	18	19	20	21
22	23	24	25	26	27	28

MARCH

M	T	W	T	F	S	S
1	2	3	4	5	6	7
8	9	10	11	12	13	14
15	16	17	18	19	20	21
22	23	24	25	26	27	28
29	30	31				

SNAP-ON

SNA ①LONG (Jan24-May5) ②SHORT (Aug1-Oct8)
③LONG (Oct9-Dec31)

Snap-On has a seasonal trend that generally follows the seasonal six month trend of the stock market, performing well from October into early May. There are some differences, with Snap-On performing much worse than the S&P 500 from August into early October. This is generally a slower time for automobile maintenance and the purchase of automobile maintenance tools.

23% gain & positive 87% of the time

After its weak summer seasonal period, Snap-On tends to perform well from October 9 to the end of the year as automobile maintenance tends to increase at this time. This strong seasonal period occurs right after its weak seasonal period and as such it has typically been best to use technical indicators to help navigate the seasonal transition.

Covid-19 Performance Update. Snap-On underperformed the S&P 500 early in 2020 and once the Covid-19 pandemic developed, it strongly underperformed. Just after the stock market bottomed in March, Snap-On started to outperform the S&P 500. Its outperformance was largely based on auto sales improving faster than expected, along with maintenance of automobiles.

(i) *SNA - stock symbol for Snap-On, which trades on the NYSE, adjusted for stock splits.*

Snap-On vs. S&P 500 1990 to 2019
Negative Short ☐   Positive Long ▦

	Jan 24 to May 5		Aug 1 to Oct 8		Oct 9 to Dec 31		Compound Growth	
Year	S&P 500	SNA	S&P 500	SNA	S&P 500	SNA	S&P 500	SNA
1990	2.0 %	8.1 %	-12.0 %	-20.3 %	5.3 %	13.4 %	-5.4 %	47.5 %
1991	15.3	7.4	-1.8	-1.9	9.6	0.8	24.0	10.3
1992	0.5	-2.2	-3.9	-4.0	6.9	3.7	3.2	5.5
1993	1.9	12.2	2.7	-11.8	1.3	-1.3	6.1	23.8
1994	-4.9	-8.8	-0.7	-5.5	0.9	-4.0	-4.7	-7.6
1995	11.7	16.3	3.6	-7.8	5.7	17.5	22.4	47.3
1996	4.7	3.3	9.5	10.7	5.7	8.8	21.2	0.3
1997	6.8	7.4	2.0	6.4	-0.4	-0.6	8.6	0.0
1998	16.5	9.4	-14.4	-17.3	28.1	18.5	27.8	52.0
1999	10.0	0.2	0.5	-7.1	10.0	-18.3	21.6	-12.3
2000	-0.6	-5.6	-1.5	-27.1	-6.3	26.7	-8.3	52.0
2001	-6.9	3.9	-12.3	-9.5	8.1	37.8	-11.7	56.8
2002	-4.9	4.1	-12.4	-17.9	10.2	26.1	-8.2	54.7
2003	4.4	14.7	4.4	2.5	7.6	11.0	17.2	24.1
2004	-1.8	7.4	1.9	-11.0	8.0	20.2	8.1	43.3
2005	0.4	-0.1	-3.1	-2.3	4.4	4.8	1.6	7.0
2006	4.9	7.4	5.7	7.0	5.1	6.0	16.5	5.8
2007	5.4	14.7	6.7	-5.4	-5.4	-2.5	6.4	17.8
2008	5.1	44.7	-22.3	-22.9	-8.3	-9.3	-25.1	61.2
2009	8.6	2.7	7.9	0.8	4.7	17.7	22.7	19.9
2010	6.8	7.2	5.8	6.0	7.9	19.5	21.9	20.4
2011	4.0	7.6	-10.6	-19.9	8.8	11.2	1.2	43.4
2012	4.0	14.5	5.6	7.4	-2.0	8.5	7.6	15.0
2013	8.0	7.4	-1.8	0.8	11.7	14.5	18.4	22.0
2014	3.1	11.8	2.0	-0.1	4.6	13.8	9.9	27.3
2015	1.8	12.7	-4.3	-1.9	1.5	6.0	-1.1	21.7
2016	7.5	3.5	-0.9	-4.4	4.0	14.0	10.8	23.1
2017	5.9	-1.8	3.2	-3.2	4.9	16.8	14.6	18.3
2018	-6.2	-20.5	2.4	5.7	-13.1	-19.0	-16.5	-39.2
2019	11.6	5.1	-2.9	-0.5	11.7	11.5	21.0	17.7
Avg.	4.2 %	6.5 %	-1.4 %	-5.1 %	4.7 %	9.1 %	7.7 %	22.6 %
Fq>0	80 %	80 %	50	30 %	80 %	77 %	73 %	87 %

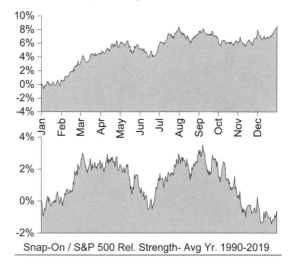

Snap-On - Avg. Year 1990-2019

Snap-On / S&P 500 Rel. Strength- Avg Yr. 1990-2019

Snap-On Performance

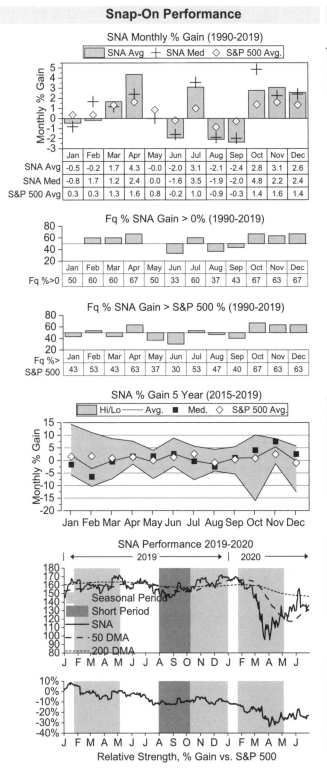

SNA Monthly % Gain (1990-2019)

Legend: SNA Avg | + SNA Med | ◇ S&P 500 Avg.

	Jan	Feb	Mar	Apr	May	Jun	Jul	Aug	Sep	Oct	Nov	Dec
SNA Avg	-0.5	-0.2	1.7	4.3	-0.0	-2.0	3.1	-2.1	-2.4	2.8	3.1	2.6
SNA Med	-0.8	1.7	1.2	2.4	0.0	-1.6	3.5	-1.9	-2.0	4.8	2.2	2.4
S&P 500 Avg	0.3	0.3	1.3	1.6	0.8	-0.2	1.0	-0.9	-0.3	1.4	1.6	1.4

Fq % SNA Gain > 0% (1990-2019)

	Jan	Feb	Mar	Apr	May	Jun	Jul	Aug	Sep	Oct	Nov	Dec
Fq %>0	50	60	60	67	50	33	60	37	43	67	63	67

Fq % SNA Gain > S&P 500 % (1990-2019)

	Jan	Feb	Mar	Apr	May	Jun	Jul	Aug	Sep	Oct	Nov	Dec
Fq %> S&P 500	43	53	43	63	37	30	53	47	40	67	63	63

SNA % Gain 5 Year (2015-2019)

Legend: Hi/Lo — Avg. ■ Med. ◇ S&P 500 Avg.

SNA Performance 2019-2020

2019 — 2020

Legend:
Seasonal Period
Short Period
— SNA
— · 50 DMA
---- 200 DMA

Relative Strength, % Gain vs. S&P 500

Market Indices & Rates Weekly Values**

Stock Markets	2019	2020
Dow	25,064	28,256
S&P500	2,707	3,226
Nasdaq	7,264	9,151
TSX	15,506	17,318
FTSE	7,020	7,286
DAX	11,181	12,982
Nikkei	20,788	23,205
Hang Seng	27,931	26,313

Commodities	2019	2020
Oil	55.26	51.56
Gold	1318.7	1584.2

Bond Yields	2019	2020
USA 5 Yr Treasury	2.51	1.32
USA 10 Yr T	2.70	1.51
USA 20 Yr T	2.88	1.83
Moody's Aaa	3.81	2.82
Moody's Baa	5.01	3.64
CAN 5 Yr T	1.86	1.28
CAN 10 Yr T	1.96	1.27

Money Market	2019	2020
USA Fed Funds	2.50	1.75
USA 3 Mo T-B	2.35	1.52
CAN tgt overnight rate	1.75	1.75
CAN 3 Mo T-B	1.66	1.64

Foreign Exchange	2019	2020
EUR/USD	1.15	1.11
GBP/USD	1.31	1.32
USD/CAD	1.31	1.32
USD/JPY	109.50	108.35

JANUARY

M	T	W	T	F	S	S
				1	2	3
4	5	6	7	8	9	10
11	12	13	14	15	16	17
18	19	20	21	22	23	24
25	26	27	28	29	30	31

FEBRUARY

M	T	W	T	F	S	S
1	2	3	4	5	6	7
8	9	10	11	12	13	14
15	16	17	18	19	20	21
22	23	24	25	26	27	28

MARCH

M	T	W	T	F	S	S
1	2	3	4	5	6	7
8	9	10	11	12	13	14
15	16	17	18	19	20	21
22	23	24	25	26	27	28
29	30	31				

FEBRUARY

	MONDAY		TUESDAY		WEDNESDAY
WEEK 05	**1** ₂₇		**2** ₂₆		**3** ₂₅
WEEK 06	**8** ₂₀		**9** ₁₉		**10** ₁₈
WEEK 07	**15** ₁₃ CAN Market Closed - Family Day USA Market Closed - Presidents' Day		**16** ₁₂		**17** ₁₁
WEEK 08	**22** ₆		**23** ₅		**24** ₄
WEEK 9	1		2		3

THURSDAY	FRIDAY
4 24	**5** 23
11 17	**12** 16
18 10	**19** 9
25 3	**26** 2
4	5

MARCH

M	T	W	T	F	S	S
1	2	3	4	5	6	7
8	9	10	11	12	13	14
15	16	17	18	19	20	21
22	23	24	25	26	27	28
29	30	31				

APRIL

M	T	W	T	F	S	S
			1	2	3	4
5	6	7	8	9	10	11
12	13	14	15	16	17	18
19	20	21	22	23	24	25
26	27	28	29	30		

MAY

M	T	W	T	F	S	S
					1	2
3	4	5	6	7	8	9
10	11	12	13	14	15	16
17	18	19	20	21	22	23
24	25	26	27	28	29	30
31						

JUNE

M	T	W	T	F	S	S
	1	2	3	4	5	6
7	8	9	10	11	12	13
14	15	16	17	18	19	20
21	22	23	24	25	26	27
28	29	30				

FEBRUARY
S U M M A R Y

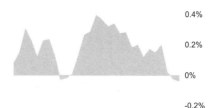

S&P500 Cumulative Daily Gains for Avg Month 1950 to 2020

	Dow Jones	S&P 500	Nasdaq	TSX Comp
Month Rank	8	10	9	5
# Up	41	39	26	22
# Down	29	31	22	13
% Pos	59	56	54	63
% Avg. Gain	0.3	0.1	0.7	1.0

Dow & S&P 1950-2019 Nasdaq 1972-2019, TSX 1985-2019

♦ Historically, over the long-term, February has been one of the weaker months of the year for the S&P 500. Over the last ten years, the S&P 500 has bucked this trend and has been positive eight out of ten times. ♦ The energy sector typically starts to outperform in late February, helping to boost the S&P/TSX Composite. ♦ The consumer discretionary sector tends to be one of the better performing sectors. ♦ In mid-February 2020, the S&P 500 and all of its major sectors moved sharply lower due to the Covid-19 pandemic.

BEST / WORST FEBRUARY BROAD MKTS. 2011-2020

BEST FEBRUARY MARKETS
♦ Nikkei 225 (2012) 10.5%
♦ Nasdaq (2015) 7.1%
♦ Nikkei (2015) 6.4%

WORST FEBRUARY MARKETS
♦ Dow (2020) -10.1%
♦ FTSE 100 (2020) -9.7%
♦ Nikkei 225 (2020) -8.9%

Index Values End of Month

	2011	2012	2013	2014	2015	2016	2017	2018	2019	2020
Dow	12,226	12,952	14,054	16,322	18,133	16,517	20,812	25,029	25,916	25,409
S&P 500	1,327	1,366	1,515	1,859	2,105	1,932	2,364	2,714	2,784	2,954
Nasdaq	2,782	2,967	3,160	4,308	4,964	4,558	5,825	7,273	7,533	8,567
TSX Comp.	14,137	12,644	12,822	14,210	15,234	12,860	15,399	15,443	15,999	16,263
Russell 1000	736	756	841	1,041	1,173	1,067	1,311	1,501	1,546	1,635
Russell 2000	823	811	911	1,183	1,233	1,034	1,387	1,512	1,576	1,476
FTSE 100	5,994	5,872	6,361	6,810	6,947	6,097	7,263	7,232	7,075	6,581
Nikkei 225	10,624	9,723	11,559	14,841	18,798	16,027	19,119	22,068	21,385	21,143

Percent Gain for February

	2011	2012	2013	2014	2015	2016	2017	2018	2019	2020
Dow	2.8	2.5	1.4	4.0	5.6	0.3	4.8	-4.3	3.7	-10.1
S&P 500	3.2	4.1	1.1	4.3	5.5	-0.4	3.7	-3.9	3.0	-8.4
Nasdaq	3.0	5.4	0.6	5.0	7.1	-1.2	3.8	-1.9	3.4	-6.4
TSX Comp.	4.3	1.5	1.1	3.8	3.8	0.3	0.1	-3.2	2.9	-6.1
Russell 1000	3.3	4.1	1.1	4.5	5.5	-0.3	3.6	-3.9	3.2	-8.3
Russell 2000	5.4	2.3	1.0	4.6	5.8	-0.1	1.8	-4.0	5.1	-8.5
FTSE 100	2.2	3.3	1.3	4.6	2.9	0.2	2.3	-4.0	1.5	-9.7
Nikkei 225	3.8	10.5	3.8	-0.5	6.4	-8.5	0.4	-4.5	2.9	-8.9

February Market Avg. Performance 2011 to 2020[1]

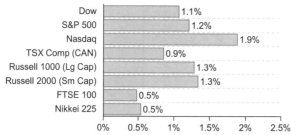

Dow	1.1%
S&P 500	1.2%
Nasdaq	1.9%
TSX Comp (CAN)	0.9%
Russell 1000 (Lg Cap)	1.3%
Russell 2000 (Sm Cap)	1.3%
FTSE 100	0.5%
Nikkei 225	0.5%

Interest Corner Feb[2]

	Fed Funds % [3]	3 Mo. T-Bill % [4]	10 Yr % [5]	20 Yr % [6]
2020	1.75	1.27	1.13	1.46
2019	2.50	2.45	2.73	2.94
2018	1.50	1.65	2.87	3.02
2017	0.75	0.53	2.36	2.70
2016	0.50	0.33	1.74	2.19

(1) Russell Data provided by Russell (2) Federal Reserve Bank of St. Louis- end of month values (3) Target rate set by FOMC (4)(5)(6) Constant yield maturities.

February 2020 % Sector Performance

GIC % Gain
- Feb 2020
- Feb 90-2020 Avg.

S&P GIC Sectors	2020 % Gain	1990-2020[1] GIC[2] % Avg Gain	1990-2020[1] Fq% Gain >S&P 500
Materials	-8.7 %	1.1 %	58 %
Consumer Discretionary	-7.7	0.8	71
Consumer Staples	-8.2	0.5	48
Industrials	-9.6	0.4	48
Information Technology	-7.4	0.3	58
Energy	-15.3	0.3	42
Financials	-11.3	-0.2	61
Health Care	-6.8	-0.6	39
Telecom	-6.3	-1.1	39
Utilities	-10.3 %	-1.2 %	29 %
S&P 500	-8.4 %	0.1 %	N/A %

Sector Commentary

♦ In February 2020, all the major sectors of the stock market were sharply negative as investors started to realize that the economy was very exposed to the measures used to combat the developing Covid-19 pandemic. ♦ The energy sector was particularly hard hit, losing 15.3%, as the demand destruction for oil impacted the sector. ♦ The health care and telecom sectors were the two best performing sectors, although both sectors were negative for the month.

Sub-Sector Commentary

♦ In February 2020, the agriculture sub-sector was sharply lower, losing 15.9%. ♦ The cyclical sub-sectors were also lower than the S&P 500 as investors adjusted to the possibility of much slower economic growth due to the developing Covid-19 pandemic. ♦ Gold was positive as falling real interest rates helped to support higher gold prices. ♦ Biotech was also positive as investors favored the sub-sector, as the need for a Covid-19 vaccine increased.

SELECTED SUB-SECTORS[3]			
SOX (1995-2020)	-4.7 %	2.6 %	65 %
Silver	-3.9	2.2	52
Retail	-5.6	1.6	71
Metals & Mining	-5.7	1.5	55
Chemicals	-8.6	1.3	68
Gold	1.6	1.1	48
Steel	-12.9	0.3	52
Transportation	-11.2	0.2	52
Railroads	-10.5	0.2	45
Automotive & Components	-12.3	0.1	42
Agriculture (1994-2020)	-15.9	-0.1	48
Banks	-13.0	-0.1	55
Homebuilders	-8.4	-0.3	55
Pharma	-8.5	-0.6	39
Biotech (1993-2020)	3.9	-1.0	48

COPPER
① Jan29 to Mar5 ② Jun24 to Jul31

Copper has a strong seasonal period early in the year as economic activity tends to increase at this time. In addition, copper demand tends to increase in China before the Chinese New Year' holidays. Investor's front run the increase in Chinese copper demand. As a result, once the Chinese economy starts to increase after the holidays, copper tends to lose momentum. From 1990 to 2019, in the period from January 29 to March 5, copper has produced an average gain of 4.1% and has been positive 67% of the time.

8% gain &
73% of the time positive

Copper also tends to perform well from late June until the end of July. The positive trend in copper somewhat aligns with strong stock market performance that tends to occur from late June into mid-July as investors move to a risk-on mode, in the period leading up to the Q2 earnings season.

From 1990 to 2019, in the period from June 24 to Jul 31, copper has produced an average gain of 3.8% and has been positive 70% of the time. It should be noted that after the strong seasonal period finishes, copper on average has declined in price in August, which tends to be one of the weaker months of the year for copper.

Covid-19 Performance Update. Copper fell in price as the Covid-19 pandemic developed, due to demand destruction taking place. As the stock market bottomed in March 2020, copper also bottomed and subsequently performed well into the summer months as economic activity increased.

ⓘ *Source: Copper. Source data: Bloomberg*

Copper vs S&P 500 - 1990 to 2019   Positive ▢

Year	Jan 29-Mar 5 S&P 500	Jan 29-Mar 5 Copper	Jun 24-Jul 31 S&P 500	Jun 24-Jul 31 Copper	Compound Growth S&P 500	Compound Growth Copper
1990	2.4 %	18.8 %	0.2 %	12.1 %	2.6 %	33.1 %
1991	12.1	4.0	2.7	0.4	15.1	4.4
1992	-2.0	2.8	5.0	6.7	2.9	9.6
1993	1.7	-4.8	1.1	4.7	2.8	-0.4
1994	-2.9	4.5	1.9	-1.9	-1.1	2.6
1995	3.2	-3.9	2.2	-2.5	5.5	-6.4
1996	5.5	3.1	-4.0	2.2	1.2	5.4
1997	4.8	4.0	8.6	-7.9	13.9	-4.2
1998	5.9	-0.2	0.1	2.5	6.0	2.3
1999	0.8	-1.5	-0.3	15.5	0.5	13.8
2000	3.6	-3.8	-0.7	7.9	2.8	3.8
2001	-8.4	-0.2	-1.2	-4.5	-9.4	-4.7
2002	1.2	5.7	-7.8	-8.3	-6.8	-3.1
2003	-3.3	1.0	0.9	7.0	-2.5	8.0
2004	2.5	18.6	-3.7	9.3	-1.3	29.6
2005	4.3	3.9	2.8	7.7	7.2	11.8
2006	0.3	1.4	2.6	13.3	2.9	14.9
2007	-3.4	1.3	-3.1	7.8	-6.4	9.2
2008	-1.5	24.8	-3.8	-3.8	-5.3	20.0
2009	-21.9	10.5	10.3	19.3	-13.9	31.9
2010	5.0	10.3	0.9	12.8	5.9	24.4
2011	3.5	2.6	0.7	11.0	4.2	13.9
2012	3.6	-0.6	3.3	3.5	7.1	2.9
2013	2.6	-3.9	5.9	0.6	8.7	-3.3
2014	4.5	-1.5	-1.6	2.4	2.8	0.8
2015	4.9	7.9	-1.0	-9.9	3.9	-2.8
2016	5.6	10.0	2.9	2.5	8.6	12.8
2017	3.9	0.3	1.3	10.2	5.2	10.5
2018	-5.3	-2.2	2.2	-6.5	-3.2	-8.5
2019	5.5	9.5	1.0	-1.4	6.6	7.9
Avg.	1.3 %	4.1 %	1.0 %	3.8 %	2.2 %	8.0 %
Fq>0	73 %	67 %	67 %	70 %	70 %	73 %

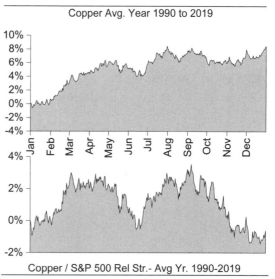

Copper Avg. Year 1990 to 2019

Copper / S&P 500 Rel Str.- Avg Yr. 1990-2019

Copper Performance

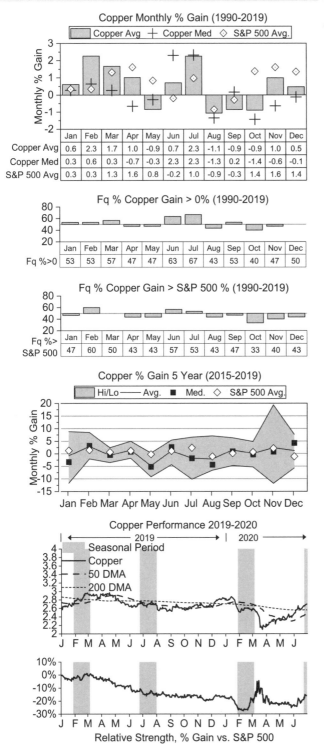

Copper Monthly % Gain (1990-2019)

Copper Avg ☐ — Copper Med ◇ S&P 500 Avg.

	Jan	Feb	Mar	Apr	May	Jun	Jul	Aug	Sep	Oct	Nov	Dec
Copper Avg	0.6	2.3	1.7	1.0	-0.9	0.7	2.3	-1.1	-0.9	-0.9	1.0	0.5
Copper Med	0.3	0.6	0.3	-0.7	-0.3	2.3	2.3	-1.3	0.2	-1.4	-0.6	-0.1
S&P 500 Avg	0.3	0.3	1.3	1.6	0.8	-0.2	1.0	-0.9	-0.3	1.4	1.6	1.4

Fq % Copper Gain > 0% (1990-2019)

	Jan	Feb	Mar	Apr	May	Jun	Jul	Aug	Sep	Oct	Nov	Dec
Fq %>0	53	53	57	47	47	63	67	43	53	40	47	50

Fq % Copper Gain > S&P 500 % (1990-2019)

	Jan	Feb	Mar	Apr	May	Jun	Jul	Aug	Sep	Oct	Nov	Dec
Fq %> S&P 500	47	60	50	43	43	57	53	43	47	33	40	43

Copper % Gain 5 Year (2015-2019)

☐ Hi/Lo — Avg. ■ Med. ◇ S&P 500 Avg.

Copper Performance 2019-2020

2019 → | 2020 →

☐ Seasonal Period
— Copper
— 50 DMA
--- 200 DMA

Relative Strength, % Gain vs. S&P 500

Market Indices & Rates
Weekly Values**

Stock Markets	2019	2020
Dow	25,106	29,103
S&P500	2,708	3,328
Nasdaq	7,298	9,521
TSX	15,633	17,655
FTSE	7,071	7,467
DAX	10,907	13,514
Nikkei	20,333	23,828
Hang Seng	27,946	27,404

Commodities	2019	2020
Oil	52.72	50.32
Gold	1314.9	1572.7

Bond Yields	2019	2020
USA 5 Yr Treasury	2.44	1.41
USA 10 Yr T	2.63	1.59
USA 20 Yr T	2.82	1.89
Moody's Aaa	3.77	2.77
Moody's Baa	4.93	3.64
CAN 5 Yr T	1.79	1.34
CAN 10 Yr T	1.88	1.33

Money Market	2019	2020
USA Fed Funds	2.50	1.75
USA 3 Mo T-B	2.38	1.53
CAN tgt overnight rate	1.75	1.75
CAN 3 Mo T-B	1.65	1.64

Foreign Exchange	2019	2020
EUR/USD	1.13	1.09
GBP/USD	1.29	1.29
USD/CAD	1.33	1.33
USD/JPY	109.73	109.75

FEBRUARY

M	T	W	T	F	S	S
1	2	3	4	5	6	7
8	9	10	11	12	13	14
15	16	17	18	19	20	21
22	23	24	25	26	27	28

MARCH

M	T	W	T	F	S	S
1	2	3	4	5	6	7
8	9	10	11	12	13	14
15	16	17	18	19	20	21
22	23	24	25	26	27	28
29	30	31				

APRIL

M	T	W	T	F	S	S
			1	2	3	4
5	6	7	8	9	10	11
12	13	14	15	16	17	18
19	20	21	22	23	24	25
26	27	28	29	30		

EASTMAN CHEMICAL COMPANY

EMN
① LONG (Jan28 to May5)
② SELL SHORT (May30-Oct27)

In its positive seasonal period from January 28 to May 5, Eastman Chemical during the period from 1994 to 2019, has produced an average 12.1% gain and has been positive 85% of the time.

In its short sell seasonal period from May 30 to October 27, in the same yearly period, Eastman Chemical has produced an average loss of 5.5% and has been positive 38% of the time.

18% growth

Eastman Chemical, in its 10-K report filed with regulators in 2013, outlines the seasonal trends in its business. "The Company's earnings are typically greater in second and third quarters." This is a bit different than many other cyclical companies, that tend to have weaker earnings over the summer months.

The net result is for Eastman Chemical to outperform into May and then underperform at the tail end of Q2, and Q3, as investors anticipate a weaker Q4 earnings report. In Q4, Eastman tends to perform at market.

Covid-19 Performance Update. Eastman Chemical started to underperform the S&P 500 in November 2019. It continued its underperformance until mid-March and started to outperform ahead of the overall stock market bottom and continued to outperform into the summer months. Its strong performance at this time was from a combination of a bounce from its underperformance since 2018 and a positive reaction to the stronger than expected economic recovery 2020.

(i) *Eastman Chemical Company manufactures and sells chemicals, fibers, and plastics, globally. It trades on the NYSE, adjusted for splits.*

Eastman Chemical* vs. S&P 500 1994 to 2019

Positive Long ▢   Negative Short ▢

Year	Jan 28 to May 5 S&P 500	Jan 28 to May 5 EMN	May 30 to Oct 27 S&P 500	May 30 to Oct 27 EMN	Compound Growth S&P 500	Compound Growth EMN
1994	-5.4	7.8 %	1.9 %	8.7 %	-3.6 %	-1.6 %
1995	10.6	11.0	10.7	2.6	22.4	8.2
1996	3.2	7.1	4.9	-21.8	8.3	30.5
1997	8.5	-1.1	3.9	2.7	12.8	-3.8
1998	15.1	18.7	-2.3	-15.3	12.4	36.8
1999	8.4	32.1	-0.4	-24.5	8.0	64.4
2000	2.4	21.9	0.1	-19.3	2.6	45.3
2001	-6.5	22.7	-12.9	-33.1	-18.6	63.2
2002	-5.3	13.1	-15.9	-21.2	-20.4	37.0
2003	9.3	-11.4	8.6	-0.6	18.7	-10.9
2004	-2.0	16.4	0.4	-1.9	-1.6	18.6
2005	-0.2	10.5	-1.7	-15.7	-1.8	27.9
2006	3.3	17.3	7.6	5.5	11.1	10.9
2007	5.9	11.8	1.1	-0.1	7.1	11.9
2008	5.8	14.9	-39.3	-55.6	-35.8	78.8
2009	6.9	52.4	15.7	34.3	23.6	0.2
2010	6.2	12.4	8.5	33.0	15.3	-24.7
2011	2.7	9.2	-3.5	-23.1	-0.8	34.5
2012	4.0	0.6	6.0	21.6	10.2	-21.1
2013	7.4	-5.6	6.8	8.4	14.7	-13.5
2014	5.8	15.5	2.2	-15.6	8.1	33.4
2015	3.0	13.1	-2.0	-6.0	0.9	19.9
2016	8.9	21.5	1.6	-8.8	10.7	32.1
2017	4.6	2.5	6.8	16.4	11.7	-14.3
2018	-7.3	2.4	-1.2	-25.0	-8.4	28.0
2019	10.5	-1.6	8.6	12.7	20.1	-14.2
Avg.	4.1 %	12.1 %	0.6 %	-5.5 %	4.9 %	18.4 %
Fq>0	77 %	85 %	65 %	38 %	69 %	69 %

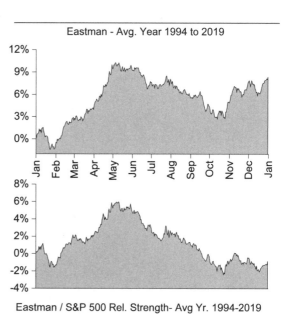

Eastman - Avg. Year 1994 to 2019

Eastman / S&P 500 Rel. Strength- Avg Yr. 1994-2019

- 21 -

Eastman Chemical Performance

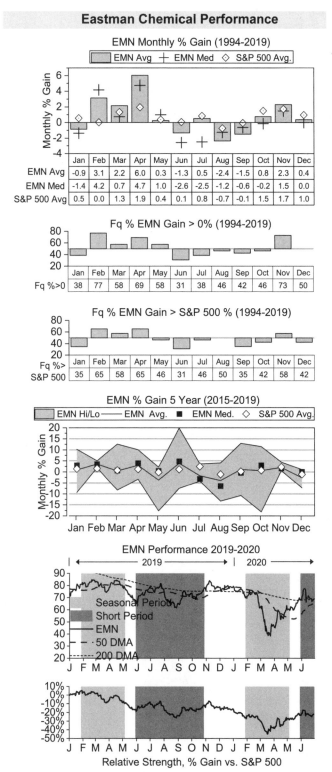

EMN Monthly % Gain (1994-2019)

Legend: EMN Avg + EMN Med ◇ S&P 500 Avg.

	Jan	Feb	Mar	Apr	May	Jun	Jul	Aug	Sep	Oct	Nov	Dec
EMN Avg	-0.9	3.1	2.2	6.0	0.3	-1.3	0.5	-2.4	-1.5	0.8	2.3	0.4
EMN Med	-1.4	4.2	0.7	4.7	1.0	-2.6	-2.5	-1.2	-0.6	-0.2	1.5	0.0
S&P 500 Avg	0.5	0.0	1.3	1.9	0.4	0.1	0.8	-0.7	-0.1	1.5	1.7	1.0

Fq % EMN Gain > 0% (1994-2019)

	Jan	Feb	Mar	Apr	May	Jun	Jul	Aug	Sep	Oct	Nov	Dec
Fq %>0	38	77	58	69	58	31	38	46	42	46	73	50

Fq % EMN Gain > S&P 500 % (1994-2019)

	Jan	Feb	Mar	Apr	May	Jun	Jul	Aug	Sep	Oct	Nov	Dec
Fq %> S&P 500	35	65	58	65	46	31	46	50	35	42	58	42

EMN % Gain 5 Year (2015-2019)

Legend: EMN Hi/Lo — EMN Avg. ■ EMN Med. ◇ S&P 500 Avg.

Jan Feb Mar Apr May Jun Jul Aug Sep Oct Nov Dec

EMN Performance 2019-2020

2019 — 2020

- Seasonal Period
- Short Period
- — EMN
- – – · 50 DMA
- ···· 200 DMA

J F M A M J J A S O N D J F M A M J

J F M A M J J A S O N D J F M A M J

Relative Strength, % Gain vs. S&P 500

WEEK 07

Market Indices & Rates
Weekly Values**

Stock Markets	2019	2020
Dow	25,883	29,398
S&P500	2,776	3,380
Nasdaq	7,472	9,731
TSX	15,838	17,848
FTSE	7,237	7,409
DAX	11,300	13,744
Nikkei	20,901	23,688
Hang Seng	27,901	27,816

Commodities	2019	2020
Oil	55.59	52.05
Gold	1316.6	1581.4

Bond Yields	2019	2020
USA 5 Yr Treasury	2.49	1.42
USA 10 Yr T	2.66	1.59
USA 20 Yr T	2.84	1.89
Moody's Aaa	3.76	2.79
Moody's Baa	4.94	3.63
CAN 5 Yr T	1.80	1.37
CAN 10 Yr T	1.90	1.37

Money Market	2019	2020
USA Fed Funds	2.50	1.75
USA 3 Mo T-B	2.38	1.55
CAN tgt overnight rate	1.75	1.75
CAN 3 Mo T-B	1.68	1.64

Foreign Exchange	2019	2020
EUR/USD	1.13	1.08
GBP/USD	1.29	1.30
USD/CAD	1.32	1.33
USD/JPY	110.47	109.78

FEBRUARY

M	T	W	T	F	S	S
1	2	3	4	5	6	7
8	9	10	11	12	13	14
15	16	17	18	19	20	21
22	23	24	25	26	27	28

MARCH

M	T	W	T	F	S	S
1	2	3	4	5	6	7
8	9	10	11	12	13	14
15	16	17	18	19	20	21
22	23	24	25	26	27	28
29	30	31				

APRIL

M	T	W	T	F	S	S
			1	2	3	4
5	6	7	8	9	10	11
12	13	14	15	16	17	18
19	20	21	22	23	24	25
26	27	28	29	30		

VALUE BETTER THAN GROWTH 2X
① Feb26-Apr19 ② Nov29-Jan6

Value vs Growth

There are different methods in assessing whether stocks are classified as value or growth. The concept of value or growth can pertain to different segments of the stock market, such as large cap or small cap. The seasonal trend analysis below is based upon the FTSE Russell, Russell 1000 Index, which is a large cap index.

Since 1991, growth stocks have on average outperformed value stocks. In the bull market that started in 2009, value stocks have underperformed growth stocks in every year up to 2019, except 2012, when value stocks outperformed by the small amount of 1.2%.

5.0% gain & 72% of the time positive

Despite the dominance of growth stocks over the last decade, value stocks on average have outperformed growth stocks in its two seasonal periods: from February 26 to April 19 and November 29 to January 6.

Both the late February to mid-April seasonal period and the late November to early January seasonally strong periods for value stocks, coincide with the strong seasonal trends for many of the cyclical sectors of the market which tend to be categorized as value.

Covid-19 Performance Update. The value sector has been underperforming the growth sector on a multi-year basis. In its seasonal period from February 26 to April 19 the value sector continued to underperform the growth sector as investors favored work-from-home (WFH) stocks that mainly fall into the growth sector.

Source: For more information on the FTSE Russell Indexes, pleaser refer to: www.ftserussell.com.

Russell 1000 Value vs Russell 1000 Growth 1991/92 to 2019/00   Positive

Year	Feb 26 Apr 19 Gr.	Value	Nov 29 Jan 6 Gr.	Value	Compound Growth Gr.	Value
1991/92	5.6 %	4.6 %	13.7 %	8.3 %	20.1 %	13.3 %
1992/93	0.0	1.7	-0.4	3.2	-0.5	4.9
1993/94	-1.5	4.0	1.0	1.3	-0.4	5.3
1994/95	-7.0	-3.1	0.5	2.5	-6.5	-0.6
1995/96	2.7	3.2	0.1	2.7	2.8	6.0
1996/97	-2.4	-1.6	-1.3	-0.6	-3.7	-2.2
1997/98	-6.1	-6.2	1.2	1.4	-4.9	-4.9
1998/99	5.2	10.0	9.6	4.1	15.3	14.5
1999/00	-0.2	8.2	-0.2	-3.1	-0.4	4.8
2000/01	1.1	12.6	-8.7	2.4	-7.7	15.3
2001/02	-0.8	1.1	3.3	5.1	2.4	6.2
2002/03	-0.9	4.7	-2.7	1.0	-3.6	5.8
2003/04	7.5	5.3	4.6	6.8	12.4	12.5
2004/05	-0.3	-1.0	0.6	0.3	0.4	-0.7
2005/06	-4.7	-4.4	2.1	2.6	-2.7	-1.8
2006/07	1.4	2.1	1.2	2.2	2.6	4.3
2007/08	0.9	1.5	-4.3	-3.6	-3.4	-2.1
2008/09	2.3	0.1	6.6	3.7	9.0	3.8
2009/10	13.8	14.8	4.4	5.1	18.8	20.6
2010/11	7.9	9.7	5.6	8.5	13.9	19.0
2011/12	-0.6	-0.2	5.4	8.7	4.8	8.4
2012/13	1.3	-0.1	2.9	5.6	4.3	5.6
2013/14	4.3	4.6	1.3	1.2	5.6	5.9
2014/15	-1.3	2.8	-3.9	-2.3	-5.2	0.4
2015/16	-1.3	-1.4	-4.9	-5.2	-6.1	-6.5
2016/17	7.2	8.9	2.8	3.9	10.3	13.2
2017/18	0.3	-2.8	4.2	4.4	4.5	1.5
2018/19	-1.7	-1.8	-7.4	-8.2	-8.9	-9.9
2019/00	5.4	2.0	3.8	1.8	9.3	3.8
Avg.	1.3 %	2.7 %	1.4 %	2.2 %	2.8 %	5.0 %
Fq>0	52 %	66 %	69 %	79 %	55 %	72 %

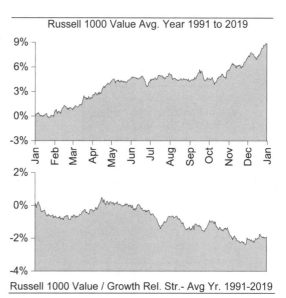

Russell 1000 Value Avg. Year 1991 to 2019

Russell 1000 Value / Growth Rel. Str.- Avg Yr. 1991-2019

Value vs. Growth Performance

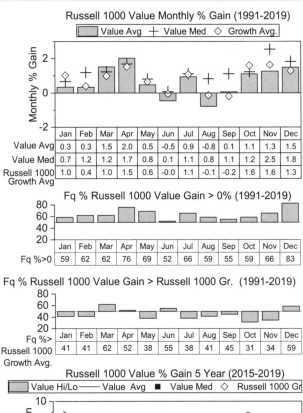

Russell 1000 Value Monthly % Gain (1991-2019)

Legend: Value Avg + Value Med ◇ Growth Avg.

	Jan	Feb	Mar	Apr	May	Jun	Jul	Aug	Sep	Oct	Nov	Dec
Value Avg	0.3	0.3	1.5	2.0	0.5	-0.5	0.9	-0.8	0.1	1.1	1.3	1.5
Value Med	0.7	1.2	1.2	1.7	0.8	0.1	1.1	0.8	1.1	1.2	2.5	1.8
Russell 1000 Growth Avg	1.0	0.4	1.0	1.5	0.6	-0.0	1.1	-0.1	-0.2	1.6	1.6	1.3

Fq % Russell 1000 Value Gain > 0% (1991-2019)

	Jan	Feb	Mar	Apr	May	Jun	Jul	Aug	Sep	Oct	Nov	Dec
Fq %>0	59	62	62	76	69	52	66	59	55	59	66	83

Fq % Russell 1000 Value Gain > Russell 1000 Gr. (1991-2019)

	Jan	Feb	Mar	Apr	May	Jun	Jul	Aug	Sep	Oct	Nov	Dec
Fq %> Russell 1000 Growth Avg.	41	41	62	52	38	55	38	41	45	31	34	59

Russell 1000 Value % Gain 5 Year (2015-2019)

Legend: Value Hi/Lo —— Value Avg ■ Value Med ◇ Russell 1000 Gr

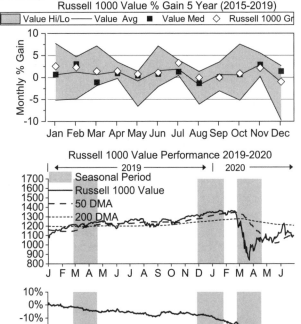

Russell 1000 Value Performance 2019-2020

Legend: Seasonal Period, Russell 1000 Value, 50 DMA, 200 DMA

Relative Strength, % Gain vs. Russell 1000 Growth

Market Indices & Rates
Weekly Values**

Stock Markets	2019	2020
Dow	26,032	28,992
S&P500	2,793	3,338
Nasdaq	7,528	9,577
TSX	16,013	17,844
FTSE	7,179	7,404
DAX	11,458	13,579
Nikkei	21,426	23,387
Hang Seng	28,816	27,309

Commodities	2019	2020
Oil	57.11	53.30
Gold	1329.1	1643.3

Bond Yields	2019	2020
USA 5 Yr Treasury	2.47	1.30
USA 10 Yr T	2.65	1.46
USA 20 Yr T	2.86	1.75
Moody's Aaa	3.81	2.74
Moody's Baa	4.90	3.55
CAN 5 Yr T	1.80	1.30
CAN 10 Yr T	1.89	1.28

Money Market	2019	2020
USA Fed Funds	2.50	1.75
USA 3 Mo T-B	2.41	1.53
CAN tgt overnight rate	1.75	1.75
CAN 3 Mo T-B	1.67	1.63

Foreign Exchange	2019	2020
EUR/USD	1.13	1.08
GBP/USD	1.31	1.30
USD/CAD	1.31	1.32
USD/JPY	110.69	111.61

FEBRUARY

M	T	W	T	F	S	S
1	2	3	4	5	6	7
8	9	10	11	12	13	14
15	16	17	18	19	20	21
22	23	24	25	26	27	28

MARCH

M	T	W	T	F	S	S
1	2	3	4	5	6	7
8	9	10	11	12	13	14
15	16	17	18	19	20	21
22	23	24	25	26	27	28
29	30	31				

APRIL

M	T	W	T	F	S	S
			1	2	3	4
5	6	7	8	9	10	11
12	13	14	15	16	17	18
19	20	21	22	23	24	25
26	27	28	29	30		

OIL STOCKS
① Feb25-May9 ② Jul24-Oct3

Oil stocks have two seasonal periods largely based upon its supply and demand cycles. The highest demand for oil on a seasonal basis occurs in May as the US driving season kicks off. Refineries prepare for this demand surge by shutting down and switching over from winter to summer gas and performing maintenance on their refineries in the late winter and early spring.

The slow down in production at this time causes an additional demand surge as the driving season approaches. Investors tend to front run this phenomenon by investing in oil stocks before the summer driving season, which has historically caused oil stocks to perform well from late February to early May.

8% gain &
positive 78% of the time

In addition, oil stocks have a second seasonal period from late July to early October. This is a minor seasonal period and is not as strong as the February to May seasonal period. This seasonal period is based upon the increased demand for oil in the winter heating season.

Covid-19 Performance Update. Oil stocks underperformed the S&P 500 as the pandemic developed in February and March due to demand destruction from Covid-19. Oil stocks outperformed into June and then continued their underperformance.

NYSE Arca Oil Index (XOI): An index designed to represent a cross section of widely held oil corporations involved in various phases of the oil industry.

For more information on the XOI index, see www.cboe.com

XOI* vs. S&P 500 1984 to 2019   Positive ▢

	Feb 25 to May 9		Jul 24 to Oct 3		Compound Growth	
Year	S&P 500	XOI	S&P 500	XOI	S&P 500	XOI
1984	1.7 %	5.6 %	9.1	9.0 %	10.9	15.1 %
1985	1.4	4.9	-4.3	6.7	-2.9	12.0
1986	6.0	7.7	-2.1	15.7	3.8	24.5
1987	3.7	25.5	6.6	-1.2	10.5	23.9
1988	-3.0	5.6	3.0	-3.6	-0.1	1.8
1989	6.3	8.1	5.6	5.7	12.2	14.2
1990	5.8	-0.6	-12.4	-0.5	-7.3	-1.1
1991	4.8	6.8	1.3	0.7	6.2	7.5
1992	0.9	5.8	-0.4	2.9	0.5	8.9
1993	0.3	6.3	3.2	7.8	3.5	14.6
1994	-4.7	3.2	1.9	-3.6	-2.9	-0.6
1995	7.3	10.3	5.2	-2.2	12.8	7.9
1996	-2.1	2.2	10.5	7.7	8.2	10.1
1997	1.8	4.7	3.0	8.9	4.9	14.0
1998	7.5	9.8	-12.0	1.4	-5.4	11.4
1999	7.3	35.4	-5.5	-2.1	1.4	32.5
2000	4.3	22.2	-3.6	12.2	0.6	37.1
2001	0.8	10.2	-10.0	-5.1	-9.3	4.5
2002	-1.5	5.3	2.7	7.3	1.1	13.0
2003	12.1	5.7	4.2	5.5	16.8	11.5
2004	-3.5	4.0	4.2	10.9	0.5	15.3
2005	-1.8	-1.0	-0.6	14.3	-2.3	13.2
2006	2.8	9.4	7.6	-8.5	10.5	0.1
2007	4.2	10.1	-0.1	-4.2	4.1	5.5
2008	2.6	7.6	-14.3	-18.1	-12.0	-11.9
2009	20.2	15.8	5.0	3.0	26.2	19.3
2010	0.5	-2.3	4.0	8.5	4.5	6.0
2011	3.1	-0.6	-18.3	-26.0	-15.8	-26.4
2012	-0.8	-13.4	7.4	6.1	6.6	-8.1
2013	7.3	3.8	-0.8	-0.8	6.5	3.0
2014	1.7	9.1	-1.0	-10.7	0.7	-2.6
2015	0.0	1.2	-7.2	-9.5	-7.1	-8.5
2016	6.7	11.1	-0.6	2.1	6.0	13.5
2017	1.2	-4.0	2.5	8.9	3.8	4.6
2018	-1.8	15.4	4.2	7.4	2.3	24.0
2019	2.8	-2.6	-3.2	-7.9	-0.4	-10.3
Avg.	2.9 %	6.9 %	-0.1 %	1.3 %	2.8 %	8.3 %
Fq>0	78 %	81 %	53 %	58 %	69 %	78 %

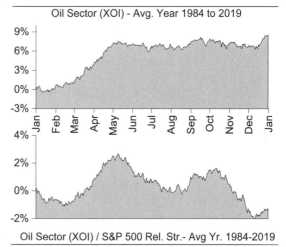

Oil Sector (XOI) - Avg. Year 1984 to 2019

Oil Sector (XOI) / S&P 500 Rel. Str.- Avg Yr. 1984-2019

NYSE Arca Oil Index (XOI) Performance

XOI Monthly % Gain (1984-2019)

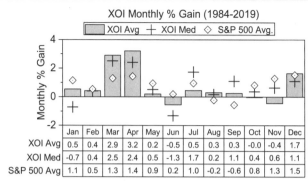

Legend: XOI Avg | + XOI Med | ◇ S&P 500 Avg.

	Jan	Feb	Mar	Apr	May	Jun	Jul	Aug	Sep	Oct	Nov	Dec
XOI Avg	0.5	0.4	2.9	3.2	0.2	-0.5	0.5	0.3	0.3	-0.0	-0.4	1.7
XOI Med	-0.7	0.4	2.5	2.4	0.5	-1.3	1.7	0.2	1.1	0.4	0.6	1.1
S&P 500 Avg	1.1	0.5	1.3	1.4	0.9	0.2	1.0	-0.2	-0.6	0.8	1.3	1.5

Fq % XOI Gain > 0% (1984-2019)

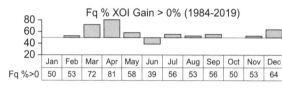

	Jan	Feb	Mar	Apr	May	Jun	Jul	Aug	Sep	Oct	Nov	Dec
Fq %>0	50	53	72	81	58	39	56	53	56	50	53	64

Fq % XOI Gain > S&P 500 % (1984-2019)

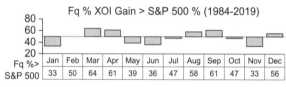

	Jan	Feb	Mar	Apr	May	Jun	Jul	Aug	Sep	Oct	Nov	Dec
Fq %> S&P 500	33	50	64	61	39	36	47	58	61	47	33	56

XOI % Gain 5 Year (2015-2019)

XOI Performance 2019-2020

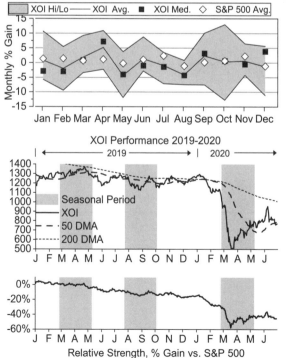

Relative Strength, % Gain vs. S&P 500

Market Indices & Rates
Weekly Values**

Stock Markets	2019	2020
Dow	26,026	25,409
S&P500	2,804	2,954
Nasdaq	7,595	8,567
TSX	16,068	16,263
FTSE	7,107	6,581
DAX	11,602	11,890
Nikkei	21,603	21,143
Hang Seng	28,812	26,130

Commodities	2019	2020
Oil	55.80	44.76
Gold	1312.0	1609.9

Bond Yields	2019	2020
USA 5 Yr Treasury	2.56	0.89
USA 10 Yr T	2.76	1.13
USA 20 Yr T	2.97	1.46
Moody's Aaa	3.90	2.70
Moody's Baa	4.98	3.51
CAN 5 Yr T	1.81	1.08
CAN 10 Yr T	1.94	1.13

Money Market	2019	2020
USA Fed Funds	2.50	1.75
USA 3 Mo T-B	2.39	1.25
CAN tgt overnight rate	1.75	1.75
CAN 3 Mo T-B	1.67	1.46

Foreign Exchange	2019	2020
EUR/USD	1.14	1.10
GBP/USD	1.32	1.28
USD/CAD	1.33	1.34
USD/JPY	111.89	107.89

FEBRUARY

M	T	W	T	F	S	S
1	2	3	4	5	6	7
8	9	10	11	12	13	14
15	16	17	18	19	20	21
22	23	24	25	26	27	28

MARCH

M	T	W	T	F	S	S
1	2	3	4	5	6	7
8	9	10	11	12	13	14
15	16	17	18	19	20	21
22	23	24	25	26	27	28
29	30	31				

APRIL

M	T	W	T	F	S	S
		1	2	3	4	
5	6	7	8	9	10	11
12	13	14	15	16	17	18
19	20	21	22	23	24	25
26	27	28	29	30		

MARCH

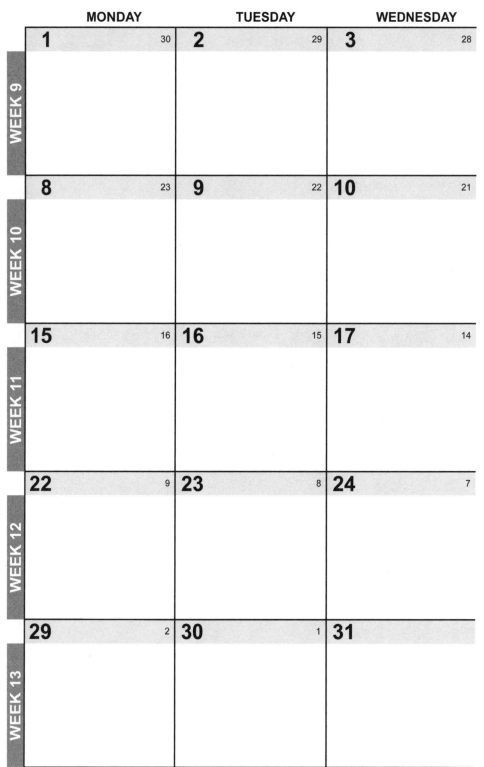

	MONDAY	TUESDAY	WEDNESDAY
WEEK 9	**1** 30	**2** 29	**3** 28
WEEK 10	**8** 23	**9** 22	**10** 21
WEEK 11	**15** 16	**16** 15	**17** 14
WEEK 12	**22** 9	**23** 8	**24** 7
WEEK 13	**29** 2	**30** 1	**31**

	THURSDAY	FRIDAY
	4 27	**5** 26
	11 20	**12** 19
	18 13	**19** 12
	25 6	**26** 5
	1	2

APRIL

M	T	W	T	F	S	S
			1	2	3	4
5	6	7	8	9	10	11
12	13	14	15	16	17	18
19	20	21	22	23	24	25
26	27	28	29	30		

MAY

M	T	W	T	F	S	S
					1	2
3	4	5	6	7	8	9
10	11	12	13	14	15	16
17	18	19	20	21	22	23
24	25	26	27	28	29	30
31						

JUNE

M	T	W	T	F	S	S
	1	2	3	4	5	6
7	8	9	10	11	12	13
14	15	16	17	18	19	20
21	22	23	24	25	26	27
28	29	30				

JULY

M	T	W	T	F	S	S
			1	2	3	4
5	6	7	8	9	10	11
12	13	14	15	16	17	18
19	20	21	22	23	24	25
26	27	28	29	30	31	

MARCH
S U M M A R Y

	Dow Jones	S&P 500	Nasdaq	TSX Comp
Month Rank	5	4	7	4
# Up	45	45	30	21
# Down	25	25	18	14
% Pos	64	64	63	60
% Avg. Gain	1.0	1.2	0.8	1.0

Dow & S&P 1950-2019, Nasdaq 1972-2019, TSX 1985-2019

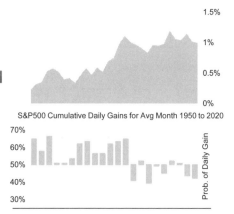

S&P500 Cumulative Daily Gains for Avg Month 1950 to 2020

♦ March tends to be a strong month for stocks. ♦ Typically, in March, it is the cyclical sectors that perform well and the defensive sectors that underperform. ♦ The energy, consumer discretionary and the financial sectors are typically strong performing sectors in March. ♦ Retail, also tends to perform well in March. ♦ The Covid-19 pandemic in 2020 created a bifurcation in the market with technology and defensive sectors outperforming the cyclicals sectors in March.

BEST / WORST MARCH BROAD MKTS. 2011-2020

BEST MARCH MARKETS
- ♦ Russell 2000 (2016) 7.7%
- ♦ Nikkei 225 (2013) 7.3%
- ♦ Dow (2016) 7.1%

WORST MARCH MARKETS
- ♦ Russell 2000 (2020) -21.9%
- ♦ TSX Comp. (2020) -17.7%
- ♦ FTSE 100 (2020) -13.8%

Index Values End of Month

	2011	2012	2013	2014	2015	2016	2017	2018	2019	2020
Dow	12,320	13,212	14,579	16,458	17,776	17,685	20,663	24,103	25,929	21,917
S&P 500	1,326	1,408	1,569	1,872	2,068	2,060	2,363	2,641	2,834	2,585
Nasdaq	2,781	3,092	3,268	4,199	4,901	4,870	5,912	7,063	7,729	7,700
TSX	14,116	12,392	12,750	14,335	14,902	13,494	15,548	15,367	16,102	13,379
Russell 1000	737	779	872	1,046	1,157	1,139	1,310	1,465	1,570	1,416
Russell 2000	844	830	952	1,173	1,253	1,114	1,386	1,529	1,540	1,153
FTSE 100	5,909	5,768	6,412	6,598	6,773	6,175	7,323	7,057	7,279	5,672
Nikkei 225	9,755	10,084	12,398	14,828	19,207	16,759	18,909	21,454	21,206	18,917

Percent Gain for March

	2011	2012	2013	2014	2015	2016	2017	2018	2019	2020
Dow	0.8	2.0	3.7	0.8	-2.0	7.1	-0.7	-3.7	0.0	-13.7
S&P 500	-0.1	3.1	3.6	0.7	-1.7	6.6	0.0	-2.7	1.8	-12.5
Nasdaq	0.0	4.2	3.4	-2.5	-1.3	6.8	1.5	-2.9	2.6	-10.1
TSX	-0.1	-2.0	-0.6	0.9	-2.2	4.9	1.0	-0.5	0.6	-17.7
Russell 1000	0.1	3.0	3.7	0.5	-1.4	6.8	-0.1	-2.4	1.6	-13.4
Russell 2000	2.4	2.4	4.4	-0.8	1.6	7.8	-0.1	1.1	-2.3	-21.9
FTSE 100	-1.4	-1.8	0.8	-3.1	-2.5	1.3	0.8	-2.4	2.9	-13.8
Nikkei 225	-8.2	3.7	7.3	-0.1	2.2	4.6	-1.1	-2.8	-0.8	-10.5

March Market Avg. Performance 2011 to 2020[1]

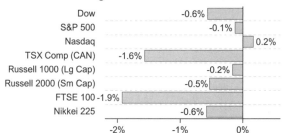

	Dow	-0.6%
	S&P 500	-0.1%
	Nasdaq	0.2%
	TSX Comp (CAN)	-1.6%
	Russell 1000 (Lg Cap)	-0.2%
	Russell 2000 (Sm Cap)	-0.5%
	FTSE 100	-1.9%
	Nikkei 225	-0.6%

Interest Corner Mar[2]

	Fed Funds %[3]	3 Mo. T-Bill %[4]	10 Yr %[5]	20 Yr %[6]
2020	0.25	0.11	0.70	1.15
2019	2.50	2.40	2.41	2.63
2018	1.75	1.73	2.74	2.85
2017	1.00	0.76	2.40	2.76
2016	0.50	0.21	1.78	2.20

(1) Russell Data provided by Russell (2) Federal Reserve Bank of St. Louis- end of month values (3) Target rate set by FOMC (4)(5)(6) Constant yield maturities.

March 2020 % Sector Performance

S&P GIC	2020	1990-2020[1]	
	GIC % Gain		
	Mar 2020		
	Mar 90-2020 Avg.		
Sectors	**% Gain**	**GIC[2] % Avg Gain**	**Fq% Gain >S&P 500**
Consumer Discretionary	-13.4 %	1.6 %	71 %
Energy	-35.0	1.1	58
Materials	-14.3	1.0	45
Telecom	-12.2	1.0	55
Industrials	-19.3	1.0	58
Financials	-21.5	0.9	55
Utilities	-10.2	0.9	55
Information Technology	-8.7	0.7	45
Consumer Staples	-5.9	0.6	52
Health Care	-4.0 %	0.2 %	32 %
S&P 500	-12.5 %	0.9 %	N/A %

-40 -30 -20 -10 0

Sector Commentary

♦ In March 2020, all of the major sectors of the stock market were negative as investors feared a substantial economic contraction due to the Covid-19 pandemic. ♦ The biggest losers were the cyclical sectors. ♦ The best performing sectors were the defensive sectors and the technology sector. The technology sector was positive and investors started to realize that a lot of the major technology companies were starting to benefit from the work from home (WFH) operations of companies. ♦ The S&P 500 found a bottom on March 23 and all of the major sectors of the stock market rallied into month end.

Sub-Sector Commentary

♦ In March 2020, the cyclical sub-sectors of the stock market were down sharply due to the developing Covid-19 pandemic. ♦ From the selected sub-sectors, biotech was the only one that was positive. Investors favored the biotech sector due to the potential benefit that some biotech companies could receive with the development of a Covid-19 vaccine.

SELECTED SUB-SECTORS[3]

Retail	-7.5 %	3.0 %	77 %
Steel	-12.9	1.7	55
Transportation	-14.9	1.4	58
Chemicals	-15.8	1.3	48
Railroads	-15.4	1.3	52
SOX (1995-2020)	-11.4	1.2	54
Silver	-18.9	0.7	45
Metals & Mining	-9.0	0.6	42
Agriculture (1994-2020)	-6.6	0.6	37
Pharma	-2.0	0.4	35
Homebuilders	-36.4	0.2	52
Banks	-27.2	0.2	45
Automotive & Components	-32.2	0.1	48
Biotech (1993-2020)	0.3	-0.6	34
Gold	-0.1	-1.0	35

NIKE – RUNS INTO EARNINGS
①Mar1-Mar20 ②Sep1-Sep25 ③Dec12-Dec24

Nike has had a strong run in the stock market since it went public in 1980. A lot of the gains in it's stock price can be accounted for in the two to three week periods leading up to its first, second and third quarters earnings reports.

Nike Inc* Seasonal Gains 1990 to 2019

Year	%	Mar 1 to Mar 20	Sep 1 to Sep 25	Dec 12 to Dec 24	Positive Compound Growth
1990	51.2 %	14.5 %	1.3 %	11.5 %	29.5 %
1991	79.8	-5.7	9.3	12.7	12.4
1992	14.7	-8.4	6.0	-2.9	-6.8
1993	-44.3	5.7	-13.5	0.6	-9.0
1994	61.4	10.4	-7.0	14.5	17.3
1995	86.6	5.3	18.8	10.7	34.4
1996	72.4	22.1	13.7	13.0	56.9
1997	-34.9	-6.1	0.9	-14.1	-18.6
1998	3.8	1.0	18.0	14.8	36.8
1999	22.2	15.6	15.1	18.2	57.3
2000	12.6	16.0	1.5	16.3	37.1
2001	0.8	-2.6	-8.7	3.7	-7.8
2002	-20.9	8.7	2.8	2.1	14.0
2003	53.9	14.0	6.0	4.4	26.1
2004	32.5	4.9	5.8	5.3	17.0
2005	-4.3	-1.8	3.0	1.3	2.5
2006	14.1	-1.5	7.1	2.6	8.3
2007	29.7	4.6	3.8	4.2	13.0
2008	-20.6	11.7	7.3	0.8	20.8
2009	29.5	8.4	5.9	2.2	17.3
2010	29.3	8.8	13.7	-2.0	21.2
2011	12.8	-12.9	2.3	-0.8	-11.6
2012	7.1	3.5	-2.3	6.2	7.4
2013	52.4	0.7	9.7	1.1	11.6
2014	22.3	1.2	1.5	-0.7	2.1
2015	30.0	5.0	11.9	0.1	17.5
2016	-18.7	2.3	-4.3	0.4	-1.8
2017	23.1	2.7	0.8	2.2	5.8
2018	18.5	-0.3	3.2	-7.4	-4.8
2019	36.6	1.1	7.5	3.0	12.0
Avg.	21.8 %	4.3 %	4.7 %	4.1 %	14.3 %

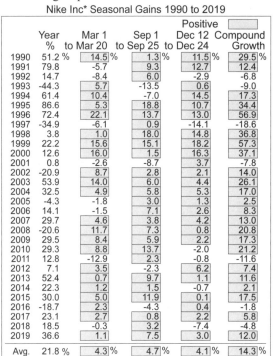

NKE - Avg. Year 1990 to 2019

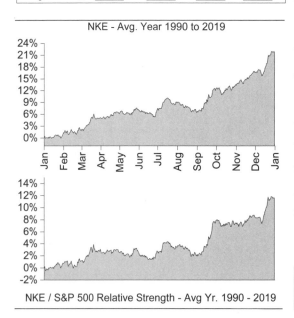

NKE / S&P 500 Relative Strength - Avg Yr. 1990 - 2019

Nike's year-end is May 31, and although from year to year the actual report dates for Nike's earnings changes, generally speaking, Nike reports its earnings in the third or fourth week in the months of March, June, September and December.

There are large differences in Nike's pattern of seasonal strength compared with the seasonal pattern of the consumer discretionary sector. First, Nike has a period of seasonal strength that includes September, a month that is not favorable to consumer discretionary stocks. Second, Nike's outperformance is focused on very short periods in the weeks leading up to three of its earnings reports. In contrast, the consumer discretionary sector has a much longer seasonal period and has a more gradual transition from its favorable seasonal period to its unfavorable seasonal period and vice versa.

From 1990 to 2019, Nike produced an average annual gain of 22%. In comparison, its three short seasonal periods within the year have produced an average compound gain of 14%. The seasonal periods for Nike, in total are approximately eight weeks and yet, they have produced most of the average annual gains of Nike. Investors have been well served investing in Nike in its seasonal periods and then running to another investment during its "off-season."

Covid-19 Performance Update. Nike managed to outperform the S&P 500 in its seasonal period in March, based upon the release of a strong earnings report. Starting in April, Nike performed at market compared to the S&P 500 in the summer months.

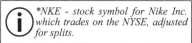

NKE - stock symbol for Nike Inc. which trades on the NYSE, adjusted for splits.

Nike Performance

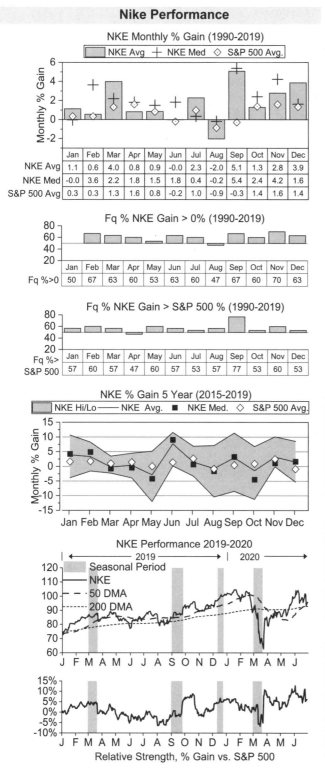

NKE Monthly % Gain (1990-2019)

NKE Avg + NKE Med ◇ S&P 500 Avg.

	Jan	Feb	Mar	Apr	May	Jun	Jul	Aug	Sep	Oct	Nov	Dec
NKE Avg	1.1	0.6	4.0	0.8	0.9	-0.0	2.3	-2.0	5.1	1.3	2.8	3.9
NKE Med	-0.0	3.6	2.2	1.8	1.5	1.8	0.4	-0.2	5.4	2.4	4.2	1.6
S&P 500 Avg	0.3	0.3	1.3	1.6	0.8	-0.2	1.0	-0.9	-0.3	1.4	1.6	1.4

Fq % NKE Gain > 0% (1990-2019)

	Jan	Feb	Mar	Apr	May	Jun	Jul	Aug	Sep	Oct	Nov	Dec
Fq %>0	50	67	63	60	53	63	60	47	67	60	70	63

Fq % NKE Gain > S&P 500 % (1990-2019)

	Jan	Feb	Mar	Apr	May	Jun	Jul	Aug	Sep	Oct	Nov	Dec
Fq %> S&P 500	57	60	57	47	60	57	53	57	77	53	60	53

NKE % Gain 5 Year (2015-2019)

NKE Hi/Lo —— NKE Avg. ■ NKE Med. ◇ S&P 500 Avg.

NKE Performance 2019-2020

Seasonal Period
NKE
50 DMA
200 DMA

Relative Strength, % Gain vs. S&P 500

WEEK 10

Market Indices & Rates
Weekly Values**

Stock Markets	2019	2020
Dow	25,450	25,865
S&P500	2,743	2,972
Nasdaq	7,408	8,576
TSX	15,996	16,175
FTSE	7,104	6,463
DAX	11,458	11,542
Nikkei	21,026	20,750
Hang Seng	28,228	26,147

Commodities	2019	2020
Oil	56.07	41.28
Gold	1296.8	1683.7

Bond Yields	2019	2020
USA 5 Yr Treasury	2.42	0.58
USA 10 Yr T	2.62	0.74
USA 20 Yr T	2.83	1.09
Moody's Aaa	3.82	2.36
Moody's Baa	4.89	3.29
CAN 5 Yr T	1.65	0.68
CAN 10 Yr T	1.77	0.73

Money Market	2019	2020
USA Fed Funds	2.50	1.25
USA 3 Mo T-B	2.41	0.45
CAN tgt overnight rate	1.75	1.25
CAN 3 Mo T-B	1.64	0.76

Foreign Exchange	2019	2020
EUR/USD	1.12	1.13
GBP/USD	1.30	1.30
USD/CAD	1.34	1.34
USD/JPY	111.17	105.39

MARCH

M	T	W	T	F	S	S
1	2	3	4	5	6	7
8	9	10	11	12	13	14
15	16	17	18	19	20	21
22	23	24	25	26	27	28
29	30	31				

APRIL

M	T	W	T	F	S	S
			1	2	3	4
5	6	7	8	9	10	11
12	13	14	15	16	17	18
19	20	21	22	23	24	25
26	27	28	29	30		

MAY

M	T	W	T	F	S	S
					1	2
3	4	5	6	7	8	9
10	11	12	13	14	15	16
17	18	19	20	21	22	23
24	25	26	27	28	29	30
31						

Loblaw is considered to be a defensive stock due to its major source of revenue coming from its grocery store business. Although Loblaw pays a healthy dividend and many Canadian investors see this as a company to hold over the long-term, on a seasonal basis Loblaw tends to perform well from late April to mid-May. This is a relatively short period, but the gains and frequency of outperformance in this period have been strong compared to the S&P/TSX Composite Index.

3.1% extra & 76% of the time better than the TSX Composite

Loblaw typically announces its Q1 earnings in late April or early May. The month of May is a transition month for the stock market from its favorable season to its unfavorable season. During this time, investors tend to favor defensive stocks. In addition, seasonally, bond yields on average have tended to decrease at this time of the year, which helps to boost stocks such as Loblaw which pays a high dividend yield.

Loblaw vs.
S&P/TSX Comp. 1996 to 2020

Apr 25 to May 18	TSX	Positive Loblaw	Diff
1996	2.0	5.3	3.3 %
1997	6.5	8.6	2.0
1998	-0.3	7.7	8.0
1999	-1.5	5.6	7.0
2000	8.2	5.8	-2.4
2001	4.8	-4.5	-9.3
2002	0.2	5.7	5.5
2003	2.8	10.1	7.3
2004	-5.8	0.2	6.1
2005	0.4	-2.8	-3.2
2006	-6.5	-1.9	4.6
2007	3.8	1.3	-2.5
2008	7.3	13.6	6.3
2009	2.2	7.9	5.6
2010	-3.9	1.1	5.0
2011	-2.6	4.0	6.6
2012	-5.8	-1.3	4.6
2013	2.8	17.9	15.1
2014	-0.3	2.2	2.5
2015	-1.9	1.6	3.6
2016	-0.3	-0.2	0.1
2017	-2.8	3.3	6.1
2018	4.4	1.9	-2.5
2019	-1.1	7.8	9.0
2020	1.5	-9.6	-11.1
Avg.	0.6 %	3.7 %	3.1 %
Fq > 0	52 %	76 %	76 %

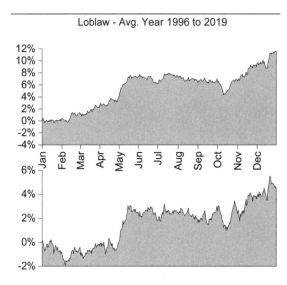

Loblaw - Avg. Year 1996 to 2019

Loblaw/ S&P/TSX Comp Rel. Strength - Avg Yr. 1996 - 2019

tends to perform poorly shortly after its strong seasonal period, extra consideration should be given to using technical analysis in exiting a position in Loblaw at the end of its seasonal period.

Covid-19 Performance Update. Loblaw outperformed the S&P/TSX Composite Index in the initial stages of the Covid-19 pandemic due to its defensive nature. In March it started to underperform, but managed to find stability in June.

It should be noted that June, which falls right after Loblaw's strong seasonal period, is one of the weaker months of the year for Loblaw. From 1996 to 2019, Loblaw produced an average loss of 1.1% and was only positive 33% of the time. Given that Loblaw

Loblaw Companies Limited, a food and pharmacy company, engages in the grocery, pharmacy, health and beauty, apparel, general merchandise, financial services, and wireless mobile products and services businesses in Canada.

Loblaw Performance

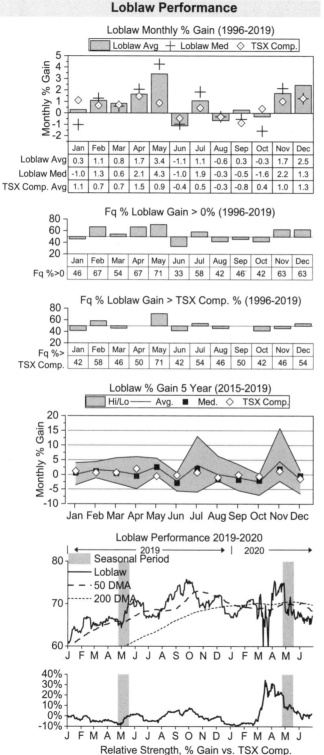

Loblaw Monthly % Gain (1996-2019)

Legend: Loblaw Avg | Loblaw Med | TSX Comp.

	Jan	Feb	Mar	Apr	May	Jun	Jul	Aug	Sep	Oct	Nov	Dec
Loblaw Avg	0.3	1.1	0.8	1.7	3.4	-1.1	1.1	-0.6	0.3	-0.3	1.7	2.5
Loblaw Med	-1.0	1.3	0.6	2.1	4.3	-1.0	1.9	-0.3	-0.5	-1.6	2.2	1.3
TSX Comp. Avg	1.1	0.7	0.7	1.5	0.9	-0.4	0.5	-0.3	-0.8	0.4	1.0	1.3

Fq % Loblaw Gain > 0% (1996-2019)

	Jan	Feb	Mar	Apr	May	Jun	Jul	Aug	Sep	Oct	Nov	Dec
Fq %>0	46	67	54	67	71	33	58	42	46	42	63	63

Fq % Loblaw Gain > TSX Comp. % (1996-2019)

	Jan	Feb	Mar	Apr	May	Jun	Jul	Aug	Sep	Oct	Nov	Dec
Fq %> TSX Comp.	42	58	46	50	71	42	54	46	50	42	46	54

Loblaw % Gain 5 Year (2015-2019)

Legend: Hi/Lo | Avg. | Med. | TSX Comp.

Loblaw Performance 2019-2020

Legend: Seasonal Period | Loblaw | 50 DMA | 200 DMA

Relative Strength, % Gain vs. TSX Comp.

Market Indices & Rates
Weekly Values**

Stock Markets	2019	2020
Dow	25,849	23,186
S&P500	2,822	2,711
Nasdaq	7,689	7,875
TSX	16,140	13,716
FTSE	7,228	5,366
DAX	11,686	9,232
Nikkei	21,451	17,431
Hang Seng	29,012	24,033

Commodities	2019	2020
Oil	58.52	31.73
Gold	1303.5	1562.8

Bond Yields	2019	2020
USA 5 Yr Treasury	2.40	0.70
USA 10 Yr T	2.59	0.94
USA 20 Yr T	2.83	1.31
Moody's Aaa	3.82	3.03
Moody's Baa	4.87	4.24
CAN 5 Yr T	1.60	0.67
CAN 10 Yr T	1.72	0.85

Money Market	2019	2020
USA Fed Funds	2.50	1.25
USA 3 Mo T-B	2.40	0.27
CAN tgt overnight rate	1.75	0.75
CAN 3 Mo T-B	1.64	0.61

Foreign Exchange	2019	2020
EUR/USD	1.13	1.11
GBP/USD	1.33	1.23
USD/CAD	1.33	1.38
USD/JPY	111.48	107.62

MARCH

M	T	W	T	F	S	S
1	2	3	4	5	6	7
8	9	10	11	12	13	14
15	16	17	18	19	20	21
22	23	24	25	26	27	28
29	30	31				

APRIL

M	T	W	T	F	S	S
			1	2	3	4
5	6	7	8	9	10	11
12	13	14	15	16	17	18
19	20	21	22	23	24	25
26	27	28	29	30		

MAY

M	T	W	T	F	S	S
					1	2
3	4	5	6	7	8	9
10	11	12	13	14	15	16
17	18	19	20	21	22	23
24	25	26	27	28	29	30
31						

NATURAL GAS – FIRES UP AND DOWN
①LONG (Mar22-Jun19) & ②LONG (Sep5-Dec21)
③SELL SHORT (Dec22-Dec31)

There are two high consumption times for natural gas: winter and summer. The colder it gets in winter, the more natural gas is consumed to keep the furnaces going. The warmer it gets in summer, the more natural gas is used to produce power for air conditioners.

On the supply side, weather plays a large factor in determining price. During the hurricane season in the Gulf of Mexico, the price of natural gas is affected by the number and severity of hurricanes.

on average increased 11.1% and has been positive 68% of the time. The price of natural gas also tends to rise between September 5 and December 21, due to the demands of the heating season. In this period, from 1995 to 2019, natural gas has produced an average gain of 33.6% and has been positive 72% of the time.

Positive 80% of the time

Natural gas tends to fall in price from December 22 to December 31. Although this is a short time period, for the years from 1995 to 2019, natural gas has produced an average loss of 3.5% and has only been positive 38% of the time. Also, in this period, when gains did occur, they were relatively small. The poor performance of natural gas at this time is largely driven by southern U.S. refiners dumping inventory on the market to help mitigate year-end taxes on their inventory.

Covid-19 Performance Update. The strong seasonal period for natural gas started as the stock market bottomed. Initially, natural gas performed well as oil wells were shut in with falling oil prices, causing supply of natural gas to fall as natural gas is often a bi-product oil production. Natural gas corrected in price in the late stages of its seasonal period. In the end, natural gas was fairly flat in its 2020 March to June seasonal period.

Natural Gas (Cash) Henry Hub LA*
Seasonal Gains 1995 to 2019

Year %	Pos. Mar 22 to Jun 19	Pos. Sep 5 to Dec 21	Neg. (Short) Dec 22 to Dec 31	Pos. Compound Growth
1995 99.4	13.0	103.0 %	1.2 %	126.7 %
1996 -27.4	-6.6	170.4	-46.2	269.2
1997 -9.4	16.8	-13.1	-6.3	7.9
1998 -13.0	-2.6	20.9	-6.7	25.7
1999 18.6	28.9	5.3	-11.2	50.9
2000 356.5	57.1	121.9	0.7	246.3
2001 -74.3	-24.1	21.5	1.5	-9.2
2002 70.0	0.6	61.3	-9.1	77.1
2003 26.4	9.5	47.1	-16.3	87.4
2004 3.6	18.2	54.6	-11.6	103.9
2005 58.4	6.3	14.5	-29.6	57.7
2006 -42.2	-1.8	17.4	-9.5	26.3
2007 30.2	9.2	32.7	2.0	42.1
2008 -21.4	52.2	-21.4	-0.9	20.6
2009 3.6	1.5	208.0	0.7	210.4
2010 -27.4	28.6	10.4	2.4	38.6
2011 -29.6	10.0	-26.1	-1.7	-17.3
2012 15.4	18.7	21.7	0.6	43.7
2013 26.3	-1.4	18.2	-0.2	16.8
2014 -31.1	7.7	-11.8	-12.9	7.2
2015 -22.8	-0.5	-36.1	35.6	-59.0
2016 59.2	46.6	21.9	5.8	68.3
2017 -3.9	-6.6	-10.4	36.0	-46.4
2018 -9.9	9.1	16.7	-7.7	37.1
2019 -34.4	-13.2	-8.5	-7.9	-14.3
Avg. 16.9 %	11.1 %	33.6 %	-3.5 %	56.5 %

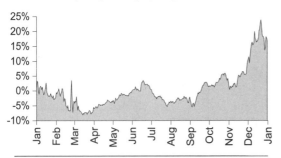

Natural Gas (Henry Hub Spot)- Avg. Year 1995 to 2019

Natural gas prices tend to rise from mid-March to mid-June ahead of the cooling season demands in the summer. From 1995 to 2019, during the period of March 22 to June 19, the spot price of natural gas has

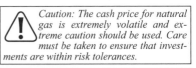

Caution: The cash price for natural gas is extremely volatile and extreme caution should be used. Care must be taken to ensure that investments are within risk tolerances.

*Source: New York Mercantile Exchange. NYMX is an exchange provider of futures and options.

Natural Gas Performance

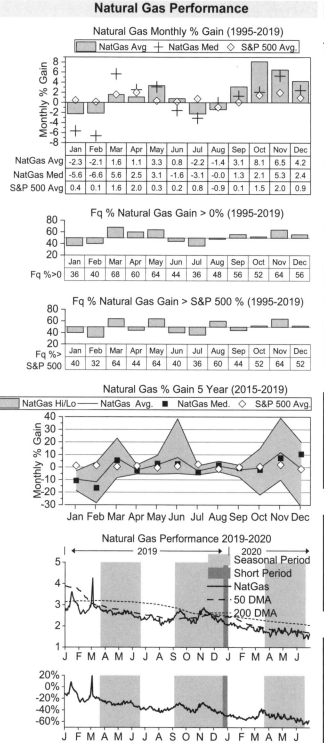

Natural Gas Monthly % Gain (1995-2019)

Legend: NatGas Avg + NatGas Med ◇ S&P 500 Avg.

	Jan	Feb	Mar	Apr	May	Jun	Jul	Aug	Sep	Oct	Nov	Dec
NatGas Avg	-2.3	-2.1	1.6	1.1	3.3	0.8	-2.2	-1.4	3.1	8.1	6.5	4.2
NatGas Med	-5.6	-6.6	5.6	2.5	3.1	-1.6	-3.1	-0.0	1.3	2.1	5.3	2.4
S&P 500 Avg	0.4	0.1	1.6	2.0	0.3	0.2	0.8	-0.9	0.1	1.5	2.0	0.9

Fq % Natural Gas Gain > 0% (1995-2019)

	Jan	Feb	Mar	Apr	May	Jun	Jul	Aug	Sep	Oct	Nov	Dec
Fq %>0	36	40	68	60	64	44	36	48	56	52	64	56

Fq % Natural Gas Gain > S&P 500 % (1995-2019)

	Jan	Feb	Mar	Apr	May	Jun	Jul	Aug	Sep	Oct	Nov	Dec
Fq %> S&P 500	40	32	64	44	64	40	36	60	44	52	64	52

Natural Gas % Gain 5 Year (2015-2019)

Legend: NatGas Hi/Lo — NatGas Avg. ■ NatGas Med. ◇ S&P 500 Avg.

Natural Gas Performance 2019-2020

Legend: 2019 | 2020 Seasonal Period, Short Period, NatGas, 50 DMA, 200 DMA

Relative Strength, % Gain vs. S&P 500

Market Indices & Rates
Weekly Values**

Stock Markets	2019	2020
Dow	25,502	19,174
S&P500	2,801	2,305
Nasdaq	7,643	6,880
TSX	16,089	11,852
FTSE	7,208	5,191
DAX	11,364	8,929
Nikkei	21,627	16,553
Hang Seng	29,113	22,805

Commodities	2019	2020
Oil	58.94	22.43
Gold	1311.3	1494.4

Bond Yields	2019	2020
USA 5 Yr Treasury	2.24	0.52
USA 10 Yr T	2.44	0.92
USA 20 Yr T	2.69	1.35
Moody's Aaa	3.67	4.12
Moody's Baa	4.74	5.15
CAN 5 Yr T	1.48	0.75
CAN 10 Yr T	1.60	0.87

Money Market	2019	2020
USA Fed Funds	2.50	0.25
USA 3 Mo T-B	2.41	0.05
CAN tgt overnight rate	1.75	0.75
CAN 3 Mo T-B	1.64	0.42

Foreign Exchange	2019	2020
EUR/USD	1.13	1.07
GBP/USD	1.32	1.16
USD/CAD	1.34	1.44
USD/JPY	109.92	110.93

MARCH

M	T	W	T	F	S	S
						1
2	3	4	5	6	7	8
9	10	11	12	13	14	15
16	17	18	19	20	21	22
23	24	25	26	27	28	29
30	31					

APRIL

M	T	W	T	F	S	S
		1	2	3	4	5
6	7	8	9	10	11	12
13	14	15	16	17	18	19
20	21	22	23	24	25	26
27	28	29	30			

MAY

M	T	W	T	F	S	S
				1	2	3
4	5	6	7	8	9	10
11	12	13	14	15	16	17
18	19	20	21	22	23	24
25	26	27	28	29	30	31

CANADIANS GIVE 3 CHEERS FOR AMERICAN HOLIDAYS

When I used to work on the retail side of the investment business, I was always amazed at how often the Canadian stock market increased on U.S. holidays, when the US market was closed.

The Canadian stock market on U.S. holidays had light volume, tended to have small increases or decreases, but usually ended the day with a gain.

0.9% average gain

How the trade works

For the three big holidays in the United States that do not exist in Canada (Memorial, Independence and U.S. Thanksgiving Days), buy at the end of the market day before the holiday (TSX Composite) and sell at the end of the U.S. holiday when the U.S markets are closed.

For U.S. investors to take advantage of this trade, they must have access to the TSX Composite. Unfortunately, SEC regulations do not allow most Americans to purchase foreign ETFs.

Generally, markets perform well around most major U.S. holidays, hence the trading strategies for U.S holidays included in this book. The typical U.S. holiday trade is to get into the stock market the day before the holiday and then exit the day after the holiday. The main reason for the strong performance around these holidays is a lack of institutional involvement in the markets, allowing bullish retail investors to push up the markets.

On the actual American holidays, economic reports are not released in the U.S. and are very seldom released in Canada. During market hours on U.S. holidays, without any strong influences, the TSX Composite tends to float, as investors wait until the next day before making any significant moves. Despite this lackadaisical action during the day, the TSX Composite tends to end the day on a gain. This is true for the three major U.S. holidays: Memorial Day, Independence Day and U.S. Thanksgiving.

From a theoretical perspective, a lot of the gain that is captured on the U.S. holidays in the Canadian stock market is realized the next day when the U.S stock market is open. This does not invalidate the *Canadians Give 3 Cheers* trade – it

presents more alternatives for the astute investor.

For example, an investor can allocate a portion of money to a standard U.S. holiday trade and another portion to the *Canadian Give 3 Cheers* version. By spreading out the exit days, the overall risk in the trade is reduced.

S&P/TSX Comp
Gain 1977-2019   Positive [   ]

	Memorial	Independence	Thanksgiving	Compound Growth
1977	0.10 %	-0.08 %	0.61 %	0.63 %
1978	-0.05	-0.16	0.57	0.36
1979	1.11	0.23	0.58	1.93
1980	1.64	0.76	0.89	3.32
1981	0.51	-0.15	1.03	1.40
1982	-0.18	-0.01	0.35	0.17
1983	0.29	0.53	0.15	0.97
1984	0.86	-0.11	0.73	1.48
1985	0.61	0.31	0.31	1.24
1986	0.23	-0.02	0.22	0.44
1987	-0.11	1.08	1.57	2.55
1988	0.44	0.08	0.58	1.11
1989	0.10	-0.12	-0.11	-0.13
1990	0.11	0.43	0.02	0.57
1991	0.02	0.18	-0.09	0.11
1992	-0.06	0.35	0.36	0.65
1993	0.42	-0.18	0.14	0.38
1994	-0.19	0.70	0.91	1.43
1995	0.14	0.25	0.29	0.68
1996	0.11	0.25	0.54	0.90
1997	1.08	-0.04	-0.85	0.18
1998	0.56	0.18	0.51	1.25
1999	0.57	1.63	1.14	3.39
2000	0.43	1.04	0.91	2.40
2001	-0.02	-0.23	0.70	0.45
2002	-0.01	0.08	0.38	0.45
2003	0.03	0.03	0.26	0.31
2004	0.84	-0.02	0.55	1.39
2005	0.56	0.39	1.48	2.45
2006	0.70	1.04	0.70	2.46
2007	0.35	-0.03	0.76	1.08
2008	0.24	-0.94	1.28	0.56
2009	0.76	0.36	-1.29	-0.18
2010	0.78	-0.92	0.34	0.19
2011	0.23	0.64	-0.75	0.12
2012	-0.09	0.55	0.44	0.90
2013	0.23	0.17	0.07	0.47
2014	0.05	0.05	-0.77	-0.67
2015	-0.09	0.30	0.16	0.38
2016	-0.13	1.48	-0.04	1.21
2017	0.03	-0.34	0.00	-0.30
2018	-0.37	0.26	-0.02	-0.14
2019	0.72	0.08	0.08	0.88
Avg	0.32 %	0.23 %	0.36 %	0.92 %
Fq > 0	74 %	65 %	81 %	88 %

- 37 -

Canadians Give 3 Cheers Performance

Market Indices & Rates
Weekly Values**

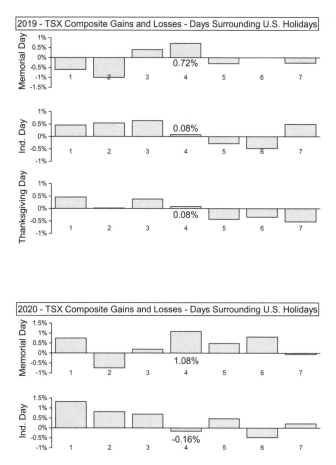

Stock Markets	2019	2020
Dow	25,929	21,637
S&P500	2,834	2,541
Nasdaq	7,729	7,502
TSX	16,102	12,688
FTSE	7,279	5,510
DAX	11,526	9,633
Nikkei	21,206	19,389
Hang Seng	29,051	23,484

Commodities	2019	2020
Oil	60.14	21.51
Gold	1295.4	1617.3

Bond Yields	2019	2020
USA 5 Yr Treasury	2.23	0.41
USA 10 Yr T	2.41	0.72
USA 20 Yr T	2.63	1.09
Moody's Aaa	3.62	2.95
Moody's Baa	4.67	4.70
CAN 5 Yr T	1.52	0.64
CAN 10 Yr T	1.62	0.74

Money Market	2019	2020
USA Fed Funds	2.50	0.25
USA 3 Mo T-B	2.35	0.03
CAN tgt overnight rate	1.75	0.25
CAN 3 Mo T-B	1.67	0.21

Foreign Exchange	2019	2020
EUR/USD	1.12	1.11
GBP/USD	1.30	1.25
USD/CAD	1.33	1.40
USD/JPY	110.86	107.94

Canadians Give 3 Cheers Performance

In 2019, the TSX Composite produced a large gain on Memorial Day, and nominal gains on Independence Day and Thanksgiving Day.

In 2020, the TSX Composite produced a large gain on Memorial Day. On Independence Day, the TSX was slightly negative.

MARCH

M	T	W	T	F	S	S
1	2	3	4	5	6	7
8	9	10	11	12	13	14
15	16	17	18	19	20	21
22	23	24	25	26	27	28
29	30	31				

APRIL

M	T	W	T	F	S	S
		1	2	3	4
5	6	7	8	9	10	11
12	13	14	15	16	17	18
19	20	21	22	23	24	25
26	27	28	29	30		

MAY

M	T	W	T	F	S	S
					1	2
3	4	5	6	7	8	9
10	11	12	13	14	15	16
17	18	19	20	21	22	23
24	25	26	27	28	29	30
31						

APRIL

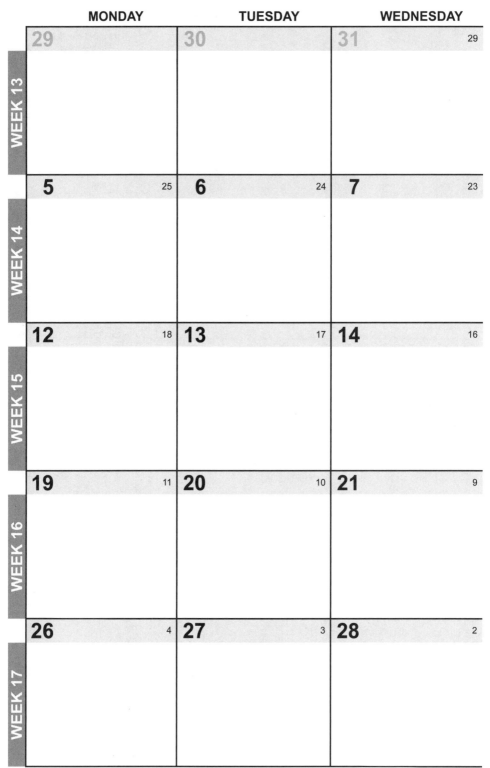

	MONDAY	TUESDAY	WEDNESDAY
WEEK 13	29	30	31 29
WEEK 14	**5** 25	**6** 24	**7** 23
WEEK 15	**12** 18	**13** 17	**14** 16
WEEK 16	**19** 11	**20** 10	**21** 9
WEEK 17	**26** 4	**27** 3	**28** 2

	THURSDAY		FRIDAY
1	29	**2**	28

USA Market Closed- Good Friday
CAN Market Closed- Good Friday

8	22	**9**	21

15	15	**16**	14

22	8	**23**	7

29	1	**30**	

MAY

M	T	W	T	F	S	S
					1	2
3	4	5	6	7	8	9
10	11	12	13	14	15	16
17	18	19	20	21	22	23
24	25	26	27	28	29	30
31						

JUNE

M	T	W	T	F	S	S
	1	2	3	4	5	6
7	8	9	10	11	12	13
14	15	16	17	18	19	20
21	22	23	24	25	26	27
28	29	30				

JULY

M	T	W	T	F	S	S
			1	2	3	4
5	6	7	8	9	10	11
12	13	14	15	16	17	18
19	20	21	22	23	24	25
26	27	28	29	30	31	

AUGUST

M	T	W	T	F	S	S
						1
2	3	4	5	6	7	8
9	10	11	12	13	14	15
16	17	18	19	20	21	22
23	24	25	26	27	28	29
30	31					

APRIL SUMMARY

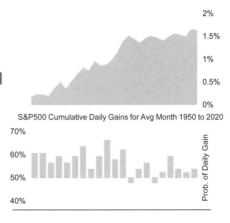

S&P500 Cumulative Daily Gains for Avg Month 1950 to 2020

	Dow Jones	S&P 500	Nasdaq	TSX Comp
Month Rank	1	3	4	6
# Up	48	49	31	22
# Down	22	21	17	13
% Pos	69	70	65	63
% Avg. Gain	1.9	1.5	1.3	0.9

Dow & S&P 1950-2019, Nasdaq 1972-2019, TSX 1985-2019

Prob. of Daily Gain

♦ The first part of April tends to be the strongest (see *18 Day Earnings Month Effect strategy*). ♦ The last part of April tends to be "flat." ♦ Overall, April tends to be a volatile month with the cyclical sectors outperforming. ♦ Due to the Federal Reserve's aggressive monetary action and government assistance to counter the Covid-19 pandemic in March and April of 2020, all of the major sectors of the stock market rallied in April.

BEST / WORST APRIL BROAD MKTS. 2011-2020

BEST APRIL MARKETS
- Nasdaq (2020) 15.4%
- Russell 2000 (2020) 13.7%
- Russell 1000 (2020) 13.1%

WORST APRIL MARKETS
- Nikkei 225 (2012) -5.6%
- Russell 2000 (2014) -3.9%
- Nikkei 225 (2014) -3.5%

Index Values End of Month

	2011	2012	2013	2014	2015	2016	2017	2018	2019	2020
Dow	12,811	13,214	14,840	16,581	17,841	17,774	20,941	24,163	26,593	24,346
S&P 500	1,364	1,398	1,598	1,884	2,086	2,065	2,384	2,648	2,946	2,912
Nasdaq	2,874	3,046	3,329	4,115	4,941	4,775	6,048	7,066	8,095	8,890
TSX	13,945	12,293	12,457	14,652	15,225	13,951	15,586	15,608	16,581	14,781
Russell 1000	758	774	887	1,050	1,164	1,144	1,322	1,468	1,632	1,602
Russell 2000	865	817	947	1,127	1,220	1,131	1,400	1,542	1,591	1,311
FTSE 100	6,070	5,738	6,430	6,780	6,961	6,242	7,204	7,509	7,418	5,901
Nikkei 225	9,850	9,521	13,861	14,304	19,520	16,666	19,197	22,468	22,259	20,194

Percent Gain for April

	2011	2012	2013	2014	2015	2016	2017	2018	2019	2020
Dow	4.0	0.0	1.8	0.7	0.4	0.5	1.3	0.2	2.6	11.1
S&P 500	2.8	-0.7	1.8	0.6	0.9	0.3	0.9	0.3	3.9	12.7
Nasdaq	3.3	-1.5	1.9	-2.0	0.8	-1.9	2.3	0.0	4.7	15.4
TSX	-1.2	-0.8	-2.3	2.2	2.2	3.4	0.2	1.6	3.0	10.5
Russell 1000	2.9	-0.7	1.7	0.4	0.6	0.4	0.9	0.2	3.9	13.1
Russell 2000	2.6	-1.6	-0.4	-3.9	-2.6	1.5	1.0	0.8	3.3	13.7
FTSE 100	2.7	-0.5	0.3	2.8	2.8	1.1	-1.6	6.4	1.9	4.0
Nikkei 225	1.0	-5.6	11.8	-3.5	1.6	-0.6	1.5	4.7	5.0	6.7

April Market Avg. Performance 2011 to 2020[1]

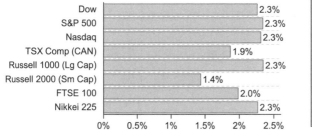

Market	Performance
Dow	2.3%
S&P 500	2.3%
Nasdaq	2.3%
TSX Comp (CAN)	1.9%
Russell 1000 (Lg Cap)	2.3%
Russell 2000 (Sm Cap)	1.4%
FTSE 100	2.0%
Nikkei 225	2.3%

Interest Corner Apr[2]

	Fed Funds %[3]	3 Mo. T-Bill %[4]	10 Yr %[5]	20 Yr %[6]
2020	0.25	0.09	0.64	1.05
2019	2.50	2.43	2.51	2.75
2018	1.75	1.87	2.95	3.01
2017	1.00	0.80	2.29	2.67
2016	0.50	0.22	1.83	2.26

(1) Russell Data provided by Russell (2) Federal Reserve Bank of St. Louis- end of month values (3) Target rate set by FOMC (4)(5)(6) Constant yield maturities.

April 2020
% Sector Performance

GIC % Gain	
Apr 2020	
Apr 90-2020 Avg.	

S&P GIC	2020	1990-2020[1]	
Sectors	% Gain	GIC[2] % Avg Gain	Fq% Gain >S&P 500
Energy	29.7 %	4.0 %	65 %
Materials	15.3	3.0	52
Consumer Discretionary	20.5	2.5	58
Financials	9.3	2.4	48
Industrials	8.7	2.4	58
Information Technology	13.7	2.2	52
Utilities	3.2	1.7	45
Health Care	12.5	1.5	48
Telecom	13.5	0.9	35
Consumer Staples	6.6 %	0.9 %	39 %
S&P 500	12.7 %	2.0 %	N/A %

Sector Commentary

♦ In April 2020, the stock market rallied sharply as investors became convinced that central bank policy and government action was going to be effective in helping the economy through the Covid-19 pandemic. Also, in late March, the number of daily cases of Covid-19 in some European countries started to fall. ♦ The end result was that most sectors of the stock market rallied sharply. Two defensive sectors, utilities and consumer staples strongly lagged the S&P 500, producing gains of 3.2% and 6.6% respectively.

Sub-Sector Commentary

♦ In April 2020, the homebuilders sub-sector was the strongest from the selected sub-sectors, producing a gain of 30.3%. ♦ The metals and mining sub-sector was next with a gain of 28.1%. ♦ As investors jumped back into the stock market, gold was only able to produce a gain of 5.8%. The Federal Reserve had reduced its key interest rate to the zero bound in March and there was little to be gained in the short-term from falling real-interest rates to drive the price of gold higher.

SELECTED SUB-SECTORS[3]			
Automotive & Components	14.4 %	5.8 %	52 %
Railroads	13.9	3.9	65
SOX (1995-2020)	14.6	3.5	50
Chemicals	15.6	3.5	74
Banks	10.2	2.9	52
Metals & Mining	28.1	2.6	42
Transportation	7.7	2.4	58
Homebuilders	30.3	2.1	45
Steel	14.4	1.9	52
Retail	22.3	1.8	52
Pharma	11.2	1.8	48
Agriculture (1994-2020)	5.6	0.9	52
Gold	5.8	0.5	42
Silver	10.1	0.4	39
Biotech (1993-2020)	10.3	0.1	34

(1) Sector data provided by Standard and Poors (2) GIC is short form for Global Industry Classification (3) Sub Sector data provided by Standard and Poors, except where marked by symbol.

18 DAY EARNINGS MONTH EFFECT
Markets Outperform 1st 18 Calendar Days of Earnings Months

Earnings season occurs the first month of every quarter. At this time, public companies report their financials for the previous quarter and give guidance on future expectations. As a result, investors tend to bid up stocks, anticipating good earnings. Earnings are a major driver of stock market prices as investors generally get in the stock market early, in anticipation of favorable results, which helps to run stock prices up in the first half of the month.

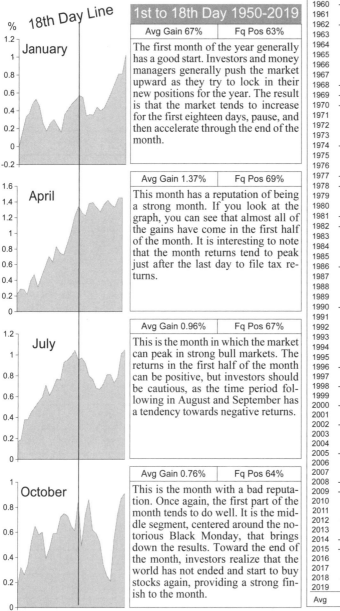

1st to 18th Day 1950-2019

Avg Gain 67%	Fq Pos 63%

January — The first month of the year generally has a good start. Investors and money managers generally push the market upward as they try to lock in their new positions for the year. The result is that the market tends to increase for the first eighteen days, pause, and then accelerate through the end of the month.

Avg Gain 1.37%	Fq Pos 69%

April — This month has a reputation of being a strong month. If you look at the graph, you can see that almost all of the gains have come in the first half of the month. It is interesting to note that the month returns tend to peak just after the last day to file tax returns.

Avg Gain 0.96%	Fq Pos 67%

July — This is the month in which the market can peak in strong bull markets. The returns in the first half of the month can be positive, but investors should be cautious, as the time period following in August and September has a tendency towards negative returns.

Avg Gain 0.76%	Fq Pos 64%

October — This is the month with a bad reputation. Once again, the first part of the month tends to do well. It is the middle segment, centered around the notorious Black Monday, that brings down the results. Toward the end of the month, investors realize that the world has not ended and start to buy stocks again, providing a strong finish to the month.

1st to 18th Day Gain S&P500			
JAN	APR	JUL	OCT
0.36 %	4.28 %	-3.56 %	2.88 %
4.75	3.41	4.39	1.76
2.02	-3.57	-0.44	-1.39
-2.07	-2.65	0.87	3.38
2.50	3.71	2.91	-1.49
-3.28	4.62	3.24	-4.63
-2.88	-1.53	4.96	2.18
-4.35	2.95	2.45	-4.93
2.78	1.45	1.17	2.80
1.09	4.47	1.23	0.79
-3.34	2.26	-2.14	1.55
2.70	1.75	-0.36	2.22
-4.42	-1.84	2.65	0.12
3.30	3.49	-1.27	2.26
2.05	1.99	2.84	0.77
2.05	2.31	1.87	1.91
1.64	2.63	2.66	2.77
6.80	1.84	3.16	-1.51
-0.94	7.63	1.87	2.09
-1.76	-0.27	-2.82	3.37
-1.24	-4.42	6.83	-0.02
1.37	3.17	0.42	-1.01
1.92	2.40	-1.22	-2.13
0.68	0.02	2.00	1.46
-2.04	0.85	-2.58	13.76
3.50	3.53	-2.09	5.95
7.55	-2.04	0.38	-3.58
-3.85	2.15	0.47	-3.18
-4.77	4.73	1.40	-2.00
3.76	0.11	-1.19	-5.22
2.90	-1.51	6.83	4.83
-0.73	-0.96	-0.34	2.59
-4.35	4.33	1.33	13.54
4.10	4.43	-2.20	1.05
1.59	-0.80	-1.16	1.20
2.44	0.10	1.32	2.72
-1.35	1.46	-5.77	3.25
9.96	-1.64	3.48	-12.16
1.94	0.12	-1.09	2.75
3.17	3.78	4.20	-2.12
-4.30	0.23	1.73	-0.10
0.61	3.53	3.83	1.20
0.42	3.06	1.83	-1.45
0.26	-0.60	-1.06	2.07
1.67	-0.74	2.46	1.07
2.27	0.93	2.52	0.52
-1.25	-0.29	-4.04	3.42
4.78	1.22	3.41	-0.33
-0.92	1.90	4.67	3.88
1.14	2.54	3.36	-2.23
-0.96	-3.80	2.69	-6.57
2.10	6.71	-1.36	2.66
-1.79	-2.00	-10.94	8.48
2.50	5.35	1.93	4.35
2.51	0.75	-3.46	-0.05
-1.32	-2.93	2.50	-4.12
2.55	1.22	0.51	3.15
1.41	4.33	-3.20	1.48
-9.75	5.11	-1.51	-19.36
-5.88	8.99	2.29	2.89
1.88	1.94	3.32	3.81
2.97	-1.56	-1.15	8.30
4.01	-1.66	0.78	1.16
4.2	-1.76	5.17	3.74
-0.52	-0.4	0.92	-4.34
-1.92	0.64	3.08	5.89
-8.0	1.68	3.21	-1.32
1.48	-0.87	1.54	1.66
4.65	2.57	3.58	-4.98
6.54	2.49	1.81	0.32
0.67 %	1.37 %	0.96 %	0.76 %

Note: the year column (1950–2019) runs alongside the JAN/APR/JUL/OCT columns, and the final row is the Avg row.

Earnings Month Effect Performance

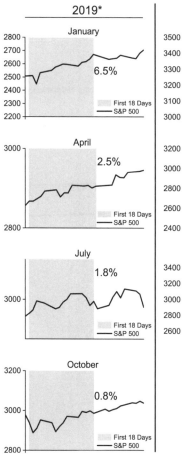

*Last day of previous month included in graph only, displayed return is for first 18 calendar days of month

Stock Markets	2019	2020
Dow	26,425	21,053
S&P500	2,893	2,489
Nasdaq	7,939	7,373
TSX	16,396	12,938
FTSE	7,447	5,416
DAX	12,010	9,526
Nikkei	21,808	17,820
Hang Seng	29,936	23,236

Commodities	2019	2020
Oil	63.08	28.34
Gold	1288.5	1613.1

Bond Yields	2019	2020
USA 5 Yr Treasury	2.31	0.39
USA 10 Yr T	2.50	0.62
USA 20 Yr T	2.72	1.05
Moody's Aaa	3.67	2.63
Moody's Baa	4.72	4.54
CAN 5 Yr T	1.57	0.59
CAN 10 Yr T	1.70	0.71

Money Market	2019	2020
USA Fed Funds	2.50	0.25
USA 3 Mo T-B	2.39	0.10
CAN tgt overnight rate	1.75	0.25
CAN 3 Mo T-B	1.67	0.17

Foreign Exchange	2019	2020
EUR/USD	1.12	1.08
GBP/USD	1.30	1.23
USD/CAD	1.34	1.42
USD/JPY	111.73	108.55

APRIL

M	T	W	T	F	S	S
			1	2	3	4
5	6	7	8	9	10	11
12	13	14	15	16	17	18
19	20	21	22	23	24	25
26	27	28	29	30		

Earnings Month Effect Performance

In 2019, the first eighteen calendar days of the earnings months were positive four out of four times. The biggest gain occurred in January.

In 2020, all of the first three earnings months were positive in the first eighteen calendar days. The first eighteen days in April were particularly strong as the stock market rebounded after Federal Reserve loose monetary policy and increased government support payments to the Covid-19 pandemic helped to increase economic growth expectations.

MAY

M	T	W	T	F	S	S
				1	2	
3	4	5	6	7	8	9
10	11	12	13	14	15	16
17	18	19	20	21	22	23
24	25	26	27	28	29	30
31						

JUNE

M	T	W	T	F	S	S
1	2	3	4	5	6	
7	8	9	10	11	12	13
14	15	16	17	18	19	20
21	22	23	24	25	26	27
28	29	30				

CONSUMER SWITCH – SELL CONSUMER DISCRETIONARY, BUY CONSUMER STAPLES
Consumer Staples Outperform Apr 23 to Oct 27

The *Consumer Switch* strategy has allowed investors to use a set portion of their account to switch between the two related consumer sectors. To use this strategy, investors take a position in the consumer discretionary sector from October 28 to April 22, and then use the proceeds to invest in the consumer staples sector from April 23 to October 27, and then repeat the cycle.

The end result has been outperformance compared with buying and holding both consumer sectors, or buying and holding the broad market.

4601% total aggregate gain

The basic premise of the strategy is that the consumer discretionary sector tends to outperform during the favorable six month period for stocks (October 28th to May 5th), when more money flows into the stock market, pushing up stock prices. On the other hand, the consumer staples sector tends to outperform when investors are looking for safety and stability of earnings in the other six months when the market tends to move into a defensive mode.

Total Gains From Apr 1990 to Apr 2020

746% — S&P 500
1233% — Con Disc
924% — Con Staples
4601% — Switch Strategy Con. Disc.- Con. Staples

* If buy date lands on weekend or holiday, then next day is used

Consumer Staples & Discretionary Switch Strategy*

Investment Period	Buy @ Beginning of Period	% Gain @ End of Period	% Gain Cumulative
90 Apr23 - 90 Oct27	Staples	8.3%	8%
90 Oct28 - 91 Apr22	Discretionary	40.0	52
91 Apr23 - 91 Oct27	Staples	0.7	53
91 Oct28 - 92 Apr22	Discretionary	16.9	78
92 Apr23 - 92 Oct27	Staples	6.9	91
92 Oct28 - 93 Apr22	Discretionary	6.3	103
93 Apr23 - 93 Oct27	Staples	5.4	114
93 Oct28 - 94 Apr22	Discretionary	-4.8	103
94 Apr23 - 94 Oct27	Staples	11.2	126
94 Oct28 - 95 Apr22	Discretionary	4.1	136
95 Apr23 - 95 Oct27	Staples	16.2	174
95 Oct28 - 96 Apr22	Discretionary	16.5	219
96 Apr23 - 96 Oct27	Staples	13.3	261
96 Oct28 - 97 Apr22	Discretionary	4.2	277
97 Apr23 - 97 Oct27	Staples	1.0	281
97 Oct28 - 98 Apr22	Discretionary	36.9	421
98 Apr23 - 98 Oct27	Staples	-0.9	417
98 Oct28 - 99 Apr22	Discretionary	40.1	624
99 Apr23 - 99 Oct27	Staples	-10.3	550
99 Oct28 - 00 Apr22	Discretionary	11.6	625
00 Apr23 - 00 Oct27	Staples	18.8	762
00 Oct28 - 01 Apr22	Discretionary	10.9	855
01 Apr23 - 01 Oct27	Staples	5.3	906
01 Oct28 - 02 Apr22	Discretionary	12.1	1027
02 Apr23 - 02 Oct27	Staples	-11.8	894
02 Oct28 - 03 Apr22	Discretionary	0.5	899
03 Apr23 - 03 Oct27	Staples	8.4	982
03 Oct28 - 04 Apr22	Discretionary	9.9	1090
04 Apr23 - 04 Oct27	Staples	-7.3	1003
04 Oct28 - 05 Apr22	Discretionary	-2.9	971
05 Apr23 - 05 Oct27	Staples	0.3	975
05 Oct28 - 06 Apr22	Discretionary	9.5	1077
06 Apr23 - 06 Oct27	Staples	10.9	1205
06 Oct28 - 07 Apr22	Discretionary	6.6	1292
07 Apr23 - 07 Oct27	Staples	3.9	1346
07 Oct28 - 08 Apr22	Discretionary	-13.7	1147
08 Apr23 - 08 Oct27	Staples	-20.9	887
08 Oct28 - 09 Apr22	Discretionary	17.6	1061
09 Apr23 - 09 Oct27	Staples	20.4	1298
09 Oct28 - 10 Apr22	Discretionary	29.1	1704
10 Apr23 - 10 Oct27	Staples	2.3	1746
10 Oct28 - 11 Apr22	Discretionary	14.0	2004
11 Apr23 - 11 Oct27	Staples	1.8	2042
11 Oct28 - 12 Apr22	Discretionary	12.1	2301
12 Apr23 - 12 Oct27	Staples	3.0	2373
12 Oct28 - 13 Apr22	Discretionary	16.7	2786
13 Apr23 - 13 Oct27	Staples	1.8	2839
13 Oct28 - 14 Apr22	Discretionary	1.9	2897
14 Apr23 - 14 Oct27	Staples	5.8	3069
14 Oct28 - 15 Apr22	Discretionary	14.7	3535
15 Apr23 - 15 Oct27	Staples	2.6	3629
15 Oct28 - 16 Apr22	Discretionary	-0.4	3616
16 Apr23 - 16 Oct27	Staples	1.1	3657
16 Oct28 - 17 Apr22	Discretionary	13.1	4149
17 Apr23 - 17 Oct27	Staples	-4.8	4016
17 Oct28 - 18 Apr22	Discretionary	11.5	4498
18 Apr23 - 18 Oct27	Staples	3.8	4832
18 Oct28 - 19 Apr22	Discretionary	14.7	5626
19 Apr22 - 19 Oct25	Staples	-8.1	4839
19 Oct28 - 20 Apr22	Discretionary	-4.7	4601

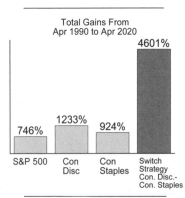

Consumer Discretionary / Consumer Staples Relative Strength Avg. Year 1990 - 2019

Consumer Switch Performance

2019

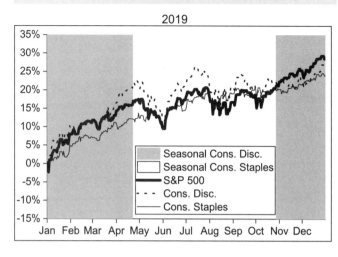

2020

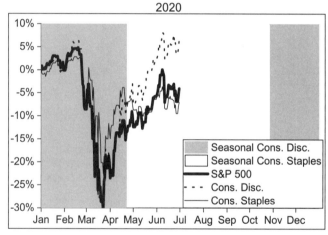

Market Indices & Rates
Weekly Values**

Stock Markets	2019	2020
Dow	26,412	23,719
S&P500	2,907	2,790
Nasdaq	7,984	8,154
TSX	16,481	14,167
FTSE	7,437	5,843
DAX	12,000	10,565
Nikkei	21,871	19,499
Hang Seng	29,910	24,300

Commodities	2019	2020
Oil	63.89	22.76
Gold	1294.3	1680.7

Bond Yields	2019	2020
USA 5 Yr Treasury	2.38	0.41
USA 10 Yr T	2.56	0.73
USA 20 Yr T	2.78	1.15
Moody's Aaa	3.71	2.46
Moody's Baa	4.71	4.34
CAN 5 Yr T	1.64	0.60
CAN 10 Yr T	1.78	0.76

Money Market	2019	2020
USA Fed Funds	2.50	0.25
USA 3 Mo T-B	2.39	0.25
CAN tgt overnight rate	1.75	0.25
CAN 3 Mo T-B	1.68	0.24

Foreign Exchange	2019	2020
EUR/USD	1.13	1.09
GBP/USD	1.31	1.25
USD/CAD	1.33	1.40
USD/JPY	112.02	108.47

APRIL

M	T	W	T	F	S	S
			1	2	3	4
5	6	7	8	9	10	11
12	13	14	15	16	17	18
19	20	21	22	23	24	25
26	27	28	29	30		

In 2020, the consumer discretionary sector performed better than the S&P 500 in its seasonal period at the beginning of the year. In its seasonal period at the end of the year, the sector underperformed as investors focused on the technology sector with its growth companies.

So far in 2020, the consumer discretionary sector has outperformed the S&P 500 in its seasonal period and the consumer staples sector has underperformed the S&P 500 in the first half of its seasonal period.

MAY

M	T	W	T	F	S	S
				1	2
3	4	5	6	7	8	9
10	11	12	13	14	15	16
17	18	19	20	21	22	23
24	25	26	27	28	29	30
31						

JUNE

M	T	W	T	F	S	S
	1	2	3	4	5	6
7	8	9	10	11	12	13
14	15	16	17	18	19	20
21	22	23	24	25	26	27
28	29	30				

U.S. GOVERNMENT BONDS (7-10 YEARS)
May 6 to October 3

The following government bond seasonal period analysis has been broken down into two contiguous periods in order to demonstrate the relative strength of the first part of the trade compared with the second part. Although both the May 6 to August 8 and the August 9 to October 3 periods provide value, the sweet spot to the government bond trade is in the latter period from August 9 to October 3.

Bonds tend to outperform from late spring into autumn for three reasons. First, governments and companies tend to raise more money through bond issuance at the beginning of the year to meet their needs for the rest of the year. With more bonds competing in the market for money, bond prices tend to decrease. Less bonds tend to be issued in late spring and early summer during their seasonal period, helping to support bond prices.

4% gain & positive 77% of the time

Second, optimistic forecasts at the beginning of the year for stronger GDP growth tend to increase inflation expectations and as a result interest rates respond by increasing. As economic growth expectations tend to decrease in the summer, interest rates respond by retreating.

Third, the stock market often peaks in May and investors rotate their money into bonds. As the demand for bonds increases, interest rates decrease and bonds increase in value. For seasonal investors looking to put their money to work in the unfavora-

Source: Barclays Capital Inc.
The U.S. Treasury: 7-10 Year is a total return index, which includes both interest and capital appreciation. For more information on fixed income indices, see www.barcap.com.

U.S. Gov. Bonds* vs. S&P 500 1998 to 2019   Positive ▢

Year	May 6 to Aug 8 S&P 500	May 6 to Aug 8 Gov. Bonds	Aug 9 to Oct 3 S&P 500	Aug 9 to Oct 3 Gov. Bonds	Total Growth S&P 500	Total Growth Gov. Bonds
1998	-2.3 %	3.3 %	-8.0 %	8.3 %	-10.1 %	11.9 %
1999	-3.5	-3.0	-1.3	0.9	-4.8	-2.1
2000	3.5	5.8	-3.8	0.9	-0.4	6.7
2001	-6.6	2.6	-9.4	4.4	-15.3	7.1
2002	-15.7	6.5	-9.6	5.0	-23.7	11.9
2003	5.5	-1.3	5.4	1.3	11.2	0.0
2004	-5.1	3.6	6.4	0.8	0.9	4.4
2005	4.3	-0.9	0.3	0.7	4.6	-0.2
2006	-4.1	2.6	4.9	2.7	0.6	5.3
2007	-0.5	-0.3	2.8	3.3	2.3	3.0
2008	-7.9	0.9	-15.2	2.4	-21.9	3.4
2009	11.8	-4.0	1.5	5.4	13.4	1.1
2010	-3.8	7.1	2.2	2.6	-1.7	9.8
2011	-16.2	7.6	-1.8	4.6	-17.7	12.6
2012	2.4	2.3	3.5	0.9	6.0	3.3
2013	5.1	-5.2	-1.1	0.3	4.0	-4.9
2014	2.5	2.3	1.9	0.1	4.4	2.4
2015	-0.6	0.6	-6.1	2.1	-6.6	2.6
2016	6.4	1.6	-0.9	-0.1	5.4	1.6
2017	3.2	1.3	2.4	-0.1	5.6	1.2
2018	7.3	0.6	2.4	-1.0	9.8	-0.4
2019	-0.2	7.1	-0.9	1.5	-1.2	8.7
Avg.	-0.6 %	1.9 %	-1.1 %	2.1 %	-1.6 %	4.1 %
Fq>0	45 %	73 %	50 %	86 %	55 %	77 %

ble six months of the year, buying bonds in the summer months fits perfectly with their strategy.

In periods when the stock market rallies in the early summer months, positive bond performance can be delayed until later in the summer, typically early August, which coincides with the bond seasonal period sweet spot, from August 9 to October 3.

Covid-19 Performance Update. US government bonds were fairly flat during their initial seasonal period starting in May, as the Federal Reserve implemented quantitative easing policies to maintain low interest rates in the market.

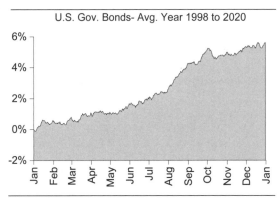

U.S. Gov. Bonds- Avg. Year 1998 to 2020

U.S. Government Bond Performance

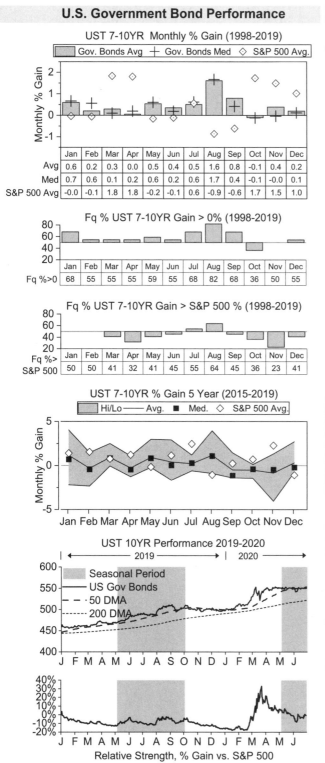

UST 7-10YR Monthly % Gain (1998-2019)

Gov. Bonds Avg — Gov. Bonds Med ◇ S&P 500 Avg.

	Jan	Feb	Mar	Apr	May	Jun	Jul	Aug	Sep	Oct	Nov	Dec
Avg	0.6	0.2	0.3	0.0	0.5	0.4	0.5	1.6	0.8	-0.1	0.4	0.2
Med	0.7	0.6	0.1	0.2	0.6	0.2	0.6	1.7	0.4	-0.1	-0.0	0.1
S&P 500 Avg	-0.0	-0.1	1.8	1.8	-0.2	-0.1	0.6	-0.9	-0.6	1.7	1.5	1.0

Fq % UST 7-10YR Gain > 0% (1998-2019)

	Jan	Feb	Mar	Apr	May	Jun	Jul	Aug	Sep	Oct	Nov	Dec
Fq %>0	68	55	55	55	59	55	68	82	68	36	50	55

Fq % UST 7-10YR Gain > S&P 500 % (1998-2019)

	Jan	Feb	Mar	Apr	May	Jun	Jul	Aug	Sep	Oct	Nov	Dec
Fq %> S&P 500	50	50	41	32	41	45	55	64	45	36	23	41

UST 7-10YR % Gain 5 Year (2015-2019)

Hi/Lo — Avg. ■ Med. ◇ S&P 500 Avg.

UST 10YR Performance 2019-2020

← 2019 → | 2020 →

Seasonal Period
— US Gov Bonds
– – 50 DMA
⋯⋯ 200 DMA

Relative Strength, % Gain vs. S&P 500

Stock Markets	2019	2020
Dow	26,560	24,242
S&P500	2,905	2,875
Nasdaq	7,998	8,650
TSX	16,613	14,360
FTSE	7,460	5,787
DAX	12,222	10,626
Nikkei	22,201	19,897
Hang Seng	29,963	24,380

Commodities	2019	2020
Oil	64.00	18.27
Gold	1275.7	1692.6

Bond Yields	2019	2020
USA 5 Yr Treasury	2.38	0.36
USA 10 Yr T	2.57	0.65
USA 20 Yr T	2.78	1.08
Moody's Aaa	3.69	2.41
Moody's Baa	4.69	3.92
CAN 5 Yr T	1.62	0.46
CAN 10 Yr T	1.77	0.65

Money Market	2019	2020
USA Fed Funds	2.50	0.25
USA 3 Mo T-B	2.37	0.12
CAN tgt overnight rate	1.75	0.25
CAN 3 Mo T-B	1.67	0.20

Foreign Exchange	2019	2020
EUR/USD	1.12	1.09
GBP/USD	1.30	1.25
USD/CAD	1.34	1.40
USD/JPY	111.92	107.54

APRIL

M	T	W	T	F	S	S
			1	2	3	4
5	6	7	8	9	10	11
12	13	14	15	16	17	18
19	20	21	22	23	24	25
26	27	28	29	30		

MAY

M	T	W	T	F	S	S
				1	2	
3	4	5	6	7	8	9
10	11	12	13	14	15	16
17	18	19	20	21	22	23
24	25	26	27	28	29	30
31						

JUNE

M	T	W	T	F	S	S
1	2	3	4	5	6	
7	8	9	10	11	12	13
14	15	16	17	18	19	20
21	22	23	24	25	26	27
28	29	30				

CAD VS US DOLLAR ①SELL SHORT (Jan6-Mar7)
②LONG (Mar15-Apr30) ③LONG(Aug12-Sep22)
④SELL SHORT (Oct13-Dec18) ⑤LONG(Dec19-Jan5)

CAD

The Canadian dollar versus the US dollar has many drivers of valuation, but two of the bigger drivers are the price of oil and the spread on the two year differential government bonds between the two countries.

Although the energy sector seasonal period does not line up exactly with the seasonality for the Canadian dollar, there is an overlap. The energy sector tends to perform well from late February into early May. Correspondingly, the Canadian dollar tends to perform well from mid-March to the end of April. In addition, the energy sector tends to perform well from late July to early October, and the Canadian dollar tends to perform well from early August to late September.

The Canadian dollar also performs well from mid-December to early January. The US dollar tends to perform poorly against most currencies in late December.

The US dollar's strongest period relative to the Canadian dollar is from mid-October to mid-December. Overall, this is one of the weaker seasonal periods for oil.

The US dollar also tends to perform well relative to the Canadian dollar from early January to early March. The US dollar tends to perform well against most major world currencies at this time.

Covid-19 Performance Update. The Canadian dollar was negative relative to the US dollar as the Covid-19 pandemic developed in 2020 and investors shifted to a risk-off mode. After the stock market bottomed, the Canadian dollar turned positive and continued to outperform the US dollar into the summer months.

Canadian Dollar vs. US Dollar 1990/91 to 2019/20

Negative Short ☐ Positive Long ☐

Year	Jan6 Mar7	Mar15 Apr30	Aug12 Sep22	Oct13 Dec18	Dec19 Jan5	Com- pound
1990/91	-2.1 %	0.8 %	-0.9 %	-0.9 %	0.5 %	3.5 %
1991/92	-0.8	0.2	0.8	-1.5	0.0	3.3
1992/93	-3.5	0.3	-3.9	-2.8	0.1	2.6
1993/94	2.5	-2.1	-0.2	-0.8	1.4	-2.6
1994/95	-2.7	-1.5	2.4	-3.3	-0.6	6.3
1995/96	-1.0	4.3	1.0	-2.9	1.5	11.1
1996/97	-1.0	0.5	0.6	-1.1	-0.2	3.0
1997/98	0.1	-2.3	0.8	-3.4	0.2	2.0
1998/99	0.3	-1.3	2.1	-0.2	2.1	2.8
1999/00	-0.4	4.6	1.6	-0.2	1.9	9.0
2001/01	-0.4	-1.0	-0.5	-0.6	1.7	1.1
2001/02	-3.3	1.4	-1.4	-0.7	-1.3	2.6
2002/03	0.8	1.5	-1.5	2.1	-0.7	-3.5
2003/04	6.7	3.0	4.3	-0.6	3.7	4.6
2004/05	-3.0	-2.8	1.9	2.1	0.3	0.1
2005/06	-0.3	-4.1	3.5	1.0	-0.3	-1.7
2006/07	1.0	3.6	0.1	-2.0	-1.4	3.3
2007/08	-0.5	6.0	5.8	-3.4	0.3	16.8
2008/09	1.2	-1.8	0.8	-2.6	1.3	1.6
2009/10	-7.6	6.7	-0.9	-3.0	2.6	20.2
2010/11	1.0	0.1	2.3	-0.4	1.8	3.7
2011/12	2.3	3.0	-3.7	-2.0	1.8	0.7
2012/13	2.2	0.5	0.9	-0.6	-0.2	-0.4
2013/14	-4.1	1.5	1.6	-3.3	0.6	11.5
2014/15	-4.1	1.3	-1.5	-3.3	-1.6	5.5
2015/16	-6.8	5.8	-1.1	-6.9	-0.3	19.2
2016/17	5.4	5.6	-2.3	-0.5	0.8	-1.1
2017/18	-1.4	-1.3	1.5	-3.0	3.6	8.5
2018/19	-3.9	0.9	0.6	-3.3	0.7	9.7
2019/20	-0.6	-0.4	0.2	0.7	0.9	0.6
Avg.	-0.8 %	1.1 %	0.5 %	-1.6 %	0.9 %	4.8 %
Fq>0	37 %	67 %	63 %	13 %	67 %	83 %

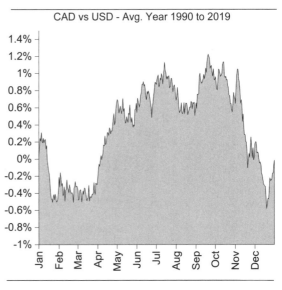

CAD vs USD - Avg. Year 1990 to 2019

CAD/USD Performance

CADUSD Monthly % Gain (1990-2019)

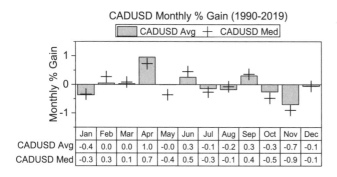

	Jan	Feb	Mar	Apr	May	Jun	Jul	Aug	Sep	Oct	Nov	Dec
CADUSD Avg	-0.4	0.0	0.0	1.0	-0.0	0.3	-0.1	-0.2	0.3	-0.3	-0.7	-0.1
CADUSD Med	-0.3	0.3	0.1	0.7	-0.4	0.5	-0.3	-0.1	0.4	-0.5	-0.9	-0.1

Fq % CADUSD Gain > 0% (1990-2019)

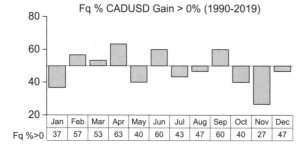

	Jan	Feb	Mar	Apr	May	Jun	Jul	Aug	Sep	Oct	Nov	Dec
Fq %>0	37	57	53	63	40	60	43	47	60	40	27	47

CADUSD % Gain 5 Year (2015-2019)

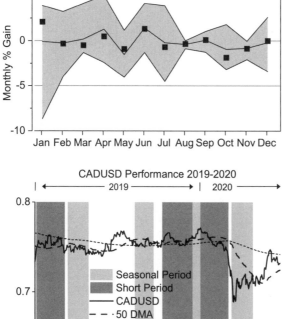

CADUSD Performance 2019-2020

Seasonal Period
Short Period
CADUSD
50 DMA
200 DMA

WEEK 17

Market Indices & Rates
Weekly Values**

Stock Markets	2019	2020
Dow	26,543	23,775
S&P500	2,940	2,837
Nasdaq	8,134	8,635
TSX	16,613	14,420
FTSE	7,428	5,752
DAX	12,315	10,336
Nikkei	22,259	19,262
Hang Seng	29,605	23,831

Commodities	2019	2020
Oil	63.30	16.04
Gold	1284.2	1715.9

Bond Yields	2019	2020
USA 5 Yr Treasury	2.29	0.36
USA 10 Yr T	2.51	0.60
USA 20 Yr T	2.74	0.98
Moody's Aaa	3.69	2.30
Moody's Baa	4.64	3.85
CAN 5 Yr T	1.53	0.44
CAN 10 Yr T	1.69	0.58

Money Market	2019	2020
USA Fed Funds	2.50	0.25
USA 3 Mo T-B	2.37	0.12
CAN tgt overnight rate	1.75	0.25
CAN 3 Mo T-B	1.67	0.23

Foreign Exchange	2019	2020
EUR/USD	1.12	1.08
GBP/USD	1.29	1.24
USD/CAD	1.35	1.41
USD/JPY	111.58	107.51

APRIL

M	T	W	T	F	S	S
			1	2	3	4
5	6	7	8	9	10	11
12	13	14	15	16	17	18
19	20	21	22	23	24	25
26	27	28	29	30		

MAY

M	T	W	T	F	S	S
					1	2
3	4	5	6	7	8	9
10	11	12	13	14	15	16
17	18	19	20	21	22	23
24	25	26	27	28	29	30
31						

JUNE

M	T	W	T	F	S	S
	1	2	3	4	5	6
7	8	9	10	11	12	13
14	15	16	17	18	19	20
21	22	23	24	25	26	27
28	29	30				

MAY

	MONDAY	TUESDAY	WEDNESDAY
WEEK 18	**3** 28	**4** 27	**5** 26
WEEK 19	**10** 21	**11** 20	**12** 19
WEEK 20	**17** 14	**18** 13	**19** 12
WEEK 21	**24** 7 CAN Market Closed- Victoria Day	**25** 6	**26** 5
WEEK 22	**31** USA Market Closed- Memorial Day	1	2

THURSDAY	FRIDAY
6 25	**7** 24
13 18	**14** 17
20 11	**21** 10
27 4	**28** 3
3	4

JUNE

M	T	W	T	F	S	S
	1	2	3	4	5	6
7	8	9	10	11	12	13
14	15	16	17	18	19	20
21	22	23	24	25	26	27
28	29	30				

JULY

M	T	W	T	F	S	S
			1	2	3	4
5	6	7	8	9	10	11
12	13	14	15	16	17	18
19	20	21	22	23	24	25
26	27	28	29	30	31	

AUGUST

M	T	W	T	F	S	S
						1
2	3	4	5	6	7	8
9	10	11	12	13	14	15
16	17	18	19	20	21	22
23	24	25	26	27	28	29
30	31					

SEPTEMBER

M	T	W	T	F	S	S
		1	2	3	4	5
6	7	8	9	10	11	12
13	14	15	16	17	18	19
20	21	22	23	24	25	26
27	28	29	30			

MAY SUMMARY

S&P500 Cumulative Daily Gains for Avg Month 1950 to 2020

	Dow Jones	S&P 500	Nasdaq	TSX Comp
Month Rank	9	8	5	2
# Up	37	41	30	21
# Down	33	29	18	14
% Pos	53	59	63	60
% Avg. Gain	-0.1	0.2	1.0	1.2

Dow & S&P 1950-2019, Nasdaq 1972-2019, TSX 1985-2019

♦ The first few days and the last few days in May tend to be strong and the period in between tends to be negative. ♦ A lot of the cyclical sectors finish their seasonal periods at the beginning of May. ♦ In May 2020, the Covid-19 rally continued without a large correction. In May, some of the economically sensitive sectors started to show continued outperformance relative to the S&P 500, as investors increased their expectations of economic growth with Covid-19 cases trending down.

BEST / WORST MAY BROAD MKTS. 2011-2020

BEST MAY MARKETS
♦ Nikkei 225 (2020) 8.3%
♦ Nasdaq (2020) 6.8%
♦ Russell 2000 (2020) 6.4%

WORST MAY MARKETS
♦ Nikkei 225 (2012) -10.3%
♦ Nasdaq (2019) -7.9%
♦ Russell 2000 (2019) -7.9%

Index Values End of Month

	2011	2012	2013	2014	2015	2016	2017	2018	2019	2020
Dow	12,570	12,393	15,116	16,717	18,011	17,787	21,009	24,416	24,815	25,383
S&P 500	1,345	1,310	1,631	1,924	2,107	2,097	2,412	2,663	2,752	3,044
Nasdaq	2,835	2,827	3,456	4,243	5,070	4,948	6,199	7,442	7,453	9,490
TSX Comp.	13,803	11,513	12,650	14,604	15,014	14,066	15,350	16,062	16,037	15,193
Russell 1000	749	724	904	1,072	1,177	1,161	1,336	1,502	1,524	1,683
Russell 2000	848	762	984	1,135	1,247	1,155	1,370	1,634	1,465	1,394
FTSE 100	5,990	5,321	6,583	6,845	6,984	6,231	7,520	7,678	7,162	6,077
Nikkei 225	9,694	8,543	13,775	14,632	20,563	17,235	19,651	22,202	20,601	21,878

Percent Gain for May

	2011	2012	2013	2014	2015	2016	2017	2018	2019	2020
Dow	-1.9	-6.2	1.9	0.8	1.0	0.1	0.3	1.0	-6.7	4.3
S&P 500	-1.4	-6.3	2.1	2.1	1.0	1.5	1.2	0.6	-6.6	4.5
Nasdaq	-1.3	-7.2	3.8	3.1	2.6	3.6	2.5	5.3	-7.9	6.8
TSX Comp.	-1.0	-6.3	1.6	-0.3	-1.4	0.8	-1.5	2.9	-3.3	2.8
Russell 1000	-1.3	-6.4	2.0	2.1	1.1	1.5	1.0	2.3	-6.6	5.1
Russell 2000	-2.0	-6.7	3.9	0.7	2.2	2.1	-2.2	5.9	-7.9	6.4
FTSE 100	-1.3	-7.3	2.4	1.0	0.3	-0.2	4.4	2.2	-3.5	3.0
Nikkei 225	-1.6	-10.3	-0.6	2.3	5.3	3.4	2.4	-1.2	-7.4	8.3

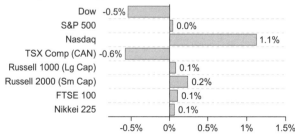

May Market Avg. Performance 2011 to 2020[1]

Dow -0.5%
S&P 500 0.0%
Nasdaq 1.1%
TSX Comp (CAN) -0.6%
Russell 1000 (Lg Cap) 0.1%
Russell 2000 (Sm Cap) 0.2%
FTSE 100 0.1%
Nikkei 225 0.1%

Interest Corner May[2]

	Fed Funds % [3]	3 Mo. T-Bill % [4]	10 Yr % [5]	20 Yr % [6]
2020	0.25	0.14	0.65	1.18
2019	2.50	2.35	2.14	2.39
2018	1.75	1.93	2.83	2.91
2017	1.00	0.98	2.21	2.60
2016	0.50	0.34	1.84	2.23

(1) Russell Data provided by Russell (2) Federal Reserve Bank of St. Louis- end of month values (3) Target rate set by FOMC (4)(5)(6) Constant yield maturities.

May 2020 % Sector Performance	GIC % Gain May 2020 May 90-2020 Avg.	S&P GIC Sectors	2020 % Gain	1990-2020[1] GIC[2] % Avg Gain	Fq% Gain >S&P 500
Cons Staples		Consumer Staples	1.4 %	1.7 %	55 %
Health Care		Health Care	3.1	1.5	52
Info Tech		Information Technology	6.8	1.5	61
Cons Disc		Consumer Discretionary	4.9	1.2	55
Financials		Financials	2.4	1.1	42
Industrials		Industrials	5.1	0.8	39
Materials		Materials	6.7	0.7	32
Utilities		Utilities	3.9	0.5	42
Telecom		Telecom	6.0	0.3	48
Energy		Energy	0.7 %	0.1 %	32 %
S&P 500		S&P 500	4.5 %	1.0 %	N/A %

Sector Commentary

♦ In May 2020, all of the major sectors of the stock market were positive. The size of the rally was less than in April. ♦ The energy sector was barely positive, producing a gain of 0.7%. ♦ The top performing sector was the information technology sector with a gain of 6.8%. Investors continued to favour sectors of the stock market that benefited from work from home stocks. ♦ The consumer discretionary sector was the next best sector, with a gain of 4.9%. Although the economy had slowed down, the consumer continued to spend money, particularly online.

Sub-Sector Commentary

♦ In May 2020, the homebuilders sub-sector performed particularly well as low interest rates helped to motivate consumer purchases of houses. ♦ Silver was a strong performer as manufacturing expectations improved. Silver also benefited from investors becoming more interested in the precious metals sector and given how cheap silver was to gold, it strongly outperformed gold in May. ♦ The banking sector was negative for the month as falling interest rates hurt the net interest margins of the banks.

SELECTED SUB-SECTORS[3]

	2020 % Gain	GIC % Avg Gain	Fq% Gain >S&P 500
Biotech (1993-2020)	4.4 %	2.0 %	66 %
Retail	4.8	1.6	58
Agriculture (1994-2020)	5.8	1.5	52
Railroads	6.8	1.4	61
Banks	-0.2	1.4	45
SOX (1995-2020)	7.0	1.0	58
Pharma	0.3	1.0	45
Chemicals	8.8	0.9	45
Transportation	6.1	0.5	52
Automotive & Components	12.1	0.4	29
Gold	1.5	0.1	48
Metals & Mining	-0.2	0.1	42
Steel	2.6	0.1	45
Silver	14.7	-0.1	45
Homebuilders	15.7	-0.5	48

DIS DISNEY–TIME TO STAY AWAY & TIME TO VISIT
①SELL SHORT (Jun5-Sep30) ②LONG(Oct1-Feb15)

Disney has two seasonal periods, one positive and one negative. The positive (strong) seasonal period for Disney, from October 1 to February 15, is stronger in magnitude than its weak seasonal period which takes place from June 5 to September 30.

Gain of 26%

According to Disney's Form 10-K filed with the Securities and Exchange Commission for the year ended September 29, 2012: "Revenues in our Media Networks segment are subject to seasonal advertising patterns... these commitments are typically satisfied during the second half of the Company's fiscal year." The media segment is the biggest driver of revenue for Disney. In addition, their other business segments are skewed towards revenue generation in the summer.

Disney's year-end occurs at the end of September and it typically reports its results in the first week of November. Investors start to increase their positions at the beginning of October in anticipation of positive year-end news.

Do not "visit" the Disney stock from June 5 to September 30. For the period from 1990 to 2019, Disney has produced an average loss of 7.0% and has only beaten the S&P 500, 30% of the time.

Covid-19 Performance Update. Disney started its weak seasonal period in early June in 2020 on a weak note as it suffered from reduced attendance in its theme parks worldwide and poor revenues from ESPN.

(i) *DIS - stock symbol for Walt Disney Company which trades on the NYSE. is a diversified worldwide entertainment company. Price is adjusted for stock splits.*

Disney vs. S&P 500 1990/91 to 2019/20

Negative Short [ ]   Positive Long [ ]

Year	Jun 5 to Sep 30 S&P 500	Jun 5 to Sep 30 Dis-ney	Oct 1 to Feb 15 S&P 500	Oct 1 to Feb 15 Dis-ney	Compound Growth S&P 500	Compound Growth Dis-ney
1990/91	-16.7 %	-29.7 %	20.6 %	30.1 %	0.5 %	68.2 %
1991/92	0.0	-3.0	6.4	25.4	6.4	29.2
1992/93	1.1	-2.7	6.4	29.7	7.6	33.1
1993/94	2.0	-14.7	3.0	23.9	5.0	42.0
1994/95	0.6	-13.2	4.7	38.5	5.3	56.6
1995/96	9.8	2.7	11.5	11.3	22.3	8.3
1996/97	2.2	5.2	17.6	23.6	20.2	17.1
1997/98	12.8	0.9	7.7	38.2	21.4	36.9
1998/99	-7.1	-30.4	21.0	39.6	12.4	82.3
1999/00	-3.4	-15.1	9.3	41.9	5.6	63.2
2001/01	-2.8	-5.4	-7.7	-15.3	-10.2	-10.7
2001/02	-17.9	-41.1	6.1	28.4	-12.9	81.1
2002/03	-21.7	-31.9	2.4	10.5	-19.8	45.8
2003/04	1.0	-2.7	15.0	33.5	16.2	37.1
2004/05	-0.7	-6.3	8.6	31.2	7.8	39.4
2005/06	2.7	-11.7	4.2	11.4	7.0	24.4
2006/07	3.7	1.0	9.1	12.2	13.1	11.1
2007/08	-0.8	-3.7	-11.6	-5.5	-12.3	-2.1
2008/09	-15.3	-10.7	-29.1	-39.7	-40.0	-33.2
2009/10	12.2	9.2	1.7	9.5	14.1	0.6
2010/11	7.2	-1.8	16.4	30.2	24.7	32.5
2011/12	-13.0	-23.4	18.7	36.8	3.3	68.8
2012/13	12.7	17.7	5.5	6.4	18.9	-12.5
2013/14	3.1	0.2	9.3	22.9	12.7	22.6
2014/15	2.3	5.7	6.3	17.0	8.8	10.4
2015/16	-8.4	-7.3	-2.9	-10.8	-11.0	-4.3
2016/17	3.3	-6.0	8.4	18.7	11.9	25.7
2017/18	3.3	-8.0	8.4	6.7	12.0	15.3
2018/19	6.1	16.7	-4.8	-3.7	1.0	-19.8
2019/20	6.2	-3.3	13.6	7.1	20.6	10.6
Avg.	-0.5 %	-7.0 %	6.2 %	17.0 %	5.8 %	25.9 %
Fq>0	63 %	30 %	83 %	83 %	80 %	77 %

Disney - Avg. Year 1990 to 2019

Disney / S&P 500 Rel. Strength- Avg Yr. 1990-2019

Disney - Performance

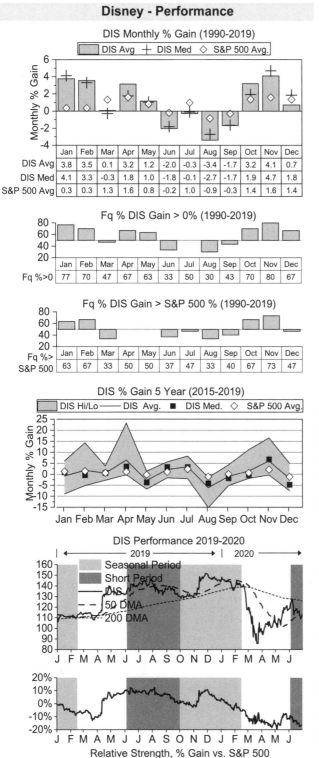

DIS Monthly % Gain (1990-2019)

	Jan	Feb	Mar	Apr	May	Jun	Jul	Aug	Sep	Oct	Nov	Dec
DIS Avg	3.8	3.5	0.1	3.2	1.2	-2.0	-0.3	-3.4	-1.7	3.2	4.1	0.7
DIS Med	4.1	3.3	-0.3	1.8	1.0	-1.8	-0.1	-2.7	-1.7	1.9	4.7	1.8
S&P 500 Avg	0.3	0.3	1.3	1.6	0.8	-0.2	1.0	-0.9	-0.3	1.4	1.6	1.4

Fq % DIS Gain > 0% (1990-2019)

	Jan	Feb	Mar	Apr	May	Jun	Jul	Aug	Sep	Oct	Nov	Dec
Fq %>0	77	70	47	67	63	33	50	30	43	70	80	67

Fq % DIS Gain > S&P 500 % (1990-2019)

	Jan	Feb	Mar	Apr	May	Jun	Jul	Aug	Sep	Oct	Nov	Dec
Fq %> S&P 500	63	67	33	50	50	37	47	33	40	67	73	47

DIS % Gain 5 Year (2015-2019)

DIS Performance 2019-2020

Relative Strength, % Gain vs. S&P 500

WEEK 18

Market Indices & Rates
Weekly Values**

Stock Markets	2019	2020
Dow	26,505	23,724
S&P500	2,946	2,831
Nasdaq	8,164	8,605
TSX	16,494	14,620
FTSE	7,381	5,763
DAX	12,413	10,862
Nikkei	0	19,619
Hang Seng	30,082	24,644

Commodities	2019	2020
Oil	61.94	19.78
Gold	1278.6	1686.3

Bond Yields	2019	2020
USA 5 Yr Treasury	2.33	0.36
USA 10 Yr T	2.54	0.64
USA 20 Yr T	2.75	1.04
Moody's Aaa	3.73	2.42
Moody's Baa	4.65	3.89
CAN 5 Yr T	1.62	0.38
CAN 10 Yr T	1.76	0.53

Money Market	2019	2020
USA Fed Funds	2.50	0.25
USA 3 Mo T-B	2.38	0.12
CAN tgt overnight rate	1.75	0.25
CAN 3 Mo T-B	1.67	0.25

Foreign Exchange	2019	2020
EUR/USD	1.12	1.10
GBP/USD	1.32	1.25
USD/CAD	1.34	1.41
USD/JPY	111.10	106.91

MAY

M	T	W	T	F	S	S
					1	2
3	4	5	6	7	8	9
10	11	12	13	14	15	16
17	18	19	20	21	22	23
24	25	26	27	28	29	30
31						

JUNE

M	T	W	T	F	S	S
	1	2	3	4	5	6
7	8	9	10	11	12	13
14	15	16	17	18	19	20
21	22	23	24	25	26	27
28	29	30				

JULY

M	T	W	T	F	S	S
		1	2	3	4	5
6	7	8	9	10	11	12
13	14	15	16	17	18	19
20	21	22	23	24	25	26
27	28	29	30	31		

The six-month cycle is the result of several factors but is mainly driven by the investor liquidity preference cycle (investors tending to decrease risk in the summer months).

Most pundits do not grasp the full value of the favorable six month period for stocks from October 28 to May 5, compared with the other six months: the unfavorable six month period.

Not only does the favorable period on average have bigger gains more frequently and smaller losses, but also on a yearly basis, outperforms the unfavorable period 72% of the time (last column in the table with YES values). There is no question which six month period seasonal investors should favor.

$1,440,905 gain on $10,000

The accompanying table uses the S&P 500 to compare the returns made from Oct 28 to May 5, to the returns made during the remainder of the year.

Starting with $10,000 and investing from October 28 to May 5 every year (October 28, 1950, to May 5, 2019) has produced a gain of $1,440,905. On the flip side, being invested from May 6 to October 27, has actually lost money. An initial investment of $10,000 has lost $1,201 over the same time period.

S&P 500 Unfavorable 6 Month Avg. Gain vs Favorable 6 Month Avg. Gain (1950-2020)

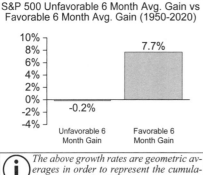

	S&P 500 % May 6 to Oct 27	$10,000 Start	S&P 500 % Oct 28 to May 5	$10,000 Start	Oct28-May5 > May6-Oct27
1950/51	8.5%	10,851	15.2%	11,517	YES
1951/52	0.2	10,870	3.7	11,947	YES
1952/53	1.8	11,067	3.9	12,413	YES
1953/54	-3.1	10,727	16.6	14,475	YES
1954/55	13.2	12,141	18.1	17,097	YES
1955/56	11.4	13,528	15.1	19,681	YES
1956/57	-4.6	12,903	0.2	19,711	YES
1957/58	-12.4	11,302	7.9	21,265	YES
1958/59	15.1	13,013	14.5	24,356	
1959/60	-0.6	12,939	-4.5	23,270	
1960/61	-2.3	12,647	24.1	28,869	YES
1961/62	2.7	12,993	-3.1	27,982	
1962/63	-17.7	10,698	28.4	35,929	YES
1963/64	5.7	11,306	9.3	39,264	YES
1964/65	5.1	11,882	5.5	41,440	YES
1965/66	3.1	12,253	-5.0	39,388	
1966/67	-8.8	11,180	17.7	46,364	YES
1967/68	0.6	11,241	3.9	48,171	YES
1968/69	5.6	11,872	0.2	48,249	
1969/70	-6.2	11,141	-19.7	38,722	
1970/71	5.8	11,782	24.9	48,346	YES
1971/72	-9.6	10,647	13.7	54,965	YES
1972/73	3.7	11,046	0.3	55,154	
1973/74	0.3	11,084	-18.0	45,205	
1974/75	-23.2	8,513	28.5	58,073	YES
1975/76	-0.4	8,480	12.4	65,290	YES
1976/77	0.9	8,554	-1.6	64,231	
1977/78	-7.8	7,890	4.5	67,146	YES
1978/79	-2.0	7,732	6.4	71,476	YES
1979/80	-0.1	7,723	5.8	75,605	YES
1980/81	20.2	9,283	1.9	77,047	
1981/82	-8.5	8,498	-1.4	76,001	YES
1982/83	15.0	9,769	21.4	92,293	YES
1983/84	0.3	9,803	-3.5	89,085	
1984/85	3.9	10,183	8.9	97,057	YES
1985/86	4.1	10,604	26.8	123,044	YES
1986/87	0.4	10,651	23.7	152,196	YES
1987/88	-21.0	8,409	11.0	168,904	YES
1988/89	7.1	9,010	10.9	187,380	YES
1989/90	8.9	9,814	1.0	189,242	
1990/91	-10.0	8,837	25.0	236,498	YES
1991/92	0.9	8,916	8.5	256,590	YES
1992/93	0.4	8,952	6.2	272,550	YES
1993/94	4.5	9,356	-2.8	264,789	
1994/95	3.2	9,656	11.6	295,636	YES
1995/96	11.5	10,762	10.7	327,219	
1996/97	9.2	11,757	18.5	387,591	YES
1997/98	5.6	12,419	27.2	493,003	YES
1998/99	-4.5	11,860	26.5	623,489	YES
1999/00	-3.8	11,415	10.5	688,842	YES
2000/01	-3.7	10,992	-8.2	632,435	
2001/02	-12.8	9,586	-2.8	614,583	YES
2002/03	-16.4	8,016	3.2	634,369	YES
2003/04	11.3	8,921	8.8	689,985	
2004/05	0.3	8,952	4.2	718,942	YES
2005/06	0.5	9,000	12.5	808,503	YES
2006/07	3.9	9,350	9.3	883,804	YES
2007/08	2.0	9,534	-8.3	810,240	
2008/09	-39.7	5,750	6.5	862,619	YES
2009/10	17.7	6,766	9.6	934,470	
2010/11	1.4	6,862	12.9	1,067,851	YES
2011/12	-3.8	6,602	6.6	1,138,103	YES
2012/13	3.1	6,809	14.3	1,301,313	YES
2013/14	9.0	7,422	7.1	1,393,667	
2014/15	4.1	7,725	6.5	1,484,478	YES
2015/16	-1.1	7,638	-0.7	1,473,513	YES
2016/17	4.0	7,985	12.5	1,649,048	YES
2017/18	7.6	8,591	3.2	1,701,662	
2018/19	-0.2	8,575	10.8	1,885,321	YES
2019/20	2.6	8,799	-5.1	1,450,905	
Total Gain (Loss)		**(1,201)**		**1,440,905**	

10% — 8% — 6% — 4% — 2% — 0% — -2% — -4%

7.7%

-0.2%

Unfavorable 6 Month Gain | Favorable 6 Month Gain

The above growth rates are geometric averages in order to represent the cumulative growth of a dollar investment over time. These figures differ from the arithmetic mean calculations used in the Six 'N' Six Take a Break Strategy, which are used to represent an average year.

6 'n' 6 Strategy Performance

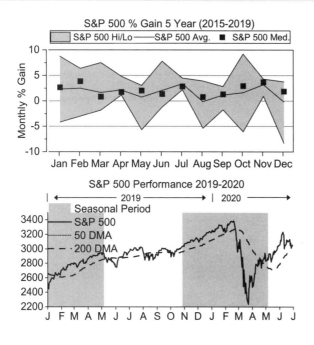

S&P 500 % Gain 5 Year (2015-2019)

S&P 500 Performance 2019-2020

Favorable vs. Unfavorable Seasons 2018-2020 (S&P 500)

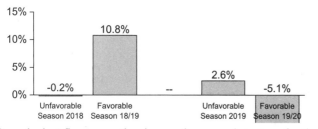

Market Indices & Rates
Weekly Values**

Stock Markets	2019	2020
Dow	25,942	24,331
S&P500	2,881	2,930
Nasdaq	7,917	9,121
TSX	16,298	14,967
FTSE	7,203	5,936
DAX	12,060	10,904
Nikkei	21,345	20,179
Hang Seng	28,550	24,230

Commodities	2019	2020
Oil	61.66	24.48
Gold	1287.1	1704.1

Bond Yields	2019	2020
USA 5 Yr Treasury	2.26	0.33
USA 10 Yr T	2.47	0.69
USA 20 Yr T	2.70	1.12
Moody's Aaa	3.72	2.54
Moody's Baa	4.67	4.06
CAN 5 Yr T	1.61	0.39
CAN 10 Yr T	1.73	0.58

Money Market	2019	2020
USA Fed Funds	2.50	0.25
USA 3 Mo T-B	2.38	0.12
CAN tgt overnight rate	1.75	0.25
CAN 3 Mo T-B	1.68	0.22

Foreign Exchange	2019	2020
EUR/USD	1.12	1.08
GBP/USD	1.30	1.24
USD/CAD	1.34	1.39
USD/JPY	109.95	106.65

Over the last five years, the six month seasonal strategy for the stock market generally has followed its seasonal pattern. The months in the six month favorable seasonal period have generally been better than the other six months of the year. The exception to this has been the performance of March, which was one of the weaker months, despite being in the favorable six-month period for stocks.

In 2018/19, the S&P 500 in its favorable six month period produced a large gain, which was stronger than its performance in the unfavorable six month period, which produced a small loss. In 2019/20, the S&P 500 in its favorable six month period was negative and was weaker compared to its performance in the unfavorable six month period which produced a small gain. The main cause of weak performance of the S&P 500 favorable period in the spring of 2020 was the Covid-19 pandemic.

MAY

M	T	W	T	F	S	S
					1	2
3	4	5	6	7	8	9
10	11	12	13	14	15	16
17	18	19	20	21	22	23
24	25	26	27	28	29	30
31						

JUNE

M	T	W	T	F	S	S
	1	2	3	4	5	6
7	8	9	10	11	12	13
14	15	16	17	18	19	20
21	22	23	24	25	26	27
28	29	30				

JULY

M	T	W	T	F	S	S
		1	2	3	4
5	6	7	8	9	10	11
12	13	14	15	16	17	18
19	20	21	22	23	24	25
26	27	28	29	30	31	

In analyzing long-term trends for the broad markets such as the S&P 500 or the TSX Composite, a large data set is preferable because it incorporates various economic cycles. The daily data set for the TSX Composite starts in 1977.

Over this time period, investors have been rewarded for following the six month cycle of investing from October 28 to May 5, versus the unfavorable six month period, May 6 to October 27.

Starting with an investment of $10,000 in 1977, investing in the unfavorable six months has produced a loss of $3,304, versus investing in the favorable six month period which has produced a gain of $219,275.

$219,275 gain on $10,000 since 1977

The TSX Composite Average Year 1977 to 2018 graph (below), indicates that the market tended to peak in mid-July or the end of August. In our book *Time In Time Out, Outsmart the Stock Market Using Calendar Investment Strategies*, Bruce Lindsay and I analyzed a number of market trends and peaks over different decades.

What we found was that the markets tend to peak at the beginning of May or mid-July. The mid-July peak was usually the result of a strong bull market in place that had a lot of momentum.

The main reason that the TSX Composite data shows a peak occurring in July-August is that the data is primarily from the biggest bull market in history, starting in 1982.

intervals, the period from October to May is far superior compared with the other half of the year. The table below illustrates the superiority of the best six months over the worst six months. Going down the table year by year, the period from October 28 to May 5 outperforms the period from May 6 to October 27 on a regular basis. In a strong bull market, investors always have the choice of using a stop loss or technical indicators to help extend the exit point past the May date.

	TSX Comp May 6 to Oct 27	$10,000 Start	TSX Comp Oct 28 to May 5	$10,000 Start
1977/78	-3.9%	9,608	13.1%	11,313
1978/79	12.1	10,775	21.3	13,728
1979/80	2.9	11,084	23.0	16,883
1980/81	22.5	13,579	-2.4	16,479
1981/82	-17.0	11,272	-18.2	13,488
1982/83	16.6	13,138	34.6	18,150
1983/84	-0.9	13,015	-1.9	17,811
1984/85	1.6	13,226	10.7	19,718
1985/86	0.5	13,299	16.5	22,978
1986/87	-1.9	13,045	24.8	28,666
1987/88	-23.4	9,992	15.3	33,050
1988/89	2.7	10,260	5.7	34,939
1989/90	7.9	11,072	-13.3	30,294
1990/91	-8.4	10,148	13.1	34,266
1991/92	-1.6	9,982	-2.0	33,571
1992/93	-2.3	9,750	15.3	38,704
1993/94	10.8	10,801	1.7	39,365
1994/95	-0.1	10,792	0.3	39,483
1995/96	1.3	10,936	18.2	46,671
1996/97	8.3	11,843	10.8	51,725
1997/98	7.3	12,707	17.0	60,510
1998/99	-22.3	9,870	17.1	70,871
1999/00	-0.2	9,853	36.9	97,009
2000/01	-2.9	9,570	-14.4	83,062
2001/02	-12.2	8,399	9.4	90,875
2002/03	-16.4	7,020	4.0	94,476
2003/04	15.1	8,079	10.3	104,252
2004/05	3.9	8,398	7.8	112,379
2005/06	8.1	9,080	19.8	134,587
2006/07	0.0	9,079	12.2	151,053
2007/08	3.8	9,426	-0.2	150,820
2008/09	-40.2	5,638	15.7	174,551
2009/10	11.9	6,307	7.4	187,526
2010/11	5.8	6,674	7.1	200,778
2011/12	-7.4	6,183	-4.8	191,207
2012/13	3.6	6,407	1.1	193,348
2013/14	7.7	6,902	9.7	212,072
2014/15	-1.6	6,795	4.9	222,404
2015/16	-9.7	6,135	-4.9	221,307
2016/17	8.8	6,676	5.0	232,470
2017/18	2.4	6,835	-1.4	229,205
2018/19	-5.3	6,733	10.8	253,932
2019/20	-0.5	6,696	-9.7	229,275
Total Gain (Loss)		**(3,304)**		**219,275**

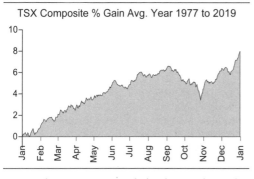

TSX Composite % Gain Avg. Year 1977 to 2019

Does a later average peak in the stock market mean that the best six month cycle does not work? No. Dividing the year up into six month

6n6 Canada Strategy Performance

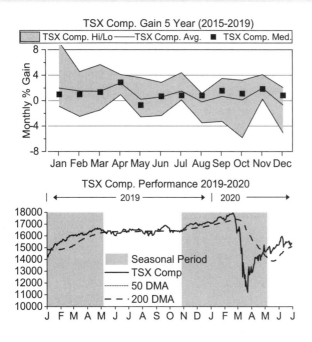

TSX Comp. Gain 5 Year (2015-2019)

TSX Comp. Hi/Lo —— TSX Comp. Avg. ■ TSX Comp. Med.

TSX Comp. Performance 2019-2020

Seasonal Period
—— TSX Comp
·········· 50 DMA
– – · 200 DMA

Market Indices & Rates
Weekly Values**

Stock Markets	2019	2020
Dow	25,764	23,685
S&P500	2,860	2,864
Nasdaq	7,816	9,015
TSX	16,402	14,639
FTSE	7,349	5,800
DAX	12,239	10,465
Nikkei	21,250	20,037
Hang Seng	27,946	23,797

Commodities	2019	2020
Oil	62.76	29.43
Gold	1280.8	1735.4

Bond Yields	2019	2020
USA 5 Yr Treasury	2.17	0.31
USA 10 Yr T	2.39	0.64
USA 20 Yr T	2.63	1.05
Moody's Aaa	3.68	2.51
Moody's Baa	4.63	4.05
CAN 5 Yr T	1.58	0.38
CAN 10 Yr T	1.69	0.54

Money Market	2019	2020
USA Fed Funds	2.50	0.25
USA 3 Mo T-B	2.34	0.12
CAN tgt overnight rate	1.75	0.25
CAN 3 Mo T-B	1.68	0.25

Foreign Exchange	2019	2020
EUR/USD	1.12	1.08
GBP/USD	1.27	1.21
USD/CAD	1.35	1.41
USD/JPY	110.08	107.06

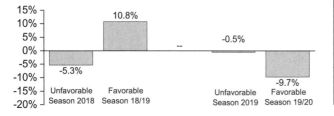

Favorable vs. Unfavorable Seasons 2018-2020 (TSX Composite)

10.8% — Favorable Season 18/19
-5.3% — Unfavorable Season 2018
-0.5% — Unfavorable Season 2019
-9.7% — Favorable Season 19/20

MAY

M	T	W	T	F	S	S
					1	2
3	4	5	6	7	8	9
10	11	12	13	14	15	16
17	18	19	20	21	22	23
24	25	26	27	28	29	30
31						

Over the last five years, the TSX Composite generally followed its six month favorable/unfavorable cycle.

In 2018, the unfavorable six month period produced a loss of 5.3% for the TSX Composite. The following six month favorable period produced a gain of 10.8%. In 2018, the unfavorable period produced a loss of 0.5% for the TSX Composite, which was better than the loss of 9.7% in the 2019/20 favorable period. The loss in the spring of 2020 favorable period was driven by investors pushing down the stock market as economies were largely shut down to fight Covid-19.

JUNE

M	T	W	T	F	S	S
	1	2	3	4	5	6
7	8	9	10	11	12	13
14	15	16	17	18	19	20
21	22	23	24	25	26	27
28	29	30				

JULY

M	T	W	T	F	S	S
			1	2	3	4
5	6	7	8	9	10	11
12	13	14	15	16	17	18
19	20	21	22	23	24	25
26	27	28	29	30	31	

COST | COSTCO – BUY AT A DISCOUNT
①May26-Jun30 ②Oct4-Dec1

Shoppers are attracted to Costco because of its consistently low prices. They take comfort in the fact that although the prices may not always be the lowest, they are consistently in the lower range.

Costco performs well in late spring into early summer, and in autumn into early winter. These two periods are considered to be transition periods where the stock market is moving to and from its unfavorable and favorable seasons. Companies such as Costco that have stable earnings are desirable at these times.

There are two times when Costco is a seasonal bargain: May 26 to June 30 and October 4 to December 1.

13% gain &
positive 96% of the time

Putting both seasonal periods together has produced a 96% positive success rate and an average gain of 13.3%. Although the earlier strong years in the 1990's skews the data to the high-side, Costco has still maintained its strong seasonal performances in both the May to June and the October to December time periods.

Covid-19 Performance Update. After strongly outperforming the S&P 500 from late February into March, the Costco underperformed the S&P 500 into June. Costco stabilized in June 2020 and started to outperform the S&P 500 into the summer months as consumers continued to spend money.

ⓘ *COST - stock symbol for Costco which trades on the Nasdaq exchange. Stock data adjusted for stock splits.*

Costco* vs. S&P 500 1994 to 2019 Positive ☐

Year	May 26 to Jun 30		Oct 4 to Dec 1		Compound Growth	
	S&P 500	COST	S&P 500	COST	S&P 500	COST
1994	-2.6 %	10.7 %	-2.8	-6.3 %	-5.3	3.7 %
1995	3.1	19.3	4.2	-2.2	7.4	16.7
1996	-1.2	9.5	9.3	15.5	8.0	26.5
1997	4.5	3.1	1.0	16.5	5.6	20.2
1998	2.1	17.6	17.2	41.1	19.7	66.0
1999	6.9	8.1	9.0	30.7	16.5	41.3
2000	5.3	10.0	-7.8	-3.6	-2.9	6.1
2001	-4.2	9.3	6.3	12.3	1.8	22.6
2002	-8.7	-0.8	14.3	4.6	4.4	3.8
2003	4.4	5.3	3.9	13.5	8.5	19.4
2004	2.5	10.3	5.3	17.4	7.9	29.4
2005	0.1	-1.5	3.1	13.9	3.2	12.2
2006	-0.2	5.0	4.7	6.0	4.5	11.3
2007	-0.8	3.8	-3.8	8.9	-4.6	12.9
2008	-7.0	-1.7	-25.8	-23.5	-30.9	-24.7
2009	3.6	-5.2	8.2	7.5	12.1	1.9
2010	-4.0	-3.0	5.2	5.0	1.0	1.9
2011	0.0	1.2	13.2	6.7	13.2	7.9
2012	3.4	12.5	-2.4	4.3	0.9	17.3
2013	-2.6	-3.3	7.6	9.6	4.7	6.0
2014	3.1	0.2	4.4	11.7	7.6	11.9
2015	-3.0	-6.0	7.8	10.6	4.6	3.9
2016	0.4	8.7	1.4	0.5	1.8	9.2
2017	0.4	-8.5	4.3	12.1	4.6	2.7
2018	-0.1	5.4	-5.7	-0.8	-5.8	4.5
2019	4.1	6.9	7.9	3.7	12.3	10.9
Avg.	0.4 %	4.5 %	3.5 %	8.3 %	3.9 %	13.3 %
Fq>0	58 %	69 %	77 %	81 %	81 %	96 %

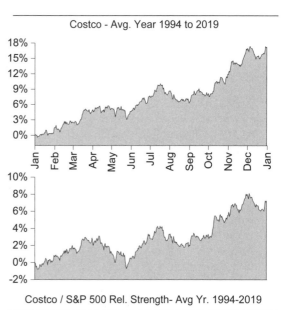

Costco - Avg. Year 1994 to 2019

Costco / S&P 500 Rel. Strength- Avg Yr. 1994-2019

Costco Performance

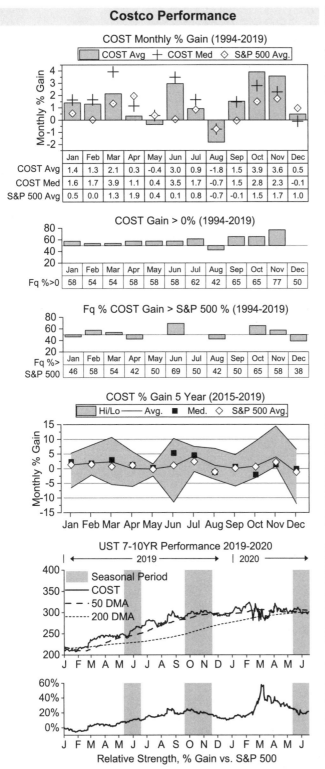

COST Monthly % Gain (1994-2019)

Legend: COST Avg + COST Med ◇ S&P 500 Avg.

	Jan	Feb	Mar	Apr	May	Jun	Jul	Aug	Sep	Oct	Nov	Dec
COST Avg	1.4	1.3	2.1	0.3	-0.4	3.0	0.9	-1.8	1.5	3.9	3.6	0.5
COST Med	1.6	1.7	3.9	1.1	0.4	3.5	1.7	-0.7	1.5	2.8	2.3	-0.1
S&P 500 Avg	0.5	0.0	1.3	1.9	0.4	0.1	0.8	-0.7	-0.1	1.5	1.7	1.0

COST Gain > 0% (1994-2019)

	Jan	Feb	Mar	Apr	May	Jun	Jul	Aug	Sep	Oct	Nov	Dec
Fq %>0	58	54	54	58	58	58	62	42	65	65	77	50

Fq % COST Gain > S&P 500 % (1994-2019)

	Jan	Feb	Mar	Apr	May	Jun	Jul	Aug	Sep	Oct	Nov	Dec
Fq %> S&P 500	46	58	54	42	50	69	50	42	50	65	58	38

COST % Gain 5 Year (2015-2019)

Legend: Hi/Lo —— Avg. ■ Med. ◇ S&P 500 Avg.

UST 7-10YR Performance 2019-2020

2019 → 2020 →

Legend: Seasonal Period, COST, 50 DMA, 200 DMA

Relative Strength, % Gain vs. S&P 500

WEEK 21

Market Indices & Rates
Weekly Values**

Stock Markets	2019	2020
Dow	25,586	24,465
S&P500	2,826	2,955
Nasdaq	7,637	9,325
TSX	16,230	14,914
FTSE	7,278	5,993
DAX	12,011	11,074
Nikkei	21,117	20,388
Hang Seng	27,354	22,930

Commodities	2019	2020
Oil	58.43	33.55
Gold	1282.5	1733.6

Bond Yields	2019	2020
USA 5 Yr Treasury	2.12	0.34
USA 10 Yr T	2.32	0.66
USA 20 Yr T	2.57	1.12
Moody's Aaa	3.64	2.41
Moody's Baa	4.63	3.84
CAN 5 Yr T	1.50	0.38
CAN 10 Yr T	1.61	0.51

Money Market	2019	2020
USA Fed Funds	2.50	0.25
USA 3 Mo T-B	2.30	0.12
CAN tgt overnight rate	1.75	0.25
CAN 3 Mo T-B	1.69	0.25

Foreign Exchange	2019	2020
EUR/USD	1.12	1.09
GBP/USD	1.27	1.22
USD/CAD	1.34	1.40
USD/JPY	109.31	107.64

MAY

M	T	W	T	F	S	S
					1	2
3	4	5	6	7	8	9
10	11	12	13	14	15	16
17	18	19	20	21	22	23
24	25	26	27	28	29	30
31						

JUNE

M	T	W	T	F	S	S
	1	2	3	4	5	6
7	8	9	10	11	12	13
14	15	16	17	18	19	20
21	22	23	24	25	26	27
28	29	30				

JULY

M	T	W	T	F	S	S
		1	2	3	4	
5	6	7	8	9	10	11
12	13	14	15	16	17	18
19	20	21	22	23	24	25
26	27	28	29	30	31	

US REITS – ONE BRICK AT A TIME

US REITS ①LONG (Mar8-Sep20)
②SELL SHORT (Sep21-Oct9)

US REITS have two seasonal periods, one positive and one negative. The positive seasonal period is much longer and lasts from March 8 to September 20, compared to the negative period which lasts just over two weeks, from September 21 to October 9.

The seasonal period for REITs generally follows the seasonal trend for government bonds, which tend to perform well from early May to early October. REITs on average turn down a bit earlier than government bonds. Although REITs benefit from lower interest rates, they do have somewhat of a positive correlation with equities. As equities tend to head lower in late September, any sign of higher interest rates at this time can strongly affect REIT prices.

13% growth & positive 79% of the time

In contrast, the weak seasonal period has produced a much smaller loss, which is beneficially for short sellers. The strong seasonal period is juxtaposed against the negative period. Although it is not suitable for most investors to short sell the negative seasonal period for REITs, the profile of this period highlights the seasonal strategy of exiting the REIT sector when it has finished its strong seasonal period.

Covid-19 Performance Update. The REIT sector was outperforming the S&P 500 from January into late February, but when the Covid-19 pandemic took hold, the sector substantially underperformed S&P 500 as the economy slowed and workers started to work from home.

ⓘ *MSCI US REIT Index (RMZ). For more information, please refer to msci.com*

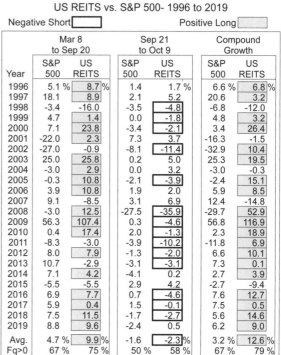

US REITS vs. S&P 500- 1996 to 2019

Negative Short ☐   Positive Long ☐

Year	Mar 8 to Sep 20 S&P 500	Mar 8 to Sep 20 US REITS	Sep 21 to Oct 9 S&P 500	Sep 21 to Oct 9 US REITS	Compound Growth S&P 500	Compound Growth US REITS
1996	5.1 %	8.7 %	1.4	1.7 %	6.6 %	6.8 %
1997	18.1	8.9	2.1	5.2	20.6	3.2
1998	-3.4	-16.0	-3.5	-4.8	-6.8	-12.0
1999	4.7	1.4	0.0	-1.8	4.8	3.2
2000	7.1	23.8	-3.4	-2.1	3.4	26.4
2001	-22.0	2.3	7.3	3.7	-16.3	-1.5
2002	-27.0	-0.9	-8.1	-11.4	-32.9	10.4
2003	25.0	25.8	0.2	5.0	25.3	19.5
2004	-3.0	2.9	0.0	3.2	-3.0	-0.3
2005	-0.3	10.8	-2.1	-3.9	-2.4	15.1
2006	3.9	10.8	1.9	2.0	5.9	8.5
2007	9.1	-8.5	3.1	6.9	12.4	-14.8
2008	-3.0	12.5	-27.5	-35.9	-29.7	52.9
2009	56.3	107.4	0.3	-4.6	56.8	116.9
2010	0.4	17.4	2.0	-1.3	2.3	18.9
2011	-8.3	-3.0	-3.9	-10.2	-11.8	6.9
2012	8.0	7.9	-1.3	-2.0	6.6	10.1
2013	10.7	-2.9	-3.1	-3.1	7.3	0.1
2014	7.1	4.2	-4.1	0.2	2.7	3.9
2015	-5.5	-5.5	2.9	4.2	-2.7	-9.4
2016	6.9	7.7	0.7	-4.6	7.6	12.7
2017	5.9	0.4	1.5	-0.1	7.5	0.5
2018	7.5	11.5	-1.7	-2.7	5.6	14.6
2019	8.8	9.6	-2.4	0.5	6.2	9.0
Avg.	4.7 %	9.9 %	-1.6	-2.3 %	3.2 %	12.6 %
Fq>0	67 %	75 %	50 %	58 %	67 %	79 %

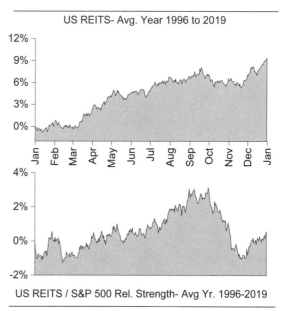

US REITS- Avg. Year 1996 to 2019

US REITS / S&P 500 Rel. Strength- Avg Yr. 1996-2019

US REITS Strategy Performance

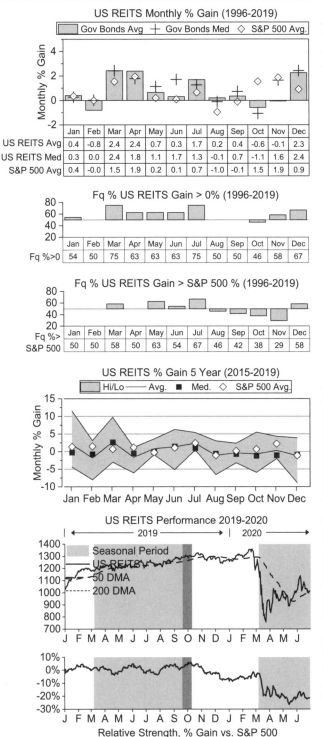

US REITS Monthly % Gain (1996-2019)

Gov Bonds Avg + Gov Bonds Med ◇ S&P 500 Avg.

	Jan	Feb	Mar	Apr	May	Jun	Jul	Aug	Sep	Oct	Nov	Dec
US REITS Avg	0.4	-0.8	2.4	2.4	0.7	0.3	1.7	0.2	0.4	-0.6	-0.1	2.3
US REITS Med	0.3	0.0	2.4	1.8	1.1	1.7	1.3	-0.1	0.7	-1.1	1.6	2.4
S&P 500 Avg	0.4	-0.0	1.5	1.9	0.2	0.1	0.7	-1.0	-0.1	1.5	1.9	0.9

Fq % US REITS Gain > 0% (1996-2019)

	Jan	Feb	Mar	Apr	May	Jun	Jul	Aug	Sep	Oct	Nov	Dec
Fq %>0	54	50	75	63	63	63	75	50	50	46	58	67

Fq % US REITS Gain > S&P 500 % (1996-2019)

	Jan	Feb	Mar	Apr	May	Jun	Jul	Aug	Sep	Oct	Nov	Dec
Fq %> S&P 500	50	50	58	50	63	54	67	46	42	38	29	58

US REITS % Gain 5 Year (2015-2019)

Hi/Lo —— Avg. ■ Med. ◇ S&P 500 Avg.

US REITS Performance 2019-2020

|← 2019 →| 2020 →|

Seasonal Period
US REITS
50 DMA
200 DMA

Relative Strength, % Gain vs. S&P 500

Market Indices & Rates
Weekly Values**

Stock Markets	2019	2020
Dow	24,815	25,383
S&P500	2,752	3,044
Nasdaq	7,453	9,490
TSX	16,037	15,193
FTSE	7,162	6,077
DAX	11,727	11,587
Nikkei	20,601	21,878
Hang Seng	26,901	22,961

Commodities	2019	2020
Oil	53.50	35.49
Gold	1295.6	1728.7

Bond Yields	2019	2020
USA 5 Yr Treasury	1.93	0.30
USA 10 Yr T	2.14	0.65
USA 20 Yr T	2.39	1.18
Moody's Aaa	3.51	2.41
Moody's Baa	4.51	3.76
CAN 5 Yr T	1.37	0.40
CAN 10 Yr T	1.49	0.53

Money Market	2019	2020
USA Fed Funds	2.50	0.25
USA 3 Mo T-B	2.30	0.14
CAN tgt overnight rate	1.75	0.25
CAN 3 Mo T-B	1.68	0.18

Foreign Exchange	2019	2020
EUR/USD	1.12	1.11
GBP/USD	1.26	1.23
USD/CAD	1.35	1.38
USD/JPY	108.29	107.83

MAY

M	T	W	T	F	S	S
					1	2
3	4	5	6	7	8	9
10	11	12	13	14	15	16
17	18	19	20	21	22	23
24	25	26	27	28	29	30
31						

JUNE

M	T	W	T	F	S	S
	1	2	3	4	5	6
7	8	9	10	11	12	13
14	15	16	17	18	19	20
21	22	23	24	25	26	27
28	29	30				

JULY

M	T	W	T	F	S	S
		1	2	3	4	
5	6	7	8	9	10	11
12	13	14	15	16	17	18
19	20	21	22	23	24	25
26	27	28	29	30	31	

JUNE

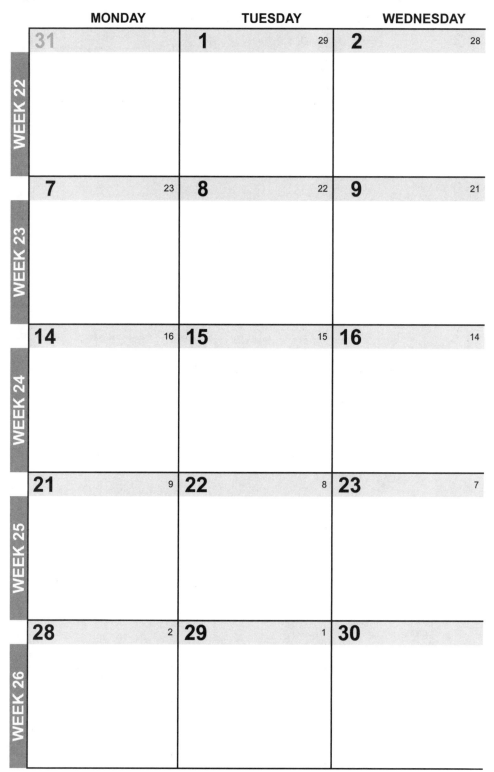

	MONDAY	TUESDAY	WEDNESDAY
WEEK 22	31	**1** 29	**2** 28
WEEK 23	**7** 23	**8** 22	**9** 21
WEEK 24	**14** 16	**15** 15	**16** 14
WEEK 25	**21** 9	**22** 8	**23** 7
WEEK 26	**28** 2	**29** 1	**30**

THURSDAY		FRIDAY	
3	27	**4**	26
10	20	**11**	19
17	13	**18**	12
24	6	**25**	5
1		2	

JULY

M	T	W	T	F	S	S
		1	2	3	4	
5	6	7	8	9	10	11
12	13	14	15	16	17	18
19	20	21	22	23	24	25
26	27	28	29	30	31	

AUGUST

M	T	W	T	F	S	S
						1
2	3	4	5	6	7	8
9	10	11	12	13	14	15
16	17	18	19	20	21	22
23	24	25	26	27	28	29
30	31					

SEPTEMBER

M	T	W	T	F	S	S
		1	2	3	4	5
6	7	8	9	10	11	12
13	14	15	16	17	18	19
20	21	22	23	24	25	26
27	28	29	30			

OCTOBER

M	T	W	T	F	S	S
				1	2	3
4	5	6	7	8	9	10
11	12	13	14	15	16	17
18	19	20	21	22	23	24
25	26	27	28	29	30	31

JUNE SUMMARY

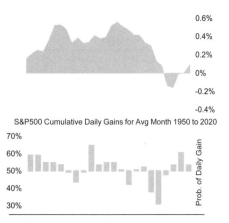

	Dow Jones	S&P 500	Nasdaq	TSX Comp
Month Rank	11	9	6	11
# Up	33	38	27	16
# Down	37	32	21	19
% Pos	47	54	56	46
% Avg. Gain	-0.2	0.1	0.8	-0.3

Dow & S&P 1950-2019, Nasdaq 1972-2019, TSX 1985-2019

S&P500 Cumulative Daily Gains for Avg Month 1950 to 2020

♦ On average, June is not a strong month for the S&P 500. From 1950 to 2019, it was the fourth worst month of the year, producing a nominal gain of 0.1%. ♦ From year to year, different sectors of the market tend to lead in June as there is not a strong consistent outperforming major sector. ♦ The last few days of June, the start of the successful *Summer Sizzler Trade,* tend to be positive. ♦ In 2020, the S&P 500 had an intern peak on June 8, and declined until late June before rallying during the period for the *Summer Sizzler Trade.*

BEST / WORST JUNE BROAD MKTS. 2011-2020

BEST JUNE MARKETS
- Nasdaq (2019) 7.4%
- Dow (2019) 7.2%
- Russell 2000 (2019) 6.9%

WORST JUNE MARKETS
- Nikkei 225 (2016) - 9.6%
- FTSE 100 (2015) - 6.6%
- FTSE 100 (2013) -5.6%

Index Values End of Month

	2011	2012	2013	2014	2015	2016	2017	2018	2019	2020
Dow	12,414	12,880	14,910	16,827	17,620	17,930	21,350	24,271	26,600	25,813
S&P 500	1,321	1,362	1,606	1,960	2,063	2,099	2,423	2,663	2,942	3,100
Nasdaq	2,774	2,935	3,403	4,408	4,987	4,843	6,140	7,510	8,006	10,059
TSX Comp.	13,301	11,597	12,129	15,146	14,553	14,065	15,182	16,278	16,382	15,515
Russell 1000	734	751	891	1,095	1,153	1,162	1,344	1,510	1,629	1,717
Russell 2000	827	798	977	1,193	1,254	1,152	1,415	1,643	1,567	1,441
FTSE 100	5,946	5,571	6,215	6,744	6,521	6,504	7,313	7,637	7,426	6,170
Nikkei 225	9,816	9,007	13,677	15,162	20,236	15,576	20,033	22,305	21,276	22,288

Percent Gain for June

	2011	2012	2013	2014	2015	2016	2017	2018	2019	2020
Dow	-1.2	3.9	-1.4	0.7	-2.2	0.8	1.6	-0.6	7.2	1.7
S&P 500	-1.8	4.0	-1.5	1.9	-2.1	0.1	0.5	0.0	6.9	1.8
Nasdaq	-2.2	3.8	-1.5	3.9	-1.6	-2.1	-0.9	0.9	7.4	6.0
TSX Comp.	-3.6	0.7	-4.1	3.7	-3.1	0.0	-1.1	1.3	2.1	2.1
Russell 1000	-1.9	3.7	-1.5	2.1	-2.0	0.1	0.5	0.5	6.9	2.1
Russell 2000	-2.5	4.8	-0.7	5.2	0.6	-0.2	3.3	0.6	6.9	3.4
FTSE 100	-0.7	4.7	-5.6	-1.5	-6.6	4.4	-2.8	-0.5	3.7	1.5
Nikkei 225	1.3	5.4	-0.7	3.6	-1.6	-9.6	1.9	0.5	3.3	1.9

June Market Avg. Performance 2011 to 2020[1]

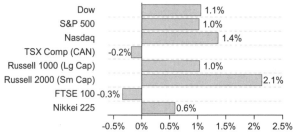

Dow	1.1%
S&P 500	1.0%
Nasdaq	1.4%
TSX Comp (CAN)	-0.2%
Russell 1000 (Lg Cap)	1.0%
Russell 2000 (Sm Cap)	2.1%
FTSE 100	-0.3%
Nikkei 225	0.6%

Interest Corner Jun[2]

	Fed Funds % [3]	3 Mo. T-Bill % [4]	10 Yr % [5]	20 Yr % [6]
2020	0.25	0.16	0.66	1.18
2019	2.50	2.12	2.00	2.31
2018	2.00	1.93	2.85	2.91
2017	1.25	1.03	2.31	2.61
2016	0.50	0.26	1.49	1.86

(1) Russell Data provided by Russell (2) Federal Reserve Bank of St. Louis- end of month values (3) Target rate set by FOMC (4)(5)(6) Constant yield maturities.

June 2020 % Sector Performance	GIC % Gain Jun 2020 / Jun 90-2020 Avg.	S&P GIC Sectors	2020 % Gain	1990-2020[1] GIC[2] % Avg Gain	Fq% Gain >S&P 500
Health Care		Health Care	-2.5 %	0.7 %	65 %
Telecom		Telecom	-0.6	0.4	58
Info Tech		Information Technology	7.1	0.1	39
Utilities		Utilities	-5.0	-0.2	48
Energy		Energy	-1.4	-0.2	42
Cons Staples		Consumer Staples	-0.7	-0.3	35
Cons Disc		Consumer Discretionary	4.9	-0.5	48
Industrials		Industrials	1.9	-0.6	45
Financials		Financials	-0.5	-0.8	39
Materials		Materials	1.9 %	-1.0 %	35 %
S&P 500		S&P 500	1.8 %	-0.1 %	N/A %

-6 -4 -2 0 2 4 6 8

Sector Commentary

♦ In June 2020, the stock market hand an interim month peak on June 8, but still managed to produce a gain of 1.8%. The information technology sector was the strongest sector with a gain of 7.1%. The next best sector was the consumer discretionary sector with a gain of 4.9%. The third best sector was the industrials sector with a gain of 1.9%. There was an unusually large gap in performance between the top two performing sectors that benefited from working from home, and the other sectors of the market. Six major sectors of the market were negative in June.

Sub-Sector Commentary

♦ In June 2020, the retail sub-sector performed particularly well with a gain of 7.0%. ♦ The metals and mining sub-sector also performed well, with a gain of 8.2%. ♦ The pharmaceutical sub-sector produced a loss of 4.7% and the biotech sub-sector produced a gain of 0.9%. Investors shifted their interest from companies potentially benefiting from Covid-19 vaccines, to other parts of the market.

SELECTED SUB-SECTORS[3]

Pharma	-4.7 %	0.7 %	65 %
Retail	7.0	0.1	58
Gold	2.3	0.1	52
Metals & Mining	8.2	0.0	55
Biotech (1993-2020)	0.9	-0.3	48
SOX (1995-2020)	7.8	-0.4	38
Steel	-2.0	-0.7	42
Railroads	-1.2	-0.9	35
Home-builders	0.9	-0.9	42
Agriculture (1994-2020)	1.5	-0.9	33
Transportation	2.9	-0.9	32
Chemicals	0.8	-1.1	35
Automotive & Components	3.0	-1.2	48
Silver	1.5	-1.6	35
Banks	-1.0	-1.6	32

(1) Sector data provided by Standard and Poors (2) GIC is short form for Global Industry Classification (3) Sub Sector data provided by Standard and Poors, except where marked by symbol.

BIOTECH SUMMER SOLSTICE
June 23 to September 13

The *Biotech Summer Solstice* trade starts on June 23 and lasts until September 13. The trade is aptly named as its outperformance starts approximately when summer solstice starts– the longest day of the year.

There are two main drivers of the trade: biotech is a good substitute for technology stocks in the summer, and investors want to take a position in the biotech sector before the autumn conferences.

Positive 82% of the time

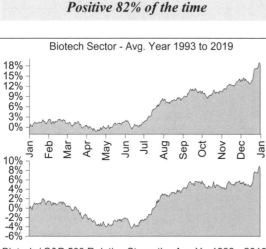

Biotech Sector - Avg. Year 1993 to 2019

Biotech / S&P 500 Relative Strength - Avg Yr. 1993 - 2019

Biotech* vs. S&P 500 1992 to 2019			
		Positive	
Jun 23 to Sep 13	S&P 500	Biotech	Diff
1992	4.0 %	17.9 %	13.8 %
1993	3.6	3.6	0.0
1994	3.2	24.2	21.0
1995	5.0	31.5	26.5
1996	2.1	7.0	4.9
1997	2.8	-18.9	-21.7
1998	-8.5	20.6	29.1
1999	0.6	64.3	63.7
2000	2.3	7.6	5.4
2001	-10.8	-3.6	7.2
2002	-10.0	8.1	18.2
2003	2.3	6.4	4.1
2004	-0.8	8.9	9.6
2005	1.4	26.0	24.5
2006	5.8	7.4	1.6
2007	-1.2	6.0	7.2
2008	-5.0	11.4	16.5
2009	16.8	7.7	-9.1
2010	2.4	2.8	0.4
2011	-8.9	-3.7	5.2
2012	9.4	15.6	6.2
2013	6.0	24.9	18.9
2014	1.2	14.8	13.6
2015	-7.6	-7.2	0.5
2016	2.0	7.3	5.3
2017	2.6	11.1	8.5
2018	5.4	7.5	2.1
2019	1.9	-4.5	-6.4
Avg	1.0 %	10.9 %	9.9 %
Fq>0	71 %	82 %	86 %

The biotechnology sector is often considered the cousin of the technology sector, a good place for speculative investments. The sectors are similar as both include concept companies (companies without a product, but with good potential).

Despite their similarity, investors view the sectors differently. The technology sector is viewed as being much more dependent on the economy compared with the biotech sector. The end product of biotechnology companies is mainly medicine, which is not economically sensitive.

As a result, in the summer months when investors tend to be more cautious, they are more willing to commit speculative money into the biotech sector, compared with the technology sector.

The biotech sector is one of the few sectors that starts its outperformance in June. This is in part because of the biotech conferences that occur in autumn and with the possibility of positive announcements, the price of biotech companies can increase dramatically. As a re-

sult, investors try to lock in positions early.

Covid-19 Performance Update. The biotech sector strongly outperformed the S&P 500 from January 2020 into May, largely based upon the possibility of Covid-19 vaccines and therapeutics being developed. In May, the biotech sector started to underperform before the start of its seasonal period, as investors started to realize that vaccines might not be available until 2021.

*Biotech SP GIC Sector # 352010: Companies primarily engaged in the research, development, manufacturing and/or marketing of products based on genetic analysis and genetic engineering.

Biotech Performance

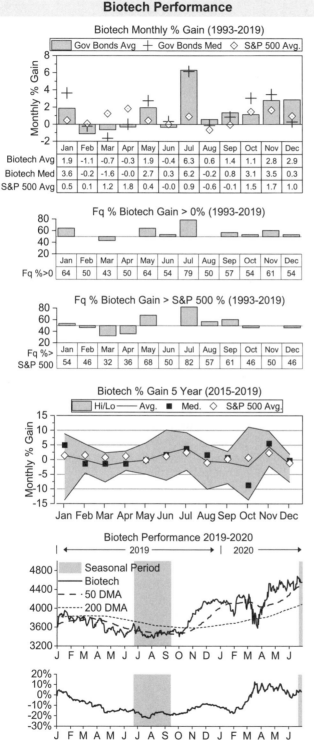

Biotech Monthly % Gain (1993-2019)

Legend: Gov Bonds Avg | Gov Bonds Med | S&P 500 Avg.

	Jan	Feb	Mar	Apr	May	Jun	Jul	Aug	Sep	Oct	Nov	Dec
Biotech Avg	1.9	-1.1	-0.7	-0.3	1.9	-0.4	6.3	0.6	1.4	1.1	2.8	2.9
Biotech Med	3.6	-0.2	-1.6	-0.0	2.7	0.3	6.2	-0.2	0.8	3.1	3.5	0.3
S&P 500 Avg	0.5	0.1	1.2	1.8	0.4	-0.0	0.9	-0.6	-0.1	1.5	1.7	1.0

Fq % Biotech Gain > 0% (1993-2019)

	Jan	Feb	Mar	Apr	May	Jun	Jul	Aug	Sep	Oct	Nov	Dec
Fq %>0	64	50	43	50	64	54	79	50	57	54	61	54

Fq % Biotech Gain > S&P 500 % (1993-2019)

	Jan	Feb	Mar	Apr	May	Jun	Jul	Aug	Sep	Oct	Nov	Dec
Fq %> S&P 500	54	46	32	36	68	50	82	57	61	46	50	46

Biotech % Gain 5 Year (2015-2019)

Legend: Hi/Lo — Avg. ■ Med. ◇ S&P 500 Avg.

Biotech Performance 2019-2020

2019 — 2020

Legend: Seasonal Period, Biotech, 50 DMA, 200 DMA

Relative Strength, % Gain vs. S&P 500

Stock Markets	2019	2020
Dow	25,984	27,111
S&P500	2,873	3,194
Nasdaq	7,742	9,814
TSX	16,231	15,854
FTSE	7,332	6,484
DAX	12,045	12,848
Nikkei	20,885	22,864
Hang Seng	26,965	24,770

Commodities	2019	2020
Oil	53.99	39.55
Gold	1340.7	1683.5

Bond Yields	2019	2020
USA 5 Yr Treasury	1.85	0.47
USA 10 Yr T	2.09	0.91
USA 20 Yr T	2.36	1.46
Moody's Aaa	3.48	2.41
Moody's Baa	4.51	3.82
CAN 5 Yr T	1.34	0.53
CAN 10 Yr T	1.46	0.73

Money Market	2019	2020
USA Fed Funds	2.50	0.25
USA 3 Mo T-B	2.23	0.15
CAN tgt overnight rate	1.75	0.25
CAN 3 Mo T-B	1.66	0.18

Foreign Exchange	2019	2020
EUR/USD	1.13	1.13
GBP/USD	1.27	1.27
USD/CAD	1.33	1.34
USD/JPY	108.19	109.59

JUNE

M	T	W	T	F	S	S
	1	2	3	4	5	6
7	8	9	10	11	12	13
14	15	16	17	18	19	20
21	22	23	24	25	26	27
28	29	30				

JULY

M	T	W	T	F	S	S
		1	2	3	4
5	6	7	8	9	10	11
12	13	14	15	16	17	18
19	20	21	22	23	24	25
26	27	28	29	30	31	

AUGUST

M	T	W	T	F	S	S
						1
2	3	4	5	6	7	8
9	10	11	12	13	14	15
16	17	18	19	20	21	22
23	24	25	26	27	28	29
30	31					

CAMECO – CHARGES DOWN AND UP

CCO ①SELL SHORT (Jun5-Aug7)
②LONG (Oct4-Jan24)

Cameco is the world's largest publicly traded uranium company. It trades on both the NYSE stock exchange (ticker: CCJ) and the Toronto Stock Exchange (ticker: CCO).

Cameco has a very narrow market for its product: countries that need uranium to power their nuclear reactors. Mining operations do not vary much throughout the year, so supply is fairly constant. In addition actual usage of uranium does not change much throughout the year as nuclear reactors are run most efficiently at one constant level over time. Yet, there is a seasonal tendency for Cameco to perform well from October 4 to January 24.

22% growth & positive 84% of the time

The seasonal trend for Cameco can be partly explained by the overall tendency of the stock market to perform well during Cameco's strong seasonal period, and poorly during Cameco's weak seasonal period.

The seasonal trend for Cameco can also be explained somewhat with buyer behavior. The World Nuclear Association (WNA) has an annual conference that takes place in the middle of September of each year. As a result of the conference, buyers tend to be reassured of the future demand of uranium, helping to give Cameco a boost starting in October. Likewise, investors often have a low interest level in Cameco in the summer months ahead of the WNA conference in mid-September.

ⓘ *Cameco Corporation is in the materials sector. Its stock symbol is CCO, which trades on the Toronto Stock Exchange, adjusted for splits.*

Cameco vs. TSX Composite Index - 1995/96 to 2019/20
Negative Short [ ]   Positive Long [ ]

Year	Jun 5 to Aug 7 TSX	Jun 5 to Aug 7 CCO	Oct 4 to Jan 24 TSX	Oct 4 to Jan 24 CCO	Compound Growth TSX	Compound Growth CCO
1995/96	3.7 %	1.8 %	8.1	42.7 %	12.1 %	40.1 %
1996/97	-3.7	-6.1	12.2	-16.5	8.0	-11.5
1997/98	8.0	1.1	-8.5	-22.6	-1.1	-23.4
1998/99	-11.3	-23.2	19.5	44.4	6.0	77.9
1999/00	-0.9	-16.9	22.0	-24.8	21.0	-12.1
2000/01	8.4	-13.7	-11.0	25.0	-3.5	42.1
2001/02	-6.4	-20.3	10.9	14.6	3.9	37.9
2002/03	-14.3	-28.6	10.6	27.9	-5.2	64.5
2003/04	2.6	4.9	14.4	35.7	17.4	29.1
2004/05	-2.1	8.9	3.8	30.6	1.7	19.0
2005/06	9.1	5.7	5.5	38.3	15.1	30.4
2006/07	0.3	-9.1	12.9	18.6	13.2	29.4
2007/08	-4.1	-30.2	-7.9	-15.7	-11.8	9.8
2008/09	-8.9	-15.0	-20.1	-6.5	-27.2	7.5
2009/10	3.9	0.5	3.5	6.2	7.5	5.6
2010/11	2.0	11.2	8.0	35.6	10.1	20.4
2011/12	-10.0	-13.7	10.2	29.0	-0.9	45.0
2012/13	4.7	9.0	3.8	12.6	8.6	2.4
2013/14	-1.4	-10.3	7.7	29.6	6.2	42.9
2014/15	2.2	-3.1	-0.1	-8.9	2.1	-6.0
2015/16	-4.8	-6.2	-7.1	-0.9	-11.6	5.3
2016/17	3.0	-17.3	6.3	54.0	9.4	80.7
2017/18	-1.2	3.7	3.5	8.0	2.3	4.0
2018/19	1.5	1.7	-4.9	4.0	-3.5	2.3
2019/20	0.6	-16.1	7.3	-11.5	8.0	2.9
Avg.	-0.8 %	-7.3 %	4.4	13.9 %	3.5 %	21.8 %
Fq>0	52 %	40 %	72 %	68 %	68 %	84 %

Covid-19 Performance Update. Cameco outperformed the S&P 500 in February. When the stock market bottomed on March 23, Cameco accelerated its outperformance into May. In May, Cameco then started to underperform the TSX Composite, giving back some of its large gains relative to the market, just ahead of its weak seasonal period starting June 5.

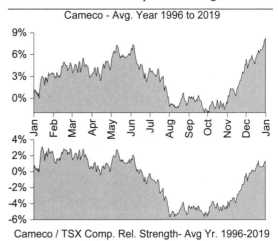

Cameco - Avg. Year 1996 to 2019

Cameco / TSX Comp. Rel. Strength- Avg Yr. 1996-2019

Cameco Performance

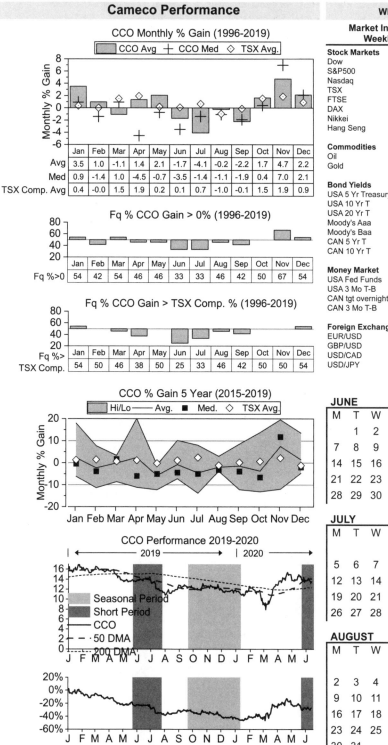

CCO Monthly % Gain (1996-2019)

CCO Avg + CCO Med ◇ TSX Avg.

	Jan	Feb	Mar	Apr	May	Jun	Jul	Aug	Sep	Oct	Nov	Dec
Avg	3.5	1.0	-1.1	1.4	2.1	-1.7	-4.1	-0.2	-2.2	1.7	4.7	2.2
Med	0.9	-1.4	1.0	-4.5	-0.7	-3.5	-1.4	-1.1	-1.9	0.4	7.0	2.1
TSX Comp. Avg	0.4	-0.0	1.5	1.9	0.2	0.1	0.7	-1.0	-0.1	1.5	1.9	0.9

Fq % CCO Gain > 0% (1996-2019)

	Jan	Feb	Mar	Apr	May	Jun	Jul	Aug	Sep	Oct	Nov	Dec
Fq %>0	54	42	54	46	46	33	33	46	42	50	67	54

Fq % CCO Gain > TSX Comp. % (1996-2019)

	Jan	Feb	Mar	Apr	May	Jun	Jul	Aug	Sep	Oct	Nov	Dec
Fq %> TSX Comp.	54	50	46	38	50	25	33	46	42	50	50	54

CCO % Gain 5 Year (2015-2019)

Hi/Lo —— Avg. ■ Med. ◇ TSX Avg.

Jan Feb Mar Apr May Jun Jul Aug Sep Oct Nov Dec

CCO Performance 2019-2020

← 2019 → | 2020 →

Seasonal Period
Short Period
—— CCO
– – · 50 DMA
······ 200 DMA

J F M A M J J A S O N D J F M A M J

Relative Strength, % Gain vs. TSX Comp.

Market Indices & Rates
Weekly Values**

Stock Markets	2019	2020
Dow	26,090	25,606
S&P500	2,887	3,041
Nasdaq	7,797	9,589
TSX	16,302	15,257
FTSE	7,346	6,105
DAX	12,096	11,949
Nikkei	21,117	22,305
Hang Seng	27,118	24,301

Commodities	2019	2020
Oil	52.51	36.26
Gold	1351.3	1733.5

Bond Yields	2019	2020
USA 5 Yr Treasury	1.85	0.33
USA 10 Yr T	2.09	0.71
USA 20 Yr T	2.38	1.24
Moody's Aaa	3.49	2.42
Moody's Baa	4.51	3.62
CAN 5 Yr T	1.33	0.37
CAN 10 Yr T	1.44	0.54

Money Market	2019	2020
USA Fed Funds	2.50	0.25
USA 3 Mo T-B	2.15	0.16
CAN tgt overnight rate	1.75	0.25
CAN 3 Mo T-B	1.67	0.18

Foreign Exchange	2019	2020
EUR/USD	1.12	1.13
GBP/USD	1.26	1.25
USD/CAD	1.34	1.36
USD/JPY	108.56	107.38

JUNE

M	T	W	T	F	S	S
	1	2	3	4	5	6
7	8	9	10	11	12	13
14	15	16	17	18	19	20
21	22	23	24	25	26	27
28	29	30				

JULY

M	T	W	T	F	S	S
			1	2	3	4
5	6	7	8	9	10	11
12	13	14	15	16	17	18
19	20	21	22	23	24	25
26	27	28	29	30	31	

AUGUST

M	T	W	T	F	S	S
						1
2	3	4	5	6	7	8
9	10	11	12	13	14	15
16	17	18	19	20	21	22
23	24	25	26	27	28	29
30	31					

SUMMER SIZZLER – THE FULL TRADE
PROFIT BEFORE & AFTER FIREWORKS
Two Market Days Before June Month End
To 5 Market Days After Independence Day

The beginning of July is a time for celebration and the markets tend to agree.

Based on previous market data, the best way to take advantage of this trend is to be invested for the two market days prior to June month end and hold until five market days after Independence Day. This time period has produced above average returns on a fairly consistent basis.

Since 1950, 1.0% avg. gain & 73% of the time positive

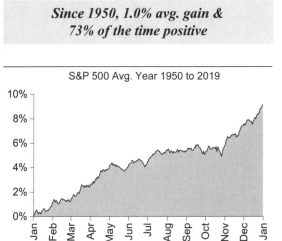

S&P 500 Avg. Year 1950 to 2019

The typical strategy to take advantage of the tendency of positive performance around Independence Day has been to invest one or two days before the holiday and take profits one or two days after the holiday.

Although this strategy has produced profits, it has left a lot of money on the table. This strategy misses out on the positive days at the end of June and on the full slate of positive days after Independence Day.

The beginning part of the *Summer Sizzler Trade's* positive trend is driven by portfolio managers who "window dress" their portfolios, buying stocks at month end that have a favorable perception in the market in order to make their portfolios look good on month and quarter end statements. This is particularly true at quarter ends. The result is typically increased buying pressure that lifts the stock market.

Depending on market conditions at the time, investors should consider extending the exit date of the *Summer Sizzler Trade* until eighteen calendar days into July. With July being an earnings month, the market can continue to rally until mid-month (see *18 Day Earnings Month Strategy*).

Covid-19 Performance Update. The stock market performed well in its 2020 Summer Sizzler period as investors anticipated that the re-opening of the economy was going to transfer into stronger than expected earnings.

S&P 500, 2 Market Days Before June Month End To 5 Market Days after Independence Day % Gain 1950 to 2020   Positive

1950	-4.4	1960	-0.1	1970	1.5	1980	1.4	1990	1.7	2000	1.8	2010	0.4	2020	5.5
1951	1.5	1961	1.7	1971	3.2	1981	-2.4	1991	1.4	2001	-2.6	2011	1.8		
1952	0.9	1962	9.8	1972	0.3	1982	-0.6	1992	2.8	2002	-4.7	2012	0.7		
1953	0.8	1963	0.5	1973	2.1	1983	1.5	1993	-0.6	2003	1.2	2013	4.5		
1954	2.9	1964	2.3	1974	-8.8	1984	-0.7	1994	0.4	2004	-1.7	2014	0.5		
1955	4.9	1965	5.0	1975	-0.2	1985	1.5	1995	1.8	2005	1.5	2015	-1.2		
1956	3.4	1966	2.1	1976	2.4	1986	-2.6	1996	-2.8	2006	2.1	2016	5.0		
1957	3.8	1967	1.3	1977	-0.6	1987	0.4	1997	3.7	2007	0.8	2017	0.2		
1958	2.0	1968	2.3	1978	0.6	1988	-0.6	1998	2.7	2008	-3.4	2018	2.8		
1959	3.3	1969	-1.5	1979	1.3	1989	0.9	1999	5.1	2009	-4.3	2019	3.0		
Avg.	1.9		2.3		0.2		-0.1		1.8		-0.9		1.8		5.5

Summer Sizzler Strategy (S&P 500) Performance

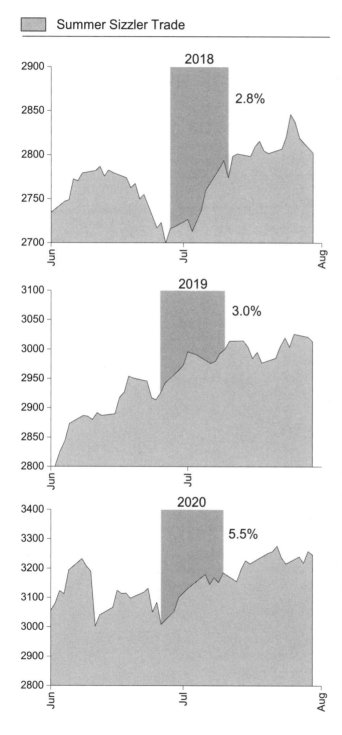

Market Indices & Rates
Weekly Values**

Stock Markets	2019	2020
Dow	26,719	25,871
S&P500	2,950	3,098
Nasdaq	8,032	9,946
TSX	16,525	15,474
FTSE	7,408	6,293
DAX	12,340	12,331
Nikkei	21,259	22,479
Hang Seng	28,474	24,644

Commodities	2019	2020
Oil	57.28	39.75
Gold	1397.2	1734.8

Bond Yields	2019	2020
USA 5 Yr Treasury	1.80	0.33
USA 10 Yr T	2.07	0.70
USA 20 Yr T	2.37	1.23
Moody's Aaa	3.36	2.43
Moody's Baa	4.42	3.57
CAN 5 Yr T	1.37	0.38
CAN 10 Yr T	1.49	0.54

Money Market	2019	2020
USA Fed Funds	2.50	0.25
USA 3 Mo T-B	2.07	0.15
CAN tgt overnight rate	1.75	0.25
CAN 3 Mo T-B	1.67	0.20

Foreign Exchange	2019	2020
EUR/USD	1.14	1.12
GBP/USD	1.27	1.24
USD/CAD	1.32	1.36
USD/JPY	107.32	106.87

JUNE

M	T	W	T	F	S	S
	1	2	3	4	5	6
7	8	9	10	11	12	13
14	15	16	17	18	19	20
21	22	23	24	25	26	27
28	29	30				

JULY

M	T	W	T	F	S	S
			1	2	3	4
5	6	7	8	9	10	11
12	13	14	15	16	17	18
19	20	21	22	23	24	25
26	27	28	29	30	31	

AUGUST

M	T	W	T	F	S	S
						1
2	3	4	5	6	7	8
9	10	11	12	13	14	15
16	17	18	19	20	21	22
23	24	25	26	27	28	29
30	31					

ORACLE
June 1 to July 1

Oracle's stock price performance exhibits a positive seasonal trend in the run-up to and after reporting on its fiscal year-end. Oracle's year-end is on May 31 and it typically reports its full-year earnings in mid-to-late June.

Selling software is instantly scalable, which provides an incentive to increase sales at year-end without disrupting operations. Oracle places a lot of emphasis on providing its sales force with incentives to increase sales before its year-end closes.

Oracle's May 31, 2020 SEC Filing 10-K Annual Report states: "Our quarterly revenues have historically been affected by a variety of seasonal factors, including the structure of our sales force incentive compensation plans, which are common in the technology industry. In each fiscal year, our total revenues and operating margins are typically highest in our fourth fiscal quarter and lowest in our first fiscal quarter."

8% gain & positive 74% of the time

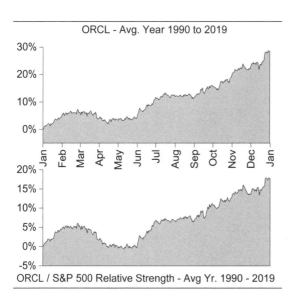

ORCL - Avg. Year 1990 to 2019

ORCL / S&P 500 Relative Strength - Avg Yr. 1990 - 2019

Investors tend to front-run Oracle's full-year earnings report pushing up Oracle's stock price. Oracle tends to be conservative in managing financial analyst expectations around year-end. The result is that its period of seasonal strength tends to last past the earnings report and finish at the beginning of July.

ORCL* vs. S&P 500 - 1990 to 2020

Jun 1 to Jun 30	S&P 500	ORCL	Positive Diff
1990	-0.9	17.1	18.0%
1991	-3.1	13.3	16.4
1992	-0.6	16.8	17.4
1993	-0.3	19.8	20.0
1994	-2.3	10.9	13.2
1995	2.1	11.2	9.0
1996	1.0	18.1	17.1
1997	5.0	4.2	-0.9
1998	5.3	1.9	-3.4
1999	6.1	52.1	46.1
2000	2.4	17.0	14.6
2001	-2.5	24.2	26.7
2002	-9.2	13.6	22.9
2003	1.9	-5.2	-7.2
2004	0.7	3.6	2.9
2005	0.2	3.8	3.6
2006	0.0	1.9	1.9
2007	-1.8	1.7	3.5
2008	-8.2	-6.7	1.5
2009	0.5	11.0	10.5
2010	-5.7	-4.5	1.2
2011	-0.4	-3.4	-3.0
2012	4.0	12.2	8.2
2013	-1.0	-10.9	-9.9
2014	2.6	-3.0	-5.6
2015	-1.4	-7.5	-6.1
2016	0.3	1.6	1.4
2017	0.5	10.5	10.0
2018	0.5	-5.7	-6.2
2019	7.7	14.6	6.9
2020	2.4	3.2	0.8
Avg	0.2%	7.7%	7.5%
Fq > 0	58%	74%	74%

Covid-19 Performance Update.

After strongly outperforming the S&P 500 during the initial stages of the pandemic March, Oracle underperformed in April, May and into early June. Oracle's relative performance compared to the S&P 500 followed its seasonal pattern and as it manged to outperform in June.

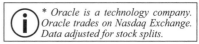

ORCL Performance

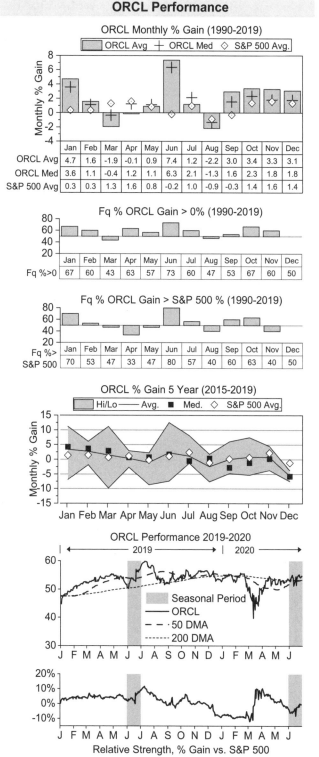

ORCL Monthly % Gain (1990-2019)

Legend: ORCL Avg ☐ | ORCL Med + | S&P 500 Avg. ◇

	Jan	Feb	Mar	Apr	May	Jun	Jul	Aug	Sep	Oct	Nov	Dec
ORCL Avg	4.7	1.6	-1.9	-0.1	0.9	7.4	1.2	-2.2	3.0	3.4	3.3	3.1
ORCL Med	3.6	1.1	-0.4	1.2	1.1	6.3	2.1	-1.3	1.6	2.3	1.8	1.8
S&P 500 Avg	0.3	0.3	1.3	1.6	0.8	-0.2	1.0	-0.9	-0.3	1.4	1.6	1.4

Fq % ORCL Gain > 0% (1990-2019)

	Jan	Feb	Mar	Apr	May	Jun	Jul	Aug	Sep	Oct	Nov	Dec
Fq %>0	67	60	43	63	57	73	60	47	53	67	60	50

Fq % ORCL Gain > S&P 500 % (1990-2019)

	Jan	Feb	Mar	Apr	May	Jun	Jul	Aug	Sep	Oct	Nov	Dec
Fq %> S&P 500	70	53	47	33	47	80	57	40	60	63	40	50

ORCL % Gain 5 Year (2015-2019)

Legend: Hi/Lo | Avg. | ■ Med. | ◇ S&P 500 Avg.

ORCL Performance 2019-2020

Seasonal Period | ORCL | — 50 DMA | ···· 200 DMA

Relative Strength, % Gain vs. S&P 500

WEEK 26

Market Indices & Rates
Weekly Values**

Stock Markets	2019	2020
Dow	26,600	25,016
S&P500	2,942	3,009
Nasdaq	8,006	9,757
TSX	16,382	15,189
FTSE	7,426	6,159
DAX	12,399	12,089
Nikkei	21,276	22,512
Hang Seng	28,543	24,550

Commodities	2019	2020
Oil	58.47	38.49
Gold	1409.0	1747.6

Bond Yields	2019	2020
USA 5 Yr Treasury	1.76	0.30
USA 10 Yr T	2.00	0.64
USA 20 Yr T	2.31	1.15
Moody's Aaa	3.25	2.35
Moody's Baa	4.31	3.56
CAN 5 Yr T	1.39	0.36
CAN 10 Yr T	1.47	0.51

Money Market	2019	2020
USA Fed Funds	2.50	0.25
USA 3 Mo T-B	2.08	0.14
CAN tgt overnight rate	1.75	0.25
CAN 3 Mo T-B	1.66	0.20

Foreign Exchange	2019	2020
EUR/USD	1.14	1.12
GBP/USD	1.27	1.23
USD/CAD	1.31	1.37
USD/JPY	107.85	107.22

JUNE

M	T	W	T	F	S	S
	1	2	3	4	5	6
7	8	9	10	11	12	13
14	15	16	17	18	19	20
21	22	23	24	25	26	27
28	29	30				

JULY

M	T	W	T	F	S	S
		1	2	3	4	
5	6	7	8	9	10	11
12	13	14	15	16	17	18
19	20	21	22	23	24	25
26	27	28	29	30	31	

AUGUST

M	T	W	T	F	S	S
						1
2	3	4	5	6	7	8
9	10	11	12	13	14	15
16	17	18	19	20	21	22
23	24	25	26	27	28	29
30	31					

JULY

	MONDAY	TUESDAY	WEDNESDAY
WEEK 26	28	29	30
WEEK 27	**5** 26 USA Market Closed - Independence Day	**6** 25	**7** 24
WEEK 28	**12** 19	**13** 18	**14** 17
WEEK 29	**19** 12	**20** 11	**21** 10
WEEK 30	**26** 5	**27** 4	**28** 3

THURSDAY	FRIDAY

1 30	**2** 29
CAN Market Closed- Canada Day	

8 23	**9** 22

15 16	**16** 15

22 9	**23** 8

29 2	**30** 1

AUGUST

M	T	W	T	F	S	S
						1
2	3	4	5	6	7	8
9	10	11	12	13	14	15
16	17	18	19	20	21	22
23	24	25	26	27	28	29
30	31					

SEPTEMBER

M	T	W	T	F	S	S
		1	2	3	4	5
6	7	8	9	10	11	12
13	14	15	16	17	18	19
20	21	22	23	24	25	26
27	28	29	30			

OCTOBER

M	T	W	T	F	S	S
				1	2	3
4	5	6	7	8	9	10
11	12	13	14	15	16	17
18	19	20	21	22	23	24
25	26	27	28	29	30	31

NOVEMBER

M	T	W	T	F	S	S
1	2	3	4	5	6	7
8	9	10	11	12	13	14
15	16	17	18	19	20	21
22	23	24	25	26	27	28
29	30					

JULY
S U M M A R Y

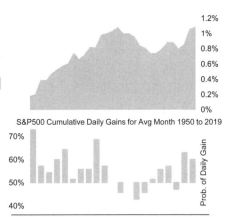

	Dow Jones	S&P 500	Nasdaq	TSX Comp
Month Rank	4	6	10	7
# Up	45	40	27	23
# Down	25	30	21	12
% Pos	64	57	56	66
% Avg. Gain	1.2	1.1	0.5	0.9

Dow & S&P 1950-2019, Nasdaq 1972-2019, TSX 1985-2019

S&P500 Cumulative Daily Gains for Avg Month 1950 to 2019

Prob. of Daily Gain

♦ When a summer rally occurs in the stock market, the gains are usually made in July. ♦ Typically, it is the first part of July that produces the gains as the market tends to rally before Independence Day and into the first eighteen calendar days (see the *18 Days Earnings Month Effect*). In 2019, July produced a strong gain of 1.3% in July. ♦ On average, volatility starts to increase in July and continues this trend into October, with August and September two of the weaker seasonal months of the year.

BEST / WORST JULY BROAD MKTS. 2010-2019

BEST JULY MARKETS
- ♦ Dow (2010) 7.1%
- ♦ FTSE 100 (2010) 6.9%
- ♦ Russell 2000 (2013) 6.9%

WORST JULY MARKETS
- ♦ Russell 2000 (2014) -6.1%
- ♦ Russell 2000 (2011) -3.7%
- ♦ Nikkei 225 (2012) -3.5%

Index Values End of Month

	2010	2011	2012	2013	2014	2015	2016	2017	2018	2019
Dow	10,466	12,143	13,009	15,500	16,563	17,690	18,432	21,891	25,415	26,864
S&P 500	1,102	1,292	1,379	1,686	1,931	2,104	2,174	2,470	2,816	2,980
Nasdaq	2,255	2,756	2,940	3,626	4,370	5,128	5,162	6,348	7,672	8,175
TSX Comp.	11,713	12,946	11,665	12,487	15,331	14,468	14,583	15,144	16,434	16,407
Russell 1000	606	718	759	937	1,076	1,174	1,204	1,369	1,560	1,652
Russell 2000	651	797	787	1,045	1,120	1,239	1,220	1,425	1,671	1,575
FTSE 100	5,258	5,815	5,635	6,621	6,730	6,696	6,724	7,372	7,749	7,587
Nikkei 225	9,537	9,833	8,695	13,668	15,621	20,585	16,569	19,925	22,554	21,522

Percent Gain for July

	2010	2011	2012	2013	2014	2015	2016	2017	2018	2019
Dow	7.1	-2.2	1.0	4.0	-1.6	0.4	2.8	2.5	4.7	1.0
S&P 500	6.9	-2.1	1.3	4.9	-1.5	2.0	3.6	1.9	3.6	1.3
Nasdaq	6.9	-0.6	0.2	6.6	-0.9	2.8	6.6	3.4	2.2	2.1
TSX Comp.	3.7	-2.7	0.6	2.9	1.2	-0.6	3.7	-0.3	1.0	0.1
Russell 1000	6.8	-2.3	1.1	5.2	-1.7	1.8	3.7	1.9	3.3	1.4
Russell 2000	6.8	-3.7	-1.4	6.9	-6.1	-1.2	5.9	0.7	1.7	0.5
FTSE 100	6.9	-2.2	1.2	6.5	-0.2	2.7	3.4	0.8	1.5	2.2
Nikkei 225	1.6	0.2	-3.5	-0.1	3.0	1.7	6.4	-0.5	1.1	1.2

July Market Avg. Performance 2010 to 2019[(1)]

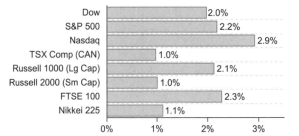

Dow	2.0%
S&P 500	2.2%
Nasdaq	2.9%
TSX Comp (CAN)	1.0%
Russell 1000 (Lg Cap)	2.1%
Russell 2000 (Sm Cap)	1.0%
FTSE 100	2.3%
Nikkei 225	1.1%

Interest Corner Jul[(2)]

	Fed Funds % [(3)]	3 Mo. T-Bill % [(4)]	10 Yr % [(5)]	20 Yr % [(6)]
2019	2.25	2.08	2.02	2.31
2018	2.00	2.03	2.96	3.03
2017	1.25	1.07	2.30	2.66
2016	0.50	0.28	1.46	1.78
2015	0.25	0.08	2.20	2.61

(1) Russell Data provided by Russell (2) Federal Reserve Bank of St. Louis- end of month values (3) Target rate set by FOMC (4)(5)(6) Constant yield maturities.

July 2019 % Sector Performance

GIC % Gain
- Jul 2019
- Jul 90-2019 Avg.

S&P GIC	2019	1990-2019[1]	
Sectors	% Gain	GIC[2] % Avg Gain	Fq% Gain >S&P 500
Financials	2.3 %	1.6 %	50 %
Information Technology	3.3	1.5	53
Materials	-0.4	1.0	53
Health Care	-1.7	1.0	47
Consumer Staples	2.3	0.9	57
Industrials	0.6	0.8	43
Energy	-1.9	0.6	57
Consumer Discretionary	0.9	0.6	50
Utilities	-0.4	0.1	43
Telecom	3.0 %	0.1 %	47 %
S&P 500	1.3 %	1.0 %	N/A %

Sector Commentary

♦ July is an earnings month and the S&P 500 was positive into the start of the earnings season in July 2019 and faded towards the end of the month. ♦ The information technology sector was the top performing sector with a gain of 3.3%. ♦ The worst performing sector was the energy sector, producing a loss of 1.9%.

Sub-Sector Commentary

♦ In July 2019, silver performed particularly well as investors continued to be attracted to precious metals. Investors continued to show a preference for silver compared to gold. ♦ Silver still managed to outperform gold, despite both the metals and mining sub-sectors producing a losses. ♦ The biotech sector produced a loss of 3.5%. The best month of the year for the biotech sub-sector has historically been July (by a long shot). In 2020, biotech performed so well against the S&P 500 in February through May that it became overstretched and underperformed in June and July.

SELECTED SUB-SECTORS[3]			
Biotech (1993-2019)	-3.5 %	6.3 %	82 %
Railroads	0.1	2.3	60
Banks	3.9	1.8	67
Silver	8.2	1.6	60
Transportation	3.5	1.4	50
Chemicals	-0.2	1.3	53
Automotive & Components	0.4	1.2	47
Retail	0.3	1.2	57
SOX (1995-2019)	5.7	1.0	48
Home-builders	1.8	0.9	47
Pharma	-4.9	0.5	50
Metals & Mining	-4.0	0.3	47
Gold	1.3	0.3	50
Steel	-1.3	0.0	47
Agriculture (1994-2019)	0.7	-0.4	46

(1) Sector data provided by Standard and Poors (2) GIC is short form for Global Industry Classification (3) Sub Sector data provided by Standard and Poors, except where marked by symbol.

GOLD SHINES

(Metal) ①Jul12-Oct9 ②Dec27-Jan26

Most of the gold produced each year is consumed in jewelery fabrication. The time of the year with the highest demand for gold is in the fourth quarter, particularly around Indian Diwali, the festival of lights. The demand for gold bullion takes place in previous months as gold fabricators purchase gold bullion to fashion into jewelery for Diwali.

6% gain &
67% of the time positive

The result is that gold bullion tends to rise from July 12 to October 9. In this period, from 1984 to 2018, gold bullion has increased on average 3.2% and has been positive 64% of the time.

In more recent years, the Chinese have become large consumers of gold and have vied with India for the top gold consuming country. The Chinese consume most of their gold around the Chinese New Year, which takes place early in the calendar year. In the yearly period from 1984 to 2019, from December 27 to January 26, gold bullion has produced an average gain of 2.4% and has been positive 61% of the time. Gains in this period have been more frequent in recent years as the Chinese population has increased its consumption of gold.

Covid-19 Performance Update. In its December 27, 2019 to January 26, 2020, gold was positive and outperformed the S&P 500. Shortly afterwards as the Covid-19 pandemic hit and central banks lowered interest rates and flooded the markets with liquidity, gold performed well and outperformed the S&P 500 until it bottomed in late March.

ⓘ *Source: Bank of England- London PM represents the close value of gold in afternoon trading in London.*

Gold* vs. S&P 500 - 1984/85 to 2019/20   Positive ▢

Year	Jul 12 to Oct 9		Dec 27 to Jan 26		Compound Growth	
	S&P 500	Gold	S&P 500	Gold	S&P 500	Gold
1984/85	7.4 %	0.5 %	6.5 %	-3.9 %	14.4 %	-3.4 %
1985/86	-5.4	4.2	-0.4	9.0	-5.7	13.5
1986/87	-2.6	25.2	9.2	4.3	6.3	30.6
1987/88	0.9	3.9	-1.0	-2.4	-0.1	1.4
1988/89	2.8	-7.5	5.0	-2.6	7.9	-10.0
1989/90	9.4	-4.2	-6.1	1.3	2.8	-3.0
1990/91	-15.5	12.1	1.6	-2.5	-14.2	9.3
1991/92	-0.1	-2.9	2.6	-1.8	2.6	-4.6
1992/93	-2.9	0.4	0.0	-0.6	-2.8	-0.2
1993/94	2.7	-8.8	1.3	-0.5	4.0	-9.3
1994/95	1.6	1.6	1.9	-0.1	3.4	1.6
1995/96	4.3	-0.1	1.2	4.8	5.5	4.7
1996/97	7.9	-0.4	1.9	-4.4	10.0	-4.7
1997/98	5.9	4.4	2.2	3.5	8.2	8.0
1998/99	-15.5	2.8	2.1	0.5	-13.7	3.3
1999/00	-4.8	25.6	-3.7	-0.5	-8.3	25.0
2000/01	-5.3	-4.5	3.0	-3.5	-2.5	-7.9
2001/02	-10.5	8.4	-1.4	0.5	-11.7	9.0
2002/03	-16.2	1.7	-3.2	6.4	-18.9	8.2
2003/04	4.1	7.8	5.4	-0.3	9.7	7.5
2004/05	0.8	3.8	-3.0	-3.5	-2.2	0.1
2005/06	-1.9	11.4	0.4	11.3	-1.5	24.0
2006/07	6.1	-8.8	0.4	4.0	6.5	-5.1
2007/08	3.1	11.0	-11.2	13.3	-8.4	25.8
2008/09	-26.6	-8.2	-4.2	7.9	-29.6	-1.0
2009/10	21.9	15.2	-3.1	0.7	18.2	16.0
2010/11	8.1	11.0	3.2	-3.3	11.5	7.3
2011/12	-12.4	6.2	4.2	7.5	-8.8	14.2
2012/13	7.5	12.5	5.9	0.5	13.7	13.1
2013/14	-1.1	1.5	-2.8	5.7	-3.9	7.2
2014/15	-2.0	-8.1	-1.5	9.0	-3.5	0.1
2015/16	-3.0	-0.7	-7.6	4.3	-10.4	3.6
2016/17	0.8	-7.3	1.5	5.2	2.2	-2.5
2017/18	4.9	5.6	7.2	7.0	12.4	13.0
2018/19	3.8	-5.3	8.0	2.8	12.1	-2.6
2019/20	-2.6	6.6	1.7	5.5	-1.1	12.5
Avg.	-0.6 %	3.2 %	0.1 %	2.4 %	0.1 %	5.7 %
Fq>0	53 %	64 %	64 %	61 %	50 %	67 %

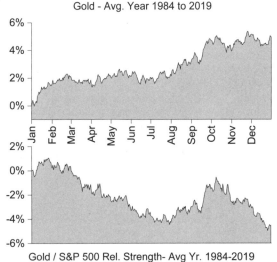

Gold - Avg. Year 1984 to 2019

Gold / S&P 500 Rel. Strength- Avg Yr. 1984-2019

Gold Performance

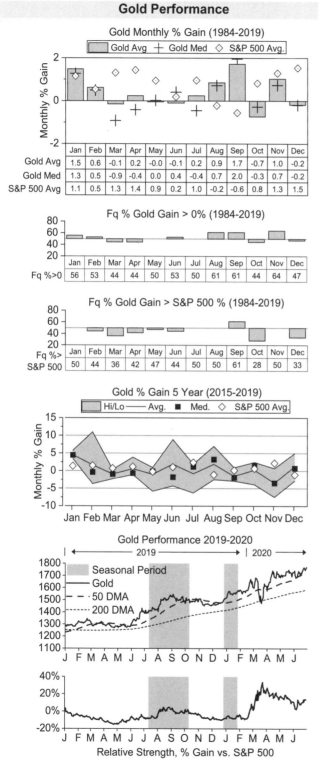

Gold Monthly % Gain (1984-2019)

Gold Avg + Gold Med ◇ S&P 500 Avg.

	Jan	Feb	Mar	Apr	May	Jun	Jul	Aug	Sep	Oct	Nov	Dec
Gold Avg	1.5	0.6	-0.1	0.2	-0.0	-0.1	0.2	0.9	1.7	-0.7	1.0	-0.2
Gold Med	1.3	0.5	-0.9	-0.4	0.0	0.4	-0.4	0.7	2.0	-0.3	0.7	-0.2
S&P 500 Avg	1.1	0.5	1.3	1.4	0.9	0.2	1.0	-0.2	-0.6	0.8	1.3	1.5

Fq % Gold Gain > 0% (1984-2019)

	Jan	Feb	Mar	Apr	May	Jun	Jul	Aug	Sep	Oct	Nov	Dec
Fq %>0	56	53	44	44	50	53	50	61	61	44	64	47

Fq % Gold Gain > S&P 500 % (1984-2019)

	Jan	Feb	Mar	Apr	May	Jun	Jul	Aug	Sep	Oct	Nov	Dec
Fq %> S&P 500	50	44	36	42	47	44	50	50	61	28	50	33

Gold % Gain 5 Year (2015-2019)

Hi/Lo — Avg. ■ Med. ◇ S&P 500 Avg.

Jan Feb Mar Apr May Jun Jul Aug Sep Oct Nov Dec

Gold Performance 2019-2020

2019 | 2020

Seasonal Period
— Gold
- - 50 DMA
···· 200 DMA

J F M A M J J A S O N D J F M A M J

Relative Strength, % Gain vs. S&P 500

Market Indices & Rates
Weekly Values**

Stock Markets	2018	2019
Dow	24,456	26,922
S&P500	2,760	2,990
Nasdaq	7,688	8,162
TSX	16,372	16,542
FTSE	7,618	7,553
DAX	12,496	12,569
Nikkei	21,788	21,746
Hang Seng	28,316	28,775

Commodities	2018	2019
Oil	73.80	57.34
Gold	1255.4	1388.7

Bond Yields	2018	2019
USA 5 Yr Treasury	2.71	1.84
USA 10 Yr T	2.82	2.04
USA 20 Yr T	2.87	2.34
Moody's Aaa	3.88	3.26
Moody's Baa	4.78	4.30
CAN 5 Yr T	2.05	1.53
CAN 10 Yr T	2.13	1.57

Money Market	2018	2019
USA Fed Funds	2.00	2.50
USA 3 Mo T-B	1.93	2.18
CAN tgt overnight rate	1.25	1.75
CAN 3 Mo T-B	1.28	1.66

Foreign Exchange	2018	2019
EUR/USD	1.17	1.12
GBP/USD	1.33	1.25
USD/CAD	1.31	1.31
USD/JPY	110.47	108.47

JULY

M	T	W	T	F	S	S
			1	2	3	4
5	6	7	8	9	10	11
12	13	14	15	16	17	18
19	20	21	22	23	24	25
26	27	28	29	30	31	

AUGUST

M	T	W	T	F	S	S
						1
2	3	4	5	6	7	8
9	10	11	12	13	14	15
16	17	18	19	20	21	22
23	24	25	26	27	28	29
30	31					

SEPTEMBER

M	T	W	T	F	S	S
	1	2	3	4	5	
6	7	8	9	10	11	12
13	14	15	16	17	18	19
20	21	22	23	24	25	26
27	28	29	30			

GOLD MINERS – DIG GAINS

(Stocks) ① Jul27-Sep25 ② Dec23-Feb14

The gold miners sector tends to perform well at approximately the same time of the year that gold bullion performs well. As gold bullion moves higher in price, gold miners benefit from their gold in the ground increasing in value.

Gold miners have their main seasonal period of strength from July 27 to September 25. Gold miners tend to perform well as gold bullion tends to increase at this time due to increased demand to make gold jewelery for fourth quarter consumption.

10% gain & 69% of the time positive

Gold miners also tend to perform well at the beginning of the year as Chinese New Year approaches. The Chinese buy a large amount of their gold in the period leading up to Chinese New Year. Over the years, this trend has become more predominant as the wealth of Chinese citizens has increased.

Combining the two gold seasonal trades together has proven to be beneficial as the frequency of gains for the combined trade increases to 6.9% with an average gain of 10.4%.

Covid-19 Pandemic Update. Gold miners finished their December 23, 2019 - February 14, 2020 seasonal period, just before the Covid-19 pandemic took its toll on the stock market. Gold miners were extremely volatile as the stock market declined into late March. Once the stock market started to rally, gold miners strongly outperformed the S&P 500 starting in late March. Gold miners benefited from increasing gold prices and a rallying stock market.

(i) *XAU- PHLX Gold Silver Index consists of 12 precious metal mining companies.*

XAU* vs. S&P 500 - 1984/85 to 2019/20   Positive ▢

Year	Jul 27 to Sep 25 S&P 500	XAU	Dec 23 to Feb 14 S&P 500	XAU	Compound Growth S&P 500	XAU
1984/85	10.4 %	20.8 %	10.2 %	10.6 %	21.6 %	33.6 %
1985/86	-6.1	-5.5	4.2	-2.0	-2.2	-7.2
1986/87	-3.5	36.9	12.4	14.4	8.5	56.6
1987/88	3.5	23.0	3.1	-15.9	6.7	3.4
1988/89	1.7	-11.9	5.4	12.1	7.2	-1.3
1989/90	1.8	10.5	-4.4	6.8	-2.7	18.1
1990/91	-13.4	3.8	9.8	-0.8	-4.9	3.1
1991/92	1.6	-11.9	6.6	9.8	8.2	-3.3
1992/93	0.7	-3.8	1.0	8.9	1.6	4.8
1993/94	1.9	-7.3	0.6	-1.4	2.5	-8.6
1994/95	1.4	18.2	5.0	-4.4	6.4	13.0
1995/96	3.6	-1.0	7.1	20.8	11.0	19.6
1996/97	7.9	-1.0	8.0	-2.2	16.4	-3.2
1997/98	-0.1	8.7	7.0	6.9	6.9	16.2
1998/99	-8.4	12.0	2.2	8.8	-6.4	21.9
1999/00	-5.2	16.9	-3.2	-1.3	-8.3	15.3
2000/01	-0.9	-2.8	0.8	-12.5	-0.2	-15.0
2001/02	-15.9	3.2	-2.5	23.7	-17.9	27.6
2002/03	-1.6	29.8	-6.8	-3.7	-8.2	25.1
2003/04	0.5	11.0	4.8	-0.8	5.3	10.1
2004/05	2.4	16.5	-0.3	-3.8	2.1	12.1
2005/06	-1.3	20.6	0.6	10.0	-0.7	32.6
2006/07	4.6	-11.8	3.2	3.7	7.9	-8.5
2007/08	2.3	14.0	-9.1	5.3	-7.0	20.1
2008/09	-3.9	-18.5	-5.1	19.2	-8.8	-2.8
2009/10	6.7	6.0	-3.8	-3.8	2.6	2.0
2010/11	3.0	14.7	5.8	-5.0	9.0	8.9
2011/12	-14.7	-13.7	7.7	3.8	-8.1	-10.4
2012/13	6.0	24.0	6.4	-7.2	12.8	15.1
2013/14	0.1	-5.6	1.1	26.8	1.2	19.8
2014/15	-0.6	-16.4	0.9	18.0	0.3	-1.3
2015/16	-7.1	-2.6	-8.5	33.7	-15.1	30.2
2016/17	-0.2	-7.0	3.4	29.1	3.2	20.0
2017/18	0.8	1.5	0.6	1.8	1.3	3.3
2018/19	2.8	-13.5	13.6	8.5	16.7	-6.0
2019/20	-1.4	4.3	4.9	4.6	3.5	9.0
Avg.	-0.6 %	4.5 %	2.6 %	6.2 %	2.0 %	10.4 %
Fq>0	56 %	56 %	75 %	61 %	64 %	69 %

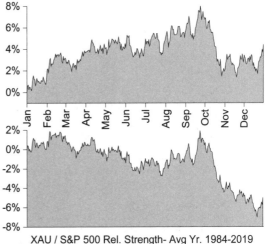

XAU - Avg. Year 1984 to 2019

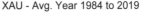

XAU / S&P 500 Rel. Strength- Avg Yr. 1984-2019

Gold Miners Performance

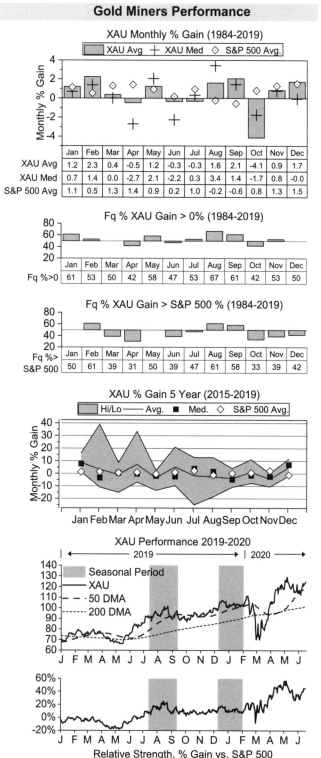

XAU Monthly % Gain (1984-2019)

XAU Avg + XAU Med ◇ S&P 500 Avg.

	Jan	Feb	Mar	Apr	May	Jun	Jul	Aug	Sep	Oct	Nov	Dec
XAU Avg	1.2	2.3	0.4	-0.5	1.2	-0.3	-0.3	1.6	2.1	-4.1	0.9	1.7
XAU Med	0.7	1.4	0.0	-2.7	2.1	-2.2	0.3	3.4	1.4	-1.7	0.8	-0.0
S&P 500 Avg	1.1	0.5	1.3	1.4	0.9	0.2	1.0	-0.2	-0.6	0.8	1.3	1.5

Fq % XAU Gain > 0% (1984-2019)

	Jan	Feb	Mar	Apr	May	Jun	Jul	Aug	Sep	Oct	Nov	Dec
Fq %>0	61	53	50	42	58	47	53	67	61	42	53	50

Fq % XAU Gain > S&P 500 % (1984-2019)

	Jan	Feb	Mar	Apr	May	Jun	Jul	Aug	Sep	Oct	Nov	Dec
Fq %> S&P 500	50	61	39	31	50	39	47	61	58	33	39	42

XAU % Gain 5 Year (2015-2019)

Hi/Lo — Avg. ■ Med. ◇ S&P 500 Avg.

XAU Performance 2019-2020

Seasonal Period
XAU
50 DMA
200 DMA

Relative Strength, % Gain vs. S&P 500

WEEK 28

**Market Indices & Rates
Weekly Values****

Stock Markets	2018	2019
Dow	25,019	27,332
S&P500	2,801	3,014
Nasdaq	7,826	8,244
TSX	16,561	16,488
FTSE	7,662	7,506
DAX	12,541	12,323
Nikkei	22,597	21,686
Hang Seng	28,525	28,472

Commodities	2018	2019
Oil	71.01	60.21
Gold	1241.7	1407.6

Bond Yields	2018	2019
USA 5 Yr Treasury	2.73	1.86
USA 10 Yr T	2.83	2.12
USA 20 Yr T	2.87	2.42
Moody's Aaa	3.80	3.34
Moody's Baa	4.73	4.37
CAN 5 Yr T	2.05	1.55
CAN 10 Yr T	2.13	1.61

Money Market	2018	2019
USA Fed Funds	2.00	2.50
USA 3 Mo T-B	1.94	2.10
CAN tgt overnight rate	1.50	1.75
CAN 3 Mo T-B	1.42	1.66

Foreign Exchange	2018	2019
EUR/USD	1.17	1.13
GBP/USD	1.32	1.26
USD/CAD	1.32	1.30
USD/JPY	112.38	107.91

JULY

M	T	W	T	F	S	S
		1	2	3	4	
5	6	7	8	9	10	11
12	13	14	15	16	17	18
19	20	21	22	23	24	25
26	27	28	29	30	31	

AUGUST

M	T	W	T	F	S	S
						1
2	3	4	5	6	7	8
9	10	11	12	13	14	15
16	17	18	19	20	21	22
23	24	25	26	27	28	29
30	31					

SEPTEMBER

M	T	W	T	F	S	S
	1	2	3	4	5	
6	7	8	9	10	11	12
13	14	15	16	17	18	19
20	21	22	23	24	25	26
27	28	29	30			

VOLATILITY INDEX
July 3rd to October 9th

The Chicago Board Options Exchange Market Volatility Index (VIX) is often referred to as a fear index as it measures investors' expectations of market volatility over the next thirty day period. The higher the VIX value, the greater the expectation of volatility and vice versa.

From 1990 to June 2019, the long-term average of the VIX is 19.4. In this time period, the VIX has bottomed at approximately 10 in the mid-90's, and the mid-2000's. In both cases, the VIX dropped below 10 for a few days.

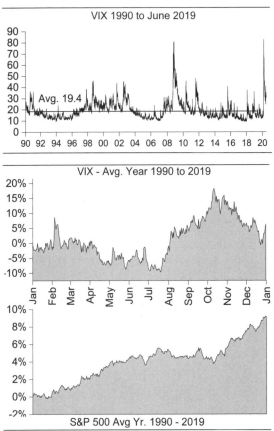

VIX 1990 to June 2019

Avg. 19.4

VIX - Avg. Year 1990 to 2019

S&P 500 Avg Yr. 1990 - 2019

VIX* vs. S&P 500 1990 to 2019

July 3 to Oct 9	S&P 500	VIX %Gain (Positive)
1990	-15.1%	88.9%
1991	-0.2	5.2
1992	-2.2	47.8
1993	3.3	6.3
1994	2.0	3.9
1995	6.2	30.5
1996	3.4	13.4
1997	7.4	13.3
1998	-14.1	138.8
1999	-4.0	9.8
2000	-3.6	22.9
2001	-14.6	85.7
2002	-18.1	45.5
2003	4.5	-1.1
2004	-0.3	-0.2
2005	0.1	28.0
2006	6.3	-10.7
2007	3.0	4.7
2008	-27.9	146.6
2009	19.5	-17.3
2010	13.9	-31.2
2011	-13.8	128.1
2012	5.6	-2.6
2013	2.6	19.2
2014	-2.4	73.4
2015	-2.9	1.7
2016	2.4	-8.7
2017	5.0	-7.6
2018	5.6	2.2
2019	-1.8	44.2
Avg	-0.1%	29.3%
Fq > 0	53%	73%

average, the VIX tends to start increasing in July, particularly after the earnings season gets underway. After mid-July, without the expectation of strong earnings ahead, investors tend to focus on economic forecasts that often become more dire in the second half of the year.

In addition, stock market analysts tend to reduce their earnings forecasts at this time. Both of these effects tend to add volatility in the markets, increasing the VIX. The VIX tends to peak in October as the stock market often starts to establishing a rising trend at this time.

Levels below 15 are often associated with investor complacency, as investors are expecting very little volatility. Very often when a stock market correction occurs in this state, it can be sharp and severe. Knowing the trends of the VIX can be useful in adjusting the amount of risk in a portfolio.

From 1990 to 2019, during the period of July 3 to October 9, the VIX has increased 73% of the time. On

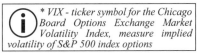

* VIX - ticker symbol for the Chicago Board Options Exchange Market Volatility Index, measure implied volatility of S&P 500 index options

VIX Performance

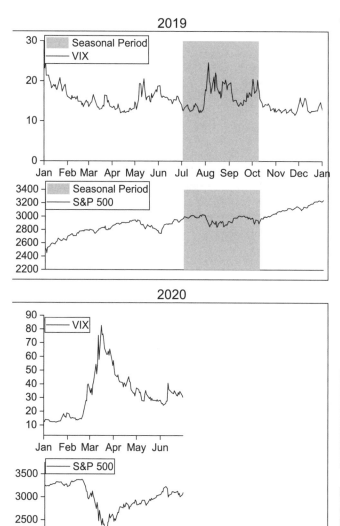

2019

2020

WEEK 29

Market Indices & Rates
Weekly Values**

Stock Markets	2018	2019
Dow	25,058	27,154
S&P500	2,802	2,977
Nasdaq	7,820	8,146
TSX	16,435	16,486
FTSE	7,679	7,509
DAX	12,561	12,260
Nikkei	22,698	21,467
Hang Seng	28,224	28,765

Commodities	2018	2019
Oil	70.46	55.63
Gold	1228.8	1439.7

Bond Yields	2018	2019
USA 5 Yr Treasury	2.77	1.80
USA 10 Yr T	2.89	2.05
USA 20 Yr T	2.96	2.35
Moody's Aaa	3.90	3.31
Moody's Baa	4.80	4.31
CAN 5 Yr T	2.08	1.42
CAN 10 Yr T	2.18	1.51

Money Market	2018	2019
USA Fed Funds	2.00	2.50
USA 3 Mo T-B	1.95	2.02
CAN tgt overnight rate	1.50	1.75
CAN 3 Mo T-B	1.39	1.65

Foreign Exchange	2018	2019
EUR/USD	1.17	1.12
GBP/USD	1.31	1.25
USD/CAD	1.31	1.31
USD/JPY	111.41	107.71

JULY

M	T	W	T	F	S	S
			1	2	3	4
5	6	7	8	9	10	11
12	13	14	15	16	17	18
19	20	21	22	23	24	25
26	27	28	29	30	31	

AUGUST

M	T	W	T	F	S	S
						1
2	3	4	5	6	7	8
9	10	11	12	13	14	15
16	17	18	19	20	21	22
23	24	25	26	27	28	29
30	31					

SEPTEMBER

M	T	W	T	F	S	S
		1	2	3	4	5
6	7	8	9	10	11	12
13	14	15	16	17	18	19
20	21	22	23	24	25	26
27	28	29	30			

In 2019, VIX increased in its seasonal period as the stock market stumbled and was fairly flat in the same period.

In 2020, VIX rose sharply in February and March as the stock market plummeted due to the Covid-19 pandemic. After the stock market bottomed on March 23 VIX declined but remained elevated despite the stock market continuing to rise.

TYSON FOODS

TSN
① LONG (Oct28-May31)
② SELL SHORT (Jun1-Jul31)

Tyson Foods has a seasonal trend that is similar to the six-month seasonal period for the broad stock market with weaker performance in the summer months.

23% growth & positive 74% of the time

Tyson Foods has an increased seasonal demand for some of its products in the spring and summer months. As a result, investors tend to front run Tyson's strong seasonal demand, favoring the stock until the end of May, which is a few weeks past the strong seasonal period for the broad stock market.

As the high demand season for Tyson Foods occurs in the summer months, the stock tends to falter relative to the S&P 500.

The juxtaposition of Tyson's strong seasonal period with its weak seasonal period, creates transitions challenges that are best navigated with the use of technical analysis

---

Covid-19 Performance Update. Tyson Foods underperformed the S&P 500 at the beginning of the year in 2020. As Covid-19 pandemic developed, Tyson Foods continued its underperformance, rallied sharply in March for a brief period and continued its underperformance into the summer months. Tyson Foods has been hit hard from the Covid-19 pandemic due to many restaurants having to close their doors.

ⓘ *Tyson Foods is a food processing and distribution company. Its stock symbol is TSN. which trades on the NYSE, adjusted for splits.*

Tyson Foods* vs. S&P 500 1989/90 to 2019/20

Positive Long ▢   Negative Short ▢

Year	Oct 28 to May 31		Jun 1 to Jul 31		Compound Growth	
	S&P 500	TSN	S&P 500	TSN	S&P 500	TSN
1989/90	7.8	51.4 %	-1.4 %	-12.9 %	6.3 %	71.0 %
1990/91	27.9	56.1	-0.5	-16.9	27.3	82.5
1991/92	8.1	-5.1	2.1	7.4	10.4	-12.1
1992/93	7.6	16.3	-0.5	-14.5	7.1	33.1
1993/94	-1.7	-6.8	0.4	11.9	-1.4	-17.8
1994/95	14.5	-6.8	5.4	10.9	20.7	-16.9
1995/96	15.4	1.0	-4.4	0.5	10.4	0.5
1996/97	21.0	2.5	12.5	2.4	36.2	0.0
1997/98	24.4	13.4	2.7	2.4	27.8	10.7
1998/99	22.2	1.9	2.1	-18.8	24.7	21.1
1999/00	9.6	-35.8	0.7	-5.1	10.3	-32.5
2000/01	-9.0	12.6	-3.6	-19.2	-12.2	34.2
2001/02	-3.4	64.2	-14.6	-14.3	-17.5	87.7
2002/03	7.3	-15.6	2.8	19.3	10.3	-31.8
2003/04	8.7	45.1	-1.7	-7.1	6.8	55.4
2004/05	5.9	26.1	3.6	1.0	9.7	24.9
2005/06	7.7	-7.0	0.5	-11.6	8.3	3.8
2006/07	11.1	55.5	-4.9	-4.4	5.7	62.5
2007/08	-8.8	19.2	-9.5	-20.9	-17.5	44.2
2008/09	8.3	66.7	7.4	-14.2	16.3	90.4
2009/10	2.4	42.5	1.1	-0.4	3.6	43.0
2010/11	13.8	21.0	-3.9	-7.7	9.3	30.3
2011/12	2.0	-0.4	5.3	-22.5	7.4	22.0
2012/13	15.5	51.1	3.4	10.5	19.4	35.3
2013/14	9.3	50.9	0.4	-12.4	9.7	69.5
2014/15	7.4	9.4	-0.2	4.5	7.3	4.5
2015/16	1.5	42.4	3.7	15.4	5.2	20.4
2016/17	13.1	-16.8	2.4	10.5	15.8	-25.5
2017/18	4.8	-5.0	4.1	-14.6	9.1	8.8
2018/19	3.5	25.5	8.3	4.8	12.1	19.5
2019/20	0.7	-21.7	7.5	0.0	8.2	-21.7
Avg.	8.3 %	17.9 %	1.0 %	-3.7 %	9.6 %	23.1 %
Fq>0	87.1 %	67.7 %	64.5 %	45.2 %	87.1 %	74.2 %

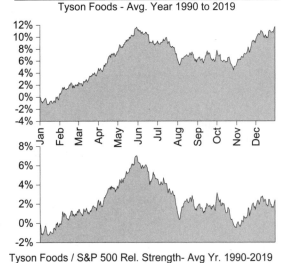

Tyson Foods - Avg. Year 1990 to 2019

Tyson Foods / S&P 500 Rel. Strength- Avg Yr. 1990-2019

Tyson Foods Performance

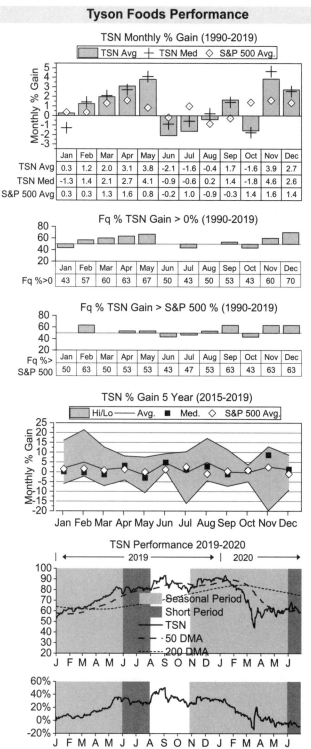

TSN Monthly % Gain (1990-2019)

Legend: TSN Avg · + TSN Med · ◇ S&P 500 Avg.

	Jan	Feb	Mar	Apr	May	Jun	Jul	Aug	Sep	Oct	Nov	Dec
TSN Avg	0.3	1.2	2.0	3.1	3.8	-2.1	-1.6	-0.4	1.7	-1.6	3.9	2.7
TSN Med	-1.3	1.4	2.1	2.7	4.1	-0.9	-0.6	0.2	1.4	-1.8	4.6	2.6
S&P 500 Avg	0.3	0.3	1.3	1.6	0.8	-0.2	1.0	-0.9	-0.3	1.4	1.6	1.4

Fq % TSN Gain > 0% (1990-2019)

	Jan	Feb	Mar	Apr	May	Jun	Jul	Aug	Sep	Oct	Nov	Dec
Fq %>0	43	57	60	63	67	50	43	50	53	43	60	70

Fq % TSN Gain > S&P 500 % (1990-2019)

	Jan	Feb	Mar	Apr	May	Jun	Jul	Aug	Sep	Oct	Nov	Dec
Fq %> S&P 500	50	63	50	53	53	43	47	53	63	43	63	63

TSN % Gain 5 Year (2015-2019)

Legend: Hi/Lo — Avg. ■ Med. ◇ S&P 500 Avg.

TSN Performance 2019-2020

Legend: Seasonal Period, Short Period, TSN, 50 DMA, 200 DMA

Relative Strength, % Gain vs. S&P 500

WEEK 30

Market Indices & Rates
Weekly Values**

Stock Markets	2018	2019
Dow	25,451	27,192
S&P500	2,819	3,026
Nasdaq	7,737	8,330
TSX	16,394	16,531
FTSE	7,701	7,549
DAX	12,860	12,420
Nikkei	22,713	21,658
Hang Seng	28,804	28,398

Commodities	2018	2019
Oil	68.69	56.20
Gold	1224.0	1420.4

Bond Yields	2018	2019
USA 5 Yr Treasury	2.84	1.85
USA 10 Yr T	2.96	2.08
USA 20 Yr T	3.03	2.38
Moody's Aaa	3.90	3.31
Moody's Baa	4.80	4.21
CAN 5 Yr T	2.21	1.40
CAN 10 Yr T	2.30	1.47

Money Market	2018	2019
USA Fed Funds	2.00	2.50
USA 3 Mo T-B	1.96	2.08
CAN tgt overnight rate	1.50	1.75
CAN 3 Mo T-B	1.41	1.65

Foreign Exchange	2018	2019
EUR/USD	1.17	1.11
GBP/USD	1.31	1.24
USD/CAD	1.31	1.32
USD/JPY	111.05	108.68

JULY

M	T	W	T	F	S	S
		1	2	3	4	
5	6	7	8	9	10	11
12	13	14	15	16	17	18
19	20	21	22	23	24	25
26	27	28	29	30	31	

AUGUST

M	T	W	T	F	S	S
						1
2	3	4	5	6	7	8
9	10	11	12	13	14	15
16	17	18	19	20	21	22
23	24	25	26	27	28	29
30	31					

SEPTEMBER

M	T	W	T	F	S	S
	1	2	3	4	5	
6	7	8	9	10	11	12
13	14	15	16	17	18	19
20	21	22	23	24	25	26
27	28	29	30			

Seasonal Investment Timeline[1]

Investment	Season		2020	2021
			O N D	J F M A M J J A S O N D
Core Positions				
S&P 500	Oct 28 - May 5			
TSX Composite	Oct 28 - May 5			
Cash	May 6 - Oct 27			
Primary Sectors				
[4]Consumer Staples	Jan 1 - Jan 22 (S)	Apr 23 - Oct 27		
Financials	Dec 15 - Apr 13			
Energy	Feb 25 - May 9	Jul 24 - Oct 3		
[2]Utilities	Jul 17 - Oct 3	Jan 1 - Mar 13 (S)		
Health Care	Aug 15 - Oct 18			
Information Tech	Oct 9 - Jan 17	Apr 16 - Apr 30		
Consumer Disc.	Oct 28 - Apr 22			
Industrials	Oct 28 - Dec 31	Jan 23- May 5		
Materials	Oct 28 - Jan 6	Jan 23 - May 5		
Small Cap	Dec 19 - Mar 7			
Secondary Sectors				
Silver Bullion	Dec 27- Feb 22			
[2]Platinum	Jan 1 - May 31			
Software Jan1 - Jan19	Jun 1 - Jun 30	Oct 10 - Dec 5		
[3]Semiconductors	Jan 1 - Mar 7	Oct 28 - Nov 6		
Canadian Dollar	Apr 1 - Apr 30	Aug 20 - Sep 25		
Biotech	Jun 23 - Sep 13			
Gold Bullion	Jul 12 - Oct 9	Dec 27 - Jan 26		
Gold Miners	Jul 27 - Sep 25	Dec 23 - Feb 14		
Agriculture	Sep 26 - Nov 11			
Transportation Jan23-Apr16	Aug 3 - Oct 9 (S)	Oct 10 - Nov 13		
Natural Gas Mar22 - Jun19	Sep 6 - Dec 21	Dec 22 - Dec 31(S)		
Airlines	Oct 3 - Nov 6	Aug 1- Aug 31 (S)		
Canadian Banks	Oct 10 - Dec 31	Jan 23 - Apr 13		
Retail	Oct 28 - Nov 29	Jan 21 - Apr 12		
Homebuilders	Oct 28 - Feb 3	Apr 27- Jun 13(S)		
Metals & Mining	Nov 19 - Jan 5	Jan 23 - May 5		
Emerging Markets	Nov 24 - April 18			
[9]Aerospace & Defense	Dec 12 - May 5			
[9]Automotive Dec14 - Jan7	Feb 24 - Apr 24	Aug 3 - Oct 3 (S)		
US REITS	Mar 8 - Sep 20	Sep 21- Oct 9 (S)		
Other Market / Sector Trades				
Nikkei 225	May 6 - Nov 19 (S)			
VIX (CBOE)	Jul 3 - Oct 9			
[7]Canadian Snowbird Trade	Oct 28 - Dec 18			
[9]Mid Caps Jan 9 - Mar 7	Jun 3 - Jun 26 (S)	Nov 23 - Dec 31		
Value vs Growth	Feb 26 - Apr 19	Nov 29 - Jan 6		
Commodities				
Copper	Jan 29 - Mar 5	Jun 24 - Jul 31		
Currency				
CAD / USD	Apr 1 - Apr 30	Aug 20 - Sep 25		
EUR / USD	Nov 17 - Dec 31			
USD / EUR	Jan 1 - Feb 7			
Fixed Income				
[3]U.S. Gov. Bonds	May 9 - Oct 3			
[3]U.S. High Yield	Nov 24 - Jan 8			
10YR Inflation Break-Even	Dec 20 - Mar 7			

Long Investment ▓▓▓▓ Short Investment (S) ☐ [1] Holiday, End of Month, Witches' Hangover, - et al not included.

[2]Thackray's 2012 Investor's Guide [3]Thackray's 2013 Investor's Guide [4]Thackray's 2014 Investor's Guide [5]Thackray's 2015 Investor's Guide [6]Thackray's 2016 Investor's Guide [7]Thackray's 2017 Investor's Guide [8]Thackray's 2018 Investor's Guide[9]Thackray's 2019 Investor's Guide

Seasonal Investment Timeline[1]

Investment	Season		2020	2021

Stocks

O N D J F M A M J J A S O N D

[9]Canadian Tire Jan1-Jan31 (S)	Feb11-Apr12	Oct28-Nov30
[8]Hasbro Jan21- April12	Jun1-Jul21(S)	Oct10-Nov26 Nov27-Dec22(S)
TJX Companies	Jan 22 - Mar 30	
[5]Caterpillar	Jan 23 - May 5	
[6]DuPont	Jan 28 - May 5	
[9]Chevron	Feb 1 - May 5	
[3]3M	Feb 3 - May 12	
[2]Suncor Energy	Feb 18 - May 9	
[4]Waste Management	Feb 24 - May 14	
[3]AMD	Feb 24 - May 5	May 6 - Jul 29 (S)
[3]GE	Mar 5 - Apr 6	
[4]Harley Davidson	Mar 9- Apr 18	Jun 22 - Jul 18
[5]Boeing	Mar 13 - Jun 15	
[5]Sysco	Apr 23 - May 30	Oct 11 - Nov 21
[5]Disney	Jun 5 - Sep 30 (S)	Oct 1 - Feb 15
[4]IBM Apr 14 - May 19	Jul 7 - Jul 30	Oct 28 - Nov 26
[3]Intel	May 6 - Jul 29	
Costco	May 26 - Jun 30	Oct 4 - Dec 1
[3]PotashCorp	Jun 23 - Jan 11	
[3]Johnson & Johnson	Jul 14 - Oct 21	
[4]Altria	Jul 19 - Dec 19	
[8]Procter and Gamble	Aug 7 - Nov 19	
[6]Archer-Daniels Midland	Aug 7 - Dec 31	
[3]Alcoa	Aug 23 - Sep 26 (S)	
[7]Carnival Cruise Lines	Sep 8 - Dec 31	
[5]Union Pacific	Oct 10 - Nov 4	Mar 11 - May 5
[6]Royal Bank	Oct 10 - Nov 28	Jan 23 - Apr 13
[6]Clorox Jan14-Mar 2	Sep 22 - Nov 17	Nov 18 - Jan 13 (S)
Nike Mar1 - Mar 20	Sep 1 - Sep 25	Dec 12 - Dec 24
[5]Campbell Soup	Sep 22 - Nov 17	
UPS	Oct 10 - Dec 8	Dec 9 - Mar 1 (S)
[8]Sun Life Financial	Oct 10 - Dec 5	
Cameco	Oct 4 - Jan 24	Jun 5 - Aug 7 (S)
Home Depot	Oct 28 - Dec 31	Jan 9 - Apr 15
McDonald's	Oct 28 - Nov 24	Jan 30 - Apr 8
[7]Estee Lauder	Oct 28 - Dec 31	Feb 1 - May 5
Eastman Chemical	Jan 28 - May 5	May 30 - Oct 27 (S)
[5]Linamar	Feb 24 - May 12	
[7]Bed Bath & Beyond	Feb 25 - Apr 8	Aug 23 - Sep 29
Amgen	Jun 23 - Sep 13	
[6]H&R Block	Oct 28 - Mar 31	Apr 1- May 16 (S)
United Technologies	Jan 23 - May 5	Oct 10 - Dec 31
[9]BKS Jan31-Mar26	Jun4-Oct27(S)	Oct28-Nov28 Nov29-Jan30(S)
Walmart	Jan 21 - Apr 12	Oct 28 - Nov 29
[9]AT&T Jan3-Feb23(S)	Sep3-Oct3	Oct4-Oct25(S) Nov15-Dec22
Sherwin-Williams	Aug 13 - Sep 23 (S)	Sep 24 - Apr 19
[9]Callaway Golf	Jan10-Apr18	Apr19-Jul28(S) Jul29-Aug14
CP Railway	Jan22-May10	Aug5-Oct2(S) Oct3-Nov10
Baker Hughes	Jan15-May11	Jun1-Jun30 (S) Aug2-Dec11(S)
Wynn Resorts	Jan21-May11	May12-Jun27(S) Oct3-Nov3
Coca-Cola Company	Apr 27 - May 27	Sep 25 - Nov 23
Snap-On	Jan 24 - May 5	Aug 1- Oct 8(S)
Loblaw	Apr 25 - May 18	
Oracle	Jun 1 - Jul 1	
Tyson Foods	Oct 28 - May 31	Jun 1 - Jul 31(S)
Lennox	Sep 6 - Oct 15 (S)	Oct 16 - Mar 16
Rogers Communications	Apr 19 - May 23	Oct 1 - Nov 7

Long Investment ▓▓▓▓▓ Short Investment (S) ☐ [1] Holiday, End of Month, Witches' Hangover, - et al not included.

[2]Thackray's 2012 Investor's Guide [3]Thackray's 2013 Investor's Guide [4]Thackray's 2014 Investor's Guide [5]Thackray's 2015 Investor's Guide
[6]Thackray's 2016 Investor's Guide [7]Thackray's 2017 Investor's Guide [8]Thackray's 2018 Investor's Guide [9]Thackray's 2018 Investor's Guide

AUGUST

	MONDAY	TUESDAY	WEDNESDAY
WEEK 31	**2** 29 CAN Market Closed- Civic Day	**3** 28	**4** 27
WEEK 32	**9** 22	**10** 21	**11** 20
WEEK 33	**16** 15	**17** 14	**18** 13
WEEK 34	**23** 8	**24** 7	**25** 6
WEEK 35	**30** 1	**31**	1

THURSDAY		FRIDAY	
5	26	**6**	25
12	19	**13**	18
19	12	**20**	11
26	5	**27**	4
2		3	

SEPTEMBER

M	T	W	T	F	S	S
		1	2	3	4	5
6	7	8	9	10	11	12
13	14	15	16	17	18	19
20	21	22	23	24	25	26
27	28	29	30			

OCTOBER

M	T	W	T	F	S	S
				1	2	3
4	5	6	7	8	9	10
11	12	13	14	15	16	17
18	19	20	21	22	23	24
25	26	27	28	29	30	31

NOVEMBER

M	T	W	T	F	S	S
1	2	3	4	5	6	7
8	9	10	11	12	13	14
15	16	17	18	19	20	21
22	23	24	25	26	27	28
29	30					

DECEMBER

M	T	W	T	F	S	S
		1	2	3	4	5
6	7	8	9	10	11	12
13	14	15	16	17	18	19
20	21	22	23	24	25	26
27	28	29	30	31		

AUGUST
S U M M A R Y

	Dow Jones	S&P 500	Nasdaq	TSX Comp
Month Rank	10	11	11	10
# Up	39	38	26	20
# Down	31	32	22	15
% Pos	56	54	54	57
% Avg. Gain	-0.1	-0.1	0.1	-0.2

Dow & S&P 1950-2019, Nasdaq 1972-2019, TSX 1985-2019

0.3%
0.2%
0.1%
0%
-0.1%
-0.2%
-0.3%

S&P500 Cumulative Daily Gains for Avg Month 1950 to 2019

70%
60%
50%
40%

Prob. of Daily Gain

♦ August is typically a marginal month and it has been the second worst month on average for the S&P 500 from 1950 to 2019. ♦ If there is a summer rally in July, it is often in jeopardy in August. ♦ In 2019, the S&P 500 consolidated for most of August, but still ended up producing a loss. ♦ The TSX Composite is usually one of the better performing markets in August, but its strength is largely dependent on oil and gold stocks. In 2019, the TSX Composite outperformed the S&P 500 in August.

BEST / WORST AUGUST BROAD MKTS. 2010-2019

BEST AUGUST MARKETS
♦ Nasdaq (2018) 5.7%
♦ Russell 2000 (2014) 4.8%
♦ Nasdaq (2014) 4.8%

WORST AUGUST MARKETS
♦ Nikkei 225 (2011) -8.9%
♦ Russell 2000 (2011) -8.8%
♦ Nikkei 225 (2015) - 8.2%

Index Values End of Month

	2010	2011	2012	2013	2014	2015	2016	2017	2018	2019
Dow	10,015	11,614	13,091	14,810	17,098	16,528	18,401	21,948	25,965	26,403
S&P 500	1,049	1,219	1,407	1,633	2,003	1,972	2,171	2,472	2,902	2,926
Nasdaq	2,114	2,579	3,067	3,590	4,580	4,777	5,213	6,429	8,110	7,963
TSX Comp.	11,914	12,769	11,949	12,654	15,626	13,859	14,598	15,212	16,263	16,442
Russell 1000	578	675	775	909	1,118	1,101	1,203	1,370	1,611	1,619
Russell 2000	602	727	812	1,011	1,174	1,159	1,240	1,405	1,741	1,495
FTSE 100	5,225	5,395	5,711	6,413	6,820	6,248	6,782	7,431	7,432	7,207
Nikkei 225	8,824	8,955	8,840	13,389	15,425	18,890	16,887	19,646	22,865	20,704

Percent Gain for August

	2010	2011	2012	2013	2014	2015	2016	2017	2018	2019
Dow	-4.3	-4.4	0.6	-4.4	3.2	-6.6	-0.2	0.3	2.2	-1.7
S&P 500	-4.7	-5.7	2.0	-3.1	3.8	-6.3	-0.1	0.1	3.0	-1.8
Nasdaq	-6.2	-6.4	4.3	-1.0	4.8	-6.9	1.0	1.3	5.7	-2.6
TSX Comp.	1.7	-1.4	2.4	1.3	1.9	-4.2	0.1	0.4	-1.0	0.2
Russell 1000	-4.7	-6.0	2.2	-3.0	3.9	-6.2	-0.1	0.1	3.2	-2.0
Russell 2000	-7.5	-8.8	3.2	-3.3	4.8	-6.4	1.6	-1.4	4.2	-5.1
FTSE 100	-0.6	-7.2	1.4	-3.1	1.3	-6.7	0.8	0.8	-4.1	-5.0
Nikkei 225	-7.5	-8.9	1.7	-2.0	-1.3	-8.2	1.9	-1.4	1.4	-3.8

August Market Avg. Performance 2010 to 2019[1]

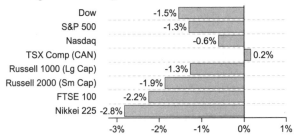

Dow	-1.5%
S&P 500	-1.3%
Nasdaq	-0.6%
TSX Comp (CAN)	0.2%
Russell 1000 (Lg Cap)	-1.3%
Russell 2000 (Sm Cap)	-1.9%
FTSE 100	-2.2%
Nikkei 225	-2.8%

Interest Corner Aug[2]

	Fed Funds %[3]	3 Mo. T-Bill %[4]	10 Yr %[5]	20 Yr %[6]
2019	2.25	0.11	1.50	1.78
2018	2.00	2.11	2.86	2.95
2017	1.25	1.01	2.12	2.47
2016	0.50	0.33	1.58	1.90
2015	0.25	0.08	2.21	2.64

(1) Russell Data provided by Russell (2) Federal Reserve Bank of St. Louis- end of month values (3) Target rate set by FOMC (4)(5)(6) Constant yield maturities.

August 2019 % Sector Performance

GIC % Gain
- Aug 2019
- Aug 90-2019 Avg.

S&P GIC Sectors	2019 % Gain	1990-2019[1] GIC[2] % Avg Gain	1990-2019[1] Fq% Gain >S&P 500
Utilities	4.7 %	0.4 %	63 %
Information Technology	-1.7	0.0	60
Consumer Staples	1.6	-0.3	60
Health Care	-0.7	-0.4	67
Consumer Discretionary	-1.4	-1.2	43
Industrials	-2.9	-1.3	37
Financials	-5.1	-1.3	37
Energy	-8.7	-1.4	43
Materials	-3.1	-1.4	43
Telecom	-1.5 %	-2.0 %	40 %
S&P 500	-1.7 %	-0.3 %	N/A %

Sector Commentary

♦ In August 2019, the defensive sectors were largely the top performing sectors. The utilities sector produced a gain of 4.7% as it benefited from declining interest rates. The consumer staples sector produced a gain of 1.6%. ♦ The cyclical sectors of the stock market produced losses. ♦ The worst performing sector of the stock market was the energy sector with a loss of 8.7%. Most sectors of the stock market produced losses in August 2019.

Sub-Sector Commentary

♦ In August 2019, the homebuilders sub-sector produced a large gain of 7.4%, which was largely driven by falling interest rates. ♦ Both gold and silver produced strong returns of 7.1% and 11.6% respectively. ♦ Silver managed to outperform gold, despite the metals and mining sub-sector producing a loss.

SELECTED SUB-SECTORS[3]

Gold	7.1 %	0.9 %	50 %
Biotech (1993-2019)	1.7	0.6	57
Homebuilders	7.4	0.4	57
Agriculture (1994-2019)	-7.4	0.0	50
SOX (1995-2019)	-2.4	-0.2	52
Silver	11.6	-0.2	50
Retail	-0.9	-0.3	60
Pharma	-0.3	-0.6	57
Banks	-7.7	-1.3	33
Chemicals	-3.9	-1.4	43
Metals & Mining	-2.6	-2.0	43
Railroads	-8.0	-2.3	43
Transportation	-5.7	-2.5	33
Automotive & Components	-6.7	-3.4	33
Steel	-9.9	-3.9	43

(1) Sector data provided by Standard and Poors (2) GIC is short form for Global Industry Classification (3) Sub Sector data provided by Standard and Poors, except where marked by symbol.

AIRLINES – DESCEND IN AUGUST SOAR IN OCTOBER
①SELL SHORT (August) ②LONG (Oct3-Nov6)

Airline flights are seasonal based upon the time of year that flights are taken. Airline flights are often used in statistics classes to demonstrate time series seasonality. There are differences between the seasonality of different airlines depending on their business model. International charter airlines have somewhat different seasonality trends compared to domestic airlines.

11% growth

It is typically best to avoid the airline sector in August; although it is still considered part of the airlines "high season," it is at the back end of the season and any benefits have probably already been incorporated into the price of stocks in the sector.

Historically, the best time for the sector has been from October 3rd to November 6th. Although this is a relatively short period, this is the sweet spot for airline sector performance. One factor driving performance at this time is that on average, it is one of the worst seasonal periods for oil prices. Oil is a large part of the cost of running airlines. Also, expectations for stronger economic growth in the next year, tend to surface at this time, helping to boost economically sensitive sectors, such as the airline sector.

Covid-19 Pandemic Update. The airline sector substantially underperformed the S&P 500 as it decreased in February and March 2020. After a brief period of the airline sector outperforming in May, due to speculation largely as the result of novice Robinhood investors, the sector continued to underperform the S&P 500.

ⓘ *The SP GICS Airlines Sector. For more information, see www.standardandpoors.com*

Airlines vs. S&P 500 1990 to 2019

Positive Long ▢   Negative Short ▢

Year	Aug 1 to Aug 31		Oct 3 to Nov 6		Compound Growth	
	S&P 500	Air-lines	S&P 500	Air-lines	S&P 500	Air-lines
1990	-9.4 %	-21.1 %	-1.1 %	0.0 %	-10.5 %	21.1 %
1991	2.0	-6.9	0.4	4.8	2.4	12.0
1992	-2.4	-11.6	1.7	14.4	-0.7	27.7
1993	3.4	3.0	-0.4	8.3	3.1	5.0
1994	3.8	2.1	-0.1	5.0	3.7	2.8
1995	0.0	-7.5	1.2	0.7	1.1	8.3
1996	1.9	0.4	4.4	5.6	6.4	5.2
1997	-5.7	-5.5	-2.3	9.3	-7.9	15.3
1998	-14.6	-20.7	13.8	16.4	-2.8	40.5
1999	-0.6	-11.4	6.8	12.6	6.1	25.4
2000	6.1	-5.4	-0.3	14.6	5.8	20.8
2001	-6.4	-11.4	6.4	3.9	-0.4	15.7
2002	0.5	2.8	11.6	31.4	12.1	27.7
2003	1.8	4.6	3.7	3.0	5.6	-1.7
2004	0.2	1.1	3.1	19.1	3.3	17.8
2005	-1.1	-7.8	-0.7	9.8	-1.8	18.3
2006	2.1	-3.7	3.6	-11.4	5.8	-8.1
2007	1.3	-3.5	-1.7	-8.8	-0.4	-5.6
2008	1.2	-2.3	-18.8	-17.2	-17.8	-15.3
2009	3.4	4.2	4.3	-6.0	7.8	-9.9
2010	-4.7	-8.3	7.0	9.7	1.9	18.8
2011	-5.7	-13.5	10.8	6.1	4.5	20.4
2012	2.0	-2.7	-1.2	1.9	0.8	4.7
2013	-3.1	-7.4	4.5	14.3	1.2	22.8
2014	3.8	8.5	4.4	19.6	8.3	9.4
2015	-6.3	-1.0	7.6	17.7	0.8	18.9
2016	-0.1	0.0	-3.8	7.4	-3.9	7.4
2017	0.1	-7.5	2.5	-0.9	2.5	6.6
2018	3.0	6.3	-5.8	-4.8	-2.9	-10.8
2019	-1.8	-5.2	6.6	10.9	4.6	16.6
Avg.	-0.8 %	-4.4 %	2.3 %	6.6 %	1.3 %	11.3 %
Fq>0	53 %	30 %	63 %	77 %	67 %	80 %

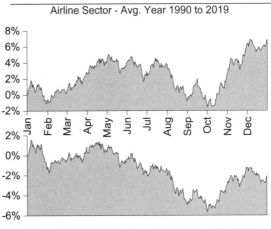

Airline Sector - Avg. Year 1990 to 2019

Airlines / S&P 500 Rel. Strength- Avg Yr. 1990-2019

Airlines Performance

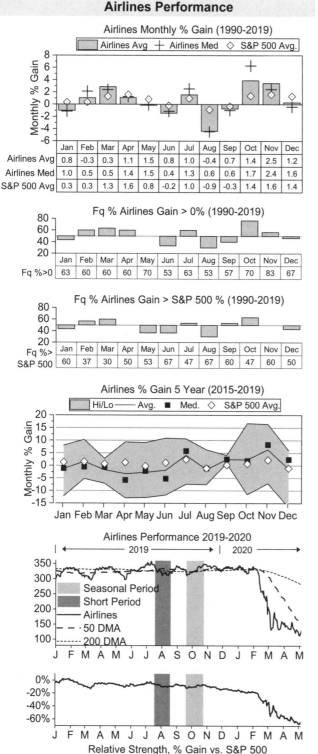

Airlines Monthly % Gain (1990-2019)

Legend: Airlines Avg · Airlines Med · S&P 500 Avg.

	Jan	Feb	Mar	Apr	May	Jun	Jul	Aug	Sep	Oct	Nov	Dec
Airlines Avg	0.8	-0.3	0.3	1.1	1.5	0.8	1.0	-0.4	0.7	1.4	2.5	1.2
Airlines Med	1.0	0.5	0.5	1.4	1.5	0.4	1.3	0.6	0.6	1.7	2.4	1.6
S&P 500 Avg	0.3	0.3	1.3	1.6	0.8	-0.2	1.0	-0.9	-0.3	1.4	1.6	1.4

Fq % Airlines Gain > 0% (1990-2019)

	Jan	Feb	Mar	Apr	May	Jun	Jul	Aug	Sep	Oct	Nov	Dec
Fq %>0	63	60	60	60	70	53	63	53	57	70	83	67

Fq % Airlines Gain > S&P 500 % (1990-2019)

	Jan	Feb	Mar	Apr	May	Jun	Jul	Aug	Sep	Oct	Nov	Dec
Fq %> S&P 500	60	37	30	50	53	67	47	67	60	47	60	50

Airlines % Gain 5 Year (2015-2019)

Legend: Hi/Lo · Avg. · Med. · S&P 500 Avg.

Airlines Performance 2019-2020

- Seasonal Period
- Short Period
- —— Airlines
- — – · 50 DMA
- ·········· 200 DMA

Relative Strength, % Gain vs. S&P 500

Market Indices & Rates
Weekly Values**

Stock Markets	2018	2019
Dow	25,463	26,485
S&P500	2,840	2,932
Nasdaq	7,812	8,004
TSX	16,420	16,272
FTSE	7,659	7,407
DAX	12,616	11,872
Nikkei	22,525	21,087
Hang Seng	27,676	26,919

Commodities	2018	2019
Oil	68.49	55.66
Gold	1216.3	1441.8

Bond Yields	2018	2019
USA 5 Yr Treasury	2.82	1.66
USA 10 Yr T	2.95	1.86
USA 20 Yr T	3.03	2.16
Moody's Aaa	3.89	3.17
Moody's Baa	4.79	4.04
CAN 5 Yr T	2.26	1.36
CAN 10 Yr T	2.35	1.37

Money Market	2018	2019
USA Fed Funds	2.00	2.25
USA 3 Mo T-B	1.97	2.02
CAN tgt overnight rate	1.50	1.75
CAN 3 Mo T-B	1.42	1.64

Foreign Exchange	2018	2019
EUR/USD	1.16	1.11
GBP/USD	1.30	1.22
USD/CAD	1.30	1.32
USD/JPY	111.25	106.59

AUGUST

M	T	W	T	F	S	S
						1
2	3	4	5	6	7	8
9	10	11	12	13	14	15
16	17	18	19	20	21	22
23	24	25	26	27	28	29
30	31					

SEPTEMBER

M	T	W	T	F	S	S
	1	2	3	4	5	
6	7	8	9	10	11	12
13	14	15	16	17	18	19
20	21	22	23	24	25	26
27	28	29	30			

OCTOBER

M	T	W	T	F	S	S
			1	2	3	
4	5	6	7	8	9	10
11	12	13	14	15	16	17
18	19	20	21	22	23	24
25	26	27	28	29	30	31

TRANSPORTATION – ON A ROLL
①LONG (Jan23-Apr16) ②SELL SHORT (Aug1-Oct9)
③LONG (Oct10-Nov13)

The transportation sector can provide a "hilly" ride as the seasonal trends rise and fall throughout the year.

Activity in the transportation sub-sectors; railroads, airlines and freight, tends to bottom in February.

15% gain

Increased transportation activity in the spring, coupled with a typically positive economic outlook in the first part of the year, creates a positive seasonal trend, starting January 23 and lasting until April 16.

The next seasonal period is a weak period, giving investors an opportunity to sell short the sector and profit from its decline lasts from August 1 to October 9.

The third seasonal period is positive and occurs from October 10 to November 13. This trend is the result of a generally improved economic outlook at this time of the year.

Covid-19 Performance Update. The transportation sector continued to underperform the S&P 500 after it bottomed in March 2020. It started to outperform in May as the economy opened up faster than expected.

(i) *The SP GICS Transportation Sector encompasses a wide range transportation based companies. For more information, see www.standardandpoors.com*

Transportation Sector* vs. S&P 500 1990 to 2019
Negative Short ☐   Positive Long ☐

Year	Jan 23 to Apr 16 S&P 500	Jan 23 to Apr 16 Trans port	Aug 1 to Oct 9 S&P 500	Aug 1 to Oct 9 Trans port	Oct 10 to Nov 13 S&P 500	Oct 10 to Nov 13 Trans port	Compound Growth S&P 500	Compound Growth Trans port
1990	4.4 %	4.1 %	-14.3 %	-19.2 %	4.1 %	3.3 %	-6.9 %	28.1 %
1991	18.1	11.4	-2.8	0.5	5.5	9.6	21.0	21.5
1992	-0.5	3.7	-5.1	-9.1	4.9	14.1	-0.9	29.1
1993	2.9	9.1	2.7	-0.3	1.1	6.4	6.9	16.5
1994	-6.0	-10.7	-0.7	-9.3	1.6	0.8	-5.2	-1.6
1995	9.6	10.5	2.9	-1.3	2.4	5.0	15.5	17.6
1996	5.2	9.4	8.9	4.9	4.9	6.1	20.1	10.4
1997	-2.9	-2.0	1.7	0.9	-5.6	-5.4	-6.7	-8.2
1998	15.1	12.2	-12.2	-16.5	14.4	12.5	15.6	47.0
1999	7.7	17.7	0.6	-11.0	4.5	4.0	13.1	35.8
2000	-5.9	-2.7	-2.0	-6.0	-3.6	13.0	-11.1	16.6
2001	12.2	0.1	-12.8	-20.0	7.8	14.1	-17.4	37.0
2002	0.8	6.9	-14.8	-11.2	13.6	8.2	-2.4	28.6
2003	0.2	0.6	4.9	4.9	1.9	8.0	7.1	3.3
2004	-0.8	-2.9	1.9	6.6	5.5	11.1	6.6	0.7
2005	-2.2	-5.1	-3.1	-0.5	3.3	9.0	-2.1	3.9
2006	2.2	13.2	5.8	6.4	2.5	3.8	10.8	9.9
2007	3.2	4.8	7.6	-0.2	-5.4	-2.9	5.0	1.9
2008	4.1	19.1	-28.2	-23.5	0.2	4.0	-25.1	52.9
2009	4.6	7.2	8.5	6.7	2.1	5.9	15.8	5.9
2010	9.2	17.4	5.8	7.9	2.9	2.5	18.9	10.9
2011	2.8	2.2	-10.6	-11.8	9.4	11.4	0.6	26.9
2012	4.1	-2.0	4.5	-3.5	-4.6	-1.1	3.8	0.3
2013	5.5	3.5	-1.7	1.8	7.6	10.9	11.5	12.7
2014	1.0	1.7	-0.1	2.6	5.8	14.9	6.6	13.8
2015	2.0	-10.0	-4.2	-0.7	0.4	-2.0	-1.9	-11.2
2016	9.1	16.4	-0.9	4.3	0.5	6.4	8.7	18.6
2017	2.5	-4.0	3.0	6.5	1.6	-2.8	7.3	-12.7
2018	-5.5	-9.0	2.3	1.2	-5.5	-4.6	-8.6	-14.2
2019	10.4	10.7	-2.0	-9.0	6.0	10.0	14.6	32.7
Avg.	3.0 %	4.5 %	-1.8 %	-3.3 %	3.0 %	5.9 %	4.0 %	14.5 %
Fq>0	73 %	70 %	47 %	43 %	83 %	80 %	63 %	83 %

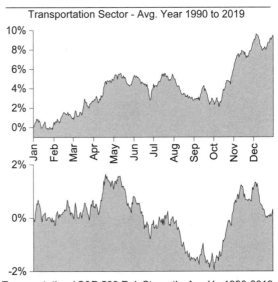

Transportation Sector - Avg. Year 1990 to 2019

Transportation / S&P 500 Rel. Strength- Avg Yr. 1990-2019

Transportation Performance

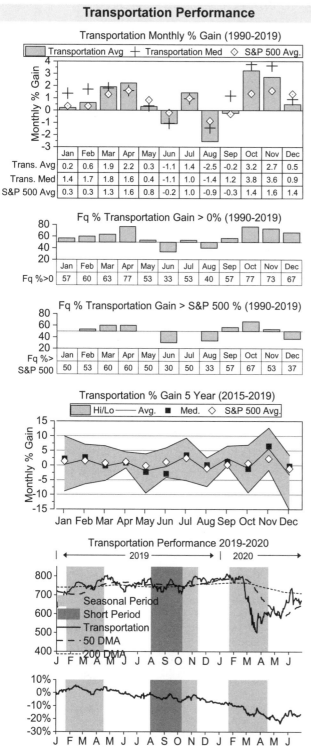

Transportation Monthly % Gain (1990-2019)

Transportation Avg + Transportation Med ◇ S&P 500 Avg.

	Jan	Feb	Mar	Apr	May	Jun	Jul	Aug	Sep	Oct	Nov	Dec
Trans. Avg	0.2	0.6	1.9	2.2	0.3	-1.1	1.4	-2.5	-0.2	3.2	2.7	0.5
Trans. Med	1.4	1.7	1.8	1.6	0.4	-1.1	1.0	-1.4	1.2	3.8	3.6	0.9
S&P 500 Avg	0.3	0.3	1.3	1.6	0.8	-0.2	1.0	-0.9	-0.3	1.4	1.6	1.4

Fq % Transportation Gain > 0% (1990-2019)

	Jan	Feb	Mar	Apr	May	Jun	Jul	Aug	Sep	Oct	Nov	Dec
Fq %>0	57	60	63	77	53	33	53	40	57	77	73	67

Fq % Transportation Gain > S&P 500 % (1990-2019)

	Jan	Feb	Mar	Apr	May	Jun	Jul	Aug	Sep	Oct	Nov	Dec
Fq %> S&P 500	50	53	60	60	50	30	50	33	57	67	53	37

Transportation % Gain 5 Year (2015-2019)

Hi/Lo —— Avg. ■ Med. ◇ S&P 500 Avg.

Transportation Performance 2019-2020

Seasonal Period
Short Period
— Transportation
- - 50 DMA
200 DMA

Relative Strength, % Gain vs. S&P 500

Market Indices & Rates
Weekly Values**

Stock Markets	2018	2019
Dow	25,313	26,287
S&P500	2,833	2,919
Nasdaq	7,839	7,959
TSX	16,327	16,341
FTSE	7,667	7,254
DAX	12,424	11,694
Nikkei	22,298	20,685
Hang Seng	28,367	25,939

Commodities	2018	2019
Oil	67.63	54.50
Gold	1214.4	1497.7

Bond Yields	2018	2019
USA 5 Yr Treasury	2.75	1.57
USA 10 Yr T	2.87	1.74
USA 20 Yr T	2.96	2.03
Moody's Aaa	3.86	3.09
Moody's Baa	4.74	3.97
CAN 5 Yr T	2.22	1.26
CAN 10 Yr T	2.30	1.27

Money Market	2018	2019
USA Fed Funds	2.00	2.25
USA 3 Mo T-B	2.01	1.96
CAN tgt overnight rate	1.50	1.75
CAN 3 Mo T-B	1.45	1.63

Foreign Exchange	2018	2019
EUR/USD	1.14	1.12
GBP/USD	1.28	1.20
USD/CAD	1.31	1.32
USD/JPY	110.83	105.69

AUGUST

M	T	W	T	F	S	S
						1
2	3	4	5	6	7	8
9	10	11	12	13	14	15
16	17	18	19	20	21	22
23	24	25	26	27	28	29
30	31					

SEPTEMBER

M	T	W	T	F	S	S
	1	2	3	4	5	
6	7	8	9	10	11	12
13	14	15	16	17	18	19
20	21	22	23	24	25	26
27	28	29	30			

OCTOBER

M	T	W	T	F	S	S
				1	2	3
4	5	6	7	8	9	10
11	12	13	14	15	16	17
18	19	20	21	22	23	24
25	26	27	28	29	30	31

AGRICULTURE MOOOVES
September 26 to November 11

The agriculture seasonal trade is the result of the major summer growing season in the northern hemisphere producing cash for growers and subsequently, increasing sales for farming suppliers typically in the fourth quarter of the year. The seasonal period for the agriculture sector occurs towards the beginning of the fourth quarter.

62% of the time
better than the S&P 500

Although this sector can represent a good opportunity, investors should be wary of the wide performance swings. Out of the twenty-six cycles from 1994 to 2019, during its seasonal period, the agriculture sector has had ten years of returns greater than +10%. In other words, this sector is very volatile.

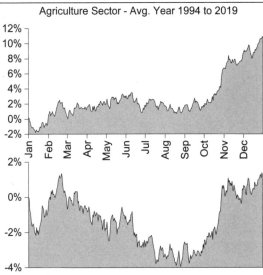

Agriculture Sector - Avg. Year 1994 to 2019

Agriculture / S&P 500 Relative Strength - Avg Yr. 1994-2019

On a year by year basis, the agriculture sector has on average produced its biggest gains during its seasonally strong period. In 2000, the agriculture sector produced a gain of 35.3%. It is interesting to note that this is the same year that the technology sector's bubble burst.

In the 2000's, after realizing that technology stocks were not going to grow to the sky, investors started to have an epiphany– that the world might be running out of food, and as a result interest in the agriculture sector started to pick up.

Agriculture* vs. S&P 500 1994 to 2019

Sep 26 to Nov 11	S&P 500	Positive Agri	Diff
1994	0.6 %	5.7 %	5.1 %
1995	1.9	12.0	10.2
1996	6.7	24.7	18.0
1997	-1.5	-6.9	-5.4
1998	7.3	-1.7	-9.0
1999	8.2	1.4	-6.8
2000	-5.1	35.3	40.4
2001	10.7	18.1	7.5
2002	4.4	13.7	9.3
2003	4.3	9.8	5.5
2004	5.7	25.0	19.2
2005	1.6	7.2	5.6
2006	4.1	-5.7	-9.9
2007	-4.2	12.6	16.8
2008	-25.7	2.3	28.0
2009	5.2	17.8	12.6
2010	5.7	-4.9	-10.6
2011	11.2	17.9	6.7
2012	-4.3	-8.2	-3.9
2013	4.7	12.2	7.5
2014	3.8	1.3	-2.5
2015	7.4	-4.7	-12.1
2016	0.0	-1.7	-1.7
2017	3.4	-8.4	-11.8
2018	-4.6	-2.8	1.8
2019	3.4	7.5	4.1
Avg.	2.1 %	6.9 %	4.8 %
Fq > 0	73 %	65 %	62 %

The world population is still increasing and imbalances in food supply and demand will continue to exist in the future, helping to support the agriculture seasonal trade.

Covid-19 Performance Update. The agriculture sector had been underperforming the S&P 500 since early 2019 and continued to underperform in the early stages of the Covid-19 crisis. The sector underperformed as farmers and companies were expected to delay purchases during the pandemic. It was not until May that the agriculture sector was able to start outperforming the S&P 500 as the economy expanded faster than expected.

The SP GICS Agriculture Sector # 30202010
For more information on the agriculture sector, see www.standardandpoors.com

Agriculture Performance

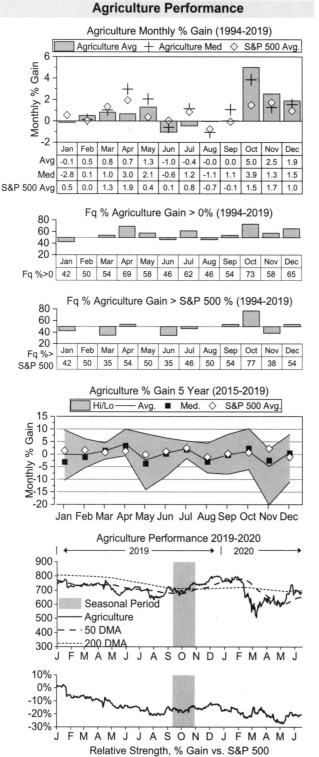

Agriculture Monthly % Gain (1994-2019)

Legend: Agriculture Avg ┼ Agriculture Med ◇ S&P 500 Avg.

	Jan	Feb	Mar	Apr	May	Jun	Jul	Aug	Sep	Oct	Nov	Dec
Avg	-0.1	0.5	0.8	0.7	1.3	-1.0	-0.4	-0.0	0.0	5.0	2.5	1.9
Med	-2.8	0.1	1.0	3.0	2.1	-0.6	1.2	-1.1	1.1	3.9	1.3	1.5
S&P 500 Avg	0.5	0.0	1.3	1.9	0.4	0.1	0.8	-0.7	-0.1	1.5	1.7	1.0

Fq % Agriculture Gain > 0% (1994-2019)

	Jan	Feb	Mar	Apr	May	Jun	Jul	Aug	Sep	Oct	Nov	Dec
Fq %>0	42	50	54	69	58	46	62	46	54	73	58	65

Fq % Agriculture Gain > S&P 500 % (1994-2019)

	Jan	Feb	Mar	Apr	May	Jun	Jul	Aug	Sep	Oct	Nov	Dec
Fq %> S&P 500	42	50	35	54	50	35	46	50	54	77	38	54

Agriculture % Gain 5 Year (2015-2019)

Legend: Hi/Lo — Avg. ■ Med. ◇ S&P 500 Avg.

Agriculture Performance 2019-2020

2019 → | 2020 →

Seasonal Period
— Agriculture
— ·50 DMA
---- 200 DMA

Relative Strength, % Gain vs. S&P 500

WEEK 33

Market Indices & Rates
Weekly Values**

Stock Markets	2018	2019
Dow	25,669	25,886
S&P500	2,850	2,889
Nasdaq	7,816	7,896
TSX	16,324	16,150
FTSE	7,559	7,117
DAX	12,211	11,563
Nikkei	22,270	20,419
Hang Seng	27,213	25,734

Commodities	2018	2019
Oil	65.91	54.87
Gold	1178.4	1515.3

Bond Yields	2018	2019
USA 5 Yr Treasury	2.75	1.42
USA 10 Yr T	2.87	1.55
USA 20 Yr T	2.95	1.82
Moody's Aaa	3.87	2.91
Moody's Baa	4.76	3.81
CAN 5 Yr T	2.20	1.20
CAN 10 Yr T	2.27	1.16

Money Market	2018	2019
USA Fed Funds	2.00	2.25
USA 3 Mo T-B	2.01	1.83
CAN tgt overnight rate	1.50	1.75
CAN 3 Mo T-B	1.48	1.64

Foreign Exchange	2018	2019
EUR/USD	1.14	1.11
GBP/USD	1.27	1.21
USD/CAD	1.31	1.33
USD/JPY	110.50	106.38

AUGUST

M	T	W	T	F	S	S
						1
2	3	4	5	6	7	8
9	10	11	12	13	14	15
16	17	18	19	20	21	22
23	24	25	26	27	28	29
30	31					

SEPTEMBER

M	T	W	T	F	S	S
	1	2	3	4	5	
6	7	8	9	10	11	12
13	14	15	16	17	18	19
20	21	22	23	24	25	26
27	28	29	30			

OCTOBER

M	T	W	T	F	S	S
			1	2	3	
4	5	6	7	8	9	10
11	12	13	14	15	16	17
18	19	20	21	22	23	24
25	26	27	28	29	30	31

LENNOX – COLD & HOT
①SELL SHORT (Sep6-Oct15) ②LONG (Oct16-Mar16)

According to Lennox International's December 2019 10-K filing, Lennox has a stronger seasonal period for its products in the second and third quarters of the year.

"Our sales and related segment profit tend to be seasonally higher in the second and third quarters of the year because summer is the peak season for sales of air conditioning equipment and services in the U.S. and Canada."

30% growth & 95% of the time positive

Lennox's stock price tends to be negative in its shoulder period (transition period) between the air conditioning season and the heating season. As a result, Lennox tends to perform poorly between September 6 to October 15.

Once its weak seasonal period ends in mid-October, Lennox tends to perform well until mid-March. As spring and summer approach, the busy time of year for Lennox, the stock typically wanes. The seasonal trend for Lennox exemplifies the approach of "buy ahead of the busy period and sell when it arrives."

Covid-19 Pandemic Update. Lennox managed to outperform the S&P 500 in its seasonal period from October 16 to March 16, 2020. Lennox outperformed in late February and early March, before underperforming in March and April. In May, Lennox managed to once again outperform the S&P 500 and continued the trend into the summer months, based upon the economy re-opening faster than expected.

> ⓘ *Lennox International Inc, designs and manufactures heating, ventilation and air conditioning products. Lennox trades on the NYSE. Symbol LII adjusted for stock splits.*

Lennox vs. S&P 500 2000 to 2019

Positive Long ▢   Negative Short ▢

Year	Sep 6 to Oct 15 S&P 500	Sep 6 to Oct 15 Lennox	Oct 16 to Mar 16 S&P 500	Oct 16 to Mar 16 Lennox	Compound Growth S&P 500	Compound Growth Lennox
2000	-8.8 %	-43.4 %	-16.3 %	47.8 %	-23.7 %	111.8 %
2001	-3.7	-12.1	7.0	40.1	3.0	57.1
2002	0.2	-16.1	-5.4	5.9	-5.2	23.0
2003	2.5	0.3	6.1	16.9	8.7	16.6
2004	-0.5	-10.5	7.2	51.3	6.7	67.2
2005	-2.6	7.7	10.0	22.3	7.2	12.9
2006	4.0	2.8	1.6	46.5	5.6	42.4
2007	5.2	-1.5	-16.8	0.6	-12.5	2.1
2008	-26.9	-25.1	-17.0	-9.0	-39.3	13.8
2009	7.9	2.2	5.7	24.9	14.1	22.1
2010	6.5	-1.3	6.9	16.1	13.8	17.6
2011	4.3	1.7	14.7	42.3	19.6	39.9
2012	2.6	-0.5	8.4	35.3	11.2	36.0
2013	2.6	6.4	8.4	23.8	11.2	15.9
2014	-7.2	-9.4	11.7	44.6	3.7	58.1
2015	5.3	0.4	0.2	12.3	5.5	11.9
2016	-2.2	-3.4	11.6	9.2	9.2	12.9
2017	3.9	9.1	7.8	17.1	12.0	6.4
2018	-4.8	-11.6	2.6	25.3	-2.3	39.8
2019	0.7	-3.7	-20.3	-17.9	-19.8	-14.8
Avg.	-0.5 %	-5.4 %	1.7 %	22.8 %	1.4 %	29.6 %
Fq>0	60 %	40 %	75 %	90 %	0.7 %	95 %

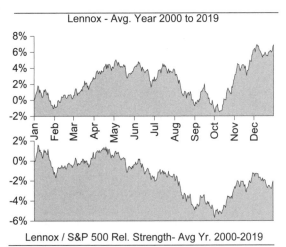

Lennox - Avg. Year 2000 to 2019

Lennox / S&P 500 Rel. Strength- Avg Yr. 2000-2019

Lennox Performance

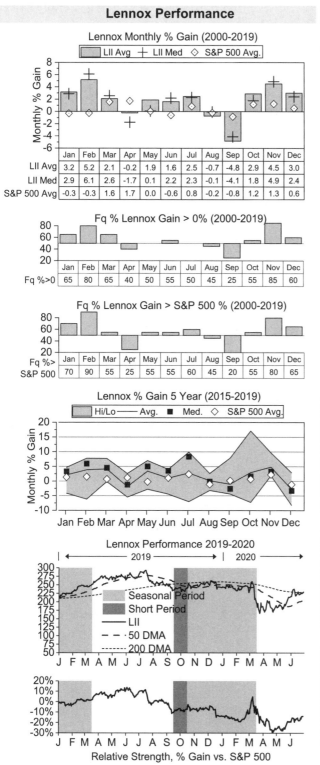

Lennox Monthly % Gain (2000-2019)

Legend: LII Avg, + LII Med, ◇ S&P 500 Avg.

	Jan	Feb	Mar	Apr	May	Jun	Jul	Aug	Sep	Oct	Nov	Dec
LII Avg	3.2	5.2	2.1	-0.2	1.9	1.6	2.5	-0.7	-4.8	2.9	4.5	3.0
LII Med	2.9	6.1	2.6	-1.7	0.1	2.2	2.3	-0.1	-4.1	1.8	4.9	2.4
S&P 500 Avg	-0.3	-0.3	1.6	1.7	0.0	-0.6	0.8	-0.2	-0.8	1.2	1.3	0.6

Fq % Lennox Gain > 0% (2000-2019)

	Jan	Feb	Mar	Apr	May	Jun	Jul	Aug	Sep	Oct	Nov	Dec
Fq %>0	65	80	65	40	50	55	50	45	25	55	85	60

Fq % Lennox Gain > S&P 500 % (2000-2019)

	Jan	Feb	Mar	Apr	May	Jun	Jul	Aug	Sep	Oct	Nov	Dec
Fq %> S&P 500	70	90	55	25	55	55	60	45	20	55	80	65

Lennox % Gain 5 Year (2015-2019)

Legend: Hi/Lo, Avg., ■ Med., ◇ S&P 500 Avg.

Lennox Performance 2019-2020

Legend: Seasonal Period, Short Period, LII, 50 DMA, 200 DMA

Relative Strength, % Gain vs. S&P 500

Market Indices & Rates
Weekly Values**

Stock Markets	2018	2019
Dow	25,790	25,629
S&P500	2,875	2,847
Nasdaq	7,946	7,752
TSX	16,356	16,038
FTSE	7,577	7,095
DAX	12,395	11,612
Nikkei	22,602	20,711
Hang Seng	27,672	26,179

Commodities	2018	2019
Oil	69.82	54.11
Gold	1197.7	1503.8

Bond Yields	2018	2019
USA 5 Yr Treasury	2.72	1.40
USA 10 Yr T	2.82	1.52
USA 20 Yr T	2.89	1.82
Moody's Aaa	3.83	2.88
Moody's Baa	4.72	3.79
CAN 5 Yr T	2.21	1.21
CAN 10 Yr T	2.26	1.17

Money Market	2018	2019
USA Fed Funds	2.00	2.25
USA 3 Mo T-B	2.05	1.93
CAN tgt overnight rate	1.50	1.75
CAN 3 Mo T-B	1.52	1.63

Foreign Exchange	2018	2019
EUR/USD	1.16	1.11
GBP/USD	1.28	1.23
USD/CAD	1.30	1.33
USD/JPY	111.24	105.39

AUGUST

M	T	W	T	F	S	S
						1
2	3	4	5	6	7	8
9	10	11	12	13	14	15
16	17	18	19	20	21	22
23	24	25	26	27	28	29
30	31					

SEPTEMBER

M	T	W	T	F	S	S
	1	2	3	4	5
6	7	8	9	10	11	12
13	14	15	16	17	18	19
20	21	22	23	24	25	26
27	28	29	30			

OCTOBER

M	T	W	T	F	S	S
				1	2	3
4	5	6	7	8	9	10
11	12	13	14	15	16	17
18	19	20	21	22	23	24
25	26	27	28	29	30	31

①LONG (May1-Aug2) ②SELL SHORT (Aug3-Aug11)
③LONG (Aug12-Oct24)

Health care stocks have traditionally been classified as defensive stocks because of their stable earnings. Pharmaceutical and other health care companies typically still perform relatively well in an economic downturn.

6% gain & positive

The health care sector has on average been one of the top performing sectors in the month of May. Although the returns tend to be lower in June and July, there is value investing in the health care sector at this time. The sector does take a pause in early August, when the stock market tends to perform poorly.

The period from August 12 to October 24 tends to be positive for the health care sector as investor interest increases ahead of the many health care conferences that take place in autumn.

Covid-19 Pandemic Update. The health care sector strongly outperformed from late February to April 2020 during the initial stages of the pandemic. As the stock market rallied in May, the health care sector started to underperform. In addition, the health care sector often becomes a "political football" in election years, which produced a further drag on the sector.

(i) *Health Care SP GIC Sector# 35: An index designed to represent a cross section of health care companies. For more information see www.standardandpoors.com.*

Health Care* vs. S&P 500 1990 to 2019
Negative Short ☐   Positive Long ▨

Year	May 1 to Aug 2		Aug 3 to Aug 11		Aug 12 to Oct 24		Compound Growth	
	S&P 500	Health Care	S&P 500	Health Care	S&P 500	Health Care	S&P 500	Health Care
1990	6.3 %	18.4 %	-4.5 %	-4.5 %	-6.8 %	2.8 %	-5.5 %	27.2 %
1991	3.2	7.9	0.0	-0.1	-0.5	1.8	2.6	9.9
1992	2.2	1.0	-1.3	-0.2	-1.2	-9.6	-0.2	-8.5
1993	2.3	-9.3	0.1	-4.2	2.8	12.2	5.2	6.0
1994	2.1	5.5	-0.4	3.6	0.4	7.4	2.2	9.2
1995	8.6	10.5	-0.7	-0.9	5.7	15.3	14.0	28.5
1996	1.3	4.7	-0.1	0.8	6.1	8.7	7.4	12.9
1997	18.2	16.3	-1.1	-3.9	0.5	6.1	17.5	28.0
1998	0.8	5.3	-4.6	-4.2	0.2	4.6	-3.7	14.8
1999	-0.5	-3.7	-2.0	-5.8	0.0	10.2	-2.5	12.2
2000	-1.0	13.0	2.3	-4.2	-5.0	7.1	-3.7	26.1
2001	-2.3	-0.1	-2.5	0.3	-8.8	0.9	-13.2	0.4
2002	-19.8	-16.1	5.1	4.8	-2.9	-1.1	-18.1	-20.9
2003	6.9	2.8	0.0	0.4	4.9	-2.3	12.2	0.0
2004	-0.1	-6.1	-2.8	-1.1	1.9	-5.5	-1.1	-10.3
2005	7.5	3.7	-0.5	-0.4	-3.1	-4.6	3.7	-0.7
2006	-2.5	3.8	-0.9	-1.8	8.7	7.3	5.1	13.2
2007	-0.7	-5.2	-1.3	-0.6	4.3	4.2	2.3	-0.6
2008	-9.0	0.7	3.6	5.2	-32.8	-23.4	-36.7	-26.9
2009	13.1	15.5	0.7	-0.5	8.6	3.4	23.7	20.0
2010	-5.1	-5.8	-3.2	-0.2	8.6	7.6	-0.3	1.6
2011	-8.0	-7.0	-6.5	-4.4	7.0	7.1	-8.0	4.0
2012	-2.4	1.4	3.0	1.8	0.2	3.7	0.8	3.3
2013	7.0	8.4	-1.1	-0.9	3.6	3.5	9.7	13.2
2014	2.2	4.6	0.6	-0.6	1.4	7.8	4.3	13.4
2015	0.9	6.7	-0.9	-1.7	-0.4	-8.0	-0.5	-0.1
2016	4.4	8.1	1.3	-0.6	-1.6	-7.1	4.2	1.0
2017	3.9	5.4	-1.5	-1.2	5.2	5.9	7.8	12.9
2018	6.8	8.5	0.2	0.4	-6.3	-2.5	0.3	5.3
2019	-0.4	1.9	-0.5	0.4	3.1	0.6	2.2	2.0
Avg.	1.5 %	3.4 %	-0.6 %	-0.8 %	0.1 %	2.1 %	1.1 %	5.5 %
Fq>0	60 %	73 %	33	30 %	60 %	70 %	60 %	70 %

Health Care Sector - Avg. Year 1990-2019

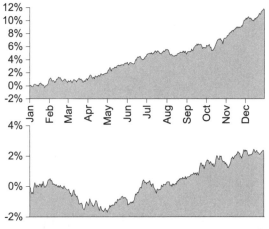

Health Care / S&P 500 Rel. Strength- Avg Yr. 1990-2019

Health Care Performance

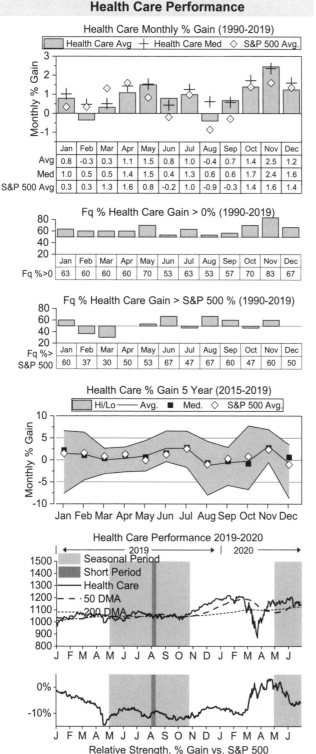

Health Care Monthly % Gain (1990-2019)

Legend: Health Care Avg + Health Care Med ◇ S&P 500 Avg.

	Jan	Feb	Mar	Apr	May	Jun	Jul	Aug	Sep	Oct	Nov	Dec
Avg	0.8	-0.3	0.3	1.1	1.5	0.8	1.0	-0.4	0.7	1.4	2.5	1.2
Med	1.0	0.5	0.5	1.4	1.5	0.4	1.3	0.6	0.6	1.7	2.4	1.6
S&P 500 Avg	0.3	0.3	1.3	1.6	0.8	-0.2	1.0	-0.9	-0.3	1.4	1.6	1.4

Fq % Health Care Gain > 0% (1990-2019)

	Jan	Feb	Mar	Apr	May	Jun	Jul	Aug	Sep	Oct	Nov	Dec
Fq %>0	63	60	60	60	70	53	63	53	57	70	83	67

Fq % Health Care Gain > S&P 500 % (1990-2019)

	Jan	Feb	Mar	Apr	May	Jun	Jul	Aug	Sep	Oct	Nov	Dec
Fq %> S&P 500	60	37	30	50	53	67	47	67	60	47	60	50

Health Care % Gain 5 Year (2015-2019)

Legend: Hi/Lo —— Avg. ■ Med. ◇ S&P 500 Avg.

Health Care Performance 2019-2020

Legend: Seasonal Period, Short Period, Health Care, 50 DMA, 200 DMA

Relative Strength, % Gain vs. S&P 500

Market Indices & Rates
Weekly Values**

Stock Markets	2018	2019
Dow	25,965	26,403
S&P500	2,902	2,926
Nasdaq	8,110	7,963
TSX	16,263	16,442
FTSE	7,432	7,207
DAX	12,364	11,939
Nikkei	22,865	20,704
Hang Seng	27,889	25,725

Commodities	2018	2019
Oil	69.80	55.10
Gold	1202.5	1528.4

Bond Yields	2018	2019
USA 5 Yr Treasury	2.74	1.39
USA 10 Yr T	2.86	1.50
USA 20 Yr T	2.95	1.78
Moody's Aaa	3.91	2.85
Moody's Baa	4.78	3.76
CAN 5 Yr T	2.17	1.19
CAN 10 Yr T	2.23	1.16

Money Market	2018	2019
USA Fed Funds	2.00	2.25
USA 3 Mo T-B	2.07	1.95
CAN tgt overnight rate	1.50	1.75
CAN 3 Mo T-B	1.53	1.62

Foreign Exchange	2018	2019
EUR/USD	1.16	1.10
GBP/USD	1.30	1.22
USD/CAD	1.30	1.33
USD/JPY	111.03	106.28

AUGUST

M	T	W	T	F	S	S
						1
2	3	4	5	6	7	8
9	10	11	12	13	14	15
16	17	18	19	20	21	22
23	24	25	26	27	28	29
30	31					

SEPTEMBER

M	T	W	T	F	S	S
	1	2	3	4	5
6	7	8	9	10	11	12
13	14	15	16	17	18	19
20	21	22	23	24	25	26
27	28	29	30			

OCTOBER

M	T	W	T	F	S	S
				1	2	3
4	5	6	7	8	9	10
11	12	13	14	15	16	17
18	19	20	21	22	23	24
25	26	27	28	29	30	31

SEPTEMBER

	MONDAY	TUESDAY	WEDNESDAY
WEEK 35	**30**	**31** 30	**1** 29
WEEK 36	**6** 24 USA Market Closed- Labor Day CAN Market Closed- Labor Day	**7** 23	**8** 22
WEEK 37	**13** 17	**14** 16	**15** 15
WEEK 38	**20** 10	**21** 9	**22** 8
WEEK 39	**27** 3	**28** 2	**29** 1

THURSDAY	FRIDAY
2 28	**3** 27
9 21	**10** 20
16 14	**17** 13
23 7	**24** 6
30	1

OCTOBER

M	T	W	T	F	S	S
				1	2	3
4	5	6	7	8	9	10
11	12	13	14	15	16	17
18	19	20	21	22	23	24
25	26	27	28	29	30	31

NOVEMBER

M	T	W	T	F	S	S
1	2	3	4	5	6	7
8	9	10	11	12	13	14
15	16	17	18	19	20	21
22	23	24	25	26	27	28
29	30					

DECEMBER

M	T	W	T	F	S	S
		1	2	3	4	5
6	7	8	9	10	11	12
13	14	15	16	17	18	19
20	21	22	23	24	25	26
27	28	29	30	31		

JANUARY

M	T	W	T	F	S	S
					1	2
3	4	5	6	7	8	9
10	11	12	13	14	15	16
17	18	19	20	21	22	23
24	25	26	27	28	29	30
31						

SEPTEMBER
S U M M A R Y

	Dow Jones	S&P 500	Nasdaq	TSX Comp
Month Rank	12	12	12	12
# Up	29	32	26	15
# Down	41	38	22	20
% Pos	41	46	54	43
% Avg. Gain	-0.7	-0.4	-0.5	-1.4

Dow & S&P 1950-2019, Nasdaq 1972-2019, TSX 1985-2019

S&P500 Cumulative Daily Gains for Avg Month 1950 to 2019

Prob. of Daily Gain

♦ September has the reputation of being the worst month of the year for the S&P 500. From 1950 to 2019, September has produced an average loss of 0.4% and has only been positive 46% of the time. ♦ In particular, the last part of September tends to be negative. ♦ The defensive sectors are typically the favored sectors in September as investors seek more stable earnings in a month that is often volatile ♦ The materials sector on average performs poorly in September and has outperformed the S&P 500 only 27% of the time from 1990 to 2019.

BEST / WORST SEPTEMBER BROAD MKTS. 2010-2019

BEST SEPTEMBER MARKETS
- ♦ Russell 2000 (2010) 12.3%
- ♦ Nasdaq (2010) 12.0%
- ♦ Russell 1000 (2010) 9.0%

WORST SEPTEMBER MARKETS
- ♦ Russell 2000 (2011) -11.4%
- ♦ TSX Comp. (2011) -9.0%
- ♦ Nikkei 225 (2015) -8.0%

Index Values End of Month

	2010	2011	2012	2013	2014	2015	2016	2017	2018	2019
Dow	10,788	10,913	13,437	15,130	17,043	16,285	18,308	22,405	26,458	26,917
S&P 500	1,141	1,131	1,441	1,682	1,972	1,920	2,168	2,519	2,914	2,977
Nasdaq	2,369	2,415	3,116	3,771	4,493	4,620	5,312	6,496	8,046	7,999
TSX Comp.	12,369	11,624	12,317	12,787	14,961	13,307	14,726	15,635	16,073	16,659
Russell 1000	630	623	794	940	1,096	1,068	1,202	1,397	1,615	1,644
Russell 2000	676	644	837	1,074	1,102	1,101	1,252	1,491	1,697	1,523
FTSE 100	5,549	5,128	5,742	6,462	6,623	6,062	6,899	7,373	7,510	7,408
Nikkei 225	9,369	8,700	8,870	14,456	16,174	17,388	16,450	20,356	24,120	21,756

Percent Gain for September

	2010	2011	2012	2013	2014	2015	2016	2017	2018	2019
Dow	7.7	-6.0	2.6	2.2	-0.3	-1.5	-0.5	2.1	1.9	1.9
S&P 500	8.8	-7.2	2.4	3.0	-1.6	-2.6	-0.1	1.9	0.4	1.7
Nasdaq	12.0	-6.4	1.6	5.1	-1.9	-3.3	1.9	1.0	-0.8	0.5
TSX Comp.	3.8	-9.0	3.1	1.1	-4.3	-4.0	0.9	2.8	-1.2	1.3
Russell 1000	9.0	-7.6	2.4	3.3	-1.9	-2.9	-0.1	2.0	0.2	1.6
Russell 2000	12.3	-11.4	3.1	6.2	-6.2	-5.1	0.9	6.1	-2.5	1.9
FTSE 100	6.2	-4.9	0.5	0.8	-2.9	-3.0	1.7	-0.8	1.0	2.8
Nikkei 225	6.2	-2.8	0.3	8.0	4.9	-8.0	-2.6	3.6	5.5	5.1

September Market Avg. Performance 2010 to 2019[1]

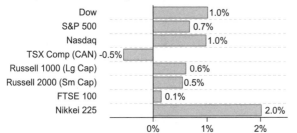

Dow	1.0%
S&P 500	0.7%
Nasdaq	1.0%
TSX Comp (CAN)	-0.5%
Russell 1000 (Lg Cap)	0.6%
Russell 2000 (Sm Cap)	0.5%
FTSE 100	0.1%
Nikkei 225	2.0%

Interest Corner Sep[2]

	Fed Funds %[3]	3 Mo. T-Bill %[4]	10 Yr %[5]	20 Yr %[6]
2019	2.00	1.88	1.68	1.94
2018	2.25	2.19	3.05	3.13
2017	1.25	1.06	2.33	2.63
2016	0.50	0.29	1.60	1.99
2015	0.25	0.00	2.06	2.51

(1) Russell Data provided by Russell (2) Federal Reserve Bank of St. Louis- end of month values (3) Target rate set by FOMC (4)(5)(6) Constant yield maturities.

September 2019
% Sector Performance

S&P GIC Sectors	2019 % Gain	1990-2019[1] GIC[2] % Avg Gain	Fq% Gain >S&P 500
Telecom	0.4 %	1.1 %	60 %
Health Care	-0.3	0.7	60
Energy	3.6	0.6	60
Utilities	4.0	0.0	37
Consumer Staples	1.3	0.0	53
Industrials	2.9	-0.2	53
Financials	4.5	-0.4	53
Information Technology	1.4	-0.6	60
Consumer Discretionary	0.7	-0.7	50
Materials	2.9 %	-1.8 %	27 %
S&P 500	1.7 %	1.4 %	N/A %

Sector Commentary

♦ In September, it is often the defensive sectors of the stock market that perform well relative to the S&P 500. In September 2019, the top performing sector was the financial sector with a gain of 4.5% ♦ The next best performing sector was the utilities sector with a gain of 4.0%. ♦ The only negative performing sector was the health care sector with a loss of 0.3%. ♦ Overall, the strength across the board for most sectors of the stock market was uncharacteristic of the performance in August.

Sub-Sector Commentary

♦ September is typically the month when precious metals tend to perform well. ♦ In September 2019, both gold and silver performed poorly. ♦ The top performing sub-sector from the list of selected sub-sectors was agriculture with a gain of 7.9%. The agriculture sub-sector typically starts outperforming the S&P 500 late in September on a seasonal basis. ♦ Homebuilders were uncharacteristically strong in September.

SELECTED SUB-SECTORS[3]

Gold	-2.8 %	2.0 %	60 %
Biotech (1993-2019)	0.8	1.4	61
Silver	-6.1	1.2	63
Pharma	0.5	0.8	57
Agriculture (1994-2019)	7.9	0.0	54
Railroads	1.8	0.0	47
Transportation	1.0	-0.2	57
Retail	0.1	-0.4	50
Banks	7.3	-0.6	53
Homebuilders	8.8	-0.7	57
Chemicals	3.7	-1.6	33
Metals & Mining	-0.8	-1.8	40
Automotive & Components	2.6	-2.0	40
SOX (1995-2019)	3.6	-2.0	48
Steel	3.9	-3.0	47

(1) Sector data provided by Standard and Poors (2) GIC is short form for Global Industry Classification (3) Sub Sector data provided by Standard and Poors, except where marked by symbol.

SHW | SHERWIN-WILLIAMS – TIME TO PAINT
①SELL SHORT (Aug13-Sep23) ②LONG(Sep24-Apr19)

Sherwin-Williams is known for its paints, stains and other coatings. Approximately 70% of its business is derived from residential orders.

In the summer months, homebuilders tend to languish with poor stock performance. Sherwin-Williams follows the same trend and tends to underperform the S&P 500 from August 13 until September 23.

Gain of 23% and positive 80% of the time

On the other hand, Sherwin-Williams tends to outperform the S&P 500 from September 24th to April 19th, This performance tendency is very similar to the seasonal trend for the homebuilders sector which tends to outperform in approximately the same time period.

It is interesting to note the contrast of large gains and losses for Sherwin-Williams, comparing the seasonally strong period to the seasonally weak period. From August 13 to September 23, from 1990 to 2019, Sherwin-Williams has produced losses of 10% or greater, four times and gains of 10% or greater only once. In comparison, from September 24 to April 19, Sherwin-Williams has produced losses of 10% or greater once and gains of 10% or greater twenty-two times.

Covid-19 Performance Update. SHW was very volatile as the stock market corrected in February and March of 2020. In April, SHW started to outperform the S&P 500 as people staying home renovated their houses and house construction showed positive signs.

ⓘ *The Sherwin-Williams Company is a consumer discretionary company. Data adjusted for stock splits.*

SHW vs. S&P 500 1990/91 to 2019/20

Negative Short ☐   Positive Long ▨

Year	Aug 13 to Sep 23 S&P 500	SHW	Sep 24 to Apr 19 S&P 500	SHW	Compound Growth S&P 500	SHW
1990/91	-7.2 %	-5.6 %	23.4 %	43.3 %	14.5 %	51.3 %
1991/92	-0.5	-5.1	7.8	24.5	7.2	30.8
1992/93	-0.1	-4.7	7.2	20.1	7.1	25.7
1993/94	2.0	8.9	-3.3	-9.2	-1.4	-17.3
1994/95	-0.5	-4.2	9.8	10.4	9.3	15.0
1995/96	4.8	-0.4	10.9	27.2	16.2	27.6
1996/97	3.1	-1.9	11.6	19.2	15.1	21.5
1997/98	2.7	-2.4	17.9	20.0	21.2	22.9
1998/99	-1.7	-31.6	21.0	54.5	18.9	103.3
1999/00	-1.4	-24.8	11.5	25.8	10.0	57.0
2001/01	-1.6	-9.0	-13.5	3.2	-14.8	12.4
2001/02	-18.9	-8.4	16.5	49.2	-5.5	61.7
2002/03	-7.8	-17.7	7.2	17.4	-1.1	38.1
2003/04	3.9	0.3	10.4	30.3	14.7	29.9
2004/05	4.2	10.1	4.0	7.7	8.4	-3.2
2005/06	-1.2	-6.9	7.8	20.0	6.5	28.2
2006/07	3.8	8.1	11.9	22.5	16.1	12.6
2007/08	5.0	-4.7	-8.9	-14.7	-4.4	-10.7
2008/09	-7.9	2.0	-26.8	-5.5	-32.6	-7.4
2009/10	5.5	-0.8	12.9	19.9	19.1	20.8
2010/11	3.8	7.3	16.7	14.3	21.1	6.0
2011/12	-3.6	-5.8	21.2	63.5	16.8	73.0
2012/13	3.9	6.1	6.5	19.3	10.6	12.0
2013/14	0.7	2.1	9.6	8.9	10.4	6.6
2014/15	2.5	3.7	5.0	29.1	7.6	24.3
2015/16	-7.1	-14.8	8.4	28.2	0.7	47.3
2016/17	-0.9	-4.3	8.0	10.1	7.0	14.8
2017/18	2.5	5.4	7.6	13.3	10.3	7.2
2018/19	3.4	6.1	-0.8	-3.7	2.5	-9.6
2019/20	3.8	5.0	-3.9	-4.6	-0.3	-9.4
Avg.	-0.2 %	-2.9 %	7.2 %	18.8 %	7.0 %	23.1 %
Fq>0	53 %	40 %	8.2 %	83 %	77 %	80 %

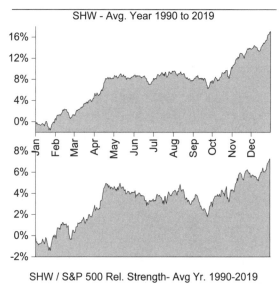

SHW - Avg. Year 1990 to 2019

SHW / S&P 500 Rel. Strength- Avg Yr. 1990-2019

Sherwin-Williams Performance

SHW Monthly % Gain (1990-2019)

Legend: SHW Avg | + SHW Med | ◇ S&P 500 Avg.

	Jan	Feb	Mar	Apr	May	Jun	Jul	Aug	Sep	Oct	Nov	Dec
SHW Avg	0.4	0.8	3.3	3.5	0.5	-0.7	1.9	-1.5	-0.6	3.0	3.3	2.8
SHW Med	1.0	0.5	1.8	5.3	0.7	-0.2	1.1	-1.0	-0.1	3.4	4.0	1.4
S&P 500 Avg	0.3	0.3	1.3	1.6	0.8	-0.2	1.0	-0.9	-0.3	1.4	1.6	1.4

Fq % SHW Gain > 0% (1990-2019)

	Jan	Feb	Mar	Apr	May	Jun	Jul	Aug	Sep	Oct	Nov	Dec
Fq %>0	60	60	63	67	50	47	57	47	47	60	77	70

Fq % SHW Gain > S&P 500 % (1990-2019)

	Jan	Feb	Mar	Apr	May	Jun	Jul	Aug	Sep	Oct	Nov	Dec
Fq %> S&P 500	53	50	67	67	47	50	53	47	50	57	63	60

SHW % Gain 5 Year (2015-2019)

Legend: Hi/Lo | Avg. | ■ Med. | ◇ S&P 500 Avg.

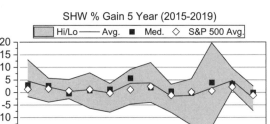

SHW Performance 2019-2020

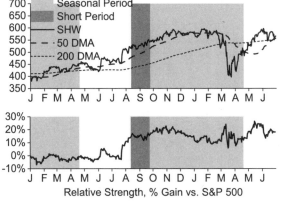

Relative Strength, % Gain vs. S&P 500

Market Indices & Rates
Weekly Values**

Stock Markets	2018	2019
Dow	25,917	26,797
S&P500	2,872	2,979
Nasdaq	7,903	8,103
TSX	16,090	16,535
FTSE	7,278	7,282
DAX	11,960	12,192
Nikkei	22,307	21,200
Hang Seng	26,973	26,691

Commodities	2018	2019
Oil	67.75	56.52
Gold	1198.9	1523.7

Bond Yields	2018	2019
USA 5 Yr Treasury	2.82	1.42
USA 10 Yr T	2.94	1.55
USA 20 Yr T	3.03	1.83
Moody's Aaa	3.99	2.91
Moody's Baa	4.87	3.81
CAN 5 Yr T	2.22	1.32
CAN 10 Yr T	2.29	1.28

Money Market	2018	2019
USA Fed Funds	2.00	2.25
USA 3 Mo T-B	2.10	1.92
CAN tgt overnight rate	1.50	1.75
CAN 3 Mo T-B	1.52	1.61

Foreign Exchange	2018	2019
EUR/USD	1.16	1.10
GBP/USD	1.29	1.23
USD/CAD	1.32	1.32
USD/JPY	110.99	106.92

SEPTEMBER

M	T	W	T	F	S	S
	1	2	3	4	5	6
7	8	9	10	11	12	13
14	15	16	17	18	19	20
21	22	23	24	25	26	27
28	29	30				

OCTOBER

M	T	W	T	F	S	S
			1	2	3	4
5	6	7	8	9	10	11
12	13	14	15	16	17	18
19	20	21	22	23	24	25
26	27	28	29	30	31	

NOVEMBER

M	T	W	T	F	S	S
						1
2	3	4	5	6	7	8
9	10	11	12	13	14	15
16	17	18	19	20	21	22
23	24	25	26	27	28	29
30						

KO COCA-COLA COMPANY
① Apr27-May27 ② Sep25-Nov23

Coca-Cola has two positive seasonal periods, one from April 27 and May 27 and the other from September 25 to November 23. Both seasonal periods occur over the two transitions periods for the broad stock market from its six-month favorable period to its unfavorable period and vice versa.

Investors are attracted to the Coca-Cola Company because of its defensive characteristics at a time when investors become concerned about market volatility, but still want to stay invested.

10% gain

The seasonal period from September 25 to November 23, from 1990 to 2019 has produced an average gain of 5.5% and has been positive 67% of the time. This average gain is slightly above the spring seasonal period, with an investment over a two month period. The stock market tends to start performing well in late October. If the stock market moves up rapidly at this time, it could be influential in mitigating the returns of the Coca-Cola Company, making the Coca-Cola trade at the end of this seasonal period sometimes less attractive.

Covid-19 Performance Update. After outperforming the S&P 500 briefly at the beginning of the Covid-19 pandemic in 2020, Coca-Cola started to underperform the S&P 500 in mid-March before the stock market bottomed. It continued its underperformance even after better than expected earnings results were announced in mid-April. In late June, Coca-Cola started stabilize relative to the S&P 500.

Source: The Coca-Cola Company is a consumer staples company. Data adjusted for stock splits.

KO* vs. S&P 500 - 1990 to 2019 — Positive ☐

Year	Apr 27 May 27 S&P 500	KO	Sep 25 Nov 23 S&P 500	KO	Compound Growth S&P 500	KO
1990	6.5 %	14.0 %	3.5 %	19.2 %	10.2 %	35.9 %
1991	-0.4	5.4	-3.0	7.6	-3.4	13.4
1992	0.8	9.0	1.6	-1.5	2.4	7.3
1993	4.4	4.1	0.7	-0.9	5.1	3.2
1994	1.2	0.3	-2.1	6.2	-0.9	6.5
1995	2.1	2.6	2.9	6.2	5.1	8.9
1996	3.8	16.9	9.2	-1.5	13.4	15.2
1997	11.0	15.9	2.0	5.2	13.2	21.8
1998	-1.4	6.3	14.0	33.1	12.3	41.4
1999	-5.8	1.5	10.0	30.4	3.6	32.4
2000	-5.7	10.4	-8.7	12.7	-13.9	24.3
2001	3.5	2.7	14.6	2.3	18.7	5.1
2002	0.7	3.2	13.6	-3.8	14.4	-0.7
2003	5.9	13.3	2.6	8.0	8.6	22.3
2004	-1.3	1.2	6.0	-0.7	4.7	0.5
2005	4.1	4.6	4.1	0.7	8.4	5.3
2006	-1.9	6.6	6.9	7.1	4.9	14.2
2007	1.4	-0.4	-5.1	9.9	-3.7	9.5
2008	-0.9	-1.3	-32.5	-12.3	-33.1	-13.4
2009	3.1	9.0	5.3	11.3	8.5	21.3
2010	-9.0	-4.7	2.8	8.5	-6.5	3.5
2011	-1.2	-0.6	2.2	-3.8	1.0	-4.4
2012	-5.9	-0.6	-3.3	-0.5	-9.0	-1.1
2013	4.3	0.3	6.3	4.9	10.9	5.3
2014	2.6	-0.6	3.3	5.3	6.0	4.7
2015	0.3	0.6	8.0	9.7	8.3	10.4
2016	0.4	0.6	1.9	-3.8	2.2	-3.3
2017	1.2	5.0	3.8	0.8	5.0	5.8
2018	2.0	-0.8	-9.8	6.4	-8.0	5.5
2019	-3.8	2.8	4.8	-2.3	0.8	0.4
Avg.	0.7 %	4.2 %	2.2 %	5.5 %	3.0 %	10.0 %
Fq>0	63 %	77 %	77 %	67 %	73 %	83 %

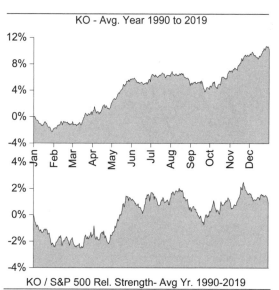

KO - Avg. Year 1990 to 2019

KO / S&P 500 Rel. Strength- Avg Yr. 1990-2019

Coca-Cola Company Performance

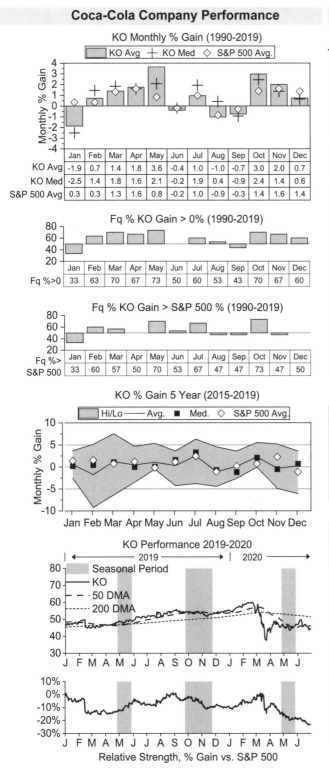

KO Monthly % Gain (1990-2019)

KO Avg + KO Med ◇ S&P 500 Avg.

	Jan	Feb	Mar	Apr	May	Jun	Jul	Aug	Sep	Oct	Nov	Dec
KO Avg	-1.9	0.7	1.4	1.8	3.6	-0.4	1.0	-1.0	-0.7	3.0	2.0	0.7
KO Med	-2.5	1.4	1.8	1.6	2.1	-0.2	1.9	0.4	-0.9	2.4	1.4	0.6
S&P 500 Avg	0.3	0.3	1.3	1.6	0.8	-0.2	1.0	-0.9	-0.3	1.4	1.6	1.4

Fq % KO Gain > 0% (1990-2019)

	Jan	Feb	Mar	Apr	May	Jun	Jul	Aug	Sep	Oct	Nov	Dec
Fq %>0	33	63	70	67	73	50	60	53	43	70	67	60

Fq % KO Gain > S&P 500 % (1990-2019)

	Jan	Feb	Mar	Apr	May	Jun	Jul	Aug	Sep	Oct	Nov	Dec
Fq %> S&P 500	33	60	57	50	70	53	67	47	47	73	47	50

KO % Gain 5 Year (2015-2019)

Hi/Lo — Avg. ■ Med. ◇ S&P 500 Avg.

KO Performance 2019-2020

← 2019 → | 2020 →

Seasonal Period
KO
50 DMA
200 DMA

Relative Strength, % Gain vs. S&P 500

Market Indices & Rates
Weekly Values**

Stock Markets	2018	2019
Dow	26,155	27,220
S&P500	2,905	3,007
Nasdaq	8,010	8,177
TSX	16,013	16,682
FTSE	7,304	7,367
DAX	12,124	12,469
Nikkei	23,095	21,988
Hang Seng	27,286	27,353

Commodities	2018	2019
Oil	68.99	54.85
Gold	1202.0	1503.1

Bond Yields	2018	2019
USA 5 Yr Treasury	2.90	1.75
USA 10 Yr T	2.99	1.90
USA 20 Yr T	3.07	2.17
Moody's Aaa	3.94	3.25
Moody's Baa	4.87	4.11
CAN 5 Yr T	2.27	1.51
CAN 10 Yr T	2.35	1.51

Money Market	2018	2019
USA Fed Funds	2.00	2.25
USA 3 Mo T-B	2.12	1.92
CAN tgt overnight rate	1.50	1.75
CAN 3 Mo T-B	1.52	1.62

Foreign Exchange	2018	2019
EUR/USD	1.16	1.11
GBP/USD	1.31	1.25
USD/CAD	1.30	1.33
USD/JPY	112.06	108.09

SEPTEMBER

M	T	W	T	F	S	S
		1	2	3	4	5
6	7	8	9	10	11	12
13	14	15	16	17	18	19
20	21	22	23	24	25	26
27	28	29	30			

OCTOBER

M	T	W	T	F	S	S
				1	2	3
4	5	6	7	8	9	10
11	12	13	14	15	16	17
18	19	20	21	22	23	24
25	26	27	28	29	30	31

NOVEMBER

M	T	W	T	F	S	S
1	2	3	4	5	6	7
8	9	10	11	12	13	14
15	16	17	18	19	20	21
22	23	24	25	26	27	28
29	30					

INFORMATION TECHNOLOGY
①Oct9-Dec5 ②Dec15-Jan17

Information technology stocks tend to get bid up at the end of the year for three reasons.

11% gain

First, a lot of companies operate with year end budgets and if they do not spend the money in their budget, they lose it. In the last few months of the year, whatever money they have, they tend to spend. The number one purchase item for this budget flush is technology equipment. Second, consumers indirectly help push up technology stocks by purchasing electronic items during the holiday season.

Third, the "Conference Effect" helps maintain the momentum of the information technology sector in January. This phenomenon is the result of investors increasing positions in a sector ahead of major conferences in order to benefit from positive announcements. In the case of the information technology sector, investors increase their holdings ahead of the Las Vegas Consumer Electronics Conference that typically occurs in the second week of January.

Covid-19 Performance Update. The technology sector strongly outperformed the S&P 500 during the Covid-19 pandemic in 2020 as many companies in the sector increased their sales with more people relying on technology as they worked from home. The technology sector also benefited from lower interest rates favoring growth companies and generally awarding them a higher valuation.

Info Tech* vs. S&P 500 1989/90 to 2019/20   Positive [ ]

Year	Oct 9 to Dec 5 S&P 500	IT	Dec 15 to Jan 17 S&P 500	IT	Compound Growth S&P 500	IT
1989/90	-2.6%	-5.7%	-3.9%	3.8%	-6.3%	-2.1%
1990/91	5.2	11.2	0.4	5.5	5.6	17.3
1991/92	-0.9	-1.4	8.9	17.6	8.0	16.0
1992/93	6.0	6.8	1.0	7.4	7.0	14.7
1993/94	1.0	6.9	2.2	8.8	3.2	16.3
1994/95	-0.4	8.5	3.3	9.6	2.9	18.9
1995/96	6.0	3.2	-1.7	-8.0	4.2	-5.1
1996/97	6.2	14.4	6.5	7.3	13.2	22.8
1997/98	1.0	-8.1	0.9	4.0	1.9	-4.4
1998/99	22.7	46.8	8.9	18.7	33.6	74.2
1999/00	7.3	18.7	4.4	9.7	12.0	30.3
2000/01	-2.3	-12.8	-0.9	-3.3	-3.1	-15.7
2001/02	10.2	31.9	1.4	2.3	11.7	34.8
2002/03	13.5	37.2	1.4	-0.6	15.1	36.4
2003/04	2.7	2.3	6.1	11.1	9.0	13.6
2004/05	6.2	11.7	-1.6	-4.1	4.5	7.1
2005/06	5.5	8.4	0.8	1.5	6.4	10.0
2006/07	4.8	6.5	0.4	0.8	5.2	7.4
2007/08	-4.4	-2.6	-9.2	-12.7	-13.1	-14.9
2008/09	-11.1	-14.2	-3.4	-1.9	-14.0	-15.8
2009/10	3.8	6.3	2.0	2.7	5.8	9.2
2010/11	5.1	7.0	4.2	4.9	9.5	12.3
2011/12	8.8	7.6	6.8	4.9	16.1	12.8
2012/13	-3.2	-6.4	4.8	4.0	1.4	-2.6
2013/14	7.8	10.2	3.6	5.5	11.7	16.3
2014/15	5.4	6.8	0.9	-0.7	6.3	6.1
2015/16	3.9	8.2	-7.0	-9.4	-3.4	-1.9
2016/17	2.4	-1.5	0.7	1.5	3.0	0.0
2017/18	3.2	4.6	5.7	6.3	9.0	11.2
2018/19	-6.4	-8.5	1.4	0.0	-5.1	-8.5
2019/20	7.8	10.0	5.1	8.9	13.2	19.7
Avg.	3.7%	6.9%	1.7%	3.4%	5.6%	10.8%
Fq > 0	74%	71%	77%	74%	81%	71%

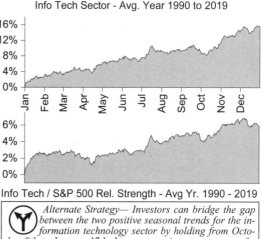

Info Tech Sector - Avg. Year 1990 to 2019

Info Tech / S&P 500 Rel. Strength - Avg Yr. 1990 - 2019

Alternate Strategy— Investors can bridge the gap between the two positive seasonal trends for the information technology sector by holding from October 9th to January 17th. Longer term investors may prefer this strategy, shorter term investors can use technical tools to determine the appropriate strategy.

*The SP GICS Information Technology Sector. For more information on the information technology sector, see www.standardandpoors.com

Information Technology Performance

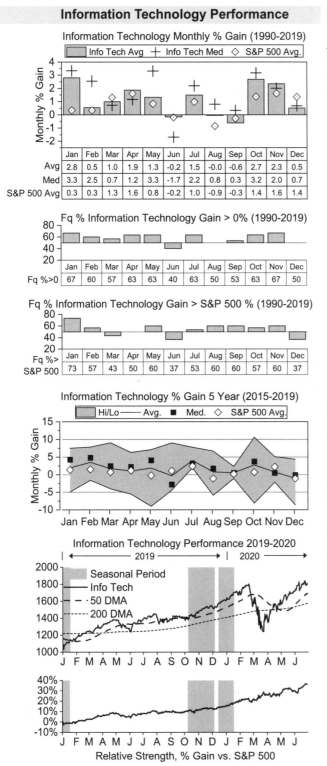

Information Technology Monthly % Gain (1990-2019)

Info Tech Avg + Info Tech Med ◇ S&P 500 Avg.

	Jan	Feb	Mar	Apr	May	Jun	Jul	Aug	Sep	Oct	Nov	Dec
Avg	2.8	0.5	1.0	1.9	1.3	-0.2	1.5	-0.0	-0.6	2.7	2.3	0.5
Med	3.3	2.5	0.7	1.2	3.3	-1.7	2.2	0.8	0.3	3.2	2.0	0.7
S&P 500 Avg	0.3	0.3	1.3	1.6	0.8	-0.2	1.0	-0.9	-0.3	1.4	1.6	1.4

Fq % Information Technology Gain > 0% (1990-2019)

	Jan	Feb	Mar	Apr	May	Jun	Jul	Aug	Sep	Oct	Nov	Dec
Fq %>0	67	60	57	63	63	40	63	50	53	63	67	50

Fq % Information Technology Gain > S&P 500 % (1990-2019)

	Jan	Feb	Mar	Apr	May	Jun	Jul	Aug	Sep	Oct	Nov	Dec
Fq %> S&P 500	73	57	43	50	60	37	53	60	60	57	60	37

Information Technology % Gain 5 Year (2015-2019)

Hi/Lo —— Avg. ■ Med. ◇ S&P 500 Avg.

Information Technology Performance 2019-2020

| 2019 | 2020 |

Seasonal Period
Info Tech
50 DMA
200 DMA

Relative Strength, % Gain vs. S&P 500

Market Indices & Rates
Weekly Values**

Stock Markets	2018	2019
Dow	26,744	26,935
S&P500	2,930	2,992
Nasdaq	7,987	8,118
TSX	16,224	16,900
FTSE	7,490	7,345
DAX	12,431	12,468
Nikkei	23,870	22,079
Hang Seng	27,954	26,436

Commodities	2018	2019
Oil	71.78	58.09
Gold	1198.7	1501.9

Bond Yields	2018	2019
USA 5 Yr Treasury	2.95	1.61
USA 10 Yr T	3.07	1.74
USA 20 Yr T	3.14	1.99
Moody's Aaa	3.99	3.03
Moody's Baa	4.90	3.93
CAN 5 Yr T	2.33	1.42
CAN 10 Yr T	2.43	1.39

Money Market	2018	2019
USA Fed Funds	2.00	2.00
USA 3 Mo T-B	2.14	1.87
CAN tgt overnight rate	1.50	1.75
CAN 3 Mo T-B	1.51	1.63

Foreign Exchange	2018	2019
EUR/USD	1.17	1.10
GBP/USD	1.31	1.25
USD/CAD	1.29	1.33
USD/JPY	112.59	107.56

SEPTEMBER

M	T	W	T	F	S	S
		1	2	3	4	5
6	7	8	9	10	11	12
13	14	15	16	17	18	19
20	21	22	23	24	25	26
27	28	29	30			

OCTOBER

M	T	W	T	F	S	S
			1	2	3	
4	5	6	7	8	9	10
11	12	13	14	15	16	17
18	19	20	21	22	23	24
25	26	27	28	29	30	31

NOVEMBER

M	T	W	T	F	S	S
1	2	3	4	5	6	7
8	9	10	11	12	13	14
15	16	17	18	19	20	21
22	23	24	25	26	27	28
29	30					

CANADIAN BANKS
①Oct10-Dec 31 ②Jan23-Apr13

The Canadian bank sector, has a strong seasonal period from October 10 to December 31 and then from January 23 to April 13.

Canadian banks have their year-end on October 31st. Why does this matter? In the past Canadian banks have announced most of their dividend increases and stock splits when they announce their typically optimistic full year fiscal reports at the end of November and beginning of December. Investors tend to push up bank stocks ahead of their earnings announcement. Canadian banks also tend to perform well in early in the year as economic reports tend to be favorable at this time.

Canadian bank returns in December have been separated out from their autumn seasonal period to show the impact of bank earnings on returns. In December, Canadian banks on average have provided gains 71% of the time, but they have underperformed the TSX Composite. If Canadian banks have performed well leading into their earnings, they often pause in December.

Covid-19 Performance Update. Canadian banks were volatile in the February-March stock market decline and underperformed the S&P/TSX Index into late May before outperforming on stronger economic growth.

(i) *Banks SP GIC Canadian Bank Sector Level 2 Represents a cross section of Canadian banking companies.*

Canadian Banks* vs. S&P 500 1989/90 to 2019/20

Positive ☐

Year	Oct 10 to Dec 31 TSX-Comp	Oct 10 to Dec 31 Cdn Banks	Jan 23 to Apr 13 TSX-Comp	Jan 23 to Apr 13 Cdn Banks	Compound Growth TSX-Comp	Compound Growth Cdn Banks	Dec 1 Dec 31 TSX-Comp	Dec 1 Dec 31 Cdn Banks
89/90	-1.7 %	-1.8 %	-6.3 %	-9.1 %	-7.9	-10.8 %	0.7 %	-1.4 %
90/91	3.7	8.9	9.8	14.6	13.9	24.8	3.4	5.5
91/92	5.2	10.2	-6.8	-11.6	-2.0	-2.6	1.9	4.6
92/93	4.1	2.5	10.7	14.4	15.2	17.3	2.1	1.8
93/94	6.3	6.8	-5.6	-13.3	0.3	-7.4	3.4	5.1
94/95	-1.8	3.4	5.0	10.0	3.1	13.8	2.9	0.9
95/96	4.9	3.5	3.6	-3.2	8.6	0.1	1.1	1.5
96/97	9.0	15.1	-6.2	0.7	2.3	15.9	-1.5	-1.9
97/98	-6.1	7.6	19.9	38.8	12.6	49.4	2.9	4.2
98/99	18.3	28.0	4.8	13.0	24.0	44.6	2.2	3.0
99/00	18.2	5.1	3.8	22.1	22.8	28.3	11.8	0.7
00/01	-14.4	1.7	-14.1	-6.7	-26.4	-5.1	1.3	9.6
01/02	11.9	6.5	2.3	8.2	14.5	15.1	3.5	3.4
02/03	16.1	21.3	-4.3	2.6	11.1	24.4	0.7	2.6
03/04	8.1	5.1	2.0	2.1	10.3	7.4	4.6	2.0
04/05	4.9	6.2	4.5	6.9	9.6	13.5	2.4	4.7
05/06	6.2	8.4	5.5	2.7	12.1	11.3	4.1	2.1
06/07	10.4	8.4	6.9	3.2	18.0	11.8	1.2	3.7
07/08	-3.0	-10.4	8.2	-3.5	5.0	-13.5	1.1	-7.7
08/09	-6.4	-14.8	9.4	24.4	2.4	6.1	-3.1	-11.2
09/10	2.7	2.4	6.7	15.2	9.6	18.0	2.6	0.1
10/11	7.2	-0.2	4.3	9.1	11.9	8.9	3.8	-0.5
11/12	3.2	3.1	-2.9	1.1	0.2	4.2	-2.0	2.7
12/13	1.3	4.4	-3.8	-2.0	-2.5	2.3	1.6	1.5
13/14	7.0	9.0	1.9	1.6	9.1	10.7	1.7	0.9
14/15	1.2	-0.9	4.2	4.4	5.4	3.5	-0.8	-4.3
15/16	-6.8	-1.5	10.4	11.0	2.8	9.4	-3.4	-3.6
16/17	5.0	11.8	-0.1	-1.5	4.9	10.2	1.4	4.3
17/18	3.1	4.4	-6.6	-8.8	-3.7	-4.8	0.9	1.1
18/19	-9.7	-11.1	8.2	2.5	-2.3	-8.8	-5.8	-6.8
19/20	4.2	0.0	-20.0	-22.8	-16.7	-22.9	-0.1	-4.0
Avg.	3.6 %	4.6 %	1.8 %	4.1 %	5.4 %	8.9 %	1.5 %	0.8 %
Fq>0	74 %	74 %	65 %	68 %	77 %	74 %	81 %	71 %

Canadian Banking Sector - Avg. Year 1990 to 2019

Cdn. Banking / TSX Comp Rel. Strength- Avg Yr. 1990-2019

Canadian Banks Performance

CDN Banks Monthly % Gain (1990-2019)

Legend: CDN Banks Avg + CDN Banks Med ◇ TSX Comp. Avg.

	Jan	Feb	Mar	Apr	May	Jun	Jul	Aug	Sep	Oct	Nov	Dec
Avg	-0.4	1.7	1.1	1.0	1.2	-0.9	1.6	-0.2	0.4	2.2	1.6	0.9
Med	-0.4	1.8	0.8	1.0	1.3	-0.4	2.3	1.0	0.6	2.1	1.3	1.7
TSX Avg	0.7	0.8	0.6	0.9	1.3	-0.6	0.7	-0.3	-1.2	0.5	0.7	1.5

Fq % CDN Banks Gain > 0% (1990-2019)

	Jan	Feb	Mar	Apr	May	Jun	Jul	Aug	Sep	Oct	Nov	Dec
Fq %>0	47	63	57	53	63	43	70	67	57	77	73	73

Fq % CDN Banks Gain > TSX Comp. % (1990-2019)

	Jan	Feb	Mar	Apr	May	Jun	Jul	Aug	Sep	Oct	Nov	Dec
Fq %> TSX Comp.	40	63	53	53	33	47	60	47	63	67	63	43

CDN Banks % Gain 5 Year (2015-2019)

Legend: Hi/Lo — Avg. ■ Med. ◇ TSX Comp. Avg.

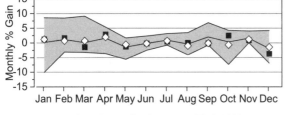

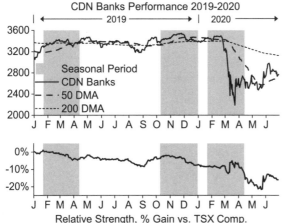

CDN Banks Performance 2019-2020

Seasonal Period — CDN Banks — 50 DMA ····· 200 DMA

Relative Strength, % Gain vs. TSX Comp.

Market Indices & Rates
Weekly Values**

Stock Markets	2018	2019
Dow	26,458	26,820
S&P500	2,914	2,962
Nasdaq	8,046	7,940
TSX	16,073	16,694
FTSE	7,510	7,426
DAX	12,247	12,381
Nikkei	24,120	21,879
Hang Seng	27,789	25,955

Commodities	2018	2019
Oil	73.25	55.91
Gold	1187.3	1489.9

Bond Yields	2018	2019
USA 5 Yr Treasury	2.94	1.56
USA 10 Yr T	3.05	1.69
USA 20 Yr T	3.13	1.95
Moody's Aaa	3.99	3.00
Moody's Baa	4.89	3.88
CAN 5 Yr T	2.34	1.40
CAN 10 Yr T	2.43	1.36

Money Market	2018	2019
USA Fed Funds	2.25	2.00
USA 3 Mo T-B	2.15	1.76
CAN tgt overnight rate	1.50	1.75
CAN 3 Mo T-B	1.59	1.65

Foreign Exchange	2018	2019
EUR/USD	1.16	1.09
GBP/USD	1.30	1.23
USD/CAD	1.29	1.32
USD/JPY	113.70	107.92

SEPTEMBER

M	T	W	T	F	S	S
	1	2	3	4	5	
6	7	8	9	10	11	12
13	14	15	16	17	18	19
20	21	22	23	24	25	26
27	28	29	30			

OCTOBER

M	T	W	T	F	S	S
				1	2	3
4	5	6	7	8	9	10
11	12	13	14	15	16	17
18	19	20	21	22	23	24
25	26	27	28	29	30	31

NOVEMBER

M	T	W	T	F	S	S
1	2	3	4	5	6	7
8	9	10	11	12	13	14
15	16	17	18	19	20	21
22	23	24	25	26	27	28
29	30					

OCTOBER

	MONDAY	TUESDAY	WEDNESDAY
WEEK 39	27	28	29
WEEK 40	**4** 27	**5** 26	**6** 25

WEEK 41	**11** 20
	
	USA Bond Market Closed-
	        Columbus Day
	
	CAN Market Closed-
	        Thanksgiving Day
		12 19	**13** 18

WEEK 42	**18** 13	**19** 12	**20** 11
WEEK 43	**25** 6	**26** 5	**27** 4

THURSDAY	FRIDAY
30 30	1 30
7 24	8 23
14 17	15 16
21 10	22 9
28 3	29 2

NOVEMBER

M	T	W	T	F	S	S
1	2	3	4	5	6	7
8	9	10	11	12	13	14
15	16	17	18	19	20	21
22	23	24	25	26	27	28
29	30					

DECEMBER

M	T	W	T	F	S	S
		1	2	3	4	5
6	7	8	9	10	11	12
13	14	15	16	17	18	19
20	21	22	23	24	25	26
27	28	29	30	31		

JANUARY

M	T	W	T	F	S	S
					1	2
3	4	5	6	7	8	9
10	11	12	13	14	15	16
17	18	19	20	21	22	23
24	25	26	27	28	29	30
31						

FEBRUARY

M	T	W	T	F	S	S
	1	2	3	4	5	6
7	8	9	10	11	12	13
14	15	16	17	18	19	20
21	22	23	24	25	26	27
28						

OCTOBER
S U M M A R Y

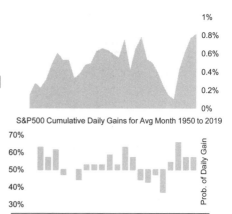

S&P500 Cumulative Daily Gains for Avg Month 1950 to 2019

	Dow Jones	S&P 500	Nasdaq	TSX Comp
Month Rank	7	7	8	9
# Up	42	42	27	22
# Down	28	28	21	13
% Pos	60	60	56	63
% Avg. Gain	0.6	0.8	0.7	0.0

Dow & S&P 1950-2019, Nasdaq 1972-2019, TSX 1985-2019

♦ October, on average, is the most volatile month of the year for the stock market and often provides opportunities for short-term traders. The first half of October tends to be positive. ♦ The second half of the month, leading up to the last four days, tends to be negative, and prone to large drops. ♦ Seasonal opportunities in mid-October include Canadian banks, technology and transportation sectors. ♦ In late October, a lot of sectors start their seasonal period, including the materials, industrials, consumer discretionary and retail sectors.

BEST / WORST OCTOBER BROAD MKTS. 2010-2019

BEST OCTOBER MARKETS
♦ Russell 2000 (2011) 15.0%
♦ Nasdaq (2011) 11.1%
♦ Russell 1000 (2011) 11.1%

WORST OCTOBER MARKETS
♦ Russell 2000 (2018) -10.9%
♦ Nasdaq (2018) -9.2%
♦ Nikkei 225 (2018) -9.1%

Index Values End of Month

	2010	2011	2012	2013	2014	2015	2016	2017	2018	2019
Dow	11,118	11,955	13,096	15,546	17,391	17,664	18,142	23,377	25,116	27,046
S&P 500	1,183	1,253	1,412	1,757	2,018	2,079	2,126	2,575	2,712	3,038
Nasdaq	2,507	2,684	2,977	3,920	4,631	5,054	5,189	6,728	7,306	8,292
TSX Comp.	12,676	12,252	12,423	13,361	14,613	13,529	14,787	16,026	15,027	16,483
Russell 1000	654	692	779	980	1,122	1,154	1,177	1,427	1,499	1,677
Russell 2000	703	741	819	1,100	1,174	1,162	1,191	1,503	1,511	1,562
FTSE 100	5,675	5,544	5,783	6,731	6,546	6,361	6,954	7,493	7,128	7,248
Nikkei 225	9,202	8,988	8,928	14,328	16,414	19,083	17,425	22,012	21,920	22,927

Percent Gain for October

	2010	2011	2012	2013	2014	2015	2016	2017	2018	2019
Dow	3.1	9.5	-2.5	2.8	2.0	8.5	-0.9	4.3	-5.1	0.5
S&P 500	3.7	10.8	-2.0	4.5	2.3	8.3	-1.9	2.2	-6.9	2.0
Nasdaq	5.9	11.1	-4.5	3.9	3.1	9.4	-2.3	3.6	-9.2	3.7
TSX Comp.	2.5	5.4	0.9	4.5	-2.3	1.7	0.4	2.5	-6.5	-1.1
Russell 1000	3.8	11.1	-1.8	4.3	2.3	8.0	-2.1	2.2	-7.2	2.0
Russell 2000	4.0	15.0	-2.2	2.5	6.5	5.6	-4.8	0.8	-10.9	2.6
FTSE 100	2.3	8.1	0.7	4.2	-1.2	4.9	0.8	1.6	-5.1	-2.2
Nikkei 225	-1.8	3.3	0.7	-0.9	1.5	9.7	5.9	8.1	-9.1	5.4

October Market Avg. Performance 2010 to 2019[1]

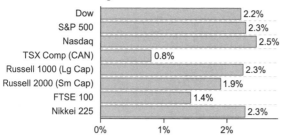

Dow	2.2%
S&P 500	2.3%
Nasdaq	2.5%
TSX Comp (CAN)	0.8%
Russell 1000 (Lg Cap)	2.3%
Russell 2000 (Sm Cap)	1.9%
FTSE 100	1.4%
Nikkei 225	2.3%

Interest Corner Oct[2]

	Fed Funds %[3]	3 Mo. T-Bill %[4]	10 Yr %[5]	20 Yr %[6]
2019	1.75	1.54	1.69	2.00
2018	2.25	2.34	3.15	3.30
2017	1.25	1.15	2.38	2.66
2016	0.50	0.34	1.84	2.25
2015	0.25	0.08	2.16	2.57

(1) Russell Data provided by Russell (2) Federal Reserve Bank of St. Louis- end of month values (3) Target rate set by FOMC (4)(5)(6) Constant yield maturities.

October 2019 % Sector Performance

S&P GIC	2019	1990-2019[1]	
Sectors	**% Gain**	**GIC[2] % Avg Gain**	**Fq% Gain >S&P 500**
Information Technology	3.8 %	2.7 %	57 %
Consumer Staples	-0.3	2.4	57
Health Care	5.0	1.4	47
Financials	2.2	1.3	50
Consumer Discretionary	0.3	1.3	47
Materials	0.0	1.0	43
Utilities	-0.8	0.9	43
Telecom	2.7	0.9	40
Industrials	1.0	0.7	37
Energy	-2.4 %	0.2 %	37 %
S&P 500	2.0 %	1.4 %	N/A %

Sector Commentary

♦ In October 2019, all of the sectors of the stock market were positive except consumer staples and energy. ♦ The health care sector was the top performing sector. In October, which is a transition month from the six-month unfavorable period for stock to the six-month favorable period, the health care sector is on average one of the top performing sectors. ♦ The consumer staples sector, which is often one of the better performing sectors, produced a small loss. ♦ The energy sector was the worst performing sector, with a loss of 2.4%. On average, the energy sector has been the worst performing sector in October since 1990.

Sub-Sector Commentary

♦ In October 2019, the biotech sub-sector was the top performing sub-sector with a gain of 9.3%. On average over the long-term, the biotech sector tends to be one of the weaker sectors. ♦ Both silver and gold performed well in October.

SELECTED SUB-SECTORS[3]			
Agriculture (1994-2019)	2.4 %	5.0 %	77 %
Transportation	0.9	3.2	67
Railroads	2.0	3.2	60
Steel	5.8	2.2	50
Pharma	4.0	1.9	57
SOX (1995-2019)	5.9	1.9	48
Chemicals	-0.4	1.8	53
Retail	2.1	1.5	57
Biotech (1993-2019)	9.3	1.1	46
Banks	4.5	1.1	43
Home-builders	2.5	0.9	40
Automotive & Components	-0.5	0.6	43
Metals & Mining	4.5	0.1	37
Gold	1.7	-0.9	23
Silver	4.6	-1.2	33

MCDONALD'S
①Oct28-Nov24 ②Jan30-Apr8

McDonald's is part of the consumer discretionary sector, but it has a slightly different seasonal pattern. Investors tend to push up the price of McDonald's stock price in autumn, but then lose interest once the holiday shopping season starts in November.

> **9% gain &**
> **81% of the time positive**

McDonald's tends to underperform the S&P 500 in December and January, but once the holiday season ends and the worst month of the year for retail comes close to finishing (January), investors warm up to the idea of McDonald's once again. McDonald's tends to perform well from January 30 to April 8.

In the summer months, investors lose interest in McDonald's and it tends to underperform the S&P 500. The time period between July 19 to August 31 tends to be very weak for McDonald's. In this time period from 1990 to 2019, McDonald's has produced an average loss of 2.3% and was only positive 40% of the time (not shown in table).

Covid-19 Pandemic Update. Initially, as stock market corrected in late February 2020, MCD outperformed the S&P 500. In early March, MCD started to underperform the S&P 500, before stabilizing and then outperforming in June.

MCD* vs. S&P 500 - 1989/90 to 2019/20   Positive ▢

Year	Oct 28 to Nov 24		Jan 30 to Apr 8		Compound Growth	
	S&P 500	MCD	S&P 500	MCD	S&P 500	MCD
1989/90	2.7 %	6.5 %	4.6 %	0.0 %	7.4 %	6.5 %
1990/91	3.4	13.3	12.8	32.2	16.6	49.2
1991/92	-2.1	-1.5	-3.9	-1.8	-5.9	-3.2
1992/93	2.2	6.8	0.7	3.9	2.9	11.0
1993/94	-0.5	2.9	-6.6	-5.8	-7.0	-3.1
1994/95	-3.4	0.9	7.7	8.1	4.0	9.1
1995/96	3.5	4.5	3.2	-5.0	6.8	-0.4
1996/97	6.8	7.3	-0.8	9.0	5.9	17.0
1997/98	8.0	11.2	11.8	27.2	20.7	41.5
1998/99	11.0	10.1	5.0	19.0	16.6	30.9
1999/00	9.3	14.9	11.5	0.7	21.8	15.7
2000/01	-2.7	13.2	-17.3	-11.1	-19.5	0.7
2001/02	4.1	-4.9	2.2	8.5	6.5	3.1
2002/03	3.7	0.8	1.6	10.2	5.3	11.0
2003/04	2.0	5.7	0.5	12.4	2.5	18.9
2004/05	5.0	4.2	0.8	-2.7	5.9	1.3
2005/06	7.4	6.9	0.9	-0.5	8.3	6.3
2006/07	1.7	1.0	1.6	5.9	3.4	6.9
2007/08	-6.2	-1.3	0.2	10.1	-5.9	8.7
2008/09	0.3	7.2	-2.4	-4.4	-2.0	2.5
2009/10	4.0	8.8	10.5	10.1	14.9	19.8
2010/11	1.3	2.6	4.1	3.8	5.5	6.4
2011/12	-9.6	-1.8	6.2	-0.1	-3.9	-1.8
2012/13	-0.2	0.4	3.7	6.9	3.5	7.3
2013/14	2.6	3.7	4.4	5.3	7.1	9.2
2014/15	5.5	5.6	3.0	3.8	8.7	9.7
2015/16	1.1	2.4	5.5	3.4	6.7	5.8
2016/17	3.4	7.2	2.7	5.8	6.1	13.4
2017/18	0.8	2.3	-8.7	-9.3	-8.0	-7.2
2018/19	-1.0	5.0	9.7	4.2	8.6	9.4
2019/20	2.9	-0.1	-16.0	-17.2	-13.6	-17.9
Avg.	2.2 %	4.7 %	1.9 %	4.3 %	4.2 %	9.3 %
Fq>0	74 %	84 %	77 %	65 %	74 %	81 %

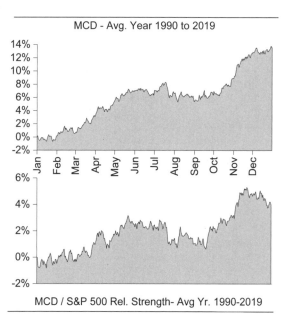

MCD - Avg. Year 1990 to 2019

MCD / S&P 500 Rel. Strength- Avg Yr. 1990-2019

ⓘ *McDonald's Corporation is in the restaurant sector. For more information, see McDonalds.com*

- 121 -

McDonald's Performance

MCD Monthly % Gain (1990-2019)

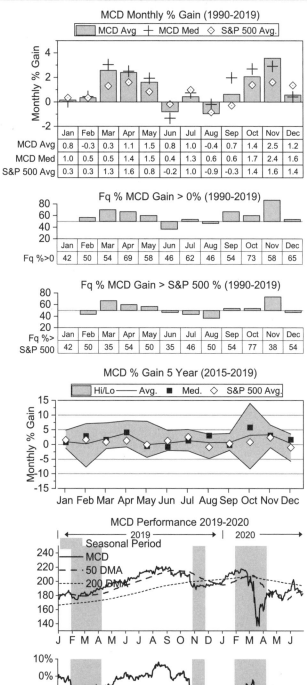

MCD Avg + MCD Med ◇ S&P 500 Avg.

	Jan	Feb	Mar	Apr	May	Jun	Jul	Aug	Sep	Oct	Nov	Dec
MCD Avg	0.8	-0.3	0.3	1.1	1.5	0.8	1.0	-0.4	0.7	1.4	2.5	1.2
MCD Med	1.0	0.5	0.5	1.4	1.5	0.4	1.3	0.6	0.6	1.7	2.4	1.6
S&P 500 Avg	0.3	0.3	1.3	1.6	0.8	-0.2	1.0	-0.9	-0.3	1.4	1.6	1.4

Fq % MCD Gain > 0% (1990-2019)

	Jan	Feb	Mar	Apr	May	Jun	Jul	Aug	Sep	Oct	Nov	Dec
Fq %>0	42	50	54	69	58	46	62	46	54	73	58	65

Fq % MCD Gain > S&P 500 % (1990-2019)

	Jan	Feb	Mar	Apr	May	Jun	Jul	Aug	Sep	Oct	Nov	Dec
Fq %> S&P 500	42	50	35	54	50	35	46	50	54	77	38	54

MCD % Gain 5 Year (2015-2019)

Hi/Lo —— Avg. ■ Med. ◇ S&P 500 Avg.

Jan Feb Mar Apr May Jun Jul Aug Sep Oct Nov Dec

MCD Performance 2019-2020

Seasonal Period
—— MCD
— — 50 DMA
···· 200 DMA

Relative Strength, % Gain vs. S&P 500

WEEK 40

Market Indices & Rates
Weekly Values**

Stock Markets	2018	2019
Dow	26,447	26,574
S&P500	2,886	2,952
Nasdaq	7,788	7,982
TSX	15,946	16,449
FTSE	7,319	7,155
DAX	12,112	12,013
Nikkei	23,784	21,410
Hang Seng	26,573	25,821

Commodities	2018	2019
Oil	74.34	52.81
Gold	1203.8	1499.2

Bond Yields	2018	2019
USA 5 Yr Treasury	3.07	1.34
USA 10 Yr T	3.23	1.52
USA 20 Yr T	3.34	1.81
Moody's Aaa	4.17	2.88
Moody's Baa	5.08	3.81
CAN 5 Yr T	2.49	1.25
CAN 10 Yr T	2.60	1.23

Money Market	2018	2019
USA Fed Funds	2.25	2.00
USA 3 Mo T-B	2.18	1.68
CAN tgt overnight rate	1.50	1.75
CAN 3 Mo T-B	1.60	1.63

Foreign Exchange	2018	2019
EUR/USD	1.15	1.10
GBP/USD	1.31	1.23
USD/CAD	1.29	1.33
USD/JPY	113.72	106.94

OCTOBER

M	T	W	T	F	S	S
				1	2	3
4	5	6	7	8	9	10
11	12	13	14	15	16	17
18	19	20	21	22	23	24
25	26	27	28	29	30	31

NOVEMBER

M	T	W	T	F	S	S
1	2	3	4	5	6	7
8	9	10	11	12	13	14
15	16	17	18	19	20	21
22	23	24	25	26	27	28
29	30					

DECEMBER

M	T	W	T	F	S	S
		1	2	3	4	5
6	7	8	9	10	11	12
13	14	15	16	17	18	19
20	21	22	23	24	25	26
27	28	29	30	31		

HOMEBUILDERS –
TIME TO BREAK & TIME TO BUILD
①SELL SHORT (Apr27-Jun13) ②LONG (Oct28-Feb3)

Historically, the best time to be in the homebuilders sector has been from October 28 to February 3. This period is the lead up to the spring build season. Investors strive to be in the sector well before the spring season takes place, which helps to push up the price of homebuilding stocks.

19% gain & positive 77% of the time

Generally, the time period outside of the strong seasonal period for homebuilders should be avoided by investors, as not only has the average performance relative to the S&P 500 been negative, but the sector has produced both large gains and losses. In other words, the risk is substantially higher that a large draw-down could occur. This is particularly true for the time period from April 27 to June 13. The weak seasonal period takes place when the spring home building season and house sales season gets underway. At this point, the sector has generally priced in expected gains.

Covid-19 Performance Update. The homebuilding sector initially underperformed the S&P 500 as the Covid-19 pandemic got underway in February and March 2020. In April, the sector stabilized relative to the S&P 500 and then started to outperform as consumers showed an increasing appetite to purchase houses with the available low interest rates. On a national level, house prices continued to increase on a year-over-year basis, despite high unemployment in the economy.

ⓘ *Homebuilders: SP GIC Sector: An index designed to represent a cross section of homebuilding companies.* For more information, see www.standardandpoors.com.

Homebuilders (HB)* vs. S&P 500 1990/91 to 2019/20
Negative Short ▭   Positive Long ▭

Year	SHORT Apr 27 to Jun 13		LONG Oct 28 to Feb 3		Compound Growth	
	S&P 500	HB.	S&P 500	HB.	S&P 500	HB.
1990/91	9.6 %	7.9 %	12.6 %	58.0 %	23.4 %	45.5 %
1991/92	-0.4	-4.8	6.6	41.2	6.2	48.0
1992/93	0.2	-11.5	6.9	26.7	7.1	41.2
1993/94	3.2	12.6	3.5	8.6	6.7	-5.1
1994/95	1.6	-4.0	2.8	-4.0	4.4	-0.2
1995/96	4.6	11.1	9.7	16.7	14.7	3.7
1996/97	2.2	10.6	12.2	6.3	14.7	-4.9
1997/98	16.7	22.6	14.7	24.8	33.9	-3.4
1998/99	-0.8	-10.6	19.4	12.4	18.4	24.2
1999/00	-4.9	-7.1	9.9	-3.9	4.5	2.9
2000/01	0.6	-3.8	-2.2	18.6	-1.6	23.1
2001/02	0.6	-17.5	1.6	43.1	2.2	68.1
2002/03	-6.2	-5.3	-4.2	6.7	-10.1	12.3
2003/04	10.0	31.5	10.2	7.6	21.2	-26.3
2004/05	0.1	-2.6	5.7	23.7	5.8	26.9
2005/06	4.3	11.9	7.2	14.8	11.8	1.1
2006/07	-6.3	-27.1	5.2	16.8	-1.4	48.4
2007/08	1.4	-7.9	-9.1	8.8	-7.8	17.4
2008/09	-2.7	-25.3	-1.2	27.7	-3.9	60.0
2009/10	9.2	-25.1	3.2	15.5	12.7	44.4
2010/11	-9.9	-22.9	10.5	12.9	-0.4	38.7
2011/12	-5.6	-11.2	4.7	35.0	-1.2	50.1
2012/13	-6.1	-9.3	7.2	13.7	0.7	24.3
2013/14	3.4	-7.2	-1.0	10.1	2.4	18.1
2014/15	3.9	4.5	4.5	7.8	8.6	3.0
2015/16	-1.1	-0.8	-7.4	-15.3	-8.5	-14.6
2016/17	-0.6	-2.3	7.7	10.9	7.1	13.5
2017/18	2.2	4.6	7.0	4.2	9.4	-0.6
2018/19	4.1	-3.6	1.8	10.2	5.9	14.2
2019/20	-1.6	2.8	7.5	7.5	5.7	4.5
Avg.	1.1 %	-3.0 %	5.2 %	15.6 %	6.4 %	19.3 %
Fq>0	60 %	33 %	80 %	90 %	73 %	77 %

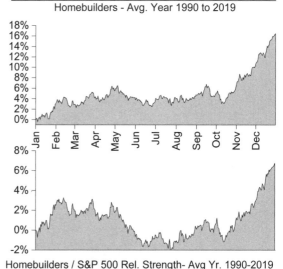

Homebuilders - Avg. Year 1990 to 2019

Homebuilders / S&P 500 Rel. Strength- Avg Yr. 1990-2019

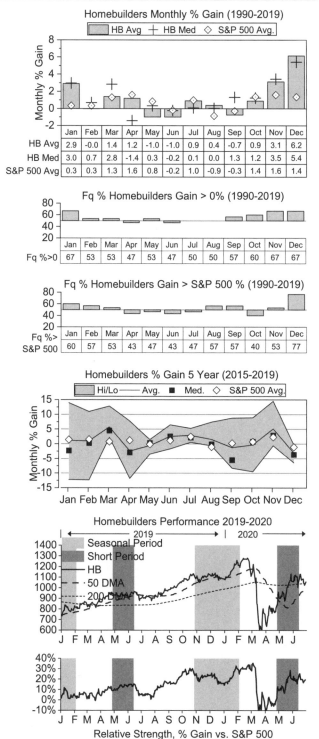

Homebuilders Performance

Market Indices & Rates
Weekly Values**

Stock Markets	2018	2019
Dow	25,340	26,817
S&P500	2,767	2,970
Nasdaq	7,497	8,057
TSX	15,414	16,415
FTSE	6,996	7,247
DAX	11,524	12,512
Nikkei	22,695	21,799
Hang Seng	25,801	26,308

Commodities	2018	2019
Oil	71.34	54.70
Gold	1219.8	1479.2

Bond Yields	2018	2019
USA 5 Yr Treasury	3.00	1.59
USA 10 Yr T	3.15	1.76
USA 20 Yr T	3.25	2.04
Moody's Aaa	4.12	3.06
Moody's Baa	5.03	3.98
CAN 5 Yr T	2.39	1.53
CAN 10 Yr T	2.50	1.52

Money Market	2018	2019
USA Fed Funds	2.25	2.00
USA 3 Mo T-B	2.23	1.65
CAN tgt overnight rate	1.50	1.75
CAN 3 Mo T-B	1.54	1.65

Foreign Exchange	2018	2019
EUR/USD	1.16	1.10
GBP/USD	1.32	1.27
USD/CAD	1.30	1.32
USD/JPY	112.21	108.29

OCTOBER
M	T	W	T	F	S	S
				1	2	3
4	5	6	7	8	9	10
11	12	13	14	15	16	17
18	19	20	21	22	23	24
25	26	27	28	29	30	31

NOVEMBER
M	T	W	T	F	S	S
1	2	3	4	5	6	7
8	9	10	11	12	13	14
15	16	17	18	19	20	21
22	23	24	25	26	27	28
29	30					

DECEMBER
M	T	W	T	F	S	S
		1	2	3	4	5
6	7	8	9	10	11	12
13	14	15	16	17	18	19
20	21	22	23	24	25	26
27	28	29	30	31		

ROGERS COMMUNICATIONS
①Apr19-May23 ②Oct1-Nov7

Rogers Communications (Rogers) has two seasonal periods. The seasonal period from mid-April to late May overlaps the transition period of the stock market from its six-month favorable period, to the six-month unfavorable period. The transition occurs in early May.

The seasonal period from the beginning of October to early November takes place in the transition period from the six-month unfavorable period for the stock market to its six-month unfavorable period. The transition occurs in late October.

On a month by month basis, October is by far the best month of the year for Rogers, producing an average gain of 7.7% from 1996 to 2019. In addition, Rogers has been positive 83% of the time in October.

15% gain & 75% of the time positive

Rogers pays a relatively high dividend. In times increased volatility or in times of increased uncertainty, investors tend to favor stocks that pay a higher dividend than the market, including Rogers. In markets that are in a turmoil, investors often rationalize that the dividend allows them to get paid while they wait.

Covid-19 Pandemic Update. Initially, as the Covid-19 pandemic developed in February and March of 2020, Rogers strongly outperformed the TSX Composite. In mid-March, started to underperform the TSX Composite and continued its underperformance into the summer months.

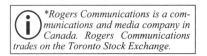

Rogers Communications is a communications and media company in Canada. Rogers Communications trades on the Toronto Stock Exchange.

RCI-B* vs. TSX Comp- 1996 to 2020 Positive ▢

Year	Apr 19 to May 23 TSX	RCI-B	Oct 1 to Nov7 TSX	RCI-B	Compound Growth TSX	RCI-B
1996	3.0 %	9.4 %	8.5 %	32.1 %	11.8 %	44.6 %
1997	10.2	0.0	-2.7	-1.2	7.3	-1.2
1998	-0.5	23.8	14.3	53.3	13.7	89.8
1999	-0.7	11.5	4.9	28.4	4.2	43.1
2000	-0.9	-3.1	-7.7	-14.7	-8.6	-17.4
2001	2.7	17.2	4.5	17.6	7.3	37.8
2002	-1.2	-5.8	3.3	34.7	2.1	26.8
2003	3.9	11.1	5.9	-0.7	10.1	10.3
2004	-5.6	1.0	2.3	12.0	-3.4	13.1
2005	1.3	10.1	-3.0	4.5	-1.7	15.0
2006	-7.3	-1.6	4.7	10.2	-3.0	8.4
2007	3.1	6.1	0.1	7.6	3.3	14.1
2008	3.4	9.1	-18.4	-5.6	-15.6	2.9
2009	5.9	13.1	-1.3	6.4	4.5	20.3
2010	-4.6	4.1	4.5	-5.2	-0.3	-1.3
2011	-0.4	8.7	7.2	6.2	6.8	15.5
2012	-4.7	-9.0	-0.7	9.5	-5.3	-0.3
2013	5.5	-6.0	4.0	6.1	9.7	-0.2
2014	1.4	3.2	-1.8	0.6	-0.4	3.9
2015	-1.0	4.8	1.9	14.1	0.8	19.6
2016	1.5	-0.4	-0.5	-5.2	1.0	-5.6
2017	-0.9	1.6	3.2	3.7	2.2	5.4
2018	3.9	9.5	-4.4	0.8	-0.7	10.4
2019	-2.7	3.3	0.9	-2.0	-1.8	1.2
Avg.	0.6 %	5.1 %	1.2 %	8.9 %	1.8 %	14.8 %
Fq>0	50 %	71 %	63 %	71 %	58 %	75 %

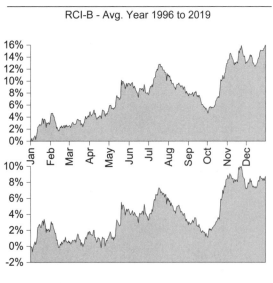

RCI-B - Avg. Year 1996 to 2019

RCI-B / S&P 500 Rel. Strength- Avg Yr. 1996-2019

Rogers Communications Performance

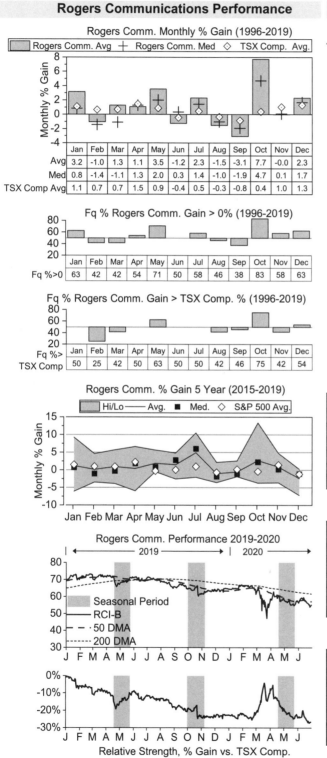

Rogers Comm. Monthly % Gain (1996-2019)

Legend: Rogers Comm. Avg + Rogers Comm. Med ◇ TSX Comp. Avg.

	Jan	Feb	Mar	Apr	May	Jun	Jul	Aug	Sep	Oct	Nov	Dec
Avg	3.2	-1.0	1.3	1.1	3.5	-1.2	2.3	-1.5	-3.1	7.7	-0.0	2.3
Med	0.8	-1.4	-1.1	1.3	2.0	0.3	1.4	-1.0	-1.9	4.7	0.1	1.7
TSX Comp Avg	1.1	0.7	0.7	1.5	0.9	-0.4	0.5	-0.3	-0.8	0.4	1.0	1.3

Fq % Rogers Comm. Gain > 0% (1996-2019)

	Jan	Feb	Mar	Apr	May	Jun	Jul	Aug	Sep	Oct	Nov	Dec
Fq %>0	63	42	42	54	71	50	58	46	38	83	58	63

Fq % Rogers Comm. Gain > TSX Comp. % (1996-2019)

	Jan	Feb	Mar	Apr	May	Jun	Jul	Aug	Sep	Oct	Nov	Dec
Fq %> TSX Comp	50	25	42	50	63	50	50	42	46	75	42	54

Rogers Comm. % Gain 5 Year (2015-2019)

Legend: Hi/Lo — Avg. ■ Med. ◇ S&P 500 Avg.

Rogers Comm. Performance 2019-2020

2019 → | 2020 →

Seasonal Period
RCI-B
50 DMA
200 DMA

Relative Strength, % Gain vs. TSX Comp.

Market Indices & Rates
Weekly Values**

Stock Markets	2018	2019
Dow	25,444	26,770
S&P500	2,768	2,986
Nasdaq	7,449	8,090
TSX	15,470	16,377
FTSE	7,050	7,151
DAX	11,554	12,634
Nikkei	22,532	22,493
Hang Seng	25,561	26,720

Commodities	2018	2019
Oil	69.12	53.78
Gold	1227.9	1490.0

Bond Yields	2018	2019
USA 5 Yr Treasury	3.05	1.56
USA 10 Yr T	3.20	1.76
USA 20 Yr T	3.31	2.06
Moody's Aaa	4.18	3.03
Moody's Baa	5.12	3.97
CAN 5 Yr T	2.40	1.55
CAN 10 Yr T	2.50	1.55

Money Market	2018	2019
USA Fed Funds	2.25	2.00
USA 3 Mo T-B	2.26	1.63
CAN tgt overnight rate	1.50	1.75
CAN 3 Mo T-B	1.66	1.67

Foreign Exchange	2018	2019
EUR/USD	1.15	1.12
GBP/USD	1.31	1.30
USD/CAD	1.31	1.31
USD/JPY	112.55	108.45

OCTOBER

M	T	W	T	F	S	S
			1	2	3
4	5	6	7	8	9	10
11	12	13	14	15	16	17
18	19	20	21	22	23	24
25	26	27	28	29	30	31

NOVEMBER

M	T	W	T	F	S	S
1	2	3	4	5	6	7
8	9	10	11	12	13	14
15	16	17	18	19	20	21
22	23	24	25	26	27	28
29	30					

DECEMBER

M	T	W	T	F	S	S
	1	2	3	4	5
6	7	8	9	10	11	12
13	14	15	16	17	18	19
20	21	22	23	24	25	26
27	28	29	30	31		

The retail sector has two strong seasonal periods. The late January to mid-April seasonal period is the result of the retail sector's response to analysts putting forward positive economic expectations for the economy and consumer spending at the beginning of the year. The retail sector also performs well at this time of the year as it bounces of a weaker period from late December to mid-January.

The second seasonal period for the retail sector occurs in the run-up period to Black Friday, from late October to late November. The retail sector tends to perform well in this period as the result of investors increasing their interest in the sector anticipating retail companies to benefit from increased sales during the holiday shopping season.

14% gain

The frequency of success in the late October to late November seasonal period is stronger than the spring seasonal period. On the other hand, the average percentage gain of spring seasonal period is stronger. Overall, the spring seasonal period when considering both frequency and gain, is the best seasonal period.

Covid-19 Performance Update. Initially, the retail sector underperformed the S&P 500 in February and March of 2020 in the Covid-19 pandemic. Starting in April, the retail sector started to outperform as "Work From Home" companies' performance more than offset companies that suffered from a "shut-in" economy. The retail sector continued its outperformance into the summer.

ⓘ *Retail SP GIC Sector # 2550: An index of retail companies.*
For more information on the retail sector, see www.standardandpoors.com.

Retail* vs. S&P 500 - 1990 to 2019   Positive ☐

Year	Jan 21 to Apr 12		Oct 28 to Nov 29		Compound Growth	
	S&P 500	Retail	S&P 500	Retail	S&P 500	Retail
1990	1.5 %	9.6 %	3.8 %	9.9 %	5.4 %	20.5 %
1991	14.5	29.9	-2.3	2.7	11.8	33.4
1992	-2.9	-2.7	2.8	5.5	-0.2	2.7
1993	3.5	-0.6	-0.6	6.3	2.9	5.7
1994	-5.8	2.0	-2.3	0.4	-7.9	2.4
1995	9.1	7.4	4.8	9.5	14.4	17.6
1996	4.1	19.7	8.0	0.4	12.4	20.2
1997	-5.0	6.0	8.9	16.9	3.5	23.9
1998	13.5	20.1	11.9	20.4	27.0	44.5
1999	8.1	23.4	8.6	14.1	17.4	40.7
2000	1.5	5.8	-2.7	9.9	-1.3	16.2
2001	-11.8	-0.5	3.2	7.9	-9.0	7.4
2002	-1.5	6.7	4.3	-1.7	2.8	4.9
2003	-3.7	6.5	2.6	2.5	-1.2	9.2
2004	0.6	6.7	4.7	7.0	5.3	14.1
2005	1.1	-1.6	6.7	9.9	7.8	8.1
2006	2.1	3.4	1.6	0.2	3.8	3.6
2007	1.2	-0.7	-4.3	-7.5	-3.1	-8.1
2008	0.6	3.5	5.6	7.5	6.2	11.3
2009	6.4	25.1	2.6	3.6	9.2	29.6
2010	5.1	15.5	0.4	5.2	5.6	21.5
2011	2.6	4.4	-7.0	-4.5	-4.5	-0.3
2012	5.5	12.1	0.3	5.1	5.8	17.8
2013	6.9	10.1	2.6	5.0	9.7	15.5
2014	-1.3	-7.1	5.4	8.9	4.1	1.2
2015	3.9	15.5	1.2	3.9	5.2	19.9
2016	10.9	9.7	3.4	2.8	14.6	12.8
2017	3.2	4.6	1.7	4.4	5.0	9.2
2018	-5.2	1.6	3.0	0.9	-2.4	2.5
2019	8.9	10.7	3.9	0.4	13.1	11.1
Avg.	2.6 %	8.2 %	2.8 %	5.2 %	5.4 %	14.0 %
Fq>0	73 %	80 %	80 %	90 %	73 %	93 %

Retail - Avg. Year 1990 to 2019

Retail / S&P 500 Rel. Strength- Avg Yr. 1990-2019

Retail Performance

Retail Monthly % Gain (1990-2019)

Legend: WMT Avg + WMT Med ◇ S&P 500 Avg.

	Jan	Feb	Mar	Apr	May	Jun	Jul	Aug	Sep	Oct	Nov	Dec
Retail Avg	0.7	1.8	3.3	1.1	1.5	-0.2	1.2	-0.3	-0.4	1.5	3.3	0.7
Retail Med	0.5	1.8	1.8	1.3	1.8	-0.5	1.3	-0.1	0.4	2.0	3.7	0.0
S&P 500 Avg	0.3	0.3	1.3	1.6	0.8	-0.2	1.0	-0.9	-0.3	1.4	1.6	1.4

Fq % Retail Gain > 0% (1990-2019)

	Jan	Feb	Mar	Apr	May	Jun	Jul	Aug	Sep	Oct	Nov	Dec
Fq %>0	53	63	73	63	63	47	63	50	53	67	83	50

Fq % Retail Gain > S&P 500 % (1990-2019)

	Jan	Feb	Mar	Apr	May	Jun	Jul	Aug	Sep	Oct	Nov	Dec
Fq %> S&P 500	57	70	77	50	57	57	57	60	50	57	67	37

Retail % Gain 5 Year (2015-2019)

Legend: Retail Hi/Lo —— Retail Avg. ■ Retail Med. ◇ S&P 500 Avg.

Jan Feb Mar Apr May Jun Jul Aug Sep Oct Nov Dec

Retail Performance 2019-2020

|← —— 2019 —— →| 2020 →

- Seasonal Period
- —— Retail
- — — 50 DMA
- ····· 200 DMA

J F M A M J J A S O N D J F M A M J

Relative Strength, % Gain vs. S&P 500

OCTOBER

M	T	W	T	F	S	S
				1	2	3
4	5	6	7	8	9	10
11	12	13	14	15	16	17
18	19	20	21	22	23	24
25	26	27	28	29	30	31

NOVEMBER

M	T	W	T	F	S	S
1	2	3	4	5	6	7
8	9	10	11	12	13	14
15	16	17	18	19	20	21
22	23	24	25	26	27	28
29	30					

DECEMBER

M	T	W	T	F	S	S
	1	2	3	4	5	
6	7	8	9	10	11	12
13	14	15	16	17	18	19
20	21	22	23	24	25	26
27	28	29	30	31		

INDUSTRIAL STRENGTH
①Oct28-Dec31 ②Jan23-May5

The industrial sector's seasonal trends are largely the same as the broad market, such as the S&P 500. Although the trends are similar, there still exists an opportunity to take advantage of the time period when the industrial sector tends to outperform.

10% gain &
positive 87% of the time

Industrials tend to outperform in the favorable six month period for the stock market, but there is an opportunity to temporarily get out of the industrial sector in order to avoid a time period when the sector has on average, decreased before turning positive again.

The overall strategy is to be invested in the industrial sector from October 28 to December 31, sell at the end of the day on the 31, and re-enter the sector to be invested from January 23 to May 5.

It should be noted that longer term investors may decide to be invested during the whole time period from October 28 to May 5. Shorter term investors may decide to use technical analysis to determine, if and when, they should temporarily sell the industrials sector during its weak period from January 1 to January 22.

Covid-19 Pandemic Update. Since 2018, the industrial sector has been underperforming the S&P 500 largely due to failed trade talks. The sector continued to underperform the S&P 500 as the stock market corrected in February and March 2020 and continued to underperform until mid-May, at which time it started to outperform largely due to the economy growing faster than expected.

Industrials* vs. S&P 500 1989/90 to 2019/20 Positive ▢

Year	Oct 28 to Dec 31 S&P 500	Ind.	Jan 23 to May 5 S&P 500	Ind.	Compound Growth S&P 500	Ind.
1989/90	5.5 %	6.9 %	2.4 %	5.5 %	8.0 %	12.7 %
1990/91	8.4	10.7	16.0	15.2	25.7	27.5
1991/92	8.6	7.2	-0.3	-1.0	8.2	6.1
1992/93	4.1	6.3	1.9	5.4	6.1	12.0
1993/94	0.4	5.1	-4.9	-6.7	-4.5	-2.0
1994/95	-1.4	-0.5	11.9	12.4	10.3	11.8
1995/96	6.3	10.7	4.6	7.6	11.1	19.1
1996/97	5.7	4.5	5.6	5.2	11.6	9.9
1997/98	10.7	10.5	15.8	11.5	28.2	23.2
1998/99	15.4	10.5	10.0	19.5	26.9	32.1
1999/00	13.3	10.8	-0.6	4.5	12.6	15.8
2000/01	-4.3	1.8	-5.7	4.7	-9.7	6.6
2001/02	3.9	8.1	-4.1	-5.3	-0.3	2.4
2002/03	-2.0	-1.3	5.5	8.6	3.4	7.1
2003/04	7.8	11.6	-2.0	-3.3	5.7	7.9
2004/05	7.7	8.7	0.4	0.2	8.1	8.9
2005/06	5.9	7.6	5.1	14.3	11.3	23.0
2006/07	3.0	3.1	5.8	6.8	9.0	10.1
2007/08	-4.4	-3.4	7.4	9.7	2.7	6.0
2008/09	4.9	7.1	9.2	6.1	16.2	13.7
2009/10	4.9	6.4	6.8	13.4	12.0	20.6
2010/11	6.4	8.1	4.0	4.9	10.6	13.5
2011/12	-2.1	-1.0	4.1	0.3	1.9	-0.7
2012/13	1.0	4.1	8.2	4.9	9.3	9.2
2013/14	5.0	7.3	2.2	1.6	7.3	9.0
2014/15	5.0	5.2	1.3	-1.0	6.3	4.1
2015/16	-1.1	-1.2	7.5	12.8	6.4	11.4
2016/17	5.0	9.7	5.6	5.0	10.9	15.2
2017/18	3.6	4.2	-6.0	-9.5	-2.6	-5.7
2018/19	-5.7	-6.7	11.9	14.2	5.5	6.6
2019/20	6.9	3.8	-13.6	-25.5	-7.7	-22.7
Avg.	4.2 %	5.4 %	3.7 %	4.6 %	8.1 %	10.1 %
Fq > 0	77 %	81 %	74 %	77 %	84 %	87 %

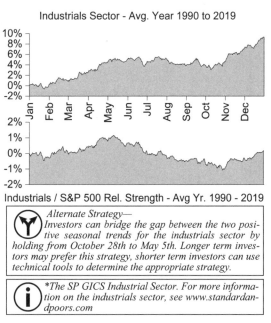

Industrials Sector - Avg. Year 1990 to 2019

Industrials / S&P 500 Rel. Strength - Avg Yr. 1990 - 2019

> **Ⓨ** *Alternate Strategy—*
> *Investors can bridge the gap between the two positive seasonal trends for the industrials sector by holding from October 28th to May 5th. Longer term investors may prefer this strategy, shorter term investors can use technical tools to determine the appropriate strategy.*

> **ⓘ** **The SP GICS Industrial Sector. For more information on the industrials sector, see www.standardandpoors.com*

Industrials Performance

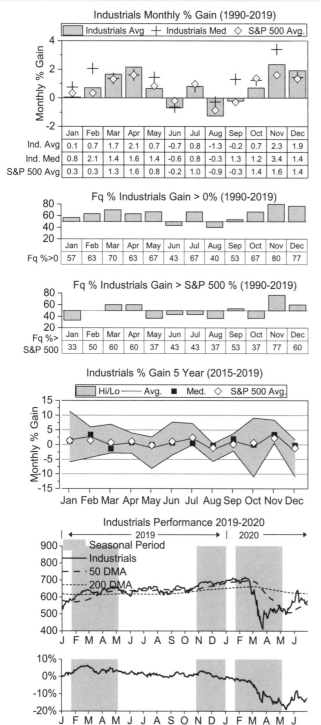

Industrials Monthly % Gain (1990-2019)

Legend: Industrials Avg | Industrials Med ◇ S&P 500 Avg.

	Jan	Feb	Mar	Apr	May	Jun	Jul	Aug	Sep	Oct	Nov	Dec
Ind. Avg	0.1	0.7	1.7	2.1	0.7	-0.7	0.8	-1.3	-0.2	0.7	2.3	1.9
Ind. Med	0.8	2.1	1.4	1.6	1.4	-0.6	0.8	-0.3	1.3	1.2	3.4	1.4
S&P 500 Avg	0.3	0.3	1.3	1.6	0.8	-0.2	1.0	-0.9	-0.3	1.4	1.6	1.4

Fq % Industrials Gain > 0% (1990-2019)

	Jan	Feb	Mar	Apr	May	Jun	Jul	Aug	Sep	Oct	Nov	Dec
Fq %>0	57	63	70	63	67	43	67	40	53	67	80	77

Fq % Industrials Gain > S&P 500 % (1990-2019)

	Jan	Feb	Mar	Apr	May	Jun	Jul	Aug	Sep	Oct	Nov	Dec
Fq %> S&P 500	33	50	60	60	37	43	43	37	53	37	77	60

Industrials % Gain 5 Year (2015-2019)

Legend: Hi/Lo — Avg. ■ Med. ◇ S&P 500 Avg.

Industrials Performance 2019-2020

Legend: Seasonal Period — Industrials · 50 DMA ·· 200 DMA

Relative Strength, % Gain vs. S&P 500

Market Indices & Rates
Weekly Values**

Stock Markets	2018	2019
Dow	25,271	27,347
S&P500	2,723	3,067
Nasdaq	7,357	8,386
TSX	15,119	16,594
FTSE	7,094	7,302
DAX	11,519	12,961
Nikkei	22,244	22,851
Hang Seng	26,486	27,101

Commodities	2018	2019
Oil	63.14	56.20
Gold	1232.1	1508.8

Bond Yields	2018	2019
USA 5 Yr Treasury	3.04	1.55
USA 10 Yr T	3.22	1.73
USA 20 Yr T	3.37	2.03
Moody's Aaa	4.27	3.02
Moody's Baa	5.24	3.89
CAN 5 Yr T	2.45	1.47
CAN 10 Yr T	2.53	1.45

Money Market	2018	2019
USA Fed Funds	2.25	1.75
USA 3 Mo T-B	2.28	1.49
CAN tgt overnight rate	1.75	1.75
CAN 3 Mo T-B	1.72	1.68

Foreign Exchange	2018	2019
EUR/USD	1.14	1.12
GBP/USD	1.30	1.29
USD/CAD	1.31	1.31
USD/JPY	113.20	108.19

OCTOBER

M	T	W	T	F	S	S
				1	2	3
4	5	6	7	8	9	10
11	12	13	14	15	16	17
18	19	20	21	22	23	24
25	26	27	28	29	30	31

NOVEMBER

M	T	W	T	F	S	S
1	2	3	4	5	6	7
8	9	10	11	12	13	14
15	16	17	18	19	20	21
22	23	24	25	26	27	28
29	30					

DECEMBER

M	T	W	T	F	S	S
	1	2	3	4	5
6	7	8	9	10	11	12
13	14	15	16	17	18	19
20	21	22	23	24	25	26
27	28	29	30	31		

NOVEMBER

	MONDAY	TUESDAY	WEDNESDAY
WEEK 44	**1** 29	**2** 28	**3** 27
WEEK 45	**8** 22	**9** 21	**10** 20
WEEK 46	**15** 15	**16** 14	**17** 13
WEEK 47	**22** 8	**23** 7	**24** 6
WEEK 48	**29** 1	**30**	1

THURSDAY	**FRIDAY**
4 26	**5** 25
11 19	**12** 18
USA Bond Market Closed- Veterans Day CAD Bond Market Closed- Remembrance Day	
18 12	**19** 11
25 5	**26** 4
USA Market Closed- Thanksgiving Day	USA Early Market Close Thanksgiving
2	3

DECEMBER

M	T	W	T	F	S	S
		1	2	3	4	5
6	7	8	9	10	11	12
13	14	15	16	17	18	19
20	21	22	23	24	25	26
27	28	29	30	31		

JANUARY

M	T	W	T	F	S	S
					1	2
3	4	5	6	7	8	9
10	11	12	13	14	15	16
17	18	19	20	21	22	23
24	25	26	27	28	29	30
31						

FEBRUARY

M	T	W	T	F	S	S
	1	2	3	4	5	6
7	8	9	10	11	12	13
14	15	16	17	18	19	20
21	22	23	24	25	26	27
28						

MARCH

M	T	W	T	F	S	S
	1	2	3	4	5	6
7	8	9	10	11	12	13
14	15	16	17	18	19	20
21	22	23	24	25	26	27
28	29	30	31			

NOVEMBER SUMMARY

S&P500 Cumulative Daily Gains for Avg Month 1950 to 2019

	Dow Jones	S&P 500	Nasdaq	TSX Comp
Month Rank	2	1	2	8
# Up	49	48	34	22
# Down	21	22	14	13
% Pos	70	69	71	63
% Avg. Gain	1.6	1.6	1.7	0.7

Dow & S&P 1950-2019, Nasdaq 1972-2019, TSX 1985-2019

♦ November, on average, is one of the better months of the year for the S&P 500. From 1950 to 2019, it has produced an average gain of 1.6% and has been positive 69% of the time. ♦ In November, the cyclical sectors tend to start increasing their relative performance compared to the S&P 500. The metals and mining sector starts its period of seasonal strength on November 19th. ♦ For investors looking for a short-term investment, the day before and the day after Thanksgiving are on average the two strongest days of the year for the S&P 500.

BEST / WORST NOVEMBER BROAD MKTS. 2010-2019

BEST NOVEMBER MARKETS
♦ Russell 2000 (2016) 11.0%
♦ Nikkei 225 (2013) 9.3%
♦ Nikkei 225 (2010) 8.0%

WORST NOVEMBER MARKETS
♦ Nikkei 225 (2011) -6.2%
♦ FTSE 100 (2010) -2.6%
♦ FTSE 100 (2016) -2.5%

Index Values End of Month

	2010	2011	2012	2013	2014	2015	2016	2017	2018	2019
Dow	11,006	12,046	13,026	16,086	17,828	17,720	19,124	24,272	25,538	28,051
S&P 500	1,181	1,247	1,416	1,806	2,068	2,080	2,199	2,648	2,760	3,141
Nasdaq	2,498	2,620	3,010	4,060	4,792	5,109	5,324	6,874	7,331	8,665
TSX Comp.	12,953	12,204	12,239	13,395	14,745	13,470	15,083	16,067	15,198	17,040
Russell 1000	654	689	783	1,005	1,149	1,155	1,221	1,467	1,526	1,737
Russell 2000	727	737	822	1,143	1,173	1,198	1,322	1,544	1,533	1,625
FTSE 100	5,528	5,505	5,867	6,651	6,723	6,356	6,784	7,327	6,980	7,347
Nikkei 225	9,937	8,435	9,446	15,662	17,460	19,747	18,308	22,725	22,351	23,294

Percent Gain for November

	2010	2011	2012	2013	2014	2015	2016	2017	2018	2019
Dow	-1.0	0.8	-0.5	3.5	2.5	0.3	5.4	3.8	1.7	3.7
S&P 500	-0.2	-0.5	0.3	2.8	2.5	0.1	3.4	2.8	1.8	3.4
Nasdaq	-0.4	-2.4	1.1	3.6	3.5	1.1	2.6	2.2	0.3	4.5
TSX Comp.	2.2	-0.4	-1.5	0.3	0.9	-0.4	2.0	0.3	1.1	3.4
Russell 1000	0.1	-0.5	0.5	2.6	2.4	0.1	3.7	2.8	1.8	3.6
Russell 2000	3.4	-0.5	0.4	3.9	0.0	3.1	11.0	2.8	1.4	4.0
FTSE 100	-2.6	-0.7	1.5	-1.2	2.7	-0.1	-2.5	-2.2	-2.1	1.4
Nikkei 225	8.0	-6.2	5.8	9.3	6.4	3.5	5.1	3.2	2.0	1.6

November Market Avg. Performance 2010 to 2019[1]

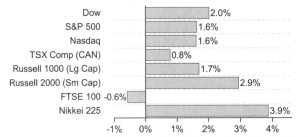

Dow	2.0%
S&P 500	1.6%
Nasdaq	1.6%
TSX Comp (CAN)	0.8%
Russell 1000 (Lg Cap)	1.7%
Russell 2000 (Sm Cap)	2.9%
FTSE 100	-0.6%
Nikkei 225	3.9%

Interest Corner Nov[2]

	Fed Funds % [3]	3 Mo. T-Bill % [4]	10 Yr % [5]	20 Yr % [6]
2019	1.75	1.59	1.78	2.07
2018	2.25	2.37	3.01	3.19
2017	1.25	1.27	2.42	2.65
2016	0.50	0.48	2.37	2.73
2015	0.25	0.22	2.21	2.63

(1) Russell Data provided by Russell (2) Federal Reserve Bank of St. Louis- end of month values (3) Target rate set by FOMC (4)(5)(6) Constant yield maturities.

November 2019 % Sector Performance

S&P GIC	2019	1990-2019[1]	
Sectors	% Gain	GIC[2] % Avg Gain	Fq% Gain >S&P 500
Consumer Discretionary	1.1 %	2.5 %	67 %
Health Care	4.8	2.5	60
Industrials	4.1	2.3	77
Information Technology	5.2	2.3	60
Materials	2.9	2.1	57
Consumer Staples	1.1	1.7	43
Financials	4.8	1.4	43
Telecom	3.7	1.2	40
Energy	1.1	0.0	27
Utilities	-2.3 %	-0.4 %	30 %
S&P 500	3.4 %	1.6 %	N/A %

Sector Commentary

♦ In November 2019, the S&P 500 managed to produce a gain of 3.4%. ♦ Information technology, which is typically one of the better performing sectors in November lived up to its reputation with a gain of 5.2%. The utilities sector has on average been the weakest sector in November since 1990. In 2019, the utilities sector was the worst performing sector with a loss of 2.3%.

Sub-Sector Commentary

♦ In November 2019, the biotech sub-sector produced a gain of 8.4%. ♦ Railroads and banks also performed well with gains of 4.1% and 5.4% respectively. ♦ Gold and silver, typically two of the weaker performers, both underperformed the S&P 500, producing losses of 3.4% and 6.0% respectively.

SELECTED SUB-SECTORS[3]

Steel	4.7 %	3.5 %	53 %
SOX (1995-2019)	4.0	3.3	60
Retail	0.3	3.3	67
Home-builders	2.9	3.1	53
Biotech (1993-2019)	8.4	2.8	50
Transportation	4.1	2.7	53
Agriculture (1994-2019)	2.1	2.5	38
Pharma	1.6	2.1	53
Chemicals	3.3	2.0	50
Railroads	5.4	2.0	60
Automotive & Components	1.0	1.7	50
Banks	5.4	1.6	50
Metals & Mining	3.1	1.6	50
Gold	-3.4	0.9	47
Silver	-6.0	0.3	43

(1) Sector data provided by Standard and Poors (2) GIC is short form for Global Industry Classification (3) Sub Sector data provided by Standard and Poors, except where marked by symbol.

MATERIAL STOCKS – MATERIAL GAINS
①Oct28-Jan6   ②Jan23-May5

The materials sector (U.S.) generally performs well during the favorable six months of the year, from the end of October to the beginning of May. The sector is economically sensitive and is leveraged to economic forecasts.

Positive 90% of the time

The materials sector has two seasonal periods. The first period is from October 28 to January 6 and the second period is from January 23 to May 5.

The time period in between the two seasonal periods, from January 7 to January 22, has had an average loss of 2.2% and only been positive 43% of the time (1990 to 2019).

Investors may decide to bridge the gap between the two seasonal periods if the materials sector has strong momentum at the beginning of January. The complete materials strategy is to be invested from October 28 to January 6, out of the sector from January 7 to the 22, and back in from January 23 to May 5.

Covid-19 Performance Update. The materials sector has been underperforming the S&P 500 since 2018. As the stock market bottomed in March 2020, the materials sector started to outperform the S&P 500. Often the materials sector and the industrials sector will outperform together, but in March the materials sector started its outperformance well before the industrial sector largely due to gold miners being included in the materials sector and performing well starting in March.

Materials* vs S&P 500 1989/90 to 2019/20 Positive ▢

Year	Oct 28 to Jan 6 S&P 500	Oct 28 to Jan 6 Mat.	Jan 23 to May 5 S&P 500	Jan 23 to May 5 Mat.	Compound Growth S&P 500	Compound Growth Mat.
1989/90	5.1 %	9.1 %	2.4 %	-3.1 %	7.7 %	5.7 %
1990/91	5.4	9.2	16.0	15.3	22.2	26.0
1991/92	8.8	1.5	-0.3	5.5	8.5	7.1
1992/93	3.8	5.6	1.9	4.3	5.8	10.2
1993/94	0.5	9.4	-4.9	-5.3	-4.4	3.6
1994/95	-1.1	-3.5	11.9	6.1	10.7	2.4
1995/96	6.4	7.6	4.6	11.1	11.3	19.5
1996/97	6.7	2.3	5.6	2.3	12.6	4.6
1997/98	10.2	1.4	15.8	20.9	27.7	22.6
1998/99	19.4	6.1	10.0	31.5	31.3	39.6
1999/00	8.2	15.7	-0.6	-7.1	7.6	7.5
2000/01	-5.9	19.2	-5.7	15.1	-11.2	37.2
2001/02	6.2	8.5	-4.1	14.9	1.8	24.7
2002/03	3.5	9.2	5.5	2.7	9.2	12.1
2003/04	9.0	16.6	-2.0	-3.0	6.8	13.1
2004/05	5.6	5.4	0.4	0.3	6.0	5.8
2005/06	9.0	16.3	5.1	14.7	14.6	33.5
2006/07	2.4	3.2	5.8	10.7	8.3	14.2
2007/08	-8.1	-5.1	7.4	16.7	-1.2	10.8
2008/09	10.1	12.0	9.2	23.3	20.3	38.1
2009/10	6.9	13.8	6.8	3.0	14.2	17.2
2010/11	7.7	11.7	4.0	4.2	12.1	16.4
2011/12	-0.5	-2.3	4.1	-2.7	3.5	-4.9
2012/13	3.9	7.2	8.2	0.0	12.3	7.2
2013/14	3.8	3.1	2.2	4.3	6.1	7.5
2014/15	2.1	-0.7	1.3	2.9	3.4	2.2
2015/16	-3.7	-6.2	7.5	18.3	3.6	11.0
2016/17	6.8	8.6	5.6	4.5	12.8	13.5
2017/18	6.3	6.4	-6.0	-8.6	-0.1	-2,8
2018/19	-4.8	1.0	11.9	7.4	6.5	8.5
2019/20	7.4	2.2	-13.6	-15.0	-7.3	-13.2
Avg.	4.6 %	6.3 %	3.7 %	6.3 %	8.5 %	12.9 %
Fq > 0	81 %	84 %	74 %	74 %	84 %	90 %

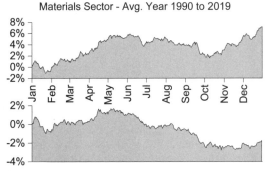

Materials Sector - Avg. Year 1990 to 2019

Materials / S&P 500 Rel. Strength - Avg Yr. 1990 - 2019

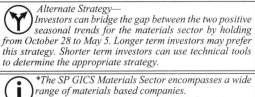

Alternate Strategy—
Investors can bridge the gap between the two positive seasonal trends for the materials sector by holding from October 28 to May 5. Longer term investors may prefer this strategy. Shorter term investors can use technical tools to determine the appropriate strategy.

The SP GICS Materials Sector encompasses a wide range of materials based companies.
For more information on the materials sector, see www.standardandpoors.com

Materials Performance

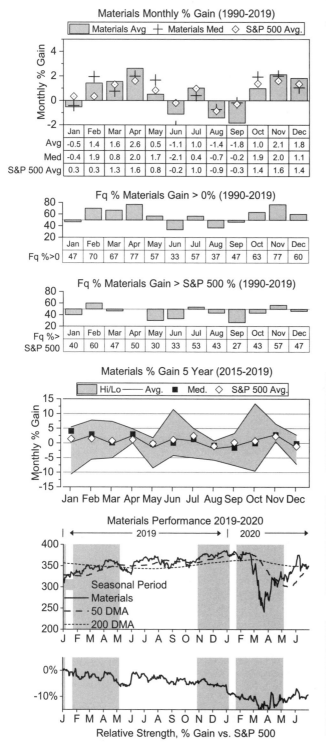

Materials Monthly % Gain (1990-2019)

Materials Avg ┼ Materials Med ◇ S&P 500 Avg.

	Jan	Feb	Mar	Apr	May	Jun	Jul	Aug	Sep	Oct	Nov	Dec
Avg	-0.5	1.4	1.6	2.6	0.5	-1.1	1.0	-1.4	-1.8	1.0	2.1	1.8
Med	-0.4	1.9	0.8	2.0	1.7	-2.1	0.4	-0.7	-0.2	1.9	2.0	1.1
S&P 500 Avg	0.3	0.3	1.3	1.6	0.8	-0.2	1.0	-0.9	-0.3	1.4	1.6	1.4

Fq % Materials Gain > 0% (1990-2019)

	Jan	Feb	Mar	Apr	May	Jun	Jul	Aug	Sep	Oct	Nov	Dec
Fq %>0	47	70	67	77	57	33	57	37	47	63	77	60

Fq % Materials Gain > S&P 500 % (1990-2019)

	Jan	Feb	Mar	Apr	May	Jun	Jul	Aug	Sep	Oct	Nov	Dec
Fq %> S&P 500	40	60	47	50	30	33	53	43	27	43	57	47

Materials % Gain 5 Year (2015-2019)

Hi/Lo ── Avg. ■ Med. ◇ S&P 500 Avg.

Materials Performance 2019-2020

Seasonal Period
Materials
50 DMA
200 DMA

Relative Strength, % Gain vs. S&P 500

Market Indices & Rates
Weekly Values**

Stock Markets	2018	2019
Dow	25,989	27,681
S&P500	2,781	3,093
Nasdaq	7,407	8,475
TSX	15,274	16,877
FTSE	7,105	7,359
DAX	11,529	13,229
Nikkei	22,250	23,392
Hang Seng	25,602	27,651

Commodities	2018	2019
Oil	60.19	57.24
Gold	1211.4	1464.2

Bond Yields	2018	2019
USA 5 Yr Treasury	3.05	1.74
USA 10 Yr T	3.19	1.94
USA 20 Yr T	3.32	2.27
Moody's Aaa	4.16	3.17
Moody's Baa	5.17	4.05
CAN 5 Yr T	2.43	1.56
CAN 10 Yr T	2.51	1.58

Money Market	2018	2019
USA Fed Funds	2.25	1.75
USA 3 Mo T-B	2.31	1.52
CAN tgt overnight rate	1.75	1.75
CAN 3 Mo T-B	1.71	1.68

Foreign Exchange	2018	2019
EUR/USD	1.13	1.10
GBP/USD	1.30	1.28
USD/CAD	1.32	1.32
USD/JPY	113.83	109.26

NOVEMBER

M	T	W	T	F	S	S
1	2	3	4	5	6	7
8	9	10	11	12	13	14
15	16	17	18	19	20	21
22	23	24	25	26	27	28
29	30					

DECEMBER

M	T	W	T	F	S	S
		1	2	3	4	5
6	7	8	9	10	11	12
13	14	15	16	17	18	19
20	21	22	23	24	25	26
27	28	29	30	31		

JANUARY

M	T	W	T	F	S	S
					1	2
3	4	5	6	7	8	9
10	11	12	13	14	15	16
17	18	19	20	21	22	23
24	25	26	27	28	29	30
31						

HOME DEPOT – BUILDING GAINS
①Oct28-Dec31 ②Jan9-Ap15

Home Depot is part of the consumer discretionary sector, and as such, has a similar seasonal period. Both Home Depot and the consumer discretionary sector start their seasonal periods on October 28. In the seasonal period from October 28 to December 31 (1989 to 2019), Home Depot has produced an average gain of 11.0% and has been positive 81% of the time

19% gain & positive 84% of the time

Home Depot has a second seasonal period from January 9 to April 15. In this period, Home Depot's strong seasonal period occurs at a similar time to the consumer discretionary and retail sectors' strong seasonal period.

Comparing the two seasonal periods, Home Depot has better performance in its October 28 to December 31 period compared to the January 9 to April 15 period.

Home Depot has a short period (January 1 to January 8) at the beginning of January where it tends to underperform the S&P 500. In this time period, during the years 1990 to 2019, on average Home Depot has lost 1.6% and has only outperformed the S&P 500, 37% of the time.

Covid-19 Performance Update. Home Depot initially underperformed the S&P 500 as the stock market corrected in February, into March 2020, but quickly started to outperform as people that were shut in their homes because of the Covid-19 pandemic increased the amount of money they spent on renovating their homesteads.

In its seasonal period of strength from January 9 to April 15, 2020, Home Depot was negative but managed to outperform the S&P 500.

HD* vs. S&P 500 1989/90 to 2019/20 Positive ☐

Year	Oct 28 to Dec 31 S&P 500	HD	Jan 9 to Apr 15 S&P 500	HD	Compound Growth S&P 500	HD
1989/90	5.5%	9.3%	-2.7%	26.2%	2.7%	37.9%
1990/91	8.4	28.8	21.1	64.2	31.2	111.4
1991/92	8.6	23.3	-0.4	-0.2	8.1	23.1
1992/93	4.1	18.4	4.5	-9.6	8.8	7.0
1993/94	0.4	1.6	-5.1	8.1	-4.7	9.8
1994/95	-1.4	3.1	10.5	-3.4	9.0	-0.4
1995/96	6.3	29.5	3.9	4.3	10.4	35.0
1996/97	5.7	-9.3	0.8	10.7	6.6	0.5
1997/98	10.7	15.4	17.1	23.6	29.5	42.7
1998/99	15.4	49.7	3.8	8.4	19.7	62.2
1999/00	13.3	48.0	-5.9	-5.1	6.6	40.4
2000/01	-4.3	26.6	-8.7	-12.7	-12.6	1.3
2001/02	3.9	26.6	-5.0	-3.7	-1.3	21.9
2002/03	-2.0	-21.5	-2.1	28.4	-4.0	0.8
2003/04	7.8	-1.4	-0.3	0.7	7.5	-0.7
2004/05	7.7	4.8	-3.7	-12.8	3.7	-8.7
2005/06	5.9	2.8	0.3	1.8	6.2	4.7
2006/07	3.0	8.3	2.8	-4.1	5.9	4.0
2007/08	-4.4	-14.1	-4.0	12.9	-8.2	-3.0
2008/09	6.4	21.7	-6.3	5.3	-0.3	28.1
2009/10	4.9	11.3	5.8	21.3	11.0	34.9
2010/11	6.4	13.5	3.8	11.0	10.4	26.0
2011/12	-2.1	13.0	7.2	18.0	5.0	33.2
2012/13	1.0	3.0	6.5	14.3	7.6	17.7
2013/14	5.0	8.0	0.3	-7.4	5.3	0.0
2014/15	5.0	10.0	2.2	6.3	7.2	16.9
2015/16	-1.1	6.3	8.3	9.0	7.1	15.8
2016/17	5.0	9.7	2.3	9.3	7.4	19.8
2017/18	3.6	13.3	-3.3	-10.0	0.1	1.9
2018/19	-5.7	-0.2	12.9	15.2	6.4	14.9
2019/20	6.9	-6.8	-14.4	-10.5	-8.5	-16.6
Avg.	4.2%	11.0%	1.7%	7.1%	5.9%	18.8%
Fq > 0	77%	81%	58%	65%	77%	84%

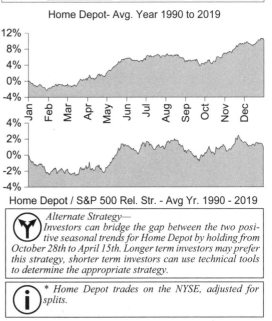

Home Depot- Avg. Year 1990 to 2019

Home Depot / S&P 500 Rel. Str. - Avg Yr. 1990 - 2019

Ⓨ *Alternate Strategy—*
Investors can bridge the gap between the two positive seasonal trends for Home Depot by holding from October 28th to April 15th. Longer term investors may prefer this strategy, shorter term investors can use technical tools to determine the appropriate strategy.

ⓘ ** Home Depot trades on the NYSE, adjusted for splits.*

Home Depot Performance

HD Monthly % Gain (1990-2019)

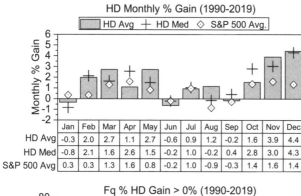

HD Avg + HD Med ◇ S&P 500 Avg.

	Jan	Feb	Mar	Apr	May	Jun	Jul	Aug	Sep	Oct	Nov	Dec
HD Avg	-0.3	2.0	2.7	1.1	2.7	-0.6	0.9	1.2	-0.2	1.6	3.9	4.4
HD Med	-0.8	2.1	1.6	2.6	1.5	-0.2	1.0	-0.2	0.4	2.8	3.0	4.3
S&P 500 Avg	0.3	0.3	1.3	1.6	0.8	-0.2	1.0	-0.9	-0.3	1.4	1.6	1.4

Fq % HD Gain > 0% (1990-2019)

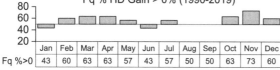

	Jan	Feb	Mar	Apr	May	Jun	Jul	Aug	Sep	Oct	Nov	Dec
Fq %>0	43	60	63	63	57	43	57	50	50	63	73	60

Fq % HD Gain > S&P 500 % (1990-2019)

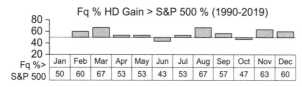

	Jan	Feb	Mar	Apr	May	Jun	Jul	Aug	Sep	Oct	Nov	Dec
Fq %> S&P 500	50	60	67	53	53	43	53	67	57	47	63	60

HD % Gain 5 Year (2015-2019)

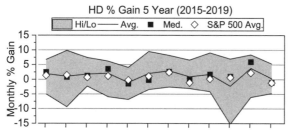

Hi/Lo —— Avg. ■ Med. ◇ S&P 500 Avg.

HD Performance 2019-2020

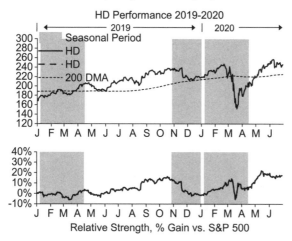

Relative Strength, % Gain vs. S&P 500

Market Indices & Rates
Weekly Values**

Stock Markets	2018	2019
Dow	25,413	28,005
S&P500	2,736	3,120
Nasdaq	7,248	8,541
TSX	15,156	17,028
FTSE	7,014	7,303
DAX	11,341	13,242
Nikkei	21,680	23,303
Hang Seng	26,184	26,327

Commodities	2018	2019
Oil	56.46	57.72
Gold	1222.4	1466.9

Bond Yields	2018	2019
USA 5 Yr Treasury	2.90	1.65
USA 10 Yr T	3.08	1.84
USA 20 Yr T	3.23	2.16
Moody's Aaa	4.21	3.10
Moody's Baa	5.21	3.97
CAN 5 Yr T	2.29	1.48
CAN 10 Yr T	2.36	1.48

Money Market	2018	2019
USA Fed Funds	2.25	1.75
USA 3 Mo T-B	2.31	1.54
CAN tgt overnight rate	1.75	1.75
CAN 3 Mo T-B	1.70	1.71

Foreign Exchange	2018	2019
EUR/USD	1.14	1.11
GBP/USD	1.28	1.29
USD/CAD	1.31	1.32
USD/JPY	112.83	108.80

NOVEMBER

M	T	W	T	F	S	S
1	2	3	4	5	6	7
8	9	10	11	12	13	14
15	16	17	18	19	20	21
22	23	24	25	26	27	28
29	30					

DECEMBER

M	T	W	T	F	S	S
		1	2	3	4	5
6	7	8	9	10	11	12
13	14	15	16	17	18	19
20	21	22	23	24	25	26
27	28	29	30	31		

JANUARY

M	T	W	T	F	S	S
					1	2
3	4	5	6	7	8	9
10	11	12	13	14	15	16
17	18	19	20	21	22	23
24	25	26	27	28	29	30
31						

METALS AND MINING – STRONG TWO TIMES
①Nov19-Jan 5　②Jan23-May5

At the macro level, the metals and mining (M&M) sector is driven by future economic growth expectations. When worldwide growth expectations are increasing, there is a greater need for raw materials, and vice versa.

Within the macro trend, the M&M sector has traditionally followed the overall market cycle of performing well from autumn until spring. This is the time of year that investors have a positive outlook on the economy and as a result, the cyclical sectors tend to outperform, including the metals and mining sector.

13% gain

The metals and mining sector has two seasonal "sweet spots" – the first from November 19 to January 5 and the second from January 23 to May 5.

Investors have the option to hold and "bridge the gap" across the two sweet spots, but over the long-term, nimble traders have been able to capture extra value by being out of the sector from January 6 to the 22.

From a portfolio perspective, it is important to consider reducing exposure at the beginning of May. The danger of holding on too long is that the sector tends not to perform well in the late summer, particularly in September.

Covid-19 Pandemic Update. The metals and mining sector started to underperform the S&P 500 in 2018. Since the bottom of the stock market in late March 2020, the metals and mining sector has only managed to moderately outperform the S&P 500.

(i) *For more information on the metals and mining sector, see www.standardandpoors.com*

Metals & Mining* vs. S&P 500
1989/90 to 2019/20　　Positive ☐

Year	Nov 19 to Jan 5 S&P 500	Nov 19 to Jan 5 M&M	Jan 23 to May 5 S&P 500	Jan 23 to May 5 M&M	Compound Growth S&P 500	Compound Growth M&M
1989/90	3.1 %	6.3 %	2.4 %	-4.6 %	5.6 %	1.4 %
1990/91	1.2	6.4	16.0	7.1	17.4	13.9
1991/92	8.9	1.0	-0.3	-1.7	8.5	-0.7
1992/93	2.7	12.5	1.9	3.2	4.7	16.1
1993/94	0.9	9.0	-4.9	-11.1	-4.1	-3.1
1994/95	-0.2	-1.2	11.9	-3.0	11.6	-4.1
1995/96	2.8	8.3	4.6	5.8	7.5	14.6
1996/97	1.5	-1.9	5.6	-1.2	7.2	-3.0
1997/98	4.1	-4.5	15.8	19.3	20.6	13.9
1998/99	8.8	-7.9	10.0	31.0	19.6	20.6
1999/00	-1.6	21.7	-0.6	-10.4	-2.2	9.1
2000/01	-5.1	17.0	-5.7	19.6	-10.5	40.0
2001/02	3.0	5.5	-4.1	12.8	-1.3	19.0
2002/03	0.9	9.3	5.5	3.2	6.4	12.8
2003/04	8.5	18.2	-2.0	-12.1	6.4	3.9
2004/05	0.0	-8.4	0.4	-4.0	0.4	-12.0
2005/06	2.0	17.3	5.1	27.3	7.2	49.4
2006/07	0.6	3.0	5.8	17.2	6.5	20.8
2007/08	-3.2	0.9	7.4	27.4	3.9	28.5
2008/09	8.0	43.8	9.2	30.6	17.9	87.8
2009/10	2.4	6.3	6.8	4.8	9.4	11.3
2010/11	6.7	15.0	4.0	-1.6	11.0	13.1
2011/12	5.4	1.2	4.1	-16.0	9.7	-15.0
2012/13	7.8	3.9	8.2	-16.8	16.6	-13.6
2013/14	2.2	1.2	2.2	2.6	4.4	3.8
2014/15	-1.5	-14.2	1.3	5.3	-0.3	-9.7
2015/16	-3.2	-3.4	7.5	76.3	4.1	70.2
2016/17	4.0	7.2	5.6	-10.8	9.8	-4.4
2017/18	6.4	24.3	-6.0	-11.5	0.0	9.9
2018/19	-7.5	-7.4	11.9	-2.6	3.5	-9.8
2019/20	3.6	9.7	-13.6	12.7	-10.5	23.6
Avg.	2.4 %	6.5 %	3.7 %	6.4 %	62 %	13.2 %
Fq > 0	77 %	74 %	74 %	55 %	81 %	68 %

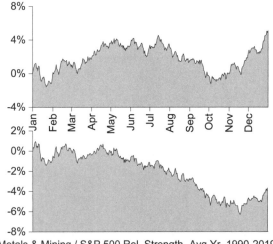

Metals & Mining - Avg. Year 1990 to 2019

Metals & Mining / S&P 500 Rel. Strength- Avg Yr. 1990-2019

Metals & Mining Performance

Metals & Mining Monthly % Gain (1990-2019)

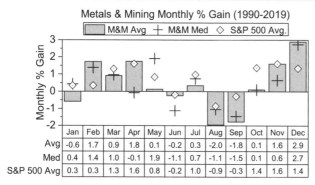

	Jan	Feb	Mar	Apr	May	Jun	Jul	Aug	Sep	Oct	Nov	Dec
Avg	-0.6	1.7	0.9	1.8	0.1	-0.2	0.3	-2.0	-1.8	0.1	1.6	2.9
Med	0.4	1.4	1.0	-0.1	1.9	-1.1	0.7	-1.1	-1.5	0.1	0.6	2.7
S&P 500 Avg	0.3	0.3	1.3	1.6	0.8	-0.2	1.0	-0.9	-0.3	1.4	1.6	1.4

Fq % Metals & Mining Gain > 0% (1990-2019)

	Jan	Feb	Mar	Apr	May	Jun	Jul	Aug	Sep	Oct	Nov	Dec
Fq %>0	57	63	57	50	53	37	57	47	40	53	60	53

Fq % Metals & Mining Gain > S&P 500 % (1990-2019)

	Jan	Feb	Mar	Apr	May	Jun	Jul	Aug	Sep	Oct	Nov	Dec
Fq %> S&P 500	43	53	40	40	43	53	47	43	40	37	50	57

Metals & Mining % Gain 5 Year (2015-2019)

Metals & Mining Performance 2019-2020

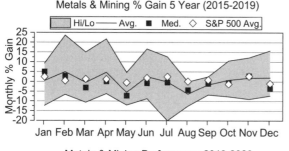

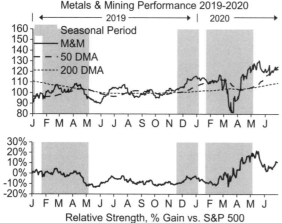

Relative Strength, % Gain vs. S&P 500

Market Indices & Rates
Weekly Values**

Stock Markets	2018	2019
Dow	24,286	27,876
S&P500	2,633	3,110
Nasdaq	6,939	8,520
TSX	15,011	16,955
FTSE	6,953	7,327
DAX	11,193	13,164
Nikkei	21,647	23,113
Hang Seng	25,928	26,595

Commodities	2018	2019
Oil	50.22	57.70
Gold	1223.7	1464.5

Bond Yields	2018	2019
USA 5 Yr Treasury	2.88	1.62
USA 10 Yr T	3.05	1.77
USA 20 Yr T	3.21	2.08
Moody's Aaa	4.18	3.03
Moody's Baa	5.23	3.91
CAN 5 Yr T	2.29	1.50
CAN 10 Yr T	2.34	1.47

Money Market	2018	2019
USA Fed Funds	2.25	1.75
USA 3 Mo T-B	2.36	1.55
CAN tgt overnight rate	1.75	1.75
CAN 3 Mo T-B	1.69	1.66

Foreign Exchange	2018	2019
EUR/USD	1.13	1.10
GBP/USD	1.28	1.28
USD/CAD	1.32	1.33
USD/JPY	112.96	108.66

NOVEMBER

M	T	W	T	F	S	S
1	2	3	4	5	6	7
8	9	10	11	12	13	14
15	16	17	18	19	20	21
22	23	24	25	26	27	28
29	30					

DECEMBER

M	T	W	T	F	S	S
		1	2	3	4	5
6	7	8	9	10	11	12
13	14	15	16	17	18	19
20	21	22	23	24	25	26
27	28	29	30	31		

JANUARY

M	T	W	T	F	S	S
					1	2
3	4	5	6	7	8	9
10	11	12	13	14	15	16
17	18	19	20	21	22	23
24	25	26	27	28	29	30
31						

UPS – DELIVERING RETURNS

UPS
① LONG (Oct10-Dec8)
② SELL SHORT (Dec9-Mar1)

In recent years, Amazon has shown an increasing interest in delivering its own packages, rather than using package delivery companies. Although this trend is expected to continue, consideration should still be given to investing in UPS in its seasonal period before Christmas, as this is when UPS would still be expected to outperform the S&P 500.

Investors look for an activity that could drive a stock price higher. In UPS' case investors typically become more interested in the stock just before the holiday season. The logic is that a busy time of year will help increase earnings, which should raise the stock price.

13% growth & positive 75% of the time

The best time to get into UPS is before most investors become excited about the stock. When maximum investor interest for the stock occurs, it has been best to exit.

"Get in before everyone else and exit once everyone is in." In other words, the seasonal trend takes advantage of human behavioral tendencies.

Investors typically do not want to invest in UPS at the times of the year when its stock price lacks a near-term catalyst. January and February are low activity months for UPS. As a result, investors tend to reduce their buying of package delivery companies at the end of the year and into the beginning of March.

Covid-19 Pandemic Update. UPS initially performed very well when the economy was shutting down and

ⓘ *UPS trades on the NYSE, adjusted for splits.*

UPS* vs. S&P 500 2000/01 to 2019/20

Positive Long ▢ Negative Short ▢

Year	Oct 10 to Dec 8 S&P 500	UPS	Dec 9 to Mar 1 S&P 500	UPS	Compound Growth S&P 500	UPS
2000/01	-2.3 %	12.0 %	-9.4 %	-12.1 %	-11.5 %	25.5 %
2001/02	9.6	12.1	-2.3	3.3	7.1	8.5
2002/03	17.4	6.5	-7.8	-10.2	8.3	17.4
2003/04	2.9	11.1	8.1	-4.9	11.3	16.5
2004/05	5.4	14.5	2.3	-11.0	7.9	27.1
2005/06	5.0	9.6	2.8	0.4	8.0	9.2
2006/07	4.4	5.6	-0.5	-10.2	3.9	16.3
2007/08	-3.9	-3.5	-11.6	-5.3	-15.0	1.6
2008/09	0.0	10.6	-19.2	-29.8	-19.2	43.5
2009/10	1.9	3.2	2.2	1.9	4.1	1.2
2010/11	5.4	6.6	6.4	0.5	12.1	6.1
2011/12	6.8	8.7	11.3	6.8	18.9	1.3
2012/13	-1.6	0.2	7.1	13.3	5.3	-13.1
2013/14	9.0	15.5	3.0	-6.5	12.3	23.0
2014/15	6.9	14.2	2.1	-7.7	9.1	22.9
2015/16	2.4	-2.4	-4.1	-2.8	-1.8	0.3
2016/17	4.3	9.4	6.7	-10.2	11.2	20.5
2017/18	4.2	2.1	1.0	-11.0	5.2	13.3
2018/19	-8.6	-10.7	6.5	6.5	-2.7	-16.5
2019/20	7.8	3.2	-6.1	-23.0	1.2	27.0
Avg.	3.9 %	6.4 %	-0.1 %	-5.6 %	3.8 %	12.6 %
Fq>0	75 %	85 %	60 %	35 %	75 %	75 %

more people were at home ordering on-line. In mid-March into April, UPS underperformed the S&P 500. At the beginning of May, once again UPS started to outperform as investors realized that the work-from-home and shop-from-home trends were more persistent than previously anticipated.

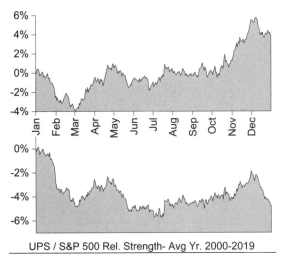

UPS - Avg. Year 2000 to 2019

UPS / S&P 500 Rel. Strength- Avg Yr. 2000-2019

- 141 -

UPS Strategy Performance

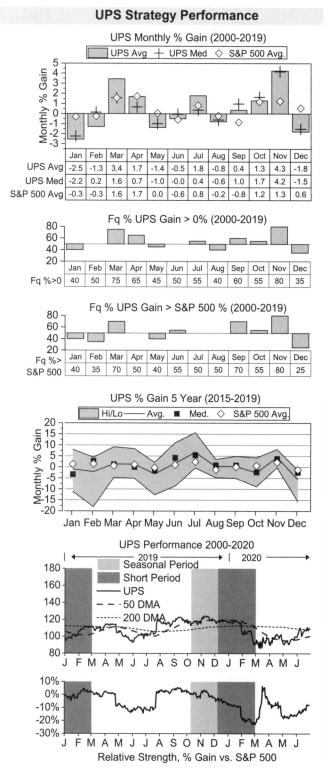

UPS Monthly % Gain (2000-2019)

Legend: UPS Avg | + UPS Med | ◇ S&P 500 Avg.

	Jan	Feb	Mar	Apr	May	Jun	Jul	Aug	Sep	Oct	Nov	Dec
UPS Avg	-2.5	-1.3	3.4	1.7	-1.4	-0.5	1.8	-0.8	0.4	1.3	4.3	-1.8
UPS Med	-2.2	0.2	1.6	0.7	-1.0	-0.0	0.4	-0.6	1.0	1.7	4.2	-1.5
S&P 500 Avg	-0.3	-0.3	1.6	1.7	0.0	-0.6	0.8	-0.2	-0.8	1.2	1.3	0.6

Fq % UPS Gain > 0% (2000-2019)

	Jan	Feb	Mar	Apr	May	Jun	Jul	Aug	Sep	Oct	Nov	Dec
Fq %>0	40	50	75	65	45	50	55	40	60	55	80	35

Fq % UPS Gain > S&P 500 % (2000-2019)

	Jan	Feb	Mar	Apr	May	Jun	Jul	Aug	Sep	Oct	Nov	Dec
Fq %> S&P 500	40	35	70	50	40	55	50	50	70	55	80	25

UPS % Gain 5 Year (2015-2019)

Legend: Hi/Lo — Avg. | ■ Med. | ◇ S&P 500 Avg.

UPS Performance 2000-2020

Legend: Seasonal Period | Short Period | UPS | – – 50 DMA | ···· 200 DMA

Relative Strength, % Gain vs. S&P 500

Market Indices & Rates
Weekly Values**

Stock Markets	2018	2019
Dow	25,538	28,051
S&P500	2,760	3,141
Nasdaq	7,331	8,665
TSX	15,198	17,040
FTSE	6,980	7,347
DAX	11,257	13,236
Nikkei	22,351	23,294
Hang Seng	26,507	26,346

Commodities	2018	2019
Oil	50.93	55.17
Gold	1217.6	1460.2

Bond Yields	2018	2019
USA 5 Yr Treasury	2.84	1.62
USA 10 Yr T	3.01	1.78
USA 20 Yr T	3.19	2.07
Moody's Aaa	4.22	2.95
Moody's Baa	5.28	3.86
CAN 5 Yr T	2.20	1.49
CAN 10 Yr T	2.27	1.46

Money Market	2018	2019
USA Fed Funds	2.25	1.75
USA 3 Mo T-B	2.32	1.56
CAN tgt overnight rate	1.75	1.75
CAN 3 Mo T-B	1.70	1.65

Foreign Exchange	2018	2019
EUR/USD	1.13	1.10
GBP/USD	1.27	1.29
USD/CAD	1.33	1.33
USD/JPY	113.57	109.49

NOVEMBER

M	T	W	T	F	S	S
1	2	3	4	5	6	7
8	9	10	11	12	13	14
15	16	17	18	19	20	21
22	23	24	25	26	27	28
29	30					

DECEMBER

M	T	W	T	F	S	S
		1	2	3	4	5
6	7	8	9	10	11	12
13	14	15	16	17	18	19
20	21	22	23	24	25	26
27	28	29	30	31		

JANUARY

M	T	W	T	F	S	S
					1	2
3	4	5	6	7	8	9
10	11	12	13	14	15	16
17	18	19	20	21	22	23
24	25	26	27	28	29	30
31						

DECEMBER

	MONDAY	TUESDAY	WEDNESDAY
WEEK 48	29	30 30	1 30
WEEK 49	6 25	7 24	8 23
WEEK 50	13 18	14 17	15 16
WEEK 51	20 11	22 10	22 9
WEEK 52	27 4 CAN Market Closed-Christmas Day USA Market Closed-Christmas Day	28 3 CAN Market Closed-Boxing Day	29 2

THURSDAY		FRIDAY	
2	29	**3**	28
9	22	**10**	21
16	15	**17**	14
23	8	**24**	7
30	1	**31**	

JANUARY

M	T	W	T	F	S	S
					1	2
3	4	5	6	7	8	9
10	11	12	13	14	15	16
17	18	19	20	21	22	23
24	25	26	27	28	29	30
31						

FEBRUARY

M	T	W	T	F	S	S
	1	2	3	4	5	6
7	8	9	10	11	12	13
14	15	16	17	18	19	20
21	22	23	24	25	26	27
28						

MARCH

M	T	W	T	F	S	S
	1	2	3	4	5	6
7	8	9	10	11	12	13
14	15	16	17	18	19	20
21	22	23	24	25	26	27
28	29	30	31			

APRIL

M	T	W	T	F	S	S
				1	2	3
4	5	6	7	8	9	10
11	12	13	14	15	16	17
18	19	20	21	22	23	24
25	26	27	28	29	30	

DECEMBER SUMMARY

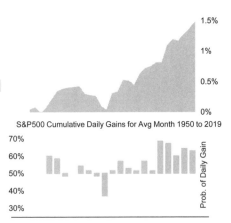

S&P500 Cumulative Daily Gains for Avg Month 1950 to 2019

	Dow Jones	S&P 500	Nasdaq	TSX Comp
Month Rank	3	2	3	1
# Up	49	52	28	29
# Down	21	18	20	6
% Pos	70	74	58	83
% Avg. Gain	1.5	1.5	1.4	1.7

Dow & S&P 1950-2019, Nasdaq 1972-2019 TSX 1985-2019

Prob. of Daily Gain

♦ December is typically one of the strongest months of the year for the S&P 500. From 1950 to 2019, the S&P 500 produced an average gain of 1.5% and was positive 74% of the time. ♦ Most of the gains for the S&P 500 tend to occur in the second half of the month. ♦ The Nasdaq tends to outperform the S&P 500 starting mid-December. ♦ The small cap sector typically starts to outperform the S&P 500 mid-month. ♦ In 2019, the S&P 500 rallied strongly for most of December.

BEST / WORST DECEMBER BROAD MKTS. 2010-2019

BEST DECEMBER MARKETS
- ♦ Nikkei 225 (2012) 10.0%
- ♦ Russell 2000 (2010) 7.8%
- ♦ FTSE 100 (2010) 6.7%

WORST DECEMBER MARKETS
- ♦ Russell 2000 (2018) -12.0%
- ♦ Nikkei 225 (2018) -10.5%
- ♦ Nasdaq (2018) -9.5%

Index Values End of Month

	2010	2011	2012	2013	2014	2015	2016	2017	2018	2019
Dow	11,578	12,218	13,104	16,577	17,823	17,425	19,763	24,719	23,327	28,538
S&P 500	1,258	1,258	1,426	1,848	2,059	2,044	2,239	2,674	2,507	3,231
Nasdaq	2,653	2,605	3,020	4,177	4,736	5,007	5,383	6,903	6,635	8,973
TSX Comp.	13,443	11,955	12,434	13,622	14,632	13,010	15,288	16,209	14,323	17,063
Russell 1000	697	693	790	1,030	1,144	1,132	1,242	1,482	1,384	1,784
Russell 2000	784	741	849	1,164	1,205	1,136	1,357	1,536	1,349	1,668
FTSE 100	5,900	5,572	5,898	6,749	6,566	6,242	7,143	7,688	6,728	7,542
Nikkei 225	10,229	8,455	10,395	16,291	17,451	19,034	19,114	22,765	20,015	23,657

Percent Gain for December

	2010	2011	2012	2013	2014	2015	2016	2017	2018	2019
Dow	5.2	1.4	0.6	3.0	0.0	-1.7	3.3	1.8	-8.7	1.7
S&P 500	6.5	0.9	0.7	2.4	-0.4	-1.8	1.8	1.0	-9.2	2.9
Nasdaq	6.2	-0.6	0.3	2.9	-1.2	-2.0	1.1	0.4	-9.5	3.5
TSX Comp.	3.8	-2.0	1.6	1.7	-0.8	-3.4	1.4	0.9	-5.8	0.1
Russell 1000	6.5	0.7	0.8	2.5	-0.4	-2.0	1.7	1.0	-9.3	2.7
Russell 2000	7.8	0.5	3.3	1.8	2.7	-5.2	2.6	-0.6	-12.0	2.7
FTSE 100	6.7	1.2	0.5	1.5	-2.3	-1.8	5.3	4.9	-3.6	2.7
Nikkei 225	2.9	0.2	10.0	4.0	-0.1	-3.6	4.4	0.2	-10.5	1.6

December Market Avg. Performance 2010 to 2019[(1)]

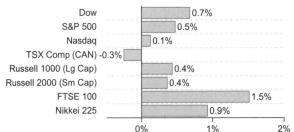

- Dow 0.7%
- S&P 500 0.5%
- Nasdaq 0.1%
- TSX Comp (CAN) -0.3%
- Russell 1000 (Lg Cap) 0.4%
- Russell 2000 (Sm Cap) 0.4%
- FTSE 100 1.5%
- Nikkei 225 0.9%

Interest Corner Dec[(2)]

	Fed Funds %[(3)]	3 Mo. T-Bill %[(4)]	10 Yr %[(5)]	20 Yr %[(6)]
2019	1.75	1.55	1.92	2.25
2018	2.50	2.45	2.69	2.87
2017	1.50	1.01	2.40	2.58
2016	0.75	0.51	2.45	2.79
2015	0.50	0.16	2.27	2.67

(1) Russell Data provided by Russell (2) Federal Reserve Bank of St. Louis- end of month values (3) Target rate set by FOMC (4)(5)(6) Constant yield maturities.

December 2019
% Sector Performance

S&P GIC	2019	1990-2019[1]	
Sectors	% Gain	GIC[2] % Avg Gain	Fq% Gain >S&P 500
Utilities	3.1 %	2.0 %	57 %
Industrials	-0.2	1.9	60
Materials	2.8	1.8	47
Telecom	1.9	1.8	57
Financials	2.5	1.8	57
Consumer Discretionary	2.7	1.4	50
Health Care	3.4	1.2	50
Consumer Staples	2.0	1.2	43
Energy	5.8	1.1	43
Information Technology	4.4 %	0.5 %	37 %
S&P 500	2.9 %	1.4 %	N/A %

Sector Commentary

♦ In December 2019, all of the major sectors were positive except the industrial sector. ♦ The strongest performing sector was the energy sector with a gain of 5.8%. Typically, the energy sector is one of the weaker sectors in December. ♦ The information technology sector also performed well with a gain of 2.9%. ♦ The utilities sector has been the strongest performing sector since 1990. In December, the utilities sector produced a gain of 3.1%.

Sub-Sector Commentary

♦ In December 2019, the metals and mining sub-sector produced a gain of 10.2%, which was much stronger than the gain for the S&P 500. ♦ The semi-conductor sector performed well with a gain of 7.7%. ♦ The homebuilders sub-sector has on average been one of the better performing sub-sectors in December. ♦ In 2019, the homebuilders sector performed poorly in December, producing a loss of 3.6%.

SELECTED SUB-SECTORS[3]			
Homebuilders	-3.6 %	6.2 %	77 %
Steel	-0.1	3.9	60
Metals & Mining	10.2	2.9	57
Biotech (1993-2019)	-0.2	2.9	46
Agriculture (1994-2019)	8.0	1.9	54
Banks	4.0	1.6	60
Chemicals	2.1	1.5	53
Silver	6.4	1.4	50
Pharma	6.2	1.1	47
Railroads	1.7	1.0	47
SOX (1995-2019)	7.7	0.9	48
Retail	2.0	0.7	37
Automotive & Components	2.0	0.6	33
Transportation	-0.2	0.5	37
Gold	3.7	0.2	37

EMERGING MARKETS (USD) – TRUNCATED SIX MONTH SEASONAL
November 24 to April 18

Emerging markets become popular periodically, mainly after they have had a strong run, or if they have suffered a major correction and investors perceive them as having a lot of value.

Markets around the world tend to have the same broad seasonal trends, including emerging markets.

Emerging markets outperform the S&P 500 more often, when the S&P 500 is increasing, and underperform when the S&P 500 is decreasing. Given that the S&P 500 has a higher probability of increasing in the favorable six-month period for stocks, from October 27 to May 5h, emerging markets will have a higher probability of outperforming the S&P 500 sometime within the six-month favorable for stocks.

4% gain & positive 68% of the time positive

Seasonal investors have benefited from concentrating their emerging market exposure in a truncated, or shorter time period within the favorable six month seasonal period. The seasonally strong period for the emerging markets sector is from November 24 to April 18.

Emerging Markets (USD)* vs. S&P 500
1989/90 to 2019/20

Nov 24 to Apr 18	S&P 500	Positive Em. Mkts.	Diff
1989/90	-0.4%	4.5	4.9%
1990/91	23.8	33.8%	10.5
1991/92	10.6	37.5	26.8
1992/93	5.6	11.8	6.2
1993/94	-4.0	3.7	7.8
1994/95	12.3	-16.4	-28.7
1995/96	7.6	14.7	7.1
1996/97	2.4	7.1	4.7
1997/98	16.6	6.7	-9.9
1998/99	11.0	18.1	7.1
1999/00	2.6	3.5	0.8
2000/01	-6.4	-4.6	1.8
2001/02	-2.3	22.3	24.5
2002/03	-4.0	0.0	4.0
2003/04	9.6	19.5	9.9
2004/05	-2.6	4.3	7.0
2005/06	3.3	24.7	21.4
2006/07	4.7	13.2	8.5
2007/08	-3.5	-0.9	2.6
2008/09	8.7	37.6	28.9
2009/10	7.8	5.6	-2.2
2010/11	10.5'	6.6	-3.9
2011/12	19.2	15.6	-3.6
2012/13	9.4	0.1	-9.3
2013/14	3.3	0.3	-3.1
2014/15	0.9	3.8	3.0
2015/16	0.4	0.3	-0.1
2016/17	6.2	11.9	5.7
2017/18	4.3	2.1	-2.2
2018/19	10.4	12.7	2.4
2019/20	-7.6	-14.0	-6.4
Avg	5.2%	9.3%	4.1%
Fq > 0	74%	84%	68%

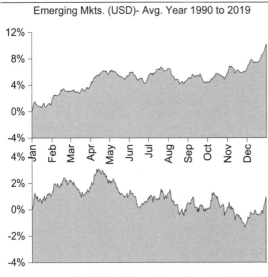

Emerging Mkts. (USD)- Avg. Year 1990 to 2019

Emerg. Mkts. (USD)/S&P 500 Rel. Str. - Avg Yr. 1990-2019

Covid-19 Performance Update. As the Covid-19 pandemic started in February 2020, investors preferred to invest in developed markets. As a result, emerging markets underperformed the S&P 500, even after the stock market bottomed in March. Emerging markets continued to underperform up until the end of May. At that time, the emerging markets started to outperform the S&P 500, but only moderately.

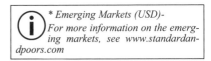

* Emerging Markets (USD)-
For more information on the emerging markets, see www.standardandpoors.com

- 147 -

Emerging Markets Performance

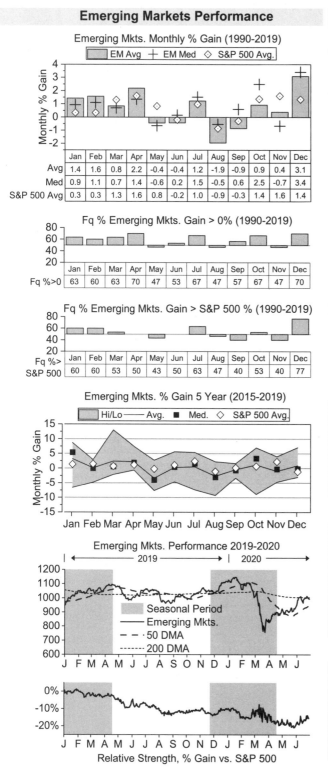

Emerging Mkts. Monthly % Gain (1990-2019)

Legend: EM Avg + EM Med ◇ S&P 500 Avg.

	Jan	Feb	Mar	Apr	May	Jun	Jul	Aug	Sep	Oct	Nov	Dec
Avg	1.4	1.6	0.8	2.2	-0.4	-0.4	1.2	-1.9	-0.9	0.9	0.4	3.1
Med	0.9	1.1	0.7	1.4	-0.6	0.2	1.5	-0.5	0.6	2.5	-0.7	3.4
S&P 500 Avg	0.3	0.3	1.3	1.6	0.8	-0.2	1.0	-0.9	-0.3	1.4	1.6	1.4

Fq % Emerging Mkts. Gain > 0% (1990-2019)

	Jan	Feb	Mar	Apr	May	Jun	Jul	Aug	Sep	Oct	Nov	Dec
Fq %>0	63	60	63	70	47	53	67	47	57	67	47	70

Fq % Emerging Mkts. Gain > S&P 500 % (1990-2019)

	Jan	Feb	Mar	Apr	May	Jun	Jul	Aug	Sep	Oct	Nov	Dec
Fq %> S&P 500	60	60	53	50	43	50	63	47	40	53	40	77

Emerging Mkts. % Gain 5 Year (2015-2019)

Legend: Hi/Lo — Avg. ■ Med. ◇ S&P 500 Avg.

Emerging Mkts. Performance 2019-2020

2019 → 2020

Seasonal Period
— Emerging Mkts.
– – 50 DMA
······ 200 DMA

Relative Strength, % Gain vs. S&P 500

Market Indices & Rates
Weekly Values**

Stock Markets	2018	2019
Dow	24,389	28,015
S&P500	2,633	3,146
Nasdaq	6,969	8,657
TSX	14,795	16,997
FTSE	6,778	7,240
DAX	10,788	13,167
Nikkei	21,679	23,354
Hang Seng	26,064	26,498

Commodities	2018	2019
Oil	52.61	59.20
Gold	1243.3	1459.7

Bond Yields	2018	
USA 5 Yr Treasury	2.70	1.67
USA 10 Yr T	2.85	1.84
USA 20 Yr T	3.01	2.14
Moody's Aaa	4.06	3.03
Moody's Baa	5.16	3.91
CAN 5 Yr T	2.01	1.59
CAN 10 Yr T	2.07	1.58

Money Market	2018	2019
USA Fed Funds	2.25	1.75
USA 3 Mo T-B	2.35	1.50
CAN tgt overnight rate	1.75	1.75
CAN 3 Mo T-B	1.63	1.65

Foreign Exchange	2018	2019
EUR/USD	1.14	1.11
GBP/USD	1.27	1.31
USD/CAD	1.33	1.33
USD/JPY	112.69	108.58

DECEMBER

M	T	W	T	F	S	S
		1	2	3	4	5
6	7	8	9	10	11	12
13	14	15	16	17	18	19
20	21	22	23	24	25	26
27	28	29	30	31		

JANUARY

M	T	W	T	F	S	S
					1	2
3	4	5	6	7	8	9
10	11	12	13	14	15	16
17	18	19	20	21	22	23
24	25	26	27	28	29	30
31						

FEBRUARY

M	T	W	T	F	S	S
	1	2	3	4	5	6
7	8	9	10	11	12	13
14	15	16	17	18	19	20
21	22	23	24	25	26	27
28						

B/E 10-YR INFLATION BREAK-EVEN (B/E) RATE
December 20th to Mar 7th

10-YR Inflation Break-Even (B/E) rate

The 10YR inflation break-even rate is representative of investors' expectations for inflation over the next ten years. It is approximately calculated by subtracting the yield on the 10 Year Treasury Inflation Protected bonds (TIPS) from the yield on 10 Year US Treasury 10 bonds.

The mantra that is inflation is dead has been prevalent in the bull market that started after the Great Financial Crash (GFC). There are undoubtedly reasons why there is downward pressure on inflation, including aging demographics and increasing productivity from computerization, but inflation is not dead.

5% increase & positive 82% of the time

There will be a time when inflation once again makes a comeback. It could be stoked by too much money printing trying to stimulate the economy or rising supply costs. The point is that at some point it will be a problem again.

Since the GFC, as inflation expectations have remained subdued, investors have on average adjusted their expectations upwards for inflation towards the end of the year and into early March of the following year. The most probably cause of this phenomenon is investors adjusting their expectations based upon overly optimistic full year analyst forecasts that generally get published at the end of the year and the beginning of the next year.

10 YR Inflation Break-Even* 2003/04 to 2019/20		
Positive		
Dec 20 to Mar 7	B/E	
2003/04	8.6	%
2004/05	4.3	
2005/06	10.3	
2006/07	2.2	
2007/08	9.4	
2008/09	440.0*	
2009/10	-1.3	
2010/11	10.1	
2011/12	13.4	
2012/13	3.2	
2013/14	3.7	
2014/15	8.9	
2015/16	1.4	
2016/17	9.1	
2017/18	11.5	
2018/19	5.6	
2019/20	-26.0	
Avg	5.1*	%
Fq > 0	82*	%

*2008/09 data has been excluded from average and frequency % positive data.

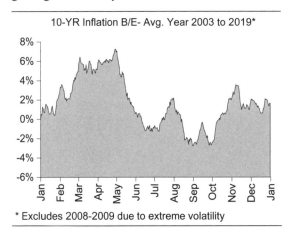

10-YR Inflation B/E- Avg. Year 2003 to 2019*

* Excludes 2008-2009 due to extreme volatility

At the retail level, one of the better methods of taking advantage of the 10YR-B/E strategy is to invest in an ETF that invests in Treasury Inflation Protected TIPS bonds and to short sell an ETF that represents the US 10YR Government bonds of the same maturity. It is important to consider the full risk of the trade, including all of the costs that go along with short selling.

Although most investors will probably not invest directly in a B/E spread trade, investors can still benefit from understanding the impact of investing in other sectors of the stock and bond markets that are affected by changing inflation expectations.

Covid-19 Performance Update. The Break-Even rate dropped sharply in late February and March 2020 as the Covid-19 pandemic caused forced shut downs of economies. As demand destruction took place, inflation expectations fell, causing the Break-Even rate to decline.

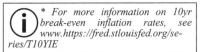
For more information on 10yr break-even inflation rates, see www.https://fred.stlouisfed.org/series/T10YIE

10YR Inflation Break-Even Performance

Market Indices & Rates
Weekly Values**

10YR Inflation Break-Even (BE) Monthly % Gain (2003-2019)*

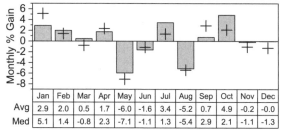

	Jan	Feb	Mar	Apr	May	Jun	Jul	Aug	Sep	Oct	Nov	Dec
Avg	2.9	2.0	0.5	1.7	-6.0	-1.6	3.4	-5.2	0.7	4.9	-0.2	-0.0
Med	5.1	1.4	-0.8	2.3	-7.1	-1.1	1.3	-5.4	2.9	2.1	-1.1	-1.3

Fq % 10YR Inflation Break-Even (BE) Gain > 0% (2003-2019)

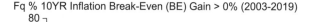

	Jan	Feb	Mar	Apr	May	Jun	Jul	Aug	Sep	Oct	Nov	Dec
Fq %>0	59	59	35	53	12	41	59	18	53	65	29	35

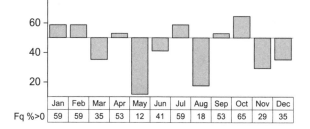

10YR Inflation Break-Even (BE) % Gain 5 Year (2003-2019)

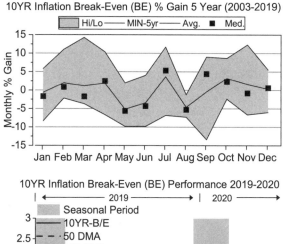

10YR Inflation Break-Even (BE) Performance 2019-2020

Stock Markets	2018	2019
Dow	24,101	28,135
S&P500	2,600	3,169
Nasdaq	6,911	8,735
TSX	14,595	17,003
FTSE	6,845	7,353
DAX	10,866	13,283
Nikkei	21,375	24,023
Hang Seng	26,095	27,688

Commodities	2018	2019
Oil	51.20	60.07
Gold	1235.4	1466.6

Bond Yields	2018	2019
USA 5 Yr Treasury	2.73	1.66
USA 10 Yr T	2.89	1.82
USA 20 Yr T	3.03	2.11
Moody's Aaa	4.02	2.97
Moody's Baa	5.14	3.84
CAN 5 Yr T	2.04	1.59
CAN 10 Yr T	2.10	1.58

Money Market	2018	2019
USA Fed Funds	2.25	1.75
USA 3 Mo T-B	2.37	1.54
CAN tgt overnight rate	1.75	1.75
CAN 3 Mo T-B	1.64	1.66

Foreign Exchange	2018	2019
EUR/USD	1.13	1.11
GBP/USD	1.26	1.33
USD/CAD	1.34	1.32
USD/JPY	113.39	109.38

DECEMBER

M	T	W	T	F	S	S
		1	2	3	4	5
6	7	8	9	10	11	12
13	14	15	16	17	18	19
20	21	22	23	24	25	26
27	28	29	30	31		

JANUARY

M	T	W	T	F	S	S
					1	2
3	4	5	6	7	8	9
10	11	12	13	14	15	16
17	18	19	20	21	22	23
24	25	26	27	28	29	30
31						

FEBRUARY

M	T	W	T	F	S	S
	1	2	3	4	5	6
7	8	9	10	11	12	13
14	15	16	17	18	19	20
21	22	23	24	25	26	27
28						

DO THE "NAZ" WITH SANTA
Nasdaq Gives More at Christmas – Dec 15th to Jan 23rd

One of the best times to invest in the major stock markets is the period around Christmas. The markets are generally positive at this time of the year as investors reposition their portfolios for the start of the new year. A lot of investors are familiar with the *Small Cap Effect* opportunity that starts approximately at this time of the year, where small caps tend to outperform from mid-December until the beginning of March (*see Small Cap Effect*), but few investors know that the last half of December and the first half of January is also a seasonally strong period for the Nasdaq.

82% of time better than S&P 500

The Nasdaq tends to perform well in the last two weeks of December, as investors typically increase their investment allocation to higher beta investments, including the Nasdaq, to finish the year.

In addition, the major sector drivers of the Nasdaq (biotech and technology), tend to perform well in the second half of December and the first half of January. Biotech tends to perform well in the last half of December, and technology tends to perform well in the first half of January. The end result is a Nasdaq Christmas trade that lasts from December 15 to January 23. In this time period, for the years 1971/72 to 2019/20, the Nasdaq has outperformed the S&P 500 by an average 2.0% per year. This rate of return is considered to be very high given that the length of the favorable period is just over one month. Even more impressive is the 81% frequency that the Nasdaq has outperformed the S&P 500.

Nasdaq vs. S&P 500 Dec 15th to Jan 23rd 1971/72 To 2019/20

Dec 15 to Jan 23	S&P 500	Positive Nasdaq	Diff
1971/72	6.1 %	7.5 %	1.3 %
1972/73	0.0	-0.7	-0.7
1973/74	4.1	6.8	2.8
1974/75	7.5	8.9	1.4
1975/76	13.0	13.8	0.9
1976/77	-1.7	2.8	4.5
1977/78	-5.1	-3.5	1.6
1978/79	4.7	6.2	1.4
1979/80	4.1	5.6	1.5
1980/81	0.8	3.3	2.5
1981/82	-6.0	-5.0	1.0
1982/83	4.7	5.5	0.8
1983/84	0.9	1.4	0.4
1984/85	9.0	13.3	4.3
1985/86	-2.7	0.8	3.5
1986/87	9.2	10.2	1.0
1987/88	1.8	9.1	7.3
1988/89	3.3	4.6	1.3
1989/90	-5.5	-3.8	1.7
1990/91	1.0	4.1	3.1
1991/92	7.9	15.2	7.2
1992/93	0.8	7.2	6.4
1993/94	2.5	5.7	3.2
1994/95	2.4	4.7	2.3
1995/96	-0.7	-1.0	-0.3
1996/97	6.7	7.3	0.6
1997/98	0.4	2.6	2.1
1998/99	7.4	18.9	11.6
1999/00	2.7	18.6	15.9
2000/01	1.5	4.1	2.6
2001/02	0.5	-1.6	-2.0
2002/03	-0.2	1.9	2.1
2003/04	6.3	9.0	2.7
2004/05	-3.0	-5.8	-2.9
2005/06	-0.7	-0.6	0.1
2006/07	0.2	-0.9	-1.1
2007/08	-8.8	-12.1	-3.3
2008/09	-5.4	-4.1	1.3
2009/10	-2.0	-0.3	1.7
2010/11	3.4	2.4	-1.0
2011/12	8.6	9.6	1.1
2012/13	5.8	6.1	0.4
2013/14	3.0	5.5	2.5
2014/15	2.5	2.2	-0.2
2015/16	-5.7	-7.3	-1.6
2016/17	0.5	2.1	1.6
2017/18	7.1	8.8	1.8
2018/19	1.5	1.7	0.2
2019/20	4.9	7.6	2.7
Avg	2.0 %	4.0 %	2.0 %
Fq > 0	71 %	73 %	82 %

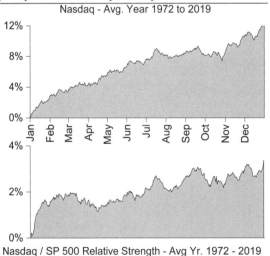

Nasdaq - Avg. Year 1972 to 2019

Nasdaq / SP 500 Relative Strength - Avg Yr. 1972 - 2019

> ⓨ *Alternate Strategy — For those investors who favor the Nasdaq, an alternative strategy is to invest in the Nasdaq at an earlier date: October 28th. Historically, on average the Nasdaq has started its outperformance at this time. The "Do the Naz with Santa" strategy focuses on the sweet spot of the Nasdaq's outperformance.*

Nasdaq Performance

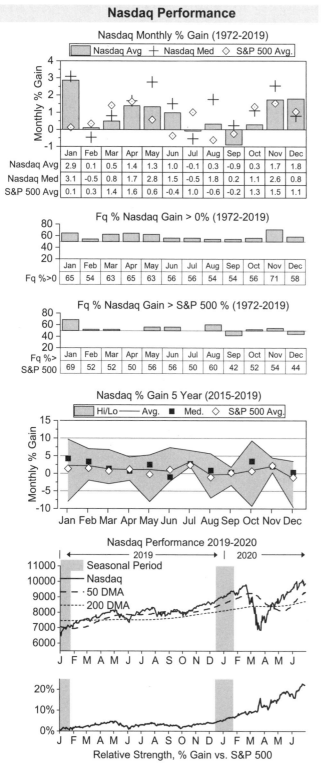

Nasdaq Monthly % Gain (1972-2019)

Legend: Nasdaq Avg | + Nasdaq Med | ◇ S&P 500 Avg.

	Jan	Feb	Mar	Apr	May	Jun	Jul	Aug	Sep	Oct	Nov	Dec
Nasdaq Avg	2.9	0.1	0.5	1.4	1.3	1.0	-0.1	0.3	-0.9	0.3	1.7	1.8
Nasdaq Med	3.1	-0.5	0.8	1.7	2.8	1.5	-0.5	1.8	0.2	1.1	2.6	0.8
S&P 500 Avg	0.1	0.3	1.4	1.6	0.6	-0.4	1.0	-0.6	-0.2	1.3	1.5	1.1

Fq % Nasdaq Gain > 0% (1972-2019)

	Jan	Feb	Mar	Apr	May	Jun	Jul	Aug	Sep	Oct	Nov	Dec
Fq %>0	65	54	63	65	63	56	56	54	54	56	71	58

Fq % Nasdaq Gain > S&P 500 % (1972-2019)

	Jan	Feb	Mar	Apr	May	Jun	Jul	Aug	Sep	Oct	Nov	Dec
Fq %> S&P 500	69	52	52	50	56	56	50	60	42	52	54	44

Nasdaq % Gain 5 Year (2015-2019)

Legend: Hi/Lo | Avg. | ■ Med. | ◇ S&P 500 Avg.

Nasdaq Performance 2019-2020

- Seasonal Period
- Nasdaq
- 50 DMA
- 200 DMA

Relative Strength, % Gain vs. S&P 500

WEEK 51

Market Indices & Rates
Weekly Values**

Stock Markets	2018	2019
Dow	22,445	28,455
S&P500	2,417	3,221
Nasdaq	6,333	8,925
TSX	13,935	17,118
FTSE	6,721	7,582
DAX	10,634	13,319
Nikkei	20,166	23,817
Hang Seng	25,753	27,871

Commodities	2018	2019
Oil	45.39	60.41
Gold	1258.2	1479.0

Bond Yields	2018	2019
USA 5 Yr Treasury	2.64	1.73
USA 10 Yr T	2.79	1.92
USA 20 Yr T	2.92	2.21
Moody's Aaa	3.97	3.01
Moody's Baa	5.10	3.88
CAN 5 Yr T	1.97	1.63
CAN 10 Yr T	2.03	1.62

Money Market	2018	2019
USA Fed Funds	2.50	1.75
USA 3 Mo T-B	2.34	1.55
CAN tgt overnight rate	1.75	1.75
CAN 3 Mo T-B	1.67	1.66

Foreign Exchange	2018	2019
EUR/USD	1.14	1.11
GBP/USD	1.26	1.30
USD/CAD	1.36	1.32
USD/JPY	111.22	109.44

DECEMBER

M	T	W	T	F	S	S
		1	2	3	4	5
6	7	8	9	10	11	12
13	14	15	16	17	18	19
20	21	22	23	24	25	26
27	28	29	30	31		

JANUARY

M	T	W	T	F	S	S
					1	2
3	4	5	6	7	8	9
10	11	12	13	14	15	16
17	18	19	20	21	22	23
24	25	26	27	28	29	30
31						

FEBRUARY

M	T	W	T	F	S	S
	1	2	3	4	5	6
7	8	9	10	11	12	13
14	15	16	17	18	19	20
21	22	23	24	25	26	27
28						

SMALL CAP (SMALL COMPANY) EFFECT
Small Companies Outperform - Dec 19 to Mar 7

At different stages of the business cycle, small capitalization companies (small caps represented by Russell 2000), perform better than large capitalization companies (large caps represented by Russell 1000).

Evidence shows that the small caps relative outperformance also has a seasonal component as they typically outperform large caps from December 19 to March 7.

3% extra and positive 76% of the time

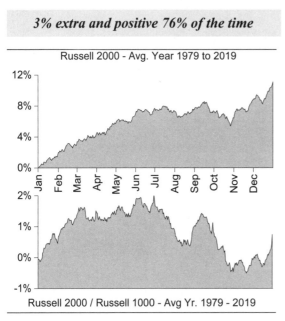

Russell 2000 - Avg. Year 1979 to 2019

Russell 2000 / Russell 1000 - Avg Yr. 1979 - 2019

In recent times, the January Effect start date has shifted to mid-December and is more pronounced for small caps as their prices are more volatile than large caps. At the beginning of the year, small cap stocks benefit from a phenomenon that I have coined, "beta out of the gate, and coast." If small cap stocks are outperforming at the beginning of the year, money managers will gravitate to the sector in order to produce returns that are above their index benchmark. Once above average returns have been "locked in," the managers then rotate from their small cap overweight positions back to index large cap positions and coast for the rest of the year with above average returns. The overall process boosts small cap stocks at the beginning of the year.

Russell 2000 vs. Russell 1000* % Gains
Dec 19th to Mar 7th 1979/80 to 2019/20

Positive ▢

Dec 19 - Mar7	Russell 1000	Russell 2000	Diff
1979/80	-1.3 %	-0.4 %	0.9 %
1980/81	-2.8	4.0	6.8
1981/82	-12.4	-12.1	0.3
1982/83	11.8	19.8	8.0
1983/84	-6.4	-7.5	-1.1
1984/85	7.7	17.1	9.4
1985/86	8.2	11.7	3.5
1986/87	17.2	21.3	4.1
1987/88	8.3	16.4	8.0
1988/89	6.9	9.1	2.5
1989/90	-2.0	-1.9	0.2
1990/91	14.6	29.0	14.4
1991/92	6.0	16.8	10.8
1992/93	1.4	5.0	3.5
1993/94	0.5	5.7	5.3
1994/95	5.3	5.5	0.2
1995/96	8.3	7.8	-0.5
1996/97	9.5	3.5	-6.0
1997/98	10.2	10.3	0.1
1998/99	7.3	0.2	-7.2
1999/00	-1.7	27.7	29.4
2000/01	-5.2	4.7	9.8
2001/02	1.6	1.9	0.4
2002/03	-6.7	-7.8	-1.0
2003/04	6.4	9.6	3.3
2004/05	2.8	0.3	-2.5
2005/06	0.8	5.6	4.7
2006/07	-1.6	-0.8	0.9
2007/08	-10.9	-12.5	-1.5
2008/09	-22.2	-26.7	-4.5
2009/10	3.6	9.1	5.5
2010/11	5.5	4.2	-1.3
2011/12	11.3	10.2	-1.1
2012/13	7.1	10.3	3.1
2013/14	4.2	6.1	2.0
2014/15	1.0	2.1	1.1
2015/16	-0.3	-2.4	-2.1
2016/17	4.8	0.8	-4.1
2017/18	1.5	1.7	0.2
2018/19	8.4	10.6	2.2
2019/20	-6.8	-12.8	-5.9
Avg.	2.5 %	5.0 %	2.5 %
Fq > 0	68 %	76 %	66 %

Covid-19 Pandemic Update. The small cap sector underperformed the S&P 500 in early 2020 and once the pandemic took place the underperformance accelerated. The seasonal period for the small cap sector ended in early March, in the early stages of the Covid-19 pandemic.

ⓘ *Russell 2000 (small cap index): The 2000 smallest companies in the Russell 3000 stock index (a broad market index). Russell 1000 (large cap index): The 1000 largest companies in the Russell 3000 stock index.*

Small Caps Performance

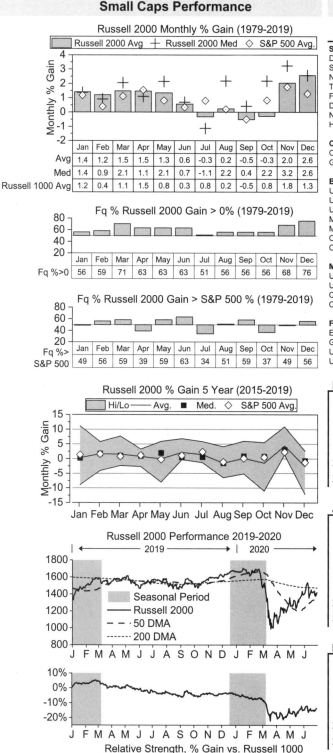

Russell 2000 Monthly % Gain (1979-2019)

Russell 2000 Avg + Russell 2000 Med ◇ S&P 500 Avg.

	Jan	Feb	Mar	Apr	May	Jun	Jul	Aug	Sep	Oct	Nov	Dec
Avg	1.4	1.2	1.5	1.5	1.3	0.6	-0.3	0.2	-0.5	-0.3	2.0	2.6
Med	1.4	0.9	2.1	1.1	2.1	0.7	-1.1	2.2	0.4	2.2	3.2	2.6
Russell 1000 Avg	1.2	0.4	1.1	1.5	0.8	0.3	0.8	0.2	-0.5	0.8	1.8	1.3

Fq % Russell 2000 Gain > 0% (1979-2019)

	Jan	Feb	Mar	Apr	May	Jun	Jul	Aug	Sep	Oct	Nov	Dec
Fq %>0	56	59	71	63	63	63	51	56	56	56	68	76

Fq % Russell 2000 Gain > S&P 500 % (1979-2019)

	Jan	Feb	Mar	Apr	May	Jun	Jul	Aug	Sep	Oct	Nov	Dec
Fq %> S&P 500	49	56	59	39	59	63	34	51	59	37	49	56

Russell 2000 % Gain 5 Year (2015-2019)

Hi/Lo — Avg. ■ Med. ◇ S&P 500 Avg.

Russell 2000 Performance 2019-2020

| ← 2019 → | | 2020 → |

Seasonal Period
— Russell 2000
– – 50 DMA
······ 200 DMA

Relative Strength, % Gain vs. Russell 1000

Market Indices & Rates
Weekly Values**

Stock Markets	2018	2019
Dow	23,062	28,645
S&P500	2,486	3,240
Nasdaq	6,585	9,007
TSX	14,222	17,168
FTSE	6,734	7,645
DAX	10,559	13,337
Nikkei	20,015	23,838
Hang Seng	25,504	28,225

Commodities	2018	2019
Oil	45.33	61.72
Gold	1279.0	1511.5

Bond Yields	2018	2019
USA 5 Yr Treasury	2.56	1.68
USA 10 Yr T	2.72	1.88
USA 20 Yr T	2.89	2.18
Moody's Aaa	4.02	2.98
Moody's Baa	5.16	3.84
CAN 5 Yr T	1.88	1.63
CAN 10 Yr T	1.95	1.60

Money Market	2018	2019
USA Fed Funds	2.50	1.75
USA 3 Mo T-B	2.35	1.54
CAN tgt overnight rate	1.75	1.75
CAN 3 Mo T-B	1.64	1.66

Foreign Exchange	2018	2019
EUR/USD	1.14	1.12
GBP/USD	1.27	1.31
USD/CAD	1.36	1.31
USD/JPY	110.27	109.44

DECEMBER

M	T	W	T	F	S	S
		1	2	3	4	5
6	7	8	9	10	11	12
13	14	15	16	17	18	19
20	21	22	23	24	25	26
27	28	29	30	31		

JANUARY

M	T	W	T	F	S	S
					1	2
3	4	5	6	7	8	9
10	11	12	13	14	15	16
17	18	19	20	21	22	23
24	25	26	27	28	29	30
31						

FEBRUARY

M	T	W	T	F	S	S
		1	2	3	4	5	6
7	8	9	10	11	12	13
14	15	16	17	18	19	20
21	22	23	24	25	26	27
28						

FINANCIALS (U.S.) YEAR END CLEAN UP
December 15th to April 13th

The main driver for the strong seasonal performance of the financial sector has been the year-end earnings of the banks that start to report in mid-January. A strong performance from mid-December has been the result of investors getting into the market early to take advantage of positive year-end earnings.

Extra 1.0% & 58% of the time better than the S&P 500

In 2014, 2015 and most of 2016, the U.S. financial sector performed "at market," producing approximately the same gain as the S&P 500. The sector strongly outperformed the stock market after Trump was elected, as investors expected to Trump to remove cumbersome financial regulations.

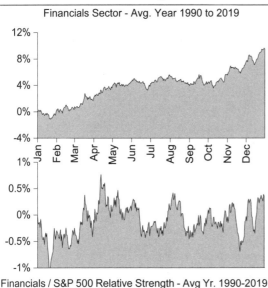

Financials Sector - Avg. Year 1990 to 2019

Financials / S&P 500 Relative Strength - Avg Yr. 1990-2019

Dec 15 to Apr 13	S&P 500	Positive Financials	Diff
1989/90	-1.9 %	-9.9 %	-8.0 %
1990/91	16.4	29.2	12.8
1991/92	5.6	9.2	3.5
1992/93	3.8	17.9	14.1
1993/94	-3.6	-0.4	3.2
1994/95	11.9	14.0	2.1
1995/96	3.2	5.5	2.3
1996/97	1.2	4.7	3.4
19/9798	16.4	19.7	3.3
1998/99	18.3	24.9	6.6
1999/00	2.7	4.0	1.3
2000/01	-11.7	-4.8	6.9
2001/02	-1.1	6.5	7.6
2002/03	-2.4	-1.8	0.6
2003/04	5.2	6.7	1.5
2004/05	-2.5	-6.2	-3.7
2005/06	1.3	1.1	-0.2
2006/07	1.9	-2.2	-4.1
2007/08	-9.2	-14.1	-4.9
2008/09	-2.4	-7.0	-4.6
2009/10	7.5	15.2	7.8
2010/11	5.9	4.6	-1.3
2011/12	13.1	20.7	7.7
2012/13	12.4	16.0	3.6
2013/14	2.3	1.0	-1.3
2014/15	4.5	1.1	-3.4
2015/16	3.0	-2.0	-5.0
2016/17	3.4	-2.0	-5.4
2017/18	0.2	-0.6	-0.7
2018/19	11.8	12.5	0.6
2019/20	-12.8	-26.2	-13.4
Avg.	3.4 %	4.4 %	1.1 %
Fq > 0	71 %	61 %	58 %

Covid-19 Performance Update. The financial sector was underperforming the S&P 500 when the Covid-19 pandemic started in 2020. The sector continued to underperform as the stock market declined in February and March as the Federal Reserve cut interest rates, hurting bank profits. The sector continued to underperform after the bottom of the stock market bottom in March.

Overall, in 2018, 2019 and 2020, the financial sector has underperformed the stock market, as US banks have been suffering from diminishing returns from lower interest rates. Generally, low interest rates decrease the banks net interest margin and profits.

Nevertheless, seasonal investors would be wise to consider concentrating their financial investments during the sector's strong seasonal period that lasts from mid-December to mid-April.

It should be noted that Canadian banks have different year-ends and different seasonal periods.

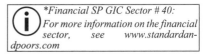

*Financial SP GIC Sector # 40:
For more information on the financial sector, see www.standardandpoors.com

Financials Performance

Financials Monthly % Gain (1990-2019)

Legend: Financials Avg + Financials Med ◇ S&P 500 Avg.

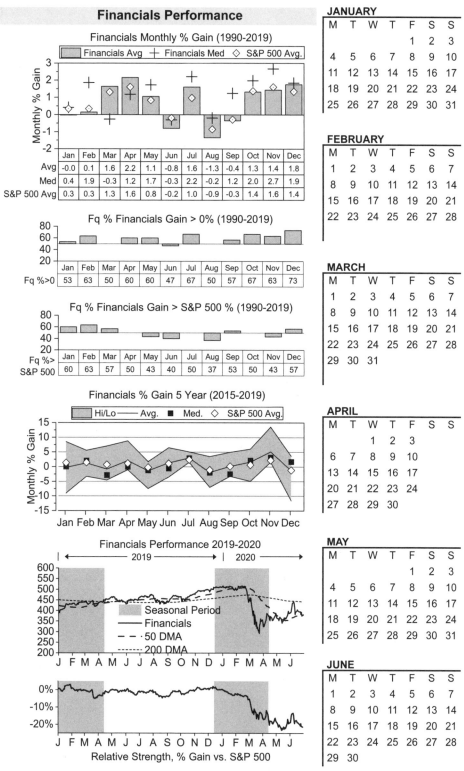

	Jan	Feb	Mar	Apr	May	Jun	Jul	Aug	Sep	Oct	Nov	Dec
Avg	-0.0	0.1	1.6	2.2	1.1	-0.8	1.6	-1.3	-0.4	1.3	1.4	1.8
Med	0.4	1.9	-0.3	1.2	1.7	-0.3	2.2	-0.2	1.2	2.0	2.7	1.9
S&P 500 Avg	0.3	0.3	1.3	1.6	0.8	-0.2	1.0	-0.9	-0.3	1.4	1.6	1.4

Fq % Financials Gain > 0% (1990-2019)

	Jan	Feb	Mar	Apr	May	Jun	Jul	Aug	Sep	Oct	Nov	Dec
Fq %>0	53	63	50	60	60	47	67	50	57	67	63	73

Fq % Financials Gain > S&P 500 % (1990-2019)

	Jan	Feb	Mar	Apr	May	Jun	Jul	Aug	Sep	Oct	Nov	Dec
Fq %> S&P 500	60	63	57	50	43	40	50	37	53	50	43	57

Financials % Gain 5 Year (2015-2019)

Legend: Hi/Lo — Avg. ■ Med. ◇ S&P 500 Avg.

Financials Performance 2019-2020

2019 — 2020

Legend: Seasonal Period — Financials − − 50 DMA ····· 200 DMA

Relative Strength, % Gain vs. S&P 500

JANUARY
M	T	W	T	F	S	S
				1	2	3
4	5	6	7	8	9	10
11	12	13	14	15	16	17
18	19	20	21	22	23	24
25	26	27	28	29	30	31

FEBRUARY
M	T	W	T	F	S	S
1	2	3	4	5	6	7
8	9	10	11	12	13	14
15	16	17	18	19	20	21
22	23	24	25	26	27	28

MARCH
M	T	W	T	F	S	S
1	2	3	4	5	6	7
8	9	10	11	12	13	14
15	16	17	18	19	20	21
22	23	24	25	26	27	28
29	30	31				

APRIL
M	T	W	T	F	S	S
		1	2	3		
6	7	8	9	10		
13	14	15	16	17		
20	21	22	23	24		
27	28	29	30			

MAY
M	T	W	T	F	S	S
				1	2	3
4	5	6	7	8	9	10
11	12	13	14	15	16	17
18	19	20	21	22	23	24
25	26	27	28	29	30	31

JUNE
M	T	W	T	F	S	S
1	2	3	4	5	6	7
8	9	10	11	12	13	14
15	16	17	18	19	20	21
22	23	24	25	26	27	28
29	30					

APPENDIX

STOCK MARKET RETURNS

S&P 500
PERCENT CHANGES

	JAN	FEB	MAR	APR	MAY	JUN
1950	1.5 %	1.0 %	0.4 %	4.5 %	3.9 %	— 5.8 %
1951	6.1	0.6	— 1.8	4.8	— 4.1	— 2.6
1952	1.6	— 3.6	4.8	— 4.3	2.3	4.6
1953	— 0.7	— 1.8	— 2.4	— 2.6	— 0.3	— 1.6
1954	5.1	0.3	3.0	4.9	3.3	0.1
1955	1.8	0.4	— 0.5	3.8	— 0.1	8.2
1956	— 3.6	3.5	6.9	— 0.2	— 6.6	3.9
1957	— 4.2	— 3.3	2.0	3.7	3.7	— 0.1
1958	4.3	2.1	3.1	3.2	1.5	2.6
1959	0.4	— 0.1	0.1	3.9	1.9	— 0.4
1960	— 7.1	0.9	— 1.4	1.8	2.7	2.0
1961	6.3	2.7	2.6	0.4	1.9	— 2.9
1962	— 3.8	1.6	— 0.6	— 6.2	— 8.6	— 8.2
1963	4.9	— 2.9	3.5	4.9	1.4	— 2.0
1964	2.7	1.0	1.5	0.6	1.1	1.6
1965	3.3	— 0.1	— 1.5	3.4	— 0.8	— 4.9
1966	0.5	— 1.8	— 2.2	2.1	— 5.4	— 1.6
1967	7.8	0.2	3.9	4.2	— 5.2	1.8
1968	— 4.4	— 3.1	0.9	8.0	1.3	0.9
1969	— 0.8	— 4.7	3.4	2.1	— 0.2	— 5.6
1970	— 7.6	5.3	0.1	— 9.0	— 6.1	— 5.0
1971	4.0	0.9	3.7	3.6	— 4.2	— 0.9
1972	1.8	2.5	0.6	0.4	1.7	— 2.2
1973	— 1.7	— 3.7	— 0.1	— 4.1	— 1.9	— 0.7
1974	— 1.0	— 0.4	— 2.3	— 3.9	— 3.4	— 1.5
1975	12.3	6.0	2.2	4.7	4.4	4.4
1976	11.8	— 1.1	3.1	— 1.1	— 1.4	4.1
1977	— 5.1	— 2.2	— 1.4	0.0	— 2.4	4.5
1978	— 6.2	— 2.5	2.5	8.5	0.4	— 1.8
1979	4.0	— 3.7	5.5	0.2	— 2.6	3.9
1980	5.8	— 0.4	— 10.2	4.1	4.7	2.7
1981	— 4.6	1.3	3.6	— 2.3	— 0.2	— 1.0
1982	— 1.8	— 6.1	— 1.0	4.0	— 3.9	— 2.0
1983	3.3	1.9	3.3	7.5	— 1.2	3.2
1984	— 0.9	— 3.9	1.3	0.5	— 5.9	1.7
1985	7.4	0.9	— 0.3	— 0.5	5.4	1.2
1986	0.2	7.1	5.3	— 1.4	5.0	1.4
1987	13.2	3.7	2.6	— 1.1	0.6	4.8
1988	4.0	4.2	— 3.3	0.9	0.3	4.3
1989	7.1	— 2.9	2.1	5.0	3.5	— 0.8
1990	— 6.9	0.9	2.4	— 2.7	9.2	— 0.9
1991	4.2	6.7	2.2	0.0	3.9	— 4.8
1992	— 2.0	1.0	— 2.2	2.8	0.1	— 1.7
1993	0.7	1.0	1.9	— 2.5	2.3	0.1
1994	3.3	— 3.0	— 4.6	1.2	1.2	— 2.7
1995	2.4	3.6	2.7	2.8	3.6	2.1
1996	3.3	0.7	0.8	1.3	2.3	0.2
1997	6.1	0.6	— 4.3	5.8	5.9	4.3
1998	1.0	7.0	5.0	0.9	— 1.9	3.9
1999	4.1	— 3.2	3.9	3.8	— 2.5	5.4
2000	— 5.1	— 2.0	9.7	— 3.1	— 2.2	2.4
2001	3.5	— 9.2	— 6.4	7.7	0.5	— 2.5
2002	— 1.6	— 2.1	3.7	— 6.1	— 0.9	— 7.2
2003	— 2.7	— 1.7	0.8	8.1	5.1	1.1
2004	1.7	1.2	— 1.6	— 1.7	1.2	1.8
2005	— 2.5	1.9	— 1.9	— 2.0	3.0	0.0
2006	2.5	0.0	1.1	1.2	— 3.1	0.0
2007	1.4	— 2.2	1.0	4.3	3.3	— 1.8
2008	— 6.1	— 3.5	— 0.6	4.8	1.1	— 8.6
2009	— 8.6	— 11.0	8.5	9.4	5.3	0.0
2010	— 3.7	2.9	5.9	1.5	— 8.2	— 5.4
2011	2.3	3.2	— 0.1	2.8	— 1.4	— 1.8
2012	4.4	4.1	3.1	— 0.7	— 6.3	4.0
2013	5.0	1.1	3.6	1.8	2.1	— 1.5
2014	— 3.6	4.3	0.7	0.6	2.1	1.9
2015	— 3.1	5.5	— 1.7	0.9	1.0	— 2.1
2016	— 5.1	— 0.4	6.6	0.3	1.5	0.1
2017	1.8	3.7	0.0	0.9	1.2	0.5
2018	5.6	— 3.9	— 2.7	0.3	2.2	0.5
2019	7.9	3.0	1.8	3.9	— 6.6	6.9
FQ POS*	43/70	39/70	45/70	49/70	41/70	38/70
% FQ POS*	61 %	56 %	64 %	70 %	59 %	54 %
AVG GAIN*	1.1 %	0.1 %	1.2 %	1.5 %	0.2 %	0.1 %
RANK GAIN*	5	10	4	3	8	9

S&P 500
PERCENT CHANGES

STOCK MKT

JUL	AUG	SEP	OCT	NOV	DEC		YEAR
0.8 %	3.3 %	5.6 %	0.4 %	− 0.1 %	4.6 %	1950	21.7 %
6.9	3.9	− 0.1	− 1.4	− 0.3	3.9	1951	16.5
1.8	− 1.5	− 2.0	− 0.1	4.6	3.5	1952	11.8
2.5	− 5.8	0.1	5.1	0.9	0.2	1953	− 6.6
5.7	− 3.4	8.3	− 1.9	8.1	5.1	1954	45.0
6.1	− 0.8	1.1	− 3.0	7.5	− 0.1	1955	26.4
5.2	− 3.8	− 4.5	0.5	− 1.1	3.5	1956	2.6
1.1	− 5.6	− 6.2	− 3.2	1.6	− 4.1	1957	− 14.3
4.3	1.2	4.8	2.5	2.2	5.2	1958	38.1
3.5	− 1.5	− 4.6	1.1	1.3	2.8	1959	8.5
− 2.5	2.6	− 6.0	− 0.2	4.0	4.6	1960	− 3.0
3.3	2.0	− 2.0	2.8	3.9	0.3	1961	23.1
6.4	1.5	− 4.8	0.4	10.2	1.3	1962	− 11.8
− 0.3	4.9	− 1.1	3.2	− 1.1	2.4	1963	18.9
1.8	− 1.6	2.9	0.8	− 0.5	0.4	1964	13.0
1.3	2.3	3.2	2.7	− 0.9	0.9	1965	9.1
− 1.3	− 7.8	− 0.7	4.8	0.3	− 0.1	1966	− 13.1
4.5	− 1.2	3.3	− 3.5	0.8	2.6	1967	20.1
− 1.8	1.1	3.9	0.7	4.8	− 4.2	1968	7.7
− 6.0	4.0	− 2.5	4.3	− 3.4	− 1.9	1969	− 11.4
7.3	4.4	3.4	− 1.2	4.7	5.7	1970	0.1
− 3.2	3.6	− 0.7	− 4.2	− 0.3	8.6	1971	10.8
0.2	3.4	− 0.5	0.9	4.6	1.2	1972	15.6
3.8	− 3.7	4.0	− 0.1	− 11.4	1.7	1973	− 17.4
− 7.8	− 9.0	− 11.9	16.3	− 5.3	− 2.0	1974	− 29.7
− 6.8	− 2.1	− 3.5	6.2	2.5	− 1.2	1975	31.5
− 0.8	− 0.5	2.3	− 2.2	− 0.8	5.2	1976	19.1
− 1.6	− 2.1	− 0.2	− 4.3	2.7	0.3	1977	− 11.5
5.4	2.6	− 0.7	− 9.2	1.7	1.5	1978	1.1
0.9	5.3	0.0	− 6.9	4.3	1.7	1979	12.3
6.5	0.6	2.5	1.6	10.2	− 3.4	1980	25.8
− 0.2	− 6.2	− 5.4	4.9	3.7	− 3.0	1981	9.7
− 2.3	11.6	0.8	11.0	3.6	1.5	1982	14.8
− 3.0	1.1	1.0	− 1.5	1.7	− 0.9	1983	17.3
− 1.6	10.6	− 0.3	0.0	− 1.5	2.2	1984	1.4
− 0.5	− 1.2	− 3.5	4.3	6.5	4.5	1985	26.3
− 5.9	7.1	− 8.5	5.5	2.1	− 2.8	1986	14.6
4.8	3.5	− 2.4	− 21.8	− 8.5	7.3	1987	2.0
− 0.5	− 3.9	4.0	2.6	− 1.9	1.5	1988	12.4
8.8	1.6	− 0.7	− 2.5	1.7	2.1	1989	27.3
− 0.5	− 9.4	− 5.1	− 0.7	6.0	2.5	1990	− 6.6
4.5	2.0	− 1.9	1.2	− 4.4	11.2	1991	26.3
3.9	− 2.4	0.9	0.2	3.0	1.0	1992	4.5
− 0.5	3.4	− 1.0	1.9	− 1.3	1.0	1993	7.1
3.1	3.8	− 2.7	2.1	− 4.0	1.2	1994	− 1.5
3.2	0.0	4.0	− 0.5	4.1	1.7	1995	34.1
− 4.6	1.9	5.4	2.6	7.3	− 2.2	1996	20.3
7.8	− 5.7	5.3	− 3.4	4.5	1.6	1997	31.0
− 1.2	− 14.6	6.2	8.0	5.9	5.6	1998	26.7
− 3.2	− 0.6	− 2.9	6.3	1.9	5.8	1999	19.5
− 1.6	6.1	− 5.3	− 0.5	− 8.0	0.4	2000	− 10.1
− 1.1	− 6.4	− 8.2	1.8	7.5	0.8	2001	− 13.0
− 7.9	0.5	− 11.0	8.6	5.7	− 6.0	2002	− 23.4
1.6	1.8	− 1.2	5.5	0.7	5.1	2003	26.4
-3.4	0.2	0.9	1.4	3.9	3.2	2004	9.0
3.6	− 1.1	0.7	− 1.8	3.5	− 0.1	2005	3.0
0.5	2.1	2.5	3.2	1.6	1.3	2006	13.6
− 3.2	1.3	3.6	1.5	− 4.4	− 0.9	2007	3.5
− 1.0	1.2	− 9.1	− 16.9	− 7.5	0.8	2008	-38.5
7.4	3.4	3.6	− 2.0	5.7	1.8	2009	23.5
6.9	− 4.7	8.8	3.7	− 0.2	6.5	2010	12.8
− 2.1	− 5.7	− 7.2	10.8	− 0.5	0.9	2011	0.0
1.3	2.0	2.4	− 2.0	0.3	0.7	2012	13.4
4.9	− 3.1	3.0	4.5	2.8	2.4	2013	29.6
− 1.5	3.8	− 1.6	2.3	2.5	− 0.4	2014	11.4
2.0	− 6.3	− 2.6	8.3	0.1	− 1.8	2015	− 0.7
3.6	− 0.1	− 0.1	− 1.9	3.4	1.8	2016	9.5
1.9	0.1	1.9	2.2	2.8	1.0	2017	19.4
3.6	3.0	0.4	− 6.9	1.8	− 9.2	2018	6.2
1.3	− 1.8	1.7	2.0	3.4	2.9	2019	28.9
40/70	38/70	32/70	42/70	48/70	52/70		51/70
57 %	54 %	46 %	60 %	69 %	74 %		73 %
1.1 %	-0.1 %	− 0.4 %	0.8 %	1.6 %	1.5 %		9.1 %
6	11	12	7	1	2		

S&P 500 MONTH CLOSING VALUES

	JAN	FEB	MAR	APR	MAY	JUN
1950	17	17	17	18	19	18
1951	22	22	21	22	22	21
1952	24	23	24	23	24	25
1953	26	26	25	25	25	24
1954	26	26	27	28	29	29
1955	37	37	37	38	38	41
1956	44	45	48	48	45	47
1957	45	43	44	46	47	47
1958	42	41	42	43	44	45
1959	55	55	55	58	59	58
1960	56	56	55	54	56	57
1961	62	63	65	65	67	65
1962	69	70	70	65	60	55
1963	66	64	67	70	71	69
1964	77	78	79	79	80	82
1965	88	87	86	89	88	84
1966	93	91	89	91	86	85
1967	87	87	90	94	89	91
1968	92	89	90	97	99	100
1969	103	98	102	104	103	98
1970	85	90	90	82	77	73
1971	96	97	100	104	100	99
1972	104	107	107	108	110	107
1973	116	112	112	107	105	104
1974	97	96	94	90	87	86
1975	77	82	83	87	91	95
1976	101	100	103	102	100	104
1977	102	100	98	98	96	100
1978	89	87	89	97	97	96
1979	100	96	102	102	99	103
1980	114	114	102	106	111	114
1981	130	131	136	133	133	131
1982	120	113	112	116	112	110
1983	145	148	153	164	162	168
1984	163	157	159	160	151	153
1985	180	181	181	180	190	192
1986	212	227	239	236	247	251
1987	274	284	292	288	290	304
1988	257	268	259	261	262	274
1989	297	289	295	310	321	318
1990	329	332	340	331	361	358
1991	344	367	375	375	390	371
1992	409	413	404	415	415	408
1993	439	443	452	440	450	451
1994	482	467	446	451	457	444
1995	470	487	501	515	533	545
1996	636	640	646	654	669	671
1997	786	791	757	801	848	885
1998	980	1049	1102	1112	1091	1134
1999	1280	1238	1286	1335	1302	1373
2000	1394	1366	1499	1452	1421	1455
2001	1366	1240	1160	1249	1256	1224
2002	1130	1107	1147	1077	1067	990
2003	856	841	848	917	964	975
2004	1131	1145	1126	1107	1121	1141
2005	1181	1204	1181	1157	1192	1191
2006	1280	1281	1295	1311	1270	1270
2007	1438	1407	1421	1482	1531	1503
2008	1379	1331	1323	1386	1400	1280
2009	826	735	798	873	919	919
2010	1074	1104	1169	1187	1089	1031
2011	1286	1327	1326	1364	1345	1321
2012	1312	1366	1408	1398	1310	1362
2013	1498	1515	1569	1598	1631	1606
2014	1783	1869	1872	1884	1924	1960
2015	1995	2105	2068	2086	2107	2063
2016	1940	1932	2060	2065	2097	2099
2017	2279	2364	2363	2384	2412	2423
2018	2824	2714	2641	2648	2705	2718
2019	2704	2784	2834	2946	2752	2942

S&P 500 MONTH CLOSING VALUES

JUL	AUG	SEP	OCT	NOV	DEC	
18	18	19	20	20	20	1950
22	23	23	23	23	24	1951
25	25	25	25	26	27	1952
25	23	23	25	25	25	1953
31	30	32	32	34	36	1954
44	43	44	42	46	45	1955
49	48	45	46	45	47	1956
48	45	42	41	42	40	1957
47	48	50	51	52	55	1958
61	60	57	58	58	60	1959
56	57	54	53	56	58	1960
67	68	67	69	71	72	1961
58	59	56	57	62	63	1962
69	73	72	74	73	75	1963
83	82	84	85	84	85	1964
85	87	90	92	92	92	1965
84	77	77	80	80	80	1966
95	94	97	93	94	96	1967
98	99	103	103	108	104	1968
92	96	93	97	94	92	1969
78	82	84	83	87	92	1970
96	99	98	94	94	102	1971
107	111	111	112	117	118	1972
108	104	108	108	96	98	1973
79	72	64	74	70	69	1974
89	87	84	89	91	90	1975
103	103	105	103	102	107	1976
99	97	97	92	95	95	1977
101	103	103	93	95	96	1978
104	109	109	102	106	108	1979
122	122	125	127	141	136	1980
131	123	116	122	126	123	1981
107	120	120	134	139	141	1982
163	164	166	164	166	165	1983
151	167	166	166	164	167	1984
191	189	182	190	202	211	1985
236	253	231	244	249	242	1986
319	330	322	252	230	247	1987
272	262	272	279	274	278	1988
346	351	349	340	346	353	1989
356	323	306	304	322	330	1990
388	395	388	392	375	417	1991
424	414	418	419	431	436	1992
448	464	459	468	462	466	1993
458	475	463	472	454	459	1994
562	562	584	582	605	616	1995
640	652	687	705	757	741	1996
954	899	947	915	955	970	1997
1121	957	1017	1099	1164	1229	1998
1329	1320	1283	1363	1389	1469	1999
1431	1518	1437	1429	1315	1320	2000
1211	1134	1041	1060	1139	1148	2001
912	916	815	886	936	880	2002
990	1008	996	1051	1058	1112	2003
1102	1104	1115	1130	1174	1212	2004
1234	1220	1229	1207	1249	1248	2005
1277	1304	1336	1378	1401	1418	2006
1455	1474	1527	1549	1481	1468	2007
1267	1283	1165	969	896	903	2008
987	1021	1057	1036	1096	1115	2009
1102	1049	1141	1183	1181	1258	2010
1292	1219	1131	1253	1247	1258	2011
1379	1407	1441	1412	1416	1426	2012
1686	1633	1682	1757	1806	1848	2013
1931	2003	1972	2018	2068	2059	2014
2104	1972	1920	2079	2080	2044	2015
2174	2171	2168	2126	2199	2239	2016
2470	2472	2519	2575	2648	2674	2017
2816	2902	2914	2712	2760	2507	2018
2980	2926	2977	3038	3141	3231	2019

STOCK MKT — DOW JONES PERCENT MONTH CHANGES

	JAN	FEB	MAR	APR	MAY	JUN
1950	0.8 %	0.8 %	1.3 %	4.0 %	4.2 %	— 6.4 %
1951	5.7	1.3	— 1.7	4.5	— 3.6	— 2.8
1952	0.6	— 3.9	3.6	— 4.4	2.1	4.3
1953	— 0.7	— 2.0	— 1.5	— 1.8	— 0.9	— 1.5
1954	4.1	0.7	3.1	5.2	2.6	1.8
1955	1.1	0.8	— 0.5	3.9	— 0.2	6.2
1956	— 3.6	2.8	5.8	0.8	— 7.4	3.1
1957	— 4.1	— 3.0	2.2	4.1	2.1	— 0.3
1958	3.3	— 2.2	1.6	2.0	1.5	3.3
1959	1.8	1.6	— 0.3	3.7	3.2	0.0
1960	— 8.4	1.2	— 2.1	— 2.4	4.0	2.4
1961	5.2	2.1	2.2	0.3	2.7	— 1.8
1962	— 4.3	1.2	— 0.2	— 5.9	— 7.8	8.5
1963	4.7	— 2.9	3.0	5.2	1.3	— 2.8
1964	2.9	1.9	1.6	— 0.3	1.2	1.3
1965	3.3	0.1	— 1.6	3.7	— 0.5	— 5.4
1966	1.5	— 3.2	— 2.8	1.0	— 5.3	— 1.6
1967	8.2	— 1.2	3.2	3.6	— 5.0	0.9
1968	— 5.5	— 1.8	0.0	8.5	— 1.4	— 0.1
1969	0.2	— 4.3	3.3	1.6	— 1.3	— 6.9
1970	— 7.0	4.5	1.0	— 6.3	— 4.8	— 2.4
1971	3.5	1.2	2.9	4.1	— 3.6	— 1.8
1972	1.3	2.9	1.4	1.4	0.7	— 3.3
1973	— 2.1	— 4.4	— 0.4	— 3.1	— 2.2	— 1.1
1974	0.6	0.6	— 1.6	— 1.2	— 4.1	0.0
1975	14.2	5.0	3.9	6.9	1.3	5.6
1976	14.4	— 0.3	2.8	— 0.3	— 2.2	2.8
1977	— 5.0	— 1.9	— 1.8	0.8	— 3.0	2.0
1978	— 7.4	— 3.6	2.1	10.5	0.4	— 2.6
1979	4.2	— 3.6	6.6	— 0.8	— 3.8	2.4
1980	4.4	— 1.5	— 9.0	4.0	4.1	2.0
1981	— 1.7	2.9	3.0	— 0.6	— 0.6	— 1.5
1982	— 0.4	— 5.4	— 0.2	3.1	— 3.4	— 0.9
1983	2.8	3.4	1.6	8.5	— 2.1	1.8
1984	— 3.0	— 5.4	0.9	0.5	— 5.6	2.5
1985	6.2	— 0.2	— 1.3	— 0.7	4.6	1.5
1986	1.6	8.8	6.4	— 1.9	5.2	0.9
1987	13.8	3.1	3.6	— 0.8	0.2	5.5
1988	1.0	5.8	— 4.0	2.2	— 0.1	5.4
1989	8.0	— 3.6	1.6	5.5	2.5	— 1.6
1990	— 5.9	1.4	3.0	— 1.9	8.3	0.1
1991	3.9	5.3	1.1	— 0.9	4.8	— 4.0
1992	1.7	1.4	— 1.0	3.8	1.1	— 2.3
1993	0.3	1.8	1.9	— 0.2	2.9	— 0.3
1994	6.0	— 3.7	— 5.1	1.3	2.1	— 3.5
1995	0.2	4.3	3.7	3.9	3.3	2.0
1996	5.4	1.7	1.9	— 0.3	1.3	0.2
1997	5.7	0.9	— 4.3	6.5	4.6	4.7
1998	0.0	8.1	3.0	3.0	— 1.8	0.6
1999	1.9	— 0.6	5.2	10.2	— 2.1	3.9
2000	— 4.5	— 7.4	7.8	— 1.7	— 2.0	— 0.7
2001	0.9	— 3.6	— 5.9	8.7	1.6	— 3.8
2002	— 1.0	1.9	2.9	— 4.4	— 0.2	— 6.9
2003	— 3.5	— 2.0	1.3	6.1	4.4	1.5
2004	0.3	0.9	— 2.1	— 1.3	— 0.4	2.4
2005	— 2.7	2.6	— 2.4	— 3.0	2.7	— 1.8
2006	1.4	1.2	1.1	2.3	— 1.7	— 0.2
2007	1.3	— 2.8	0.7	5.7	4.3	— 1.6
2008	— 4.6	— 3.0	0.0	4.5	— 1.4	— 10.2
2009	— 8.8	— 11.7	7.7	7.3	4.1	— 0.6
2010	— 3.5	2.6	5.1	1.4	— 7.9	— 3.6
2011	2.7	2.8	0.8	4.0	— 1.9	— 1.2
2012	3.4	3.8	2.0	0.0	— 6.2	3.9
2013	5.8	4.8	3.7	1.8	1.9	— 1.4
2014	— 5.3	5.8	0.8	0.7	0.8	0.7
2015	— 3.7	6.8	— 2.0	0.4	1.0	— 2.2
2016	— 5.5	0.3	7.1	0.5	0.1	0.8
2017	0.5	4.8	— 0.7	1.3	0.3	1.6
2018	5.8	— 4.3	— 3.7	0.2	1.0	— 0.6
2019	7.2	3.7	0.0	2.6	— 6.7	7.2
FQ POS	45/70	41/70	45/70	48/70	37/70	33/70
% FQ POS	64 %	59 %	64 %	698 %	53 %	47 %
AVG GAIN	1.0 %	0.3 %	1.1 %	1.9 %	-0.1 %	— 0.2 %
RANK GAIN	6	8	5	1	9	11

DOW JONES PERCENT MONTH CHANGES 🇺🇸 STOCK MKT

JUL	AUG	SEP	OCT	NOV	DEC	YEAR	
0.1 %	3.6 %	4.4 %	— 0.6 %	1.2 %	3.4 %	**1950**	17.6 %
6.3	4.8	0.3	— 3.2	— 0.4	3.0	**1951**	14.4
1.9	— 1.6	— 1.6	— 0.5	5.4	2.9	**1952**	8.4
2.6	— 5.2	1.1	4.5	2.0	— 0.2	**1953**	— 3.8
4.3	— 3.5	7.4	— 2.3	9.9	4.6	**1954**	44.0
3.2	0.5	— 0.3	— 2.5	6.2	1.1	**1955**	20.8
5.1	— 3.1	— 5.3	1.0	— 1.5	5.6	**1956**	2.3
1.0	— 4.7	— 5.8	— 3.4	2.0	— 3.2	**1957**	— 12.8
5.2	1.1	4.6	2.1	2.6	4.7	**1958**	34.0
4.9	— 1.6	— 4.9	2.4	1.9	3.1	**1959**	16.4
— 3.7	1.5	— 7.3	0.1	2.9	3.1	**1960**	— 9.3
3.1	2.1	— 2.6	0.4	2.5	1.3	**1961**	18.7
6.5	1.9	— 5.0	1.9	10.1	0.4	**1962**	— 10.8
— 1.6	4.9	0.5	3.1	— 0.6	1.7	**1963**	17.0
1.2	— 0.3	4.4	— 0.3	0.3	— 0.1	**1964**	14.6
1.6	1.3	4.2	3.2	— 1.5	2.4	**1965**	10.9
— 2.6	— 7.0	— 1.8	4.2	— 1.9	— 0.7	**1966**	— 18.9
5.1	— 0.3	2.8	— 5.1	— 0.4	3.3	**1967**	15.2
— 1.6	1.5	4.4	1.8	3.4	— 4.2	**1968**	4.3
— 6.6	2.6	— 2.8	5.3	— 5.1	— 1.5	**1969**	— 15.2
7.4	4.2	— 0.5	— 0.7	5.1	5.6	**1970**	4.8
— 3.7	4.6	— 1.2	— 5.4	— 0.9	7.1	**1971**	6.1
— 0.5	4.2	— 1.1	0.2	6.6	0.2	**1972**	14.6
3.9	— 4.2	6.7	1.0	— 14.0	3.5	**1973**	— 16.6
— 5.6	— 10.4	— 10.4	9.5	— 7.0	— 0.4	**1974**	— 27.6
— 5.4	0.5	— 5.0	5.3	3.0	— 1.0	**1975**	38.3
— 1.8	— 1.1	1.7	— 2.6	— 1.8	6.1	**1976**	17.9
— 2.9	— 3.2	— 1.7	— 3.4	1.4	0.2	**1977**	— 17.3
5.3	1.7	— 1.3	— 8.5	0.8	0.8	**1978**	— 3.2
0.5	4.9	— 1.0	— 7.2	0.8	2.0	**1979**	4.2
7.8	— 0.3	0.0	— 0.8	7.4	— 2.9	**1980**	14.9
— 2.5	— 7.4	— 3.6	0.3	4.3	— 1.6	**1981**	9.2
— 0.4	11.5	— 0.6	10.6	4.8	0.7	**1982**	19.6
— 1.9	1.4	1.4	— 0.6	4.1	— 1.4	**1983**	20.3
— 1.5	9.8	— 1.4	0.1	— 1.5	1.9	**1984**	3.7
0.9	— 1.0	— 0.4	3.4	7.1	5.1	**1985**	27.7
— 6.2	6.9	— 6.9	6.2	1.9	— 1.0	**1986**	22.6
6.4	3.5	— 2.5	— 23.2	— 8.0	5.7	**1987**	2.3
— 0.6	— 4.6	4.0	1.7	— 1.6	2.6	**1988**	11.9
9.0	2.9	— 1.6	— 1.8	2.3	1.7	**1989**	27.0
0.9	— 10.0	— 6.2	— 0.4	4.8	2.9	**1990**	— 4.3
4.1	0.6	— 0.9	1.7	— 5.7	9.5	**1991**	20.3
2.3	— 4.0	0.4	— 1.4	2.4	— 0.1	**1992**	4.2
0.7	3.2	— 2.6	3.5	0.1	1.9	**1993**	13.7
3.8	4.0	— 1.8	1.7	— 4.3	2.5	**1994**	2.1
3.3	— 2.1	3.9	— 0.7	6.7	0.8	**1995**	33.5
— 2.2	1.6	4.7	2.5	8.2	— 1.1	**1996**	26.0
7.2	— 7.3	4.2	— 6.3	5.1	1.1	**1997**	22.6
— 0.8	— 15.1	4.0	9.6	6.1	0.7	**1998**	16.1
— 2.9	1.6	— 4.5	3.8	1.4	5.3	**1999**	24.7
0.7	6.6	— 5.0	3.0	— 5.1	3.6	**2000**	— 5.8
0.2	— 5.4	— 11.1	2.6	8.6	1.7	**2001**	— 7.1
— 5.5	— 0.8	— 12.4	10.6	5.9	— 6.2	**2002**	— 16.8
2.8	2.0	— 1.5	5.7	— 0.2	6.9	**2003**	25.3
— 2.8	0.3	— 0.9	— 0.5	4.0	3.4	**2004**	3.1
3.6	— 1.5	0.8	— 1.2	3.5	— 0.8	**2005**	— 0.6
0.3	1.7	2.6	3.4	1.2	2.0	**2006**	16.3
— 1.5	1.1	4.0	0.2	— 4.0	— 0.8	**2007**	6.4
0.2	1.5	— 6.0	— 14.1	— 5.3	— 0.6	**2008**	— 33.8
8.6	3.5	2.3	0.0	6.5	0.8	**2009**	18.8
7.1	— 4.3	7.7	3.1	— 1.0	5.2	**2010**	11.0
— 2.2	— 4.4	— 6.0	9.5	0.8	1.4	**2011**	5.5
1.0	0.6	2.6	— 2.5	— 0.5	0.6	**2012**	7.3
4.0	— 4.4	2.2	2.8	3.5	3.0	**2013**	26.5
— 1.6	3.2	— 0.3	2.0	2.5	0.0	**2014**	7.5
0.4	— 6.6	— 1.5	8.5	0.3	— 2.2	**2015**	— 2.2
2.8	— 0.2	— 0.5	— 0.9	5.4	3.3	**2016**	13.4
2.5	0.3	2.1	4.3	3.8	1.8	**2017**	25.1
4.7	2.2	1.9	— 5.1	1.7	— 8.7	**2018**	— 5.6
1.0	— 1.7	1.9	0.5	3.7	1.7	**2019**	22.3
45/70	39/70	29/70	42/70	49/70	49/70		50/70
64 %	56 %	41 %	60 %	70 %	70 %		71 %
1.2 %	— 0.1 %	— 0.7 %	0.6 %	1.6 %	1.5 %		8.3 %
4	10	12	7	2	3		

DOW JONES
MONTH CLOSING VALUES

	JAN	FEB	MAR	APR	MAY	JUN
1950	202	203	206	214	223	209
1951	249	252	248	259	250	243
1952	271	260	270	258	263	274
1953	290	284	280	275	272	268
1954	292	295	304	319	328	334
1955	409	412	410	426	425	451
1956	471	484	512	516	478	493
1957	479	465	475	494	505	503
1958	450	440	447	456	463	478
1959	594	604	602	624	644	644
1960	623	630	617	602	626	641
1961	648	662	677	679	697	684
1962	700	708	707	665	613	561
1963	683	663	683	718	727	707
1964	785	800	813	811	821	832
1965	903	904	889	922	918	868
1966	984	952	925	934	884	870
1967	850	839	866	897	853	860
1968	856	841	841	912	899	898
1969	946	905	936	950	938	873
1970	744	778	786	736	700	684
1971	869	879	904	942	908	891
1972	902	928	941	954	961	929
1973	999	955	951	921	901	892
1974	856	861	847	837	802	802
1975	704	739	768	821	832	879
1976	975	973	1000	997	975	1003
1977	954	936	919	927	899	916
1978	770	742	757	837	841	819
1979	839	809	862	855	822	842
1980	876	863	786	817	851	868
1981	947	975	1004	998	992	977
1982	871	824	823	848	820	812
1983	1076	1113	1130	1226	1200	1222
1984	1221	1155	1165	1171	1105	1132
1985	1287	1284	1267	1258	1315	1336
1986	1571	1709	1819	1784	1877	1893
1987	2158	2224	2305	2286	2292	2419
1988	1958	2072	1988	2032	2031	2142
1989	2342	2258	2294	2419	2480	2440
1990	2591	2627	2707	2657	2877	2881
1991	2736	2882	2914	2888	3028	2907
1992	3223	3268	3236	3359	3397	3319
1993	3310	3371	3435	3428	3527	3516
1994	3978	3832	3636	3682	3758	3625
1995	3844	4011	4158	4321	4465	4556
1996	5395	5486	5587	5569	5643	5655
1997	6813	6878	6584	7009	7331	7673
1998	7907	8546	8800	9063	8900	8952
1999	9359	9307	9786	10789	10560	10971
2000	10941	10128	10922	10734	10522	10448
2001	10887	10495	9879	10735	10912	10502
2002	9920	10106	10404	9946	9925	9243
2003	8054	7891	7992	8480	8850	8985
2004	10488	10584	10358	10226	10188	10435
2005	10490	10766	10504	10193	10467	10275
2006	10865	10993	11109	11367	11168	11150
2007	12622	12269	12354	13063	13628	13409
2008	12650	12266	12263	12820	12638	11350
2009	8001	7063	7609	8168	8500	8447
2010	10067	10325	10857	11009	10137	9774
2011	11892	12226	12320	12811	12570	12414
2012	12633	12952	13212	13214	12393	12880
2013	13861	14054	14579	14840	15116	14910
2014	15699	16322	16458	16581	16717	16827
2015	17165	18133	17776	17841	18011	17620
2016	16466	16517	17685	17774	17787	17930
2017	19864	20812	20663	20941	21009	21350
2018	26149	25029	24103	24163	24416	24271
2019	25000	25916	25929	26593	24815	26600

DOW JONES
MONTH CLOSING VALUES — STOCK MKT

JUL	AUG	SEP	OCT	NOV	DEC	
209	217	226	225	228	235	1950
258	270	271	262	261	269	1951
280	275	271	269	284	292	1952
275	261	264	276	281	281	1953
348	336	361	352	387	404	1954
466	468	467	455	483	488	1955
518	502	475	480	473	500	1956
509	484	456	441	450	436	1957
503	509	532	543	558	584	1958
675	664	632	647	659	679	1959
617	626	580	580	597	616	1960
705	720	701	704	722	731	1961
598	609	579	590	649	652	1962
695	729	733	755	751	763	1963
841	839	875	873	875	874	1964
882	893	931	961	947	969	1965
847	788	774	807	792	786	1966
904	901	927	880	876	905	1967
883	896	936	952	985	944	1968
816	837	813	856	812	800	1969
734	765	761	756	794	839	1970
858	898	887	839	831	890	1971
925	964	953	956	1018	1020	1972
926	888	947	957	822	851	1973
757	679	608	666	619	616	1974
832	835	794	836	861	852	1975
985	974	990	965	947	1005	1976
890	862	847	818	830	831	1977
862	877	866	793	799	805	1978
846	888	879	816	822	839	1979
935	933	932	925	993	964	1980
952	882	850	853	889	875	1981
809	901	896	992	1039	1047	1982
1199	1216	1233	1225	1276	1259	1983
1115	1224	1207	1207	1189	1212	1984
1348	1334	1329	1374	1472	1547	1985
1775	1898	1768	1878	1914	1896	1986
2572	2663	2596	1994	1834	1939	1987
2129	2032	2113	2149	2115	2169	1988
2661	2737	2693	2645	2706	2753	1989
2905	2614	2453	2442	2560	2634	1990
3025	3044	3017	3069	2895	3169	1991
3394	3257	3272	3226	3305	3301	1992
3540	3651	3555	3681	3684	3754	1993
3765	3913	3843	3908	3739	3834	1994
4709	4611	4789	4756	5075	5117	1995
5529	5616	5882	6029	6522	6448	1996
8223	7622	7945	7442	7823	7908	1997
8883	7539	7843	8592	9117	9181	1998
10655	10829	10337	10730	10878	11453	1999
10522	11215	10651	10971	10415	10788	2000
10523	9950	8848	9075	9852	10022	2001
8737	8664	7592	8397	8896	8342	2002
9234	9416	9275	9801	9782	10454	2003
10140	10174	10080	10027	10428	10783	2004
10641	10482	10569	10440	10806	10718	2005
11186	11381	11679	12801	12222	12463	2006
13212	13358	13896	13930	13372	13265	2007
11378	11544	10851	9325	8829	8776	2008
9172	9496	9712	9713	10345	10428	2009
10466	10015	10788	11118	11006	11578	2010
12143	11614	10913	11955	12046	12218	2011
13009	13091	13437	13096	13026	13104	2012
15500	14810	15130	15546	16086	16577	2013
16563	17098	17043	17391	17828	17823	2014
17690	16528	16285	17664	17720	17425	2015
18432	18401	18308	18142	19124	19763	2016
21891	21948	22405	23377	24272	24719	2017
25415	25965	26458	25166	25538	23327	2018
26864	26403	26917	27046	28051	28538	2019

🇺🇸 **NASDAQ PERCENT MONTH CHANGES**

	JAN	FEB	MAR	APR	MAY	JUN
1972	4.2	5.5	2.2	2.5	0.9	− 1.8
1973	− 4.0	− 6.2	− 2.4	− 8.2	− 4.8	− 1.6
1974	3.0	− 0.6	− 2.2	− 5.9	− 7.7	− 5.3
1975	16.6	4.6	3.6	3.8	5.8	4.7
1976	12.1	3.7	0.4	− 0.6	− 2.3	2.6
1977	− 2.4	− 1.0	− 0.5	1.4	0.1	4.3
1978	− 4.0	0.6	4.7	8.5	4.4	0.0
1979	6.6	− 2.6	7.5	1.6	− 1.8	5.1
1980	7.0	− 2.3	− 17.1	6.9	7.5	4.9
1981	− 2.2	0.1	6.1	3.1	3.1	− 3.5
1982	− 3.8	− 4.8	− 2.1	5.2	− 3.3	− 4.1
1983	6.9	5.0	3.9	8.2	5.3	3.2
1984	− 3.7	− 5.9	− 0.7	− 1.3	− 5.9	2.9
1985	12.8	2.0	− 1.8	0.5	3.6	1.9
1986	3.4	7.1	4.2	2.3	4.4	1.3
1987	12.4	8.4	1.2	− 2.9	− 0.3	2.0
1988	4.3	6.5	2.1	1.2	− 2.3	6.6
1989	5.2	− 0.4	1.8	5.1	4.3	− 2.4
1990	− 8.6	2.4	2.3	− 3.5	9.3	0.7
1991	10.8	9.4	6.4	0.5	4.4	− 6.0
1992	5.8	2.1	− 4.7	− 4.2	1.1	− 3.7
1993	2.9	− 3.7	2.9	− 4.2	5.9	0.5
1994	3.0	− 1.0	− 6.2	− 1.3	0.2	− 4.0
1995	0.4	5.1	3.0	3.3	2.4	8.0
1996	0.7	3.8	0.1	8.1	4.4	− 4.7
1997	6.9	− 5.1	− 6.7	3.2	11.1	3.0
1998	3.1	9.3	3.7	1.8	− 4.8	6.5
1999	14.3	− 8.7	7.6	3.3	− 2.8	8.7
2000	− 3.2	19.2	− 2.6	− 15.6	− 11.9	16.6
2001	12.2	− 22.4	− 14.5	15.0	− 0.3	2.4
2002	− 0.8	− 10.5	6.6	− 8.5	− 4.3	− 9.4
2003	− 1.1	1.3	0.3	9.2	9.0	1.7
2004	3.1	− 1.8	− 1.8	− 3.7	3.5	3.1
2005	− 5.2	− 0.5	− 2.6	− 3.9	7.6	− 0.5
2006	4.6	− 1.1	2.6	− 0.7	− 6.2	− 0.3
2007	2.0	− 1.9	0.2	4.3	3.1	0.0
2008	− 9.9	− 5.0	0.3	5.9	4.6	− 9.1
2009	− 6.4	− 6.7	10.9	12.3	3.3	3.4
2010	− 5.4	4.2	7.1	2.6	− 8.3	− 6.5
2011	1.8	3.0	0.0	3.3	− 1.3	− 2.2
2012	8.0	5.4	4.2	− 1.5	− 7.2	3.8
2013	4.1	0.6	3.4	1.9	3.8	− 1.5
2014	− 1.7	5.0	− 2.5	− 2.0	3.1	3.9
2015	− 2.1	7.1	− 1.3	0.8	2.6	− 1.6
2016	− 7.9	− 1.2	6.8	− 1.9	3.6	− 2.1
2017	4.3	3.8	1.5	2.3	2.5	− 0.9
2018	7.4	− 1.9	− 2.9	0.0	5.3	0.9
2019	9.7	3.4	2.6	4.7	− 7.9	7.4
FQ POS	31/48	26/48	30/48	31/48	30/48	27/48
% FQ POS	65 %	54 %	63 %	65 %	63 %	56 %
AVG GAIN	2.7 %	0.7 %	0.8 %	1.3 %	1.0 %	0.8 %
RANK GAIN	1	9	7	4	5	6

NASDAQ PERCENT MONTH CHANGES 🇺🇸 STOCK MKT

JUL	AUG	SEP	OCT	NOV	DEC	YEAR	
— 1.8	1.7	— 0.3	0.5	2.1	0.6	**1972**	17.2
7.6	— 3.5	6.0	— 0.9	— 15.1	— 1.4	**1973**	— 31.1
— 7.9	— 10.9	— 10.7	17.2	— 3.5	— 5.0	**1974**	— 35.1
— 4.4	— 5.0	— 5.9	3.6	2.4	— 1.5	**1975**	29.8
1.1	— 1.7	1.7	— 1.0	0.9	7.4	**1976**	26.1
0.9	— 0.5	0.7	— 3.3	5.8	1.8	**1977**	7.3
5.0	6.9	— 1.6	— 16.4	3.2	2.9	**1978**	12.3
2.3	6.4	— 0.3	— 9.6	6.4	4.8	**1979**	28.1
8.9	5.7	3.4	2.7	8.0	— 2.8	**1980**	33.9
— 1.9	— 7.5	— 8.0	8.4	3.1	— 2.7	**1981**	— 3.2
— 2.3	6.2	5.6	13.3	9.3	0.0	**1982**	18.7
— 4.6	— 3.8	1.4	— 7.4	4.1	— 2.5	**1983**	19.9
— 4.2	10.9	— 1.8	— 1.2	— 1.9	1.9	**1984**	— 11.3
1.7	— 1.2	— 5.8	4.4	7.4	3.5	**1985**	31.5
— 8.4	3.1	— 8.4	2.9	— 0.3	— 3.0	**1986**	7.4
2.4	4.6	— 2.4	— 27.2	— 5.6	8.3	**1987**	— 5.2
— 1.9	— 2.8	2.9	— 1.3	— 2.9	2.7	**1988**	15.4
4.2	3.4	0.8	— 3.7	0.1	— 0.3	**1989**	19.2
— 5.2	— 13.0	— 9.6	— 4.3	8.9	4.1	**1990**	— 17.8
5.5	4.7	0.2	3.1	— 3.5	11.9	**1991**	56.9
3.1	— 3.0	3.6	3.8	7.9	3.7	**1992**	15.5
0.1	5.4	2.7	2.2	— 3.2	3.0	**1993**	14.7
2.3	6.0	— 0.2	1.7	— 3.5	0.2	**1994**	— 3.2
7.3	1.9	2.3	— 0.7	2.2	— 0.7	**1995**	39.9
— 8.8	5.6	7.5	— 0.4	5.8	— 0.1	**1996**	22.7
10.5	— 0.4	6.2	— -5.5	0.4	— 1.9	**1997**	21.6
— 1.2	— 19.9	13.0	4.6	10.1	12.5	**1998**	39.6
— 1.8	3.8	0.2	8.0	12.5	22.0	**1999**	85.6
— 5.0	11.7	— 12.7	— 8.3	— 22.9	— 4.9	**2000**	— 39.3
— 6.2	— 10.9	— 17.0	12.8	14.2	1.0	**2001**	— 21.1
— 9.2	— 1.0	— 10.9	13.5	11.2	— 9.7	**2002**	— 31.5
6.9	4.3	— 1.3	8.1	1.5	2.2	**2003**	50.0
— 7.8	— 2.6	3.2	4.1	6.2	3.7	**2004**	8.6
6.2	— 1.5	0.0	— 1.5	5.3	— 1.2	**2005**	1.4
— 3.7	4.4	3.4	4.8	2.7	— 0.7	**2006**	9.5
— 2.2	2.0	4.0	5.8	— 6.9	— 0.3	**2007**	9.8
1.4	1.8	— 11.6	— 17.7	— 10.8	2.7	**2008**	— 40.5
7.8	1.5	5.6	— 3.6	4.9	5.8	**2009**	43.9
6.9	— 6.2	12.0	5.9	— 0.4	6.2	**2010**	16.9
— 0.6	— 6.4	— 6.4	11.1	— 2.4	— 0.6	**2011**	— 1.8
0.2	4.3	1.6	— 4.5	1.1	0.3	**2012**	15.9
6.6	— 1.0	5.1	3.9	3.6	2.9	**2013**	38.3
— 0.9	4.8	— 1.9	3.1	3.5	— 1.2	**2014**	13.4
2.8	— 6.9	— 3.3	9.4	1.1	— 2.0	**2015**	5.7
6.6	1.0	1.9	— 2.3	2.6	1.1	**2016**	7.5
3.4	1.3	1.0	3.6	2.2	0.4	**2017**	28.2
2.2	5.7	— 0.8	— 9.2	0.3	— 9.5	**2018**	— 3.9
2.1	— 2.6	0.5	3.7	4.5	3.5	**2019**	35.2
27/48	26/48	26/48	27/48	34/48	28/48		35/48
56 %	54 %	54 %	56 %	71 %	58 %		73 %
0.5 %	0.1 %	— 0.5 %	0.7 %	1.7 %	1.4 %		12.6 %
10	11	12	8	2	3		

NASDAQ MONTH
CLOSING VALUES

	JAN	FEB	MAR	APR	MAY	JUN
1972	119	125	128	131	133	130
1973	128	120	117	108	103	101
1974	95	94	92	87	80	76
1975	70	73	76	79	83	87
1976	87	90	91	90	88	90
1977	96	95	94	95	96	100
1978	101	101	106	115	120	120
1979	126	123	132	134	131	138
1980	162	158	131	140	150	158
1981	198	198	210	217	223	216
1982	188	179	176	185	179	171
1983	248	261	271	293	309	319
1984	268	253	251	247	233	240
1985	279	284	279	281	291	296
1986	336	360	375	383	400	406
1987	392	425	430	418	417	425
1988	345	367	375	379	370	395
1989	401	400	407	428	446	435
1990	416	426	436	420	459	462
1991	414	453	482	485	506	476
1992	620	633	604	579	585	564
1993	696	671	690	661	701	704
1994	800	793	743	734	735	706
1995	755	794	817	844	865	933
1996	1060	1100	1101	1191	1243	1185
1997	1380	1309	1222	1261	1400	1442
1998	1619	1771	1836	1868	1779	1895
1999	2506	2288	2461	2543	2471	2686
2000	3940	4697	4573	3861	3401	3966
2001	2773	2152	1840	2116	2110	2161
2002	1934	1731	1845	1688	1616	1463
2003	1321	1338	1341	1464	1596	1623
2004	2066	2030	1994	1920	1987	2048
2005	2062	2052	1999	1922	2068	2057
2006	2306	2281	2340	2323	2179	2172
2007	2464	2416	2422	2525	2605	2603
2008	2390	2271	2279	2413	2523	2293
2009	1476	1378	1529	1717	1774	1835
2010	2147	2238	2398	2461	2257	2109
2011	2700	2782	2781	2874	2835	2774
2012	2814	2967	3092	3046	2827	2935
2013	3142	3160	3268	3329	3456	3403
2014	4104	4308	4199	4115	4243	4408
2015	4635	4964	4901	4941	5070	4987
2016	4614	4558	4870	4775	4948	4843
2017	5615	5825	5912	6048	6199	6140
2018	7411	7273	7063	7066	7442	7510
2019	7282	7533	7729	8095	7453	8006

NASDAQ MONTH CLOSING VALUES 🟦🟥 STOCK MKT

JUL	AUG	SEP	OCT	NOV	DEC	
128	130	130	130	133	134	**1972**
109	105	111	110	94	92	**1973**
70	62	56	65	63	60	**1974**
83	79	74	77	79	78	**1975**
91	90	91	90	91	98	**1976**
101	100	101	98	103	105	**1977**
126	135	133	111	115	118	**1978**
141	150	150	136	144	151	**1979**
172	182	188	193	208	202	**1980**
212	196	180	195	201	196	**1981**
167	178	188	213	232	232	**1982**
304	292	297	275	286	279	**1983**
230	255	250	247	242	247	**1984**
301	298	280	293	314	325	**1985**
371	383	351	361	360	349	**1986**
435	455	444	323	305	331	**1987**
387	377	388	383	372	381	**1988**
454	469	473	456	456	455	**1989**
438	381	345	330	359	374	**1990**
502	526	527	543	524	586	**1991**
581	563	583	605	653	677	**1992**
705	743	763	779	754	777	**1993**
722	766	764	777	750	752	**1994**
1001	1020	1044	1036	1059	1052	**1995**
1081	1142	1227	1222	1293	1291	**1996**
1594	1587	1686	1594	1601	1570	**1997**
1872	1499	1694	1771	1950	2193	**1998**
2638	2739	2746	2966	3336	4069	**1999**
3767	4206	3673	3370	2598	2471	**2000**
2027	1805	1499	1690	1931	1950	**2001**
1328	1315	1172	1330	1479	1336	**2002**
1735	1810	1787	1932	1960	2003	**2003**
1887	1838	1897	1975	2097	2175	**2004**
2185	2152	2152	2120	2233	2205	**2005**
2091	2184	2258	2367	2432	2415	**2006**
2546	2596	2702	2859	2661	2652	**2007**
2326	2368	2092	1721	1536	1577	**2008**
1979	2009	2122	2045	2145	2269	**2009**
2255	2114	2369	2507	2498	2653	**2010**
2756	2579	2415	2684	2620	2605	**2011**
2940	3067	3116	2977	3010	3020	**2012**
3626	3590	3771	3920	4060	4177	**2013**
4370	4580	4493	4631	4792	4736	**2014**
5128	4777	4620	5054	5109	5007	**2015**
5162	5213	5312	5189	5324	5383	**2016**
6348	6429	6496	6728	6874	6903	**2017**
7672	8110	8046	7306	7331	6635	**2018**
8175	7963	7999	8292	8665	8973	**2019**

S&P/TSX MONTH PERCENT CHANGES

	JAN	FEB	MAR	APR	MAY	JUN
1985	8.1	0.0	0.7	0.8	3.8	— 0.8
1986	— 1.7	0.5	6.7	1.1	1.4	— 1.2
1987	9.2	4.5	6.9	— 0.6	— 0.9	1.5
1988	— 3.3	4.8	3.4	0.8	— 2.7	5.9
1989	6.7	— 1.2	0.2	1.4	2.2	1.5
1990	— 6.7	— 0.5	— 1.3	— 8.2	6.7	— 0.6
1991	0.5	5.8	1.0	-0.8	2.2	— 2.3
1992	2.4	— 0.4	— 4.7	— 1.7	1.0	0.0
1993	— 1.3	4.4	4.4	5.2	2.5	2.2
1994	5.4	— 2.9	— 2.1	— 1.4	1.4	— 7.0
1995	— 4.7	2.7	4.6	— -0.8	4.0	1.8
1996	5.4	— 0.7	0.8	3.5	1.9	— 3.9
1997	3.1	0.8	— 5.0	2.2	6.8	0.9
1998	0.0	5.9	6.6	1.4	— 1.0	— 2.9
1999	3.8	— 6.2	4.5	6.3	— 2.5	2.5
2000	0.8	7.6	3.7	— 1.2	— 1.0	10.2
2001	4.3	— 13.3	— 5.8	4.5	2.7	— 5.2
2002	— 0.5	— 0.1	2.8	— 2.4	— 0.1	— 6.7
2003	— 0.7	— 0.2	— 3.2	3.8	4.2	1.8
2004	3.7	3.1	— 2.3	— 4.0	2.1	1.5
2005	— 0.5	5.0	— 0.6	— 3.5	3.6	3.1
2006	6.0	— 2.2	3.6	0.8	— 3.8	— 1.1
2007	1.0	0.1	0.9	1.9	4.8	— 1.1
2008	— 4.9	3.3	— 1.7	4.4	5.6	— 1.7
2009	— 3.3	— 6.6	7.4	6.9	11.2	0.0
2010	— 5.5	4.8	3.5	1.4	— 3.7	— 4.0
2011	0.8	4.3	— 0.1	— 1.2	— 1.0	— 3.6
2012	4.2	1.5	— 2.0	— 0.8	— 6.3	0.7
2013	2.0	1.1	— 0.6	— 2.3	1.6	— 4.1
2014	0.5	3.8	0.9	2.2	— 0.3	3.7
2015	0.3	3.8	— 2.2	2.2	— 1.4	— 3.1
2016	— 1.4	0.3	4.9	3.4	0.8	0.0
2017	0.6	0.1	1.0	0.2	— 1.5	— 1.1
2018	— 1.6	— 3.2	— 0.5	1.6	2.9	1.3
2019	8.5	2.9	0.6	3.0	— 3.3	2.1
FQ POS	22/35	22/35	21/35	22/35	21/35	16/35
% FQ POS	63 %	63 %	60 %	63 %	60 %	46 %
AVG GAIN	1.2 %	1.0 %	1.0 %	0.9 %	1.2 %	-0.3 %
RANK GAIN	3	5	4	6	2	11

S&P/TSX MONTH PERCENT CHANGES | STOCK MKT

JUL	AUG	SEP	OCT	NOV	DEC		YEAR
2.4	1.5	— 6.7	1.6	6.8	1.3	**1985**	20.5
— 4.9	3.2	— 1.6	1.6	0.7	0.6	**1986**	6.0
7.8	— 0.9	— 2.3	— 22.6	— 1.4	6.1	**1987**	3.1
— 1.9	— 2.7	— 0.1	3.4	— 3.0	2.9	**1988**	7.3
5.6	1.0	— 1.7	— 0.6	0.6	0.7	**1989**	17.1
0.5	— 6.0	— 5.6	— 2.5	2.3	3.4	**1990**	— 18.0
2.1	— 0.6	— 3.7	3.8	— 1.9	1.9	**1991**	7.8
1.6	— 1.2	— 3.1	1.2	— 1.6	2.1	**1992**	— 4.6
0.0	4.3	— 3.6	6.6	— 1.8	3.4	**1993**	29.0
3.8	4.1	0.1	— 1.4	— 4.6	2.9	**1994**	— 2.5
1.9	— 2.1	0.3	— 1.6	4.5	1.1	**1995**	11.9
— 2.3	4.3	2.9	5.8	7.5	— 1.5	**1996**	25.7
6.8	— 3.9	6.5	— 2.8	— 4.8	2.9	**1997**	13.0
— 5.9	— 20.2	1.5	10.6	2.2	2.2	**1998**	— 3.2
1.0	— 1.6	— 0.2	4.3	3.6	11.9	**1999**	29.7
2.1	8.1	— 7.7	— 7.1	— 8.5	1.3	**2000**	6.2
— 0.6	— 3.8	— 7.6	0.7	7.8	3.5	**2001**	— 13.9
— 7.6	0.1	— 6.5	1.1	5.1	0.7	**2002**	— 14.0
3.9	3.6	— 1.3	4.7	1.1	4.6	**2003**	24.3
— 1.0	— 1.0	3.5	2.3	1.8	2.4	**2004**	12.5
5.3	2.4	3.2	— 5.7	4.2	4.1	**2005**	21.9
1.9	2.1	— 2.6	5.0	3.3	1.2	**2006**	14.5
— 0.3	— 1.5	3.2	3.7	— 6.4	1.1	**2007**	7.2
— 6.0	1.3	— 14.7	— 16.9	— 5.0	— 3.1	**2008**	— 35.0
4.0	0.8	4.8	— 4.2	4.9	2.6	**2009**	30.7
3.7	1.7	3.8	2.5	2.2	3.8	**2010**	14.4
— 2.7	— 1.4	— 9.0	5.4	— 0.4	— 2.0	**2011**	— 11.1
0.6	2.4	3.1	0.9	— 1.5	1.6	**2012**	4.0
2.9	1.3	1.1	4.5	0.3	1.7	**2013**	9.6
1.2	1.9	— 4.3	— 2.3	0.9	— 0.8	**2014**	7.4
— 0.6	— 4.2	— 4.0	1.7	— 0.4	— 3.4	**2015**	— 11.1
3.7	0.1	0.9	0.4	2.0	1.4	**2016**	17.5
— 0.3	0.4	2.8	2.5	0.3	0.9	**2017**	6.0
1.0	— 1.0	— 1.2	— 6.5	1.1	— 5.8	**2018**	— 11.8
0.1	0.2	1.3	— 1.1	3.4	0.1	**2019**	19.1
23/35	20/35	15/35	22/35	22/35	29/35		25/35
66 %	57 %	431 %	63 %	63 %	83 %		71 %
0.9 %	— 0.2 %	— 1.4 %	0.0 %	0.7 %	1.7 %		6.9 %
7	10	12	9	8	1		

S&P/TSX MONTH CLOSING VALUES

	JAN	FEB	MAR	APR	MAY	JUN
1985	2595	2595	2613	2635	2736	2713
1986	2843	2856	3047	3079	3122	3086
1987	3349	3499	3739	3717	3685	3740
1988	3057	3205	3314	3340	3249	3441
1989	3617	3572	3578	3628	3707	3761
1990	3704	3687	3640	3341	3565	3544
1991	3273	3462	3496	3469	3546	3466
1992	3596	3582	3412	3356	3388	3388
1993	3305	3452	3602	3789	3883	3966
1994	4555	4424	4330	4267	4327	4025
1995	4018	4125	4314	4280	4449	4527
1996	4968	4934	4971	5147	5246	5044
1997	6110	6158	5850	5977	6382	6438
1998	6700	7093	7559	7665	7590	7367
1999	6730	6313	6598	7015	6842	7010
2000	8481	9129	9462	9348	9252	10196
2001	9322	8079	7608	7947	8162	7736
2002	7649	7638	7852	7663	7656	7146
2003	6570	6555	6343	6586	6860	6983
2004	8521	8789	8586	8244	8417	8546
2005	9204	9668	9612	9275	9607	9903
2006	11946	11688	12111	12204	11745	11613
2007	13034	13045	13166	13417	14057	13907
2008	13155	13583	13350	13937	14715	14467
2009	8695	8123	8720	9325	10370	10375
2010	11094	11630	12038	12211	11763	11294
2011	13552	14137	14116	13945	13803	13301
2012	12452	12644	12392	12293	11513	11597
2013	12685	12822	12750	12457	12650	12129
2014	13695	14210	14335	14652	14604	15146
2015	14674	15234	14902	15225	15014	14553
2016	12822	12860	13494	13951	14066	14065
2017	15386	15399	15548	15586	15350	15182
2018	15952	15443	15367	15608	16062	16278
2019	15541	15999	16102	16581	16037	16382

JUL	AUG	SEP	OCT	NOV	DEC	
2779	2820	2632	2675	2857	2893	1985
2935	3028	2979	3027	3047	3066	1986
4030	3994	3902	3019	2978	3160	1987
3377	3286	3284	3396	3295	3390	1988
3971	4010	3943	3919	3943	3970	1989
3561	3346	3159	3081	3151	3257	1990
3540	3518	3388	3516	3449	3512	1991
3443	3403	3298	3336	3283	3350	1992
3967	4138	3991	4256	4180	4321	1993
4179	4350	4354	4292	4093	4214	1994
4615	4517	4530	4459	4661	4714	1995
4929	5143	5291	5599	6017	5927	1996
6878	6612	7040	6842	6513	6699	1997
6931	5531	5614	6208	6344	6486	1998
7081	6971	6958	7256	7520	8414	1999
10406	11248	10378	9640	8820	8934	2000
7690	7399	6839	6886	7426	7688	2001
6605	6612	6180	6249	6570	6615	2002
7258	7517	7421	7773	7859	8221	2003
8458	8377	8668	8871	9030	9247	2004
10423	10669	11012	10383	10824	11272	2005
11831	12074	11761	12345	12752	12908	2006
13869	13660	14099	14625	13689	13833	2007
13593	13771	11753	9763	9271	8988	2008
10787	10868	11935	10911	11447	11746	2009
11713	11914	12369	12676	12953	13443	2010
12946	12769	11624	12252	12204	11955	2011
11665	11949	12317	12423	12239	12434	2012
12487	12654	12787	13361	13395	13622	2013
15331	15626	14961	14613	14745	14632	2014
14468	13859	13307	13529	13470	13010	2015
14583	14598	14726	14787	15083	15288	2016
15144	15212	15635	16026	16067	16209	2017
16434	16263	16073	15027	15198	14323	2018
16407	16442	16659	16483	17040	17063	2019

10 BEST

10 WORST

YEARS

	Close	Change	Change
1954	36	11 pt	45.0 %
1958	55	15	38.1
1995	616	157	34.1
1975	90	22	31.5
1997	970	230	31.0
2013	1848	422	29.6
2019	3231	724	28.9
1989	353	76	27.3
1998	1229	259	26.7
1955	45	10	26.4

YEARS

	Close	Change	Change
2008	903	− 566 pt	− 38.5 %
1974	69	− 29	− 29.7
2002	880	− 268	− 23.4
1973	98	− 21	− 17.4
1957	40	− 7	− 14.3
1966	80	− 12	− 13.1
2001	1148	− 172	− 13.0
1962	63	− 8	− 11.8
1977	95	− 12	− 11.5
1969	92	− 12	− 11.4

MONTHS

	Close	Change	Change
Oct 1974	74	10 pt	16.3 %
Aug 1982	120	12	11.6
Dec 1991	417	42	11.2
Oct 1982	134	13	11.0
Oct 2011	1253	122	10.8
Aug 1984	167	16	10.6
Nov 1980	141	13	10.2
Nov 1962	62	6	10.2
Mar 2000	1499	132	9.7
Apr 2009	798	75	9.4

MONTHS

	Close	Change	Change
Oct 1987	252	− 70 pt	− 21.8 %
Oct 2008	969	− 196	− 16.8
Aug 1998	957	− 163	− 14.6
Sep 1974	64	− 9	− 11.9
Nov 1973	96	− 12	− 11.4
Sep 2002	815	− 101	− 11.0
Feb 2009	735	− 91	− 11.0
Mar 1980	102	− 12	− 10.2
Aug 1990	323	− 34	− 9.4
Feb 2001	1240	− 126	− 9.2

DAYS

		Close	Change	Change
Mon	2008 Oct 13	1003	104 pt	11.6 %
Tue	2008 Oct 28	941	92	10.8
Wed	1987 Oct 21	258	22	9.1
Mon	2009 Mar 23	883	54	7.1
Thu	2008 Nov 13	911	59	6.9
Mon	2008 Nov 24	852	52	6.5
Tues	2009 Mar 10	720	43	6.4
Fri	2008 Nov 21	800	48	6.3
Wed	2002 Jul 24	843	46	5.7
Tue	2008 Sep 30	1166	60	5.4

DAYS

		Close	Change	Change
Mon	1987 Oct 19	225	− 58 pt	− 20.5 %
Wed	2008 Oct 15	908	− 90	− 9.0
Mon	2008 Dec 01	816	− 80	− 8.9
Mon	2008 Sep 29	1106	− 107	− 8.8
Mon	1987 Oct 26	228	− 21	− 8.3
Thu	2008 Oct 09	910	− 75	− 7.6
Mon	1997 Oct 27	877	− 65	− 6.9
Mon	1998 Aug 31	957	− 70	− 6.8
Fri	1988 Jan 8	243	− 18	− 6.8
Thu	2008 Nov 20	752	− 54	− 6.7

10 BEST

10 WORST

YEARS

	Close	Change	Change
1954	404	124 pt	44.0 %
1975	852	236	38.3
1958	584	148	34.0
1995	5117	1283	33.5
1985	1547	335	27.7
1989	2753	585	27.0
2013	16577	3473	26.5
1996	6448	1331	26.0
2003	10454	2112	25.3
1999	11453	2272	25.2

YEARS

	Close	Change	Change
2008	8776	− 4488 pt	− 33.8 %
1974	616	− 235	− 27.6
1966	786	− 184	− 18.9
1977	831	− 174	− 17.3
2002	8342	− 1680	− 16.8
1973	851	− 169	− 16.6
1969	800	− 143	− 15.2
1957	436	− 64	− 12.8
1962	652	− 79	− 10.8
1960	616	− 64	− 9.3

MONTHS

	Close	Change	Change
Aug 1982	901	93 pt	11.5 %
Oct 1982	992	95	10.6
Oct 2002	8397	805	10.6
Apr 1978	837	80	10.5
Apr 1999	10789	1003	10.2
Nov 1962	649	60	10.1
Nov 1954	387	35	9.9
Aug 1984	1224	109	9.8
Oct 1998	8592	750	9.6
Oct 2011	11955	1042	9.5

MONTHS

	Close	Change	Change
Oct 1987	1994	− 603 pt	− 23.2 %
Aug 1998	7539	− 1344	− 15.1
Oct 2008	9325	− 1526	− 14.1
Nov 1973	822	− 134	− 14.0
Sep 2002	7592	− 1072	− 12.4
Feb 2009	7063	− 938	− 11.7
Sep 2001	8848	− 1102	− 11.1
Sep 1974	608	− 71	− 10.4
Aug 1974	679	− 79	− 10.4
Jun 2008	11350	− 1288	− 10.2

DAYS

		Close	Change	Change
Mon	2008 Oct 13	9388	936 pt	11.1 %
Tue	2008 Oct 28	9065	889	10.9
Wed	1987 Oct 21	2028	187	10.2
Mon	2009 Mar 23	7776	497	6.8
Thu	2008 Nov 13	8835	553	6.7
Fri	2008 Nov 21	8046	494	6.5
Wed	2002 Jul 24	8191	489	6.3
Tue	1987 Oct 20	1841	102	5.9
Tue	2009 Mar 10	6926	379	5.8
Mon	2002 Jul 29	8712	448	5.4

DAYS

		Close	Change	Change
Mon	1987 Oct 19	1739	− 508 pt	− 22.6 %
Mon	1987 Oct 26	1794	− 157	− 8.0
Wed	2008 Oct 15	8578	− 733	− 7.9
Mon	2008 Dec 01	8149	− 680	− 7.7
Thu	2008 Oct 09	8579	− 679	− 7.3
Mon	1997 Oct 27	8366	− 554	− 7.2
Mon	2001 Sep 17	8921	− 685	− 7.1
Mon	2008 Sep 29	10365	− 778	− 7.0
Fri	1989 Oct 13	2569	− 191	− 6.9
Fri	1988 Jan 8	1911	− 141	− 6.9

10 BEST

10 WORST

YEARS

	Close	Change	Change
1999	4069	1877 pt	85.6 %
1991	586	213	56.9
2003	2003	668	50.0
2009	2269	692	43.9
1995	1052	300	39.9
1998	2193	622	39.6
2013	4161	1157	38.3
2019	8973	2337	35.2
1980	202	51	33.9
1985	325	78	31.5

YEARS

	Close	Change	Change
2008	1577	– 1075 pt	– 40.5 %
2000	2471	– 1599	– 39.3
1974	60	– 32	– 35.1
2002	1336	– 615	– 31.5
1973	92	– 42	– 31.1
2001	1950	– 520	– 21.1
1990	374	– 81	– 17.8
1984	247	– 32	– 11.3
1987	331	– 18	– 5.2
2018	6635	– 268	– 3.9

MONTHS

	Close	Change	Change
Dec 1999	4069	733 pt	22.0 %
Feb 2000	4697	756	19.2
Oct 1974	65	10	17.2
Jun 2000	3966	565	16.6
Apr 2001	2116	276	15.0
Nov 2001	1931	240	14.2
Oct 2002	1330	158	13.5
Oct 1982	1771	25	13.3
Sep 1998	1694	195	13.0
Oct 2001	1690	191	12.8

MONTHS

	Close	Change	Change
Oct 1987	323	– 121 pt	– 27.2 %
Nov 2000	2598	– 772	– 22.9
Feb 2001	2152	– 621	– 22.4
Aug 1998	1499	– 373	– 19.9
Oct 2008	1721	– 371	– 17.7
Mar 1980	131	– 27	– 17.1
Sep 2001	1499	– 307	– 17.0
Oct 1978	111	– 22	– 16.4
Apr 2000	3861	– 712	– 15.6
Nov 1973	94	– 17	– 15.1

DAYS

		Close	Change	Change
Wed	2001 Jan 3	2617	325 pt	14.2 %
Mon	2008 Oct 13	1844	195	11.8
Tue	2000 Dec 5	2890	274	10.5
Tue	2008 Oct 28	1649	144	9.5
Thu	2001 Apr 5	1785	146	8.9
Wed	2001 Apr 18	2079	156	8.1
Tue	2000 May 30	3459	254	7.9
Fri	2000 Oct 13	3317	242	7.9
Thu	2000 Oct 19	3419	247	7.8
Wed	2002 May 8	1696	122	7.8

DAYS

		Close	Change	Change
Mon	1987 Oct 19	360	– 46 pt	– 11.3 %
Fri	2000 Apr 14	3321	– 355	– 9.7
Mon	2008 Sep 29	1984	– 200	– 9.1
Mon	1987 Oct 26	299	– 30	– 9.0
Tue	1987 Oct 20	328	– 32	– 9.0
Mon	2008 Dec 01	1398	– 138	– 9.0
Mon	1998 Aug 31	1499	– 140	– 8.6
Wed	2008 Oct 15	1628	– 151	– 8.5
Mon	2000 Apr 03	4224	– 349	– 7.6
Tue	2001 Jan 02	2292	– 179	– 7.2

10 BEST

10 WORST

YEARS

	Close	Change	Change
2009	8414	2758 pt	30.7 %
1999	4321	1928	29.7
1993	5927	971	29.0
1996	8221	1213	25.7
2003	11272	1606	24.3
2005	2893	2026	21.9
1985	3970	500	20.8
2019	17063	1842	27.4
1989	12908	580	17.1
2006	6699	1636	14.5

YEARS

	Close	Change	Change
2008	8988	− 4845 pt	− 35.0 %
1990	3257	− 713	− 18.0
2002	6615	− 1074	− 14.0
2001	7688	− 1245	− 13.9
2018	14323	− 1886	− 11.6
2015	13010	− 1622	− 11.1
2011	11955	− 1488	− 11.1
1992	3350	− 162	− 4.6
1998	6486	− 214	− 3.2
1994	4214	− 108	− 2.5

MONTHS

	Close	Change	Change
Dec 1999	8414	891 pt	11.8 %
May 2009	8500	1045	11.2
Oct 1998	6208	594	10.6
Jun 2000	10196	943	10.2
Jan 1985	2595	195	8.1
Aug 2000	11248	842	8.1
Nov 2001	7426	540	7.8
Jul 1987	4030	290	7.8
Feb 2000	9129	648	7.6
Nov 1996	6017	418	7.5

MONTHS

	Close	Change	Change
Oct 1987	3019	− 883 pt	− 22.6 %
Aug 1998	5531	− 1401	− 20.2
Oct 2008	9763	− 1990	− 16.9
Sep 2008	11753	− 2018	− 14.7
Feb 2001	8079	− 1243	− 13.3
Sep 2011	11624	− 1145	− 9.0
Nov 2000	8820	− 820	− 8.5
Apr 1990	3341	− 299	− 8.2
Sep 2000	10378	− 870	− 7.7
Sep 2001	6839	− 561	− 7.6

DAYS

		Close	Change	Change
Tue	2008 Oct 14	9956	891 pt	9.8 %
Wed	1987 Oct 21	3246	269	9.0
Mon	2008 Oct 20	10251	689	7.2
Tue	2008 Oct 28	9152	614	7.2
Fri	2008 Sep 19	12913	848	7.0
Fri	2008 Nov 28	9271	517	5.9
Fri	2008 Nov 21	8155	431	5.6
Mon	2008 Dec 08	8567	450	5.5
Mon	2009 Mar 23	8959	452	5.3
Fri	1987 Oct 30	3019	147	5.1

DAYS

		Close	Change	Change
Mon	1987 Oct 19	3192	− 407 pt	− 11.3 %
Mon	2008 Dec 01	8406	− 864	− 9.3
Thu	2008 Nov 20	7725	− 766	− 9.0
Mon	2008 Oct 27	8537	− 757	− 8.1
Wed	2000 Oct 25	9512	− 840	− 8.1
Mon	1987 Oct 26	2846	− 233	− 7.6
Thu	2008 Oct 02	10901	− 814	− 6.9
Mon	2008 Sep 29	11285	− 841	− 6.9
Tue	1987 Oct 20	2977	− 215	− 6.7
Fri	2001 Feb 16	8393	− 574	− 6.4

BOND YIELDS

	JAN	FEB	MAR	APR	MAY	JUN
1954	2.48	2.47	2.37	2.29	2.37	2.38
1955	2.61	2.65	2.68	2.75	2.76	2.78
1956	2.9	2.84	2.96	3.18	3.07	3
1957	3.46	3.34	3.41	3.48	3.6	3.8
1958	3.09	3.05	2.98	2.88	2.92	2.97
1959	4.02	3.96	3.99	4.12	4.31	4.34
1960	4.72	4.49	4.25	4.28	4.35	4.15
1961	3.84	3.78	3.74	3.78	3.71	3.88
1962	4.08	4.04	3.93	3.84	3.87	3.91
1963	3.83	3.92	3.93	3.97	3.93	3.99
1964	4.17	4.15	4.22	4.23	4.2	4.17
1965	4.19	4.21	4.21	4.2	4.21	4.21
1966	4.61	4.83	4.87	4.75	4.78	4.81
1967	4.58	4.63	4.54	4.59	4.85	5.02
1968	5.53	5.56	5.74	5.64	5.87	5.72
1969	6.04	6.19	6.3	6.17	6.32	6.57
1970	7.79	7.24	7.07	7.39	7.91	7.84
1971	6.24	6.11	5.7	5.83	6.39	6.52
1972	5.95	6.08	6.07	6.19	6.13	6.11
1973	6.46	6.64	6.71	6.67	6.85	6.9
1974	6.99	6.96	7.21	7.51	7.58	7.54
1975	7.5	7.39	7.73	8.23	8.06	7.86
1976	7.74	7.79	7.73	7.56	7.9	7.86
1977	7.21	7.39	7.46	7.37	7.46	7.28
1978	7.96	8.03	8.04	8.15	8.35	8.46
1979	9.1	9.1	9.12	9.18	9.25	8.91
1980	10.8	12.41	12.75	11.47	10.18	9.78
1981	12.57	13.19	13.12	13.68	14.1	13.47
1982	14.59	14.43	13.86	13.87	13.62	14.3
1983	10.46	10.72	10.51	10.4	10.38	10.85
1984	11.67	11.84	12.32	12.63	13.41	13.56
1985	11.38	11.51	11.86	11.43	10.85	10.16
1986	9.19	8.7	7.78	7.3	7.71	7.8
1987	7.08	7.25	7.25	8.02	8.61	8.4
1988	8.67	8.21	8.37	8.72	9.09	8.92
1989	9.09	9.17	9.36	9.18	8.86	8.28
1990	8.21	8.47	8.59	8.79	8.76	8.48
1991	8.09	7.85	8.11	8.04	8.07	8.28
1992	7.03	7.34	7.54	7.48	7.39	7.26
1993	6.6	6.26	5.98	5.97	6.04	5.96
1994	5.75	5.97	6.48	6.97	7.18	7.1
1995	7.78	7.47	7.2	7.06	6.63	6.17
1996	5.65	5.81	6.27	6.51	6.74	6.91
1997	6.58	6.42	6.69	6.89	6.71	6.49
1998	5.54	5.57	5.65	5.64	5.65	5.5
1999	4.72	5	5.23	5.18	5.54	5.9
2000	6.66	6.52	6.26	5.99	6.44	6.1
2001	5.16	5.1	4.89	5.14	5.39	5.28
2002	5.04	4.91	5.28	5.21	5.16	4.93
2003	4.05	3.9	3.81	3.96	3.57	3.33
2004	4.15	4.08	3.83	4.35	4.72	4.73
2005	4.22	4.17	4.5	4.34	4.14	4.00
2006	4.42	4.57	4.72	4.99	5.11	5.11
2007	4.76	4.72	4.56	4.69	4.75	5.10
2008	3.74	3.74	3.51	3.68	3.88	4.10
2009	2.52	2.87	2.82	2.93	3.29	3.72
2010	3.73	3.69	3.73	3.85	3.42	3.20
2011	3.39	3.58	3.41	3.46	3.17	3.00
2012	1.97	1.97	2.17	2.05	1.80	1.62
2013	1.91	1.98	1.96	1.76	1.93	2.30
2014	2.86	2.71	2.72	2.71	2.56	2.60
2015	1.88	1.98	2.04	1.94	2.20	2.36
2016	2.09	1.78	1.89	1.81	1.81	1.64
2017	2.43	2.42	2.48	2.30	2.30	2.19
2018	2.58	2.86	2.84	2.87	2.98	2.91
2019	2.71	2.68	2.57	2.53	2.40	2.07

* Source: Federal Reserve Bank of St. Louis, monthly data calculated as average of business days

10 YEAR TREASURY  BOND YIELDS

JUL	AUG	SEP	OCT	NOV	DEC	
2.3	2.36	2.38	2.43	2.48	2.51	**1954**
2.9	2.97	2.97	2.88	2.89	2.96	**1955**
3.11	3.33	3.38	3.34	3.49	3.59	**1956**
3.93	3.93	3.92	3.97	3.72	3.21	**1957**
3.2	3.54	3.76	3.8	3.74	3.86	**1958**
4.4	4.43	4.68	4.53	4.53	4.69	**1959**
3.9	3.8	3.8	3.89	3.93	3.84	**1960**
3.92	4.04	3.98	3.92	3.94	4.06	**1961**
4.01	3.98	3.98	3.93	3.92	3.86	**1962**
4.02	4	4.08	4.11	4.12	4.13	**1963**
4.19	4.19	4.2	4.19	4.15	4.18	**1964**
4.2	4.25	4.29	4.35	4.45	4.62	**1965**
5.02	5.22	5.18	5.01	5.16	4.84	**1966**
5.16	5.28	5.3	5.48	5.75	5.7	**1967**
5.5	5.42	5.46	5.58	5.7	6.03	**1968**
6.72	6.69	7.16	7.1	7.14	7.65	**1969**
7.46	7.53	7.39	7.33	6.84	6.39	**1970**
6.73	6.58	6.14	5.93	5.81	5.93	**1971**
6.11	6.21	6.55	6.48	6.28	6.36	**1972**
7.13	7.4	7.09	6.79	6.73	6.74	**1973**
7.81	8.04	8.04	7.9	7.68	7.43	**1974**
8.06	8.4	8.43	8.14	8.05	8	**1975**
7.83	7.77	7.59	7.41	7.29	6.87	**1976**
7.33	7.4	7.34	7.52	7.58	7.69	**1977**
8.64	8.41	8.42	8.64	8.81	9.01	**1978**
8.95	9.03	9.33	10.3	10.65	10.39	**1979**
10.25	11.1	11.51	11.75	12.68	12.84	**1980**
14.28	14.94	15.32	15.15	13.39	13.72	**1981**
13.95	13.06	12.34	10.91	10.55	10.54	**1982**
11.38	11.85	11.65	11.54	11.69	11.83	**1983**
13.36	12.72	12.52	12.16	11.57	11.5	**1984**
10.31	10.33	10.37	10.24	9.78	9.26	**1985**
7.3	7.17	7.45	7.43	7.25	7.11	**1986**
8.45	8.76	9.42	9.52	8.86	8.99	**1987**
9.06	9.26	8.98	8.8	8.96	9.11	**1988**
8.02	8.11	8.19	8.01	7.87	7.84	**1989**
8.47	8.75	8.89	8.72	8.39	8.08	**1990**
8.27	7.9	7.65	7.53	7.42	7.09	**1991**
6.84	6.59	6.42	6.59	6.87	6.77	**1992**
5.81	5.68	5.36	5.33	5.72	5.77	**1993**
7.3	7.24	7.46	7.74	7.96	7.81	**1994**
6.28	6.49	6.2	6.04	5.93	5.71	**1995**
6.87	6.64	6.83	6.53	6.2	6.3	**1996**
6.22	6.3	6.21	6.03	5.88	5.81	**1997**
5.46	5.34	4.81	4.53	4.83	4.65	**1998**
5.79	5.94	5.92	6.11	6.03	6.28	**1999**
6.05	5.83	5.8	5.74	5.72	5.24	**2000**
5.24	4.97	4.73	4.57	4.65	5.09	**2001**
4.65	4.26	3.87	3.94	4.05	4.03	**2002**
3.98	4.45	4.27	4.29	4.3	4.27	**2003**
4.5	4.28	4.13	4.1	4.19	4.23	**2004**
4.18	4.26	4.20	4.46	4.54	4.47	**2005**
5.09	4.88	4.72	4.73	4.60	4.56	**2006**
5.00	4.67	4.52	4.53	4.15	4.10	**2007**
4.01	3.89	3.69	3.81	3.53	2.42	**2008**
3.56	3.59	3.40	3.39	3.40	3.59	**2009**
3.01	2.70	2.65	2.54	2.76	3.29	**2010**
3.00	2.30	1.98	2.15	2.01	1.98	**2011**
1.53	1.68	1.72	1.75	1.65	1.72	**2012**
2.58	2.74	2.81	2.62	2.72	2.90	**2013**
2.54	2.42	2.53	2.30	2.33	2.21	**2014**
2.32	2.17	2.17	2.07	2.26	2.24	**2015**
1.50	1.56	1.63	1.76	2.14	2.49	**2016**
2.32	2.21	2.20	2.36	2.35	2.40	**2017**
2.89	2.89	3.00	3.15	3.12	2.83	**2018**
2.06	1.63	1.70	1.71	1.81	1.86	**2019**

5 YEAR TREASURY*

	JAN	FEB	MAR	APR	MAY	JUN
1954	2.17	2.04	1.93	1.87	1.92	1.92
1955	2.32	2.38	2.48	2.55	2.56	2.59
1956	2.84	2.74	2.93	3.20	3.08	2.97
1957	3.47	3.39	3.46	3.53	3.64	3.83
1958	2.88	2.78	2.64	2.46	2.41	2.46
1959	4.01	3.96	3.99	4.12	4.35	4.50
1960	4.92	4.69	4.31	4.29	4.49	4.12
1961	3.67	3.66	3.60	3.57	3.47	3.81
1962	3.94	3.89	3.68	3.60	3.66	3.64
1963	3.58	3.66	3.68	3.74	3.72	3.81
1964	4.07	4.03	4.14	4.15	4.05	4.02
1965	4.10	4.15	4.15	4.15	4.15	4.15
1966	4.86	4.98	4.92	4.83	4.89	4.97
1967	4.70	4.74	4.54	4.51	4.75	5.01
1968	5.54	5.59	5.76	5.69	6.04	5.85
1969	6.25	6.34	6.41	6.30	6.54	6.75
1970	8.17	7.82	7.21	7.50	7.97	7.85
1971	5.89	5.56	5.00	5.65	6.28	6.53
1972	5.59	5.69	5.87	6.17	5.85	5.91
1973	6.34	6.60	6.80	6.67	6.80	6.69
1974	6.95	6.82	7.31	7.92	8.18	8.10
1975	7.41	7.11	7.30	7.99	7.72	7.51
1976	7.46	7.45	7.49	7.25	7.59	7.61
1977	6.58	6.83	6.93	6.79	6.94	6.76
1978	7.77	7.83	7.86	7.98	8.18	8.36
1979	9.20	9.13	9.20	9.25	9.24	8.85
1980	10.74	12.60	13.47	11.84	9.95	9.21
1981	12.77	13.41	13.41	13.99	14.63	13.95
1982	14.65	14.54	13.98	14.00	13.75	14.43
1983	10.03	10.26	10.08	10.02	10.03	10.63
1984	11.37	11.54	12.02	12.37	13.17	13.48
1985	10.93	11.13	11.52	11.01	10.34	9.60
1986	8.68	8.34	7.46	7.05	7.52	7.64
1987	6.64	6.79	6.79	7.57	8.26	8.02
1988	8.18	7.71	7.83	8.19	8.58	8.49
1989	9.15	9.27	9.51	9.30	8.91	8.29
1990	8.12	8.42	8.60	8.77	8.74	8.43
1991	7.70	7.47	7.77	7.70	7.70	7.94
1992	6.24	6.58	6.95	6.78	6.69	6.48
1993	5.83	5.43	5.19	5.13	5.20	5.22
1994	5.09	5.40	5.94	6.52	6.78	6.70
1995	7.76	7.37	7.05	6.86	6.41	5.93
1996	5.36	5.38	5.97	6.30	6.48	6.69
1997	6.33	6.20	6.54	6.76	6.57	6.38
1998	5.42	5.49	5.61	5.61	5.63	5.52
1999	4.60	4.91	5.14	5.08	5.44	5.81
2000	6.58	6.68	6.50	6.26	6.69	6.30
2001	4.86	4.89	4.64	4.76	4.93	4.81
2002	4.34	4.30	4.74	4.65	4.49	4.19
2003	3.05	2.90	2.78	2.93	2.52	2.27
2004	3.12	3.07	2.79	3.39	3.85	3.93
2005	3.71	3.77	4.17	4.00	3.85	3.77
2006	4.35	4.57	4.72	4.90	5.00	5.07
2007	4.75	4.71	4.48	4.59	4.67	5.03
2008	2.98	2.78	2.48	2.84	3.15	3.49
2009	1.60	1.87	1.82	1.86	2.13	2.71
2010	2.48	2.36	2.43	2.58	2.18	2.00
2011	1.99	2.26	2.11	2.17	1.84	1.58
2012	0.84	0.83	1.02	0.89	0.76	0.71
2013	0.81	0.85	0.82	0.71	0.84	1.20
2014	1.65	1.52	1.64	1.70	1.59	1.68
2015	1.37	1.47	1.52	1.35	1.54	1.68
2016	1.52	1.22	1.38	1.26	1.30	1.17
2017	1.92	1.90	2.01	1.82	1.84	1.77
2018	2.38	2.60	2.63	2.70	2.82	2.78
2019	2.54	2.49	2.37	2.33	2.19	1.83

* Source: Federal Reserve Bank of St. Louis, monthly data calculated as average of business days

5 YEAR TREASURY  BOND YIELDS

JUL	AUG	SEP	OCT	NOV	DEC	
1.85	1.90	1.96	2.02	2.09	2.16	**1954**
2.72	2.86	2.85	2.76	2.81	2.93	**1955**
3.12	3.41	3.47	3.40	3.56	3.70	**1956**
4.00	4.00	4.03	4.08	3.72	3.08	**1957**
2.77	3.29	3.69	3.78	3.70	3.82	**1958**
4.58	4.57	4.90	4.72	4.75	5.01	**1959**
3.79	3.62	3.61	3.76	3.81	3.67	**1960**
3.84	3.96	3.90	3.80	3.82	3.91	**1961**
3.80	3.71	3.70	3.64	3.60	3.56	**1962**
3.89	3.89	3.96	3.97	4.01	4.04	**1963**
4.03	4.05	4.08	4.07	4.04	4.09	**1964**
4.15	4.20	4.25	4.34	4.46	4.72	**1965**
5.17	5.50	5.50	5.27	5.36	5.00	**1966**
5.23	5.31	5.40	5.57	5.78	5.75	**1967**
5.60	5.50	5.48	5.55	5.66	6.12	**1968**
7.01	7.03	7.57	7.51	7.53	7.96	**1969**
7.59	7.57	7.29	7.12	6.47	5.95	**1970**
6.85	6.55	6.14	5.93	5.78	5.69	**1971**
5.97	6.02	6.25	6.18	6.12	6.16	**1972**
7.33	7.63	7.05	6.77	6.92	6.80	**1973**
8.38	8.63	8.37	7.97	7.68	7.31	**1974**
7.92	8.33	8.37	7.97	7.80	7.76	**1975**
7.49	7.31	7.13	6.75	6.52	6.10	**1976**
6.84	7.03	7.04	7.32	7.34	7.48	**1977**
8.54	8.33	8.43	8.61	8.84	9.08	**1978**
8.90	9.06	9.41	10.63	10.93	10.42	**1979**
9.53	10.84	11.62	11.86	12.83	13.25	**1980**
14.79	15.56	15.93	15.41	13.38	13.60	**1981**
14.07	13.00	12.25	10.80	10.38	10.22	**1982**
11.21	11.63	11.43	11.28	11.41	11.54	**1983**
13.27	12.68	12.53	12.06	11.33	11.07	**1984**
9.70	9.81	9.81	9.69	9.28	8.73	**1985**
7.06	6.80	6.92	6.83	6.76	6.67	**1986**
8.01	8.32	8.94	9.08	8.35	8.45	**1987**
8.66	8.94	8.69	8.51	8.79	9.09	**1988**
7.83	8.09	8.17	7.97	7.81	7.75	**1989**
8.33	8.44	8.51	8.33	8.02	7.73	**1990**
7.91	7.43	7.14	6.87	6.62	6.19	**1991**
5.84	5.60	5.38	5.60	6.04	6.08	**1992**
5.09	5.03	4.73	4.71	5.06	5.15	**1993**
6.91	6.88	7.08	7.40	7.72	7.78	**1994**
6.01	6.24	6.00	5.86	5.69	5.51	**1995**
6.64	6.39	6.60	6.27	5.97	6.07	**1996**
6.12	6.16	6.11	5.93	5.80	5.77	**1997**
5.46	5.27	4.62	4.18	4.54	4.45	**1998**
5.68	5.84	5.80	6.03	5.97	6.19	**1999**
6.18	6.06	5.93	5.78	5.70	5.17	**2000**
4.76	4.57	4.12	3.91	3.97	4.39	**2001**
3.81	3.29	2.94	2.95	3.05	3.03	**2002**
2.87	3.37	3.18	3.19	3.29	3.27	**2003**
3.69	3.47	3.36	3.35	3.53	3.60	**2004**
3.98	4.12	4.01	4.33	4.45	4.39	**2005**
5.04	4.82	4.67	4.69	4.58	4.53	**2006**
4.88	4.43	4.20	4.20	3.67	3.49	**2007**
3.30	3.14	2.88	2.73	2.29	1.52	**2008**
2.46	2.57	2.37	2.33	2.23	2.34	**2009**
1.76	1.47	1.41	1.18	1.35	1.93	**2010**
1.54	1.02	0.90	1.06	0.91	0.89	**2011**
0.62	0.71	0.67	0.71	0.67	0.70	**2012**
1.40	1.52	1.60	1.37	1.37	1.58	**2013**
1.70	1.63	1.77	1.55	1.62	1.64	**2014**
1.63	1.54	1.49	1.39	1.67	1.70	**2015**
1.07	1.13	1.18	1.27	1.60	1.96	**2016**
1.87	1.78	1.80	1.98	2.05	2.18	**2017**
2.78	2.77	2.89	3.00	2.95	2.68	**2018**
1.83	1.49	1.57	1.53	1.64	1.68	**2019**

BOND YIELDS 🇺🇸 3 MONTH TREASURY

	JAN	FEB	MAR	APR	MAY	JUN
1982	12.92	14.28	13.31	13.34	12.71	13.08
1983	8.12	8.39	8.66	8.51	8.50	9.14
1984	9.26	9.46	9.89	10.07	10.22	10.26
1985	8.02	8.56	8.83	8.22	7.73	7.18
1986	7.30	7.29	6.76	6.24	6.33	6.40
1987	5.58	5.75	5.77	5.82	5.85	5.85
1988	6.00	5.84	5.87	6.08	6.45	6.66
1999	8.56	8.84	9.14	8.96	8.74	8.43
1990	7.90	8.00	8.17	8.04	8.01	7.99
1991	6.41	6.12	6.09	5.83	5.63	5.75
1992	3.91	3.95	4.14	3.84	3.72	3.75
1993	3.07	2.99	3.01	2.93	3.03	3.14
1994	3.04	3.33	3.59	3.78	4.27	4.25
1995	5.90	5.94	5.91	5.84	5.85	5.64
1996	5.15	4.96	5.10	5.09	5.15	5.23
1997	5.17	5.14	5.28	5.30	5.20	5.07
1998	5.18	5.23	5.16	5.08	5.14	5.12
1999	4.45	4.56	4.57	4.41	4.63	4.72
2000	5.50	5.73	5.86	5.82	5.99	5.86
2001	5.29	5.01	4.54	3.97	3.70	3.57
2002	1.68	1.76	1.83	1.75	1.76	1.73
2003	1.19	1.19	1.15	1.15	1.09	0.94
2004	0.90	0.94	0.95	0.96	1.04	1.29
2005	2.37	2.58	2.80	2.84	2.90	3.04
2006	4.34	4.54	4.63	4.72	4.84	4.92
2007	5.11	5.16	5.08	5.01	4.87	4.74
2008	2.82	2.17	1.28	1.31	1.76	1.89
2009	0.13	0.30	0.22	0.16	0.18	0.18
2010	0.06	0.11	0.15	0.16	0.16	0.12
2011	0.15	0.13	0.10	0.06	0.04	0.04
2012	0.03	0.09	0.08	0.08	0.09	0.09
2013	0.07	0.10	0.09	0.06	0.04	0.05
2014	0.04	0.05	0.05	0.03	0.03	0.04
2015	0.03	0.02	0.03	0.02	0.02	0.02
2016	0.26	0.31	0.30	0.23	0.28	0.27
2017	0.52	0.53	0.75	0.81	0.90	1.00
2018	1.43	1.59	1.73	1.79	1.90	1.94
2019	2.42	2.44	2.45	2.43	2.40	2.22

* Source: Federal Reserve Bank of St. Louis, monthly data calculated as average of business days

3 MONTH TREASURY 🇺🇸 BOND YIELDS

JUL	AUG	SEP	OCT	NOV	DEC	
11.86	9.00	8.19	7.97	8.35	8.20	**1982**
9.45	9.74	9.36	8.99	9.11	9.36	**1983**
10.53	10.90	10.80	10.12	8.92	8.34	**1984**
7.32	7.37	7.33	7.40	7.48	7.33	**1985**
6.00	5.69	5.35	5.32	5.50	5.68	**1986**
5.88	6.23	6.62	6.35	5.89	5.96	**1987**
6.95	7.30	7.48	7.60	8.03	8.35	**1988**
8.15	8.17	8.01	7.90	7.94	7.88	**1999**
7.87	7.69	7.60	7.40	7.29	6.95	**1990**
5.75	5.50	5.37	5.14	4.69	4.18	**1991**
3.28	3.20	2.97	2.93	3.21	3.29	**1992**
3.11	3.09	3.01	3.09	3.18	3.13	**1993**
4.46	4.61	4.75	5.10	5.45	5.76	**1994**
5.59	5.57	5.43	5.44	5.52	5.29	**1995**
5.30	5.19	5.24	5.12	5.17	5.04	**1996**
5.19	5.28	5.08	5.11	5.28	5.30	**1997**
5.09	5.04	4.74	4.07	4.53	4.50	**1998**
4.69	4.87	4.82	5.02	5.23	5.36	**1999**
6.14	6.28	6.18	6.29	6.36	5.94	**2000**
3.59	3.44	2.69	2.20	1.91	1.72	**2001**
1.71	1.65	1.66	1.61	1.25	1.21	**2002**
0.92	0.97	0.96	0.94	0.95	0.91	**2003**
1.36	1.50	1.68	1.79	2.11	2.22	**2004**
3.29	3.52	3.49	3.79	3.97	3.97	**2005**
5.08	5.09	4.93	5.05	5.07	4.97	**2006**
4.96	4.32	3.99	4.00	3.35	3.07	**2007**
1.66	1.75	1.15	0.69	0.19	0.03	**2008**
0.18	0.17	0.12	0.07	0.05	0.05	**2009**
0.16	0.16	0.15	0.13	0.14	0.14	**2010**
0.04	0.02	0.01	0.02	0.01	0.01	**2011**
0.10	0.10	0.11	0.10	0.09	0.07	**2012**
0.04	0.04	0.02	0.05	0.07	0.07	**2013**
0.03	0.03	0.02	0.02	0.02	0.03	**2014**
0.03	0.07	0.02	0.02	0.13	0.23	**2015**
0.30	0.30	0.29	0.33	0.45	0.51	**2016**
1.09	1.03	1.05	1.09	1.25	1.34	**2017**
1.99	2.07	2.17	2.29	2.37	2.41	**2018**
2.15	1.99	1.93	1.68	1.57	1.57	**2019**

MOODY'S SEASONED CORPORATE Aaa*

	JAN	FEB	MAR	APR	MAY	JUN
1950	2.57	2.58	2.58	2.60	2.61	2.62
1951	2.66	2.66	2.78	2.87	2.89	2.94
1952	2.98	2.93	2.96	2.93	2.93	2.94
1953	3.02	3.07	3.12	3.23	3.34	3.40
1954	3.06	2.95	2.86	2.85	2.88	2.90
1955	2.93	2.93	3.02	3.01	3.04	3.05
1956	3.11	3.08	3.10	3.24	3.28	3.26
1957	3.77	3.67	3.66	3.67	3.74	3.91
1958	3.60	3.59	3.63	3.60	3.57	3.57
1959	4.12	4.14	4.13	4.23	4.37	4.46
1960	4.61	4.56	4.49	4.45	4.46	4.45
1961	4.32	4.27	4.22	4.25	4.27	4.33
1962	4.42	4.42	4.39	4.33	4.28	4.28
1963	4.21	4.19	4.19	4.21	4.22	4.23
1964	4.39	4.36	4.38	4.40	4.41	4.41
1965	4.43	4.41	4.42	4.43	4.44	4.46
1966	4.74	4.78	4.92	4.96	4.98	5.07
1967	5.20	5.03	5.13	5.11	5.24	5.44
1968	6.17	6.10	6.11	6.21	6.27	6.28
1969	6.59	6.66	6.85	6.89	6.79	6.98
1970	7.91	7.93	7.84	7.83	8.11	8.48
1971	7.36	7.08	7.21	7.25	7.53	7.64
1972	7.19	7.27	7.24	7.30	7.30	7.23
1973	7.15	7.22	7.29	7.26	7.29	7.37
1974	7.83	7.85	8.01	8.25	8.37	8.47
1975	8.83	8.62	8.67	8.95	8.90	8.77
1976	8.60	8.55	8.52	8.40	8.58	8.62
1977	7.96	8.04	8.10	8.04	8.05	7.95
1978	8.41	8.47	8.47	8.56	8.69	8.76
1979	9.25	9.26	9.37	9.38	9.50	9.29
1980	11.09	12.38	12.96	12.04	10.99	10.58
1981	12.81	13.35	13.33	13.88	14.32	13.75
1982	15.18	15.27	14.58	14.46	14.26	14.81
1983	11.79	12.01	11.73	11.51	11.46	11.74
1984	12.20	12.08	12.57	12.81	13.28	13.55
1985	12.08	12.13	12.56	12.23	11.72	10.94
1986	10.05	9.67	9.00	8.79	9.09	9.13
1987	8.36	8.38	8.36	8.85	9.33	9.32
1988	9.88	9.40	9.39	9.67	9.90	9.86
1989	9.62	9.64	9.80	9.79	9.57	9.10
1990	8.99	9.22	9.37	9.46	9.47	9.26
1991	9.04	8.83	8.93	8.86	8.86	9.01
1992	8.20	8.29	8.35	8.33	8.28	8.22
1993	7.91	7.71	7.58	7.46	7.43	7.33
1994	6.92	7.08	7.48	7.88	7.99	7.97
1995	8.46	8.26	8.12	8.03	7.65	7.30
1996	6.81	6.99	7.35	7.50	7.62	7.71
1997	7.42	7.31	7.55	7.73	7.58	7.41
1998	6.61	6.67	6.72	6.69	6.69	6.53
1999	6.24	6.40	6.62	6.64	6.93	7.23
2000	7.78	7.68	7.68	7.64	7.99	7.67
2001	7.15	7.10	6.98	7.20	7.29	7.18
2002	6.55	6.51	6.81	6.76	6.75	6.63
2003	6.17	5.95	5.89	5.74	5.22	4.97
2004	5.54	5.50	5.33	5.73	6.04	6.01
2005	5.36	5.20	5.40	5.33	5.15	4.96
2006	5.29	5.35	5.53	5.84	5.95	5.89
2007	5.40	5.39	5.30	5.47	5.47	5.79
2008	5.33	5.53	5.51	5.55	5.57	5.68
2009	5.05	5.27	5.50	5.39	5.54	5.61
2010	5.26	5.35	5.27	5.29	4.96	4.88
2011	5.04	5.22	5.13	5.16	4.96	4.99
2012	3.85	3.85	3.99	3.96	3.80	3.64
2013	3.80	3.90	3.93	3.73	3.89	4.27
2014	4.49	4.45	4.38	4.24	4.16	4.25
2015	3.46	3.61	3.64	3.52	3.98	4.19
2016	4.00	3.96	3.82	3.62	3.65	3.50
2017	3.92	3.95	4.01	3.87	3.85	3.68
2018	3.55	3.82	3.87	3.85	4.00	3.96
2019	3.93	3.79	3.77	3.69	3.67	3.42

* Source: Federal Reserve Bank of St. Louis, monthly data calculated as average of business days

MOODY'S SEASONED CORPORATE Aaa BOND YIELDS

JUL	AUG	SEP	OCT	NOV	DEC	
2.65	2.61	2.64	2.67	2.67	2.67	**1950**
2.94	2.88	2.84	2.89	2.96	3.01	**1951**
2.95	2.94	2.95	3.01	2.98	2.97	**1952**
3.28	3.24	3.29	3.16	3.11	3.13	**1953**
2.89	2.87	2.89	2.87	2.89	2.90	**1954**
3.06	3.11	3.13	3.10	3.10	3.15	**1955**
3.28	3.43	3.56	3.59	3.69	3.75	**1956**
3.99	4.10	4.12	4.10	4.08	3.81	**1957**
3.67	3.85	4.09	4.11	4.09	4.08	**1958**
4.47	4.43	4.52	4.57	4.56	4.58	**1959**
4.41	4.28	4.25	4.30	4.31	4.35	**1960**
4.41	4.45	4.45	4.42	4.39	4.42	**1961**
4.34	4.35	4.32	4.28	4.25	4.24	**1962**
4.26	4.29	4.31	4.32	4.33	4.35	**1963**
4.40	4.41	4.42	4.42	4.43	4.44	**1964**
4.48	4.49	4.52	4.56	4.60	4.68	**1965**
5.16	5.31	5.49	5.41	5.35	5.39	**1966**
5.58	5.62	5.65	5.82	6.07	6.19	**1967**
6.24	6.02	5.97	6.09	6.19	6.45	**1968**
7.08	6.97	7.14	7.33	7.35	7.72	**1969**
8.44	8.13	8.09	8.03	8.05	7.64	**1970**
7.64	7.59	7.44	7.39	7.26	7.25	**1971**
7.21	7.19	7.22	7.21	7.12	7.08	**1972**
7.45	7.68	7.63	7.60	7.67	7.68	**1973**
8.72	9.00	9.24	9.27	8.89	8.89	**1974**
8.84	8.95	8.95	8.86	8.78	8.79	**1975**
8.56	8.45	8.38	8.32	8.25	7.98	**1976**
7.94	7.98	7.92	8.04	8.08	8.19	**1977**
8.88	8.69	8.69	8.89	9.03	9.16	**1978**
9.20	9.23	9.44	10.13	10.76	10.74	**1979**
11.07	11.64	12.02	12.31	12.97	13.21	**1980**
14.38	14.89	15.49	15.40	14.22	14.23	**1981**
14.61	13.71	12.94	12.12	11.68	11.83	**1982**
12.15	12.51	12.37	12.25	12.41	12.57	**1983**
13.44	12.87	12.66	12.63	12.29	12.13	**1984**
10.97	11.05	11.07	11.02	10.55	10.16	**1985**
8.88	8.72	8.89	8.86	8.68	8.49	**1986**
9.42	9.67	10.18	10.52	10.01	10.11	**1987**
9.96	10.11	9.82	9.51	9.45	9.57	**1988**
8.93	8.96	9.01	8.92	8.89	8.86	**1989**
9.24	9.41	9.56	9.53	9.30	9.05	**1990**
9.00	8.75	8.61	8.55	8.48	8.31	**1991**
8.07	7.95	7.92	7.99	8.10	7.98	**1992**
7.17	6.85	6.66	6.67	6.93	6.93	**1993**
8.11	8.07	8.34	8.57	8.68	8.46	**1994**
7.41	7.57	7.32	7.12	7.02	6.82	**1995**
7.65	7.46	7.66	7.39	7.10	7.20	**1996**
7.14	7.22	7.15	7.00	6.87	6.76	**1997**
6.55	6.52	6.40	6.37	6.41	6.22	**1998**
7.19	7.40	7.39	7.55	7.36	7.55	**1999**
7.65	7.55	7.62	7.55	7.45	7.21	**2000**
7.13	7.02	7.17	7.03	6.97	6.77	**2001**
6.53	6.37	6.15	6.32	6.31	6.21	**2002**
5.49	5.88	5.72	5.70	5.65	5.62	**2003**
5.82	5.65	5.46	5.47	5.52	5.47	**2004**
5.06	5.09	5.13	5.35	5.42	5.37	**2005**
5.85	5.68	5.51	5.51	5.33	5.32	**2006**
5.73	5.79	5.74	5.66	5.44	5.49	**2007**
5.67	5.64	5.65	6.28	6.12	5.05	**2008**
5.41	5.26	5.13	5.15	5.19	5.26	**2009**
4.72	4.49	4.53	4.68	4.87	5.02	**2010**
4.93	4.37	4.09	3.98	3.87	3.93	**2011**
3.40	3.48	3.49	3.47	3.50	3.65	**2012**
4.34	4.54	4.64	4.53	4.63	4.62	**2013**
4.16	4.08	4.11	3.92	3.92	3.79	**2014**
4.15	4.04	4.07	3.95	4.06	3.97	**2015**
3.28	3.32	3.41	3.51	3.86	4.06	**2016**
3.70	3.63	3.63	3.60	3.57	3.51	**2017**
3.87	3.88	3.98	4.14	4.22	4.02	**2018**
3.29	2.98	3.03	3.01	3.06	3.01	**2019**

MOODY'S SEASONED CORPORATE Baa*

	JAN	FEB	MAR	APR	MAY	JUN
1950	3.24	3.24	3.24	3.23	3.25	3.28
1951	3.17	3.16	3.23	3.35	3.40	3.49
1952	3.59	3.53	3.51	3.50	3.49	3.50
1953	3.51	3.53	3.57	3.65	3.78	3.86
1954	3.71	3.61	3.51	3.47	3.47	3.49
1955	3.45	3.47	3.48	3.49	3.50	3.51
1956	3.60	3.58	3.60	3.68	3.73	3.76
1957	4.49	4.47	4.43	4.44	4.52	4.63
1958	4.83	4.66	4.68	4.67	4.62	4.55
1959	4.87	4.89	4.85	4.86	4.96	5.04
1960	5.34	5.34	5.25	5.20	5.28	5.26
1961	5.10	5.07	5.02	5.01	5.01	5.03
1962	5.08	5.07	5.04	5.02	5.00	5.02
1963	4.91	4.89	4.88	4.87	4.85	4.84
1964	4.83	4.83	4.83	4.85	4.85	4.85
1965	4.80	4.78	4.78	4.80	4.81	4.85
1966	5.06	5.12	5.32	5.41	5.48	5.58
1967	5.97	5.82	5.85	5.83	5.96	6.15
1968	6.84	6.80	6.85	6.97	7.03	7.07
1969	7.32	7.30	7.51	7.54	7.52	7.70
1970	8.86	8.78	8.63	8.70	8.98	9.25
1971	8.74	8.39	8.46	8.45	8.62	8.75
1972	8.23	8.23	8.24	8.24	8.23	8.20
1973	7.90	7.97	8.03	8.09	8.06	8.13
1974	8.48	8.53	8.62	8.87	9.05	9.27
1975	10.81	10.65	10.48	10.58	10.69	10.62
1976	10.41	10.24	10.12	9.94	9.86	9.89
1977	9.08	9.12	9.12	9.07	9.01	8.91
1978	9.17	9.20	9.22	9.32	9.49	9.60
1979	10.13	10.08	10.26	10.33	10.47	10.38
1980	12.42	13.57	14.45	14.19	13.17	12.71
1981	15.03	15.37	15.34	15.56	15.95	15.80
1982	17.10	17.18	16.82	16.78	16.64	16.92
1983	13.94	13.95	13.61	13.29	13.09	13.37
1984	13.65	13.59	13.99	14.31	14.74	15.05
1985	13.26	13.23	13.69	13.51	13.15	12.40
1986	11.44	11.11	10.50	10.19	10.29	10.34
1987	9.72	9.65	9.61	10.04	10.51	10.52
1988	11.07	10.62	10.57	10.90	11.04	11.00
1989	10.65	10.61	10.67	10.61	10.46	10.03
1990	9.94	10.14	10.21	10.30	10.41	10.22
1991	10.45	10.07	10.09	9.94	9.86	9.96
1992	9.13	9.23	9.25	9.21	9.13	9.05
1993	8.67	8.39	8.15	8.14	8.21	8.07
1994	7.65	7.76	8.13	8.52	8.62	8.65
1995	9.08	8.85	8.70	8.60	8.20	7.90
1996	7.47	7.63	8.03	8.19	8.30	8.40
1997	8.09	7.94	8.18	8.34	8.20	8.02
1998	7.19	7.25	7.32	7.33	7.30	7.13
1999	7.29	7.39	7.53	7.48	7.72	8.02
2000	8.33	8.29	8.37	8.40	8.90	8.48
2001	7.93	7.87	7.84	8.07	8.07	7.97
2002	7.87	7.89	8.11	8.03	8.09	7.95
2003	7.35	7.06	6.95	6.85	6.38	6.19
2004	6.44	6.27	6.11	6.46	6.75	6.78
2005	6.02	5.82	6.06	6.05	6.01	5.86
2006	6.24	6.27	6.41	6.68	6.75	6.78
2007	6.34	6.28	6.27	6.39	6.39	6.70
2008	6.54	6.82	6.89	6.97	6.93	7.07
2009	8.14	8.08	8.42	8.39	8.06	7.50
2010	6.25	6.34	6.27	6.25	6.05	6.23
2011	6.09	6.15	6.03	6.02	5.78	5.75
2012	5.23	5.14	5.23	5.19	5.07	5.02
2013	4.73	4.85	4.85	4.59	4.73	5.19
2014	5.19	5.10	5.06	4.90	4.76	4.80
2015	4.45	4.51	4.54	4.48	4.89	5.13
2016	5.45	5.34	5.13	4.79	4.68	4.53
2017	4.66	4.64	4.68	4.57	4.55	4.37
2018	4.26	4.51	4.64	4.67	4.83	4.83
2019	5.12	4.95	4.84	4.70	4.63	4.46

* Source: Federal Reserve Bank of St. Louis, monthly data calculated as average of business days

MOODY'S SEASONED CORPORATE Baa* BOND YIELDS

JUL	AUG	SEP	OCT	NOV	DEC	
3.32	3.23	3.21	3.22	3.22	3.20	**1950**
3.53	3.50	3.46	3.50	3.56	3.61	**1951**
3.50	3.51	3.52	3.54	3.53	3.51	**1952**
3.86	3.85	3.88	3.82	3.75	3.74	**1953**
3.50	3.49	3.47	3.46	3.45	3.45	**1954**
3.52	3.56	3.59	3.59	3.58	3.62	**1955**
3.80	3.93	4.07	4.17	4.24	4.37	**1956**
4.73	4.82	4.93	4.99	5.09	5.03	**1957**
4.53	4.67	4.87	4.92	4.87	4.85	**1958**
5.08	5.09	5.18	5.28	5.26	5.28	**1959**
5.22	5.08	5.01	5.11	5.08	5.10	**1960**
5.09	5.11	5.12	5.13	5.11	5.10	**1961**
5.05	5.06	5.03	4.99	4.96	4.92	**1962**
4.84	4.83	4.84	4.83	4.84	4.85	**1963**
4.83	4.82	4.82	4.81	4.81	4.81	**1964**
4.88	4.88	4.91	4.93	4.95	5.02	**1965**
5.68	5.83	6.09	6.10	6.13	6.18	**1966**
6.26	6.33	6.40	6.52	6.72	6.93	**1967**
6.98	6.82	6.79	6.84	7.01	7.23	**1968**
7.84	7.86	8.05	8.22	8.25	8.65	**1969**
9.40	9.44	9.39	9.33	9.38	9.12	**1970**
8.76	8.76	8.59	8.48	8.38	8.38	**1971**
8.23	8.19	8.09	8.06	7.99	7.93	**1972**
8.24	8.53	8.63	8.41	8.42	8.48	**1973**
9.48	9.77	10.18	10.48	10.60	10.63	**1974**
10.55	10.59	10.61	10.62	10.56	10.56	**1975**
9.82	9.64	9.40	9.29	9.23	9.12	**1976**
8.87	8.82	8.80	8.89	8.95	8.99	**1977**
9.60	9.48	9.42	9.59	9.83	9.94	**1978**
10.29	10.35	10.54	11.40	11.99	12.06	**1979**
12.65	13.15	13.70	14.23	14.64	15.14	**1980**
16.17	16.34	16.92	17.11	16.39	16.55	**1981**
16.80	16.32	15.63	14.73	14.30	14.14	**1982**
13.39	13.64	13.55	13.46	13.61	13.75	**1983**
15.15	14.63	14.35	13.94	13.48	13.40	**1984**
12.43	12.50	12.48	12.36	11.99	11.58	**1985**
10.16	10.18	10.20	10.24	10.07	9.97	**1986**
10.61	10.80	11.31	11.62	11.23	11.29	**1987**
11.11	11.21	10.90	10.41	10.48	10.65	**1988**
9.87	9.88	9.91	9.81	9.81	9.82	**1989**
10.20	10.41	10.64	10.74	10.62	10.43	**1990**
9.89	9.65	9.51	9.49	9.45	9.26	**1991**
8.84	8.65	8.62	8.84	8.96	8.81	**1992**
7.93	7.60	7.34	7.31	7.66	7.69	**1993**
8.80	8.74	8.98	9.20	9.32	9.10	**1994**
8.04	8.19	7.93	7.75	7.68	7.49	**1995**
8.35	8.18	8.35	8.07	7.79	7.89	**1996**
7.75	7.82	7.70	7.57	7.42	7.32	**1997**
7.15	7.14	7.09	7.18	7.34	7.23	**1998**
7.95	8.15	8.20	8.38	8.15	8.19	**1999**
8.35	8.26	8.35	8.34	8.28	8.02	**2000**
7.97	7.85	8.03	7.91	7.81	8.05	**2001**
7.90	7.58	7.40	7.73	7.62	7.45	**2002**
6.62	7.01	6.79	6.73	6.66	6.60	**2003**
6.62	6.46	6.27	6.21	6.20	6.15	**2004**
5.95	5.96	6.03	6.30	6.39	6.32	**2005**
6.76	6.59	6.43	6.42	6.20	6.22	**2006**
6.65	6.65	6.59	6.48	6.40	6.65	**2007**
7.16	7.15	7.31	8.88	9.21	8.43	**2008**
7.09	6.58	6.31	6.29	6.32	6.37	**2009**
6.01	5.66	5.66	5.72	5.92	6.10	**2010**
5.76	5.36	5.27	5.37	5.14	5.25	**2011**
4.87	4.91	4.84	4.58	4.51	4.63	**2012**
5.32	5.42	5.47	5.31	5.38	5.38	**2013**
4.73	4.69	4.80	4.69	4.79	4.74	**2014**
5.20	5.19	5.34	5.34	5.46	5.46	**2015**
4.22	4.24	4.31	4.38	4.71	4.83	**2016**
4.39	4.31	4.30	4.32	4.27	4.22	**2017**
4.79	4.77	4.88	5.07	5.22	5.13	**2018**
4.28	3.87	3.91	3.92	3.94	3.88	**2019**

COMMODITIES

OIL - WEST TEXAS INTERMEDIATE
CLOSING VALUES $ / bbl

	JAN	FEB	MAR	APR	MAY	JUN
1950	2.6	2.6	2.6	2.6	2.6	2.6
1951	2.6	2.6	2.6	2.6	2.6	2.6
1952	2.6	2.6	2.6	2.6	2.6	2.6
1953	2.6	2.6	2.6	2.6	2.6	2.8
1954	2.8	2.8	2.8	2.8	2.8	2.8
1955	2.8	2.8	2.8	2.8	2.8	2.8
1956	2.8	2.8	2.8	2.8	2.8	2.8
1957	2.8	3.1	3.1	3.1	3.1	3.1
1958	3.1	3.1	3.1	3.1	3.1	3.1
1959	3.0	3.0	3.0	3.0	3.0	3.0
1960	3.0	3.0	3.0	3.0	3.0	3.0
1961	3.0	3.0	3.0	3.0	3.0	3.0
1962	3.0	3.0	3.0	3.0	3.0	3.0
1963	3.0	3.0	3.0	3.0	3.0	3.0
1964	3.0	3.0	3.0	3.0	3.0	3.0
1965	2.9	2.9	2.9	2.9	2.9	2.9
1966	2.9	2.9	2.9	2.9	2.9	2.9
1967	3.0	3.0	3.0	3.0	3.0	3.0
1968	3.1	3.1	3.1	3.1	3.1	3.1
1969	3.1	3.1	3.3	3.4	3.4	3.4
1970	3.4	3.4	3.4	3.4	3.4	3.4
1971	3.6	3.6	3.6	3.6	3.6	3.6
1972	3.6	3.6	3.6	3.6	3.6	3.6
1973	3.6	3.6	3.6	3.6	3.6	3.6
1974	10.1	10.1	10.1	10.1	10.1	10.1
1975	11.2	11.2	11.2	11.2	11.2	11.2
1976	11.2	12.0	12.1	12.2	12.2	12.2
1977	13.9	13.9	13.9	13.9	13.9	13.9
1978	14.9	14.9	14.9	14.9	14.9	14.9
1979	14.9	15.9	15.9	15.9	18.1	19.1
1980	32.5	37.0	38.0	39.5	39.5	39.5
1981	38.0	38.0	38.0	38.0	38.0	36.0
1982	33.9	31.6	28.5	33.5	35.9	35.1
1983	31.2	29.0	28.8	30.6	30.0	31.0
1984	29.7	30.1	30.8	30.6	30.5	30.0
1985	25.6	27.3	28.2	28.8	27.6	27.1
1986	22.9	15.4	12.6	12.8	15.4	13.5
1987	18.7	17.7	18.3	18.6	19.4	20.0
1988	17.2	16.8	16.2	17.9	17.4	16.5
1989	18.0	17.8	19.4	21.0	20.0	20.0
1990	22.6	22.1	20.4	18.6	18.2	16.9
1991	25.0	20.5	19.9	20.8	21.2	20.2
1992	18.8	19.0	18.9	20.2	20.9	22.4
1993	19.1	20.1	20.3	20.3	19.9	19.1
1994	15.0	14.8	14.7	16.4	17.9	19.1
1995	18.0	18.5	18.6	19.9	19.7	18.4
1996	18.9	19.1	21.4	23.6	21.3	20.5
1997	25.2	22.2	21.0	19.7	20.8	19.2
1998	16.7	16.1	15.0	15.4	14.9	13.7
1999	12.5	12.0	14.7	17.3	17.8	17.9
2000	27.2	29.4	29.9	25.7	28.8	31.8
2001	29.6	29.6	27.2	27.4	28.6	27.6
2002	19.7	20.7	24.4	26.3	27.0	25.5
2003	32.9	35.9	33.6	28.3	28.1	30.7
2004	34.3	34.7	36.8	36.7	40.3	38.0
2005	46.8	48.0	54.3	53.0	49.8	56.3
2006	65.5	61.6	62.9	69.7	70.9	71.0
2007	54.6	59.3	60.6	64.0	63.5	67.5
2008	93.0	95.4	105.6	112.6	125.4	133.9
2009	41.7	39.2	48.0	49.8	59.2	69.7
2010	78.2	76.4	81.2	84.5	73.8	75.4
2011	89.4	89.6	102.9	110.0	101.3	96.3
2012	100.3	102.3	106.2	103.3	94.7	82.3
2013	94.8	95.3	92.9	92.0	94.5	95.8
2014	94.6	100.8	100.8	102.1	102.2	105.8
2015	47.2	50.6	47.8	54.5	59.3	59.8
2016	31.7	30.3	37.6	40.8	46.7	48.8
2017	52.5	53.5	49.3	51.1	48.5	45.2
2018	63.7	62.2	62.7	66.3	70.0	67.9
2019	51.4	55.0	58.2	63.9	60.8	54.7

* Source: Federal Reserve

OIL - WEST TEXAS INTERMEDIATE
CLOSING VALUES $ / bbl
COMMODITIES

JUL	AUG	SEP	OCT	NOV	DEC	
2.6	2.6	2.6	2.6	2.6	2.6	1950
2.6	2.6	2.6	2.6	2.6	2.6	1951
2.6	2.6	2.6	2.6	2.6	2.6	1952
2.8	2.8	2.8	2.8	2.8	2.8	1953
2.8	2.8	2.8	2.8	2.8	2.8	1954
2.8	2.8	2.8	2.8	2.8	2.8	1955
2.8	2.8	2.8	2.8	2.8	2.8	1956
3.1	3.1	3.1	3.1	3.1	3.0	1957
3.1	3.1	3.1	3.1	3.0	3.0	1958
3.0	3.0	3.0	3.0	3.0	3.0	1959
3.0	3.0	3.0	3.0	3.0	3.0	1960
3.0	3.0	3.0	3.0	3.0	3.0	1961
3.0	3.0	3.0	3.0	3.0	3.0	1962
3.0	3.0	3.0	3.0	3.0	3.0	1963
2.9	2.9	2.9	2.9	2.9	2.9	1964
2.9	2.9	2.9	2.9	2.9	2.9	1965
2.9	2.9	3.0	3.0	3.0	3.0	1966
3.0	3.1	3.1	3.1	3.1	3.1	1967
3.1	3.1	3.1	3.1	3.1	3.1	1968
3.4	3.4	3.4	3.4	3.4	3.4	1969
3.3	3.3	3.3	3.3	3.3	3.6	1970
3.6	3.6	3.6	3.6	3.6	3.6	1971
3.6	3.6	3.6	3.6	3.6	3.6	1972
3.6	4.3	4.3	4.3	4.3	4.3	1973
10.1	10.1	10.1	11.2	11.2	11.2	1974
11.2	11.2	11.2	11.2	11.2	11.2	1975
12.2	12.2	13.9	13.9	13.9	13.9	1976
13.9	14.9	14.9	14.9	14.9	14.9	1977
14.9	14.9	14.9	14.9	14.9	14.9	1978
21.8	26.5	28.5	29.0	31.0	32.5	1979
39.5	38.0	36.0	36.0	36.0	37.0	1980
36.0	36.0	36.0	35.0	36.0	35.0	1981
34.2	34.0	35.6	35.7	34.2	31.7	1982
31.7	31.9	31.1	30.4	29.8	29.2	1983
28.8	29.3	29.3	28.8	28.1	25.4	1984
27.3	27.8	28.3	29.5	30.8	27.2	1985
11.6	15.1	14.9	14.9	15.2	16.1	1986
21.4	20.3	19.5	19.8	18.9	17.2	1987
15.5	15.5	14.5	13.8	14.0	16.3	1988
19.6	18.5	19.6	20.1	19.8	21.1	1989
18.6	27.2	33.7	35.9	32.3	27.3	1990
21.4	21.7	21.9	23.2	22.5	19.5	1991
21.8	21.4	21.9	21.7	20.3	19.4	1992
17.9	18.0	17.5	18.1	16.7	14.5	1993
19.7	18.4	17.5	17.7	18.1	17.2	1994
17.3	18.0	18.2	17.4	18.0	19.0	1995
21.3	22.0	24.0	24.9	23.7	25.4	1996
19.6	19.9	19.8	21.3	20.2	18.3	1997
14.1	13.4	15.0	14.4	12.9	11.3	1998
20.1	21.3	23.9	22.6	25.0	26.1	1999
29.8	31.2	33.9	33.1	34.4	28.5	2000
26.5	27.5	25.9	22.2	19.7	19.3	2001
26.9	28.4	29.7	28.9	26.3	29.4	2002
30.8	31.6	28.3	30.3	31.1	32.2	2003
40.7	44.9	46.0	53.1	48.5	43.3	2004
58.7	65.0	65.6	62.4	58.3	59.4	2005
74.4	73.1	63.9	58.9	59.4	62.0	2006
74.2	72.4	79.9	86.2	94.6	91.7	2007
133.4	116.6	103.9	76.7	57.4	41.0	2008
64.1	71.1	69.5	75.6	78.1	74.3	2009
76.4	76.8	75.3	81.9	84.1	89.0	2010
97.2	86.3	85.6	86.4	97.2	98.6	2011
87.9	94.2	94.7	89.6	86.7	88.3	2012
104.7	106.6	106.3	100.5	93.9	97.6	2013
103.6	96.5	93.2	84.4	75.8	59.3	2014
50.9	42.9	45.5	46.2	42.4	37.2	2015
44.7	44.7	45.2	49.8	45.7	52.0	2016
46.6	48.0	49.8	51.6	56.6	57.9	2017
71.0	68.1	70.2	70.8	57.1	49.5	2018
57.4	54.8	57.0	54.0	57.0	59.9	2019

GOLD $US/OZ LONDON PM MONTH CLOSE

	JAN	FEB	MAR	APR	MAY	JUN
1970	34.9	35.0	35.1	35.6	36.0	35.4
1971	37.9	38.7	38.9	39.0	40.5	40.1
1972	45.8	48.3	48.3	49.0	54.6	62.1
1973	65.1	74.2	84.4	90.5	102.0	120.1
1974	129.2	150.2	168.4	172.2	163.3	154.1
1975	175.8	181.8	178.2	167.0	167.0	166.3
1976	128.2	132.3	129.6	128.4	125.5	123.8
1977	132.3	142.8	148.9	147.3	143.0	143.0
1978	175.8	182.3	181.6	170.9	184.2	183.1
1979	233.7	251.3	240.1	245.3	274.6	277.5
1980	653.0	637.0	494.5	518.0	535.5	653.5
1981	506.5	489.0	513.8	482.8	479.3	426.0
1982	387.0	362.6	320.0	361.3	325.3	317.5
1983	499.5	408.5	414.8	429.3	437.5	416.0
1984	373.8	394.3	388.5	375.8	384.3	373.1
1985	306.7	287.8	329.3	321.4	314.0	317.8
1986	350.5	338.2	344.0	345.8	343.2	345.5
1987	400.5	405.9	405.9	453.3	451.0	447.3
1988	458.0	426.2	457.0	449.0	455.5	436.6
1989	394.0	387.0	383.2	377.6	361.8	373.0
1990	415.1	407.7	368.5	367.8	363.1	352.2
1991	366.0	362.7	355.7	357.8	360.4	368.4
1992	354.1	353.1	341.7	336.4	337.5	343.4
1993	330.5	327.6	337.8	354.3	374.8	378.5
1994	377.9	381.6	389.2	376.5	387.6	388.3
1995	374.9	376.4	392.0	389.8	384.3	387.1
1996	405.6	400.7	396.4	391.3	390.6	382.0
1997	345.5	358.6	348.2	340.2	345.6	334.6
1998	304.9	297.4	301.0	310.7	293.6	296.3
1999	285.4	287.1	279.5	286.6	268.6	261.0
2000	283.3	293.7	276.8	275.1	272.3	288.2
2001	264.5	266.7	257.7	263.2	267.5	270.6
2002	282.3	296.9	301.4	308.2	326.6	318.5
2003	367.5	347.5	334.9	336.8	361.4	346.0
2004	399.8	395.9	423.7	388.5	393.3	395.8
2005	422.2	435.5	427.5	435.7	414.5	437.1
2006	568.8	556.0	582.0	644.0	653.0	613.5
2007	650.5	664.2	661.8	677.0	659.1	650.5
2008	923.3	971.5	933.5	871.0	885.8	930.3
2009	919.5	952.0	916.5	883.3	975.5	934.5
2010	1078.5	1108.3	1115.5	1179.3	1207.5	1244.0
2011	1327.0	1411.0	1439.0	1535.5	1536.5	1505.5
2012	1744.0	1770.0	1662.5	1651.3	1558.0	1598.5
2013	1664.8	1588.5	1598.3	1469.0	1394.5	1192.0
2014	1251.0	1326.5	1291.75	1288.5	1250.5	1315.0
2015	1260.3	1214.0	1187.0	1180.3	1191.4	1171.0
2016	1111.8	1234.9	1237.0	1285.7	1212.1	1320.8
2017	1212.8	1255.0	1244.9	1266.4	1266.2	1242.3
2018	1345.1	1317.9	1323.9	1313.2	1305.4	1250.5
2019	1323.3	1319.2	1295.4	1282.3	1295.6	1409.0

* Source: Bank of England

GOLD $US/OZ LONDON PM MONTH CLOSE
COMMODITIES

JUL	AUG	SEP	OCT	NOV	DEC	
35.3	35.4	36.2	37.5	37.4	37.4	1970
41.0	42.7	42.0	42.5	42.9	43.5	1971
65.7	67.0	65.5	64.9	62.9	63.9	1972
120.2	106.8	103.0	100.1	94.8	106.7	1973
143.0	154.6	151.8	158.8	181.7	183.9	1974
166.7	159.8	141.3	142.9	138.2	140.3	1975
112.5	104.0	116.0	123.2	130.3	134.5	1976
144.1	146.0	154.1	161.5	160.1	165.0	1977
200.3	208.7	217.1	242.6	193.4	226.0	1978
296.5	315.1	397.3	382.0	415.7	512.0	1979
614.3	631.3	666.8	629.0	619.8	589.8	1980
406.0	425.5	428.8	427.0	414.5	397.5	1981
342.9	411.5	397.0	423.3	436.0	456.9	1982
422.0	414.3	405.0	382.0	405.0	382.4	1983
342.4	348.3	343.8	333.5	329.0	309.0	1984
327.5	333.3	326.5	325.1	325.3	326.8	1985
357.5	384.7	423.2	401.0	383.5	388.8	1986
462.5	453.4	459.5	468.8	492.5	484.1	1987
436.8	427.8	397.7	412.4	422.6	410.3	1988
368.3	359.8	366.5	375.3	408.2	398.6	1989
372.3	387.8	408.4	379.5	384.9	386.2	1990
362.9	347.4	354.9	357.5	366.3	353.2	1991
357.9	340.0	349.0	339.3	334.2	332.9	1992
401.8	371.6	355.5	369.6	370.9	391.8	1993
384.0	385.8	394.9	383.9	383.1	383.3	1994
383.4	382.4	384.0	382.7	387.8	387.0	1995
385.3	386.5	379.0	379.5	371.3	369.3	1996
326.4	325.4	332.1	311.4	296.8	290.2	1997
288.9	273.4	293.9	292.3	294.7	287.8	1998
255.6	254.8	299.0	299.1	291.4	290.3	1999
276.8	277.0	273.7	264.5	269.1	274.5	2000
265.9	273.0	293.1	278.8	275.5	276.5	2001
304.7	312.8	323.7	316.9	319.1	347.2	2002
354.8	375.6	388.0	386.3	398.4	416.3	2003
391.4	407.3	415.7	425.6	453.4	435.6	2004
429.0	433.3	473.3	470.8	495.7	513.0	2005
632.5	623.5	599.3	603.8	646.7	632.0	2006
665.5	672.0	743.0	789.5	783.5	833.8	2007
918.0	833.0	884.5	730.8	814.5	869.8	2008
939.0	955.5	995.8	1040.0	1175.8	1087.5	2009
1169.0	1246.0	1307.0	1346.8	1383.5	1405.5	2010
1628.5	1813.5	1620.0	1722.0	1746.0	1531.0	2011
1622.0	1648.5	1776.0	1719.0	1726.0	1657.5	2012
1314.5	1394.8	1326.5	1324.0	1253.0	1204.5	2013
1285.3	1285.8	1216.5	1164.8	1282.8	1206.0	2014
1098.4	1135.0	1114.0	1142.4	1061.9	1060.0	2015
1342.0	1309.3	1322.5	1272.0	1178.1	1145.9	2016
1267.6	1311.8	1283.1	1270.2	1280.2	1291.0	2017
1221.0	1202.5	1187.3	1215.0	1217.6	1279.0	2018
1427.6	1528.4	1485.3	1511.0	1460.2	1514.8	2019

FOREIGN EXCHANGE

	JAN		FEB		MAR		APR		MAY		JUN	
	US/ CDN	CDN /US	US/ CDN	CDN /US	US/ CDN	CDN /US	US/ CDN	CDN /US	US/ CDN	CDN /US	US/ CDN	CDN /US
1971	1.01	0.99	1.01	0.99	1.01	0.99	1.01	0.99	1.01	0.99	1.02	0.98
1972	1.01	0.99	1.00	1.00	1.00	1.00	1.00	1.00	0.99	1.01	0.98	1.02
1973	1.00	1.00	1.00	1.00	1.00	1.00	1.00	1.00	1.00	1.00	1.00	1.00
1974	0.99	1.01	0.98	1.02	0.97	1.03	0.97	1.03	0.96	1.04	0.97	1.03
1975	0.99	1.01	1.00	1.00	1.00	1.00	1.01	0.99	1.03	0.97	1.03	0.97
1976	1.01	0.99	0.99	1.01	0.99	1.01	0.98	1.02	0.98	1.02	0.97	1.03
1977	1.01	0.99	1.03	0.97	1.05	0.95	1.05	0.95	1.05	0.95	1.06	0.95
1978	1.10	0.91	1.11	0.90	1.13	0.89	1.14	0.88	1.12	0.89	1.12	0.89
1979	1.19	0.84	1.20	0.84	1.17	0.85	1.15	0.87	1.16	0.87	1.17	0.85
1980	1.16	0.86	1.16	0.87	1.17	0.85	1.19	0.84	1.17	0.85	1.15	0.87
1981	1.19	0.84	1.20	0.83	1.19	0.84	1.19	0.84	1.20	0.83	1.20	0.83
1982	1.19	0.84	1.21	0.82	1.22	0.82	1.23	0.82	1.23	0.81	1.28	0.78
1983	1.23	0.81	1.23	0.81	1.23	0.82	1.23	0.81	1.23	0.81	1.23	0.81
1984	1.25	0.80	1.25	0.80	1.27	0.79	1.28	0.78	1.29	0.77	1.30	0.77
1985	1.32	0.76	1.35	0.74	1.38	0.72	1.37	0.73	1.38	0.73	1.37	0.73
1986	1.41	0.71	1.40	0.71	1.40	0.71	1.39	0.72	1.38	0.73	1.39	0.72
1987	1.36	0.73	1.33	0.75	1.32	0.76	1.32	0.76	1.34	0.75	1.34	0.75
1988	1.29	0.78	1.27	0.79	1.25	0.80	1.24	0.81	1.24	0.81	1.22	0.82
1989	1.19	0.84	1.19	0.84	1.20	0.84	1.19	0.84	1.19	0.84	1.20	0.83
1990	1.17	0.85	1.20	0.84	1.18	0.85	1.16	0.86	1.17	0.85	1.17	0.85
1991	1.16	0.87	1.15	0.87	1.16	0.86	1.15	0.87	1.15	0.87	1.14	0.87
1992	1.16	0.86	1.18	0.85	1.19	0.84	1.19	0.84	1.20	0.83	1.20	0.84
1993	1.28	0.78	1.26	0.79	1.25	0.80	1.26	0.79	1.27	0.79	1.28	0.78
1994	1.32	0.76	1.34	0.74	1.36	0.73	1.38	0.72	1.38	0.72	1.38	0.72
1995	1.41	0.71	1.40	0.71	1.41	0.71	1.38	0.73	1.36	0.73	1.38	0.73
1996	1.37	0.73	1.38	0.73	1.37	0.73	1.36	0.74	1.37	0.73	1.37	0.73
1997	1.35	0.74	1.36	0.74	1.37	0.73	1.39	0.72	1.38	0.72	1.38	0.72
1998	1.44	0.69	1.43	0.70	1.42	0.71	1.43	0.70	1.45	0.69	1.47	0.68
1999	1.52	0.66	1.50	0.67	1.52	0.66	1.49	0.67	1.46	0.68	1.47	0.68
2000	1.45	0.69	1.45	0.69	1.46	0.68	1.47	0.68	1.50	0.67	1.48	0.68
2001	1.50	0.67	1.52	0.66	1.56	0.64	1.56	0.64	1.54	0.65	1.52	0.66
2002	1.60	0.63	1.60	0.63	1.59	0.63	1.58	0.63	1.55	0.65	1.53	0.65
2003	1.54	0.65	1.51	0.66	1.48	0.68	1.46	0.69	1.38	0.72	1.35	0.74
2004	1.30	0.77	1.33	0.75	1.33	0.75	1.34	0.75	1.38	0.73	1.36	0.74
2005	1.22	0.82	1.24	0.81	1.22	0.82	1.24	0.81	1.26	0.80	1.24	0.81
2006	1.16	0.86	1.15	0.87	1.16	0.86	1.14	0.87	1.11	0.90	1.11	0.90
2007	1.18	0.85	1.17	0.85	1.17	0.86	1.14	0.88	1.10	0.91	1.07	0.94
2008	1.01	0.99	1.00	1.00	1.00	1.00	1.01	0.99	1.00	1.00	1.02	0.98
2009	1.22	0.82	1.25	0.80	1.26	0.79	1.22	0.82	1.15	0.87	1.13	0.89
2010	1.04	0.96	1.06	0.95	1.02	0.98	1.01	0.99	1.04	0.96	1.04	0.96
2011	0.99	1.01	0.99	1.01	0.98	1.02	0.96	1.04	0.97	1.03	0.98	1.02
2012	1.01	0.99	1.00	1.00	0.99	1.01	0.99	1.01	1.01	0.99	1.03	0.97
2013	0.99	1.01	1.01	0.99	1.02	.098	1.02	0.98	1.02	0.98	1.03	0.97
2014	1.09	0.91	1.11	0.90	1.11	0.90	1.10	0.91	1.09	0.92	1.08	0.92
2015	1.21	0.82	1.25	0.80	1.26	0.79	1.23	0.81	1.22	0.82	1.24	0.81
2016	1.42	0.70	1.38	0.72	1.32	0.76	1,28	0.78	1.29	0.77	1.29	0.78
2017	1.30	0.77	1.32	0.75	1.33	0.75	1.37	0.73	1.35	0.74	1.30	0.77
2018	1.24	0.80	1.26	0.79	1.29	0.77	1.27	0.79	1.29	0.78	1.31	0.76
2019	1.33	0.75	1.32	0.76	1.34	0.75	1.34	0.75	1.35	0.74	1.33	0.75

Source: Federal Reserve: Avg of daily rates, noon buying rates in New York City for transfers payable in foreign currencies

US DOLLAR vs CDN DOLLAR MONTHLY AVG. VALUES

JUL US/CDN	JUL CDN/US	AUG US/CDN	AUG CDN/US	SEP US/CDN	SEP CDN/US	OCT US/CDN	OCT CDN/US	NOV US/CDN	NOV CDN/US	DEC US/CDN	DEC CDN/US	
1.02	0.98	1.01	0.99	1.01	0.99	1.00	1.00	1.00	1.00	1.00	1.00	1971
0.98	1.02	0.98	1.02	0.98	1.02	0.98	1.02	0.99	1.01	1.00	1.00	1972
1.00	1.00	1.00	1.00	1.01	0.99	1.00	1.00	1.00	1.00	1.00	1.00	1973
0.98	1.02	0.98	1.02	0.99	1.01	0.98	1.02	0.99	1.01	0.99	1.01	1974
1.03	0.97	1.04	0.97	1.03	0.97	1.03	0.98	1.01	0.99	1.01	0.99	1975
0.97	1.03	0.99	1.01	0.98	1.03	0.97	1.03	0.99	1.01	1.02	0.98	1976
1.06	0.94	1.08	0.93	1.07	0.93	1.10	0.91	1.11	0.90	1.10	0.91	1977
1.12	0.89	1.14	0.88	1.17	0.86	1.18	0.85	1.17	0.85	1.18	0.85	1978
1.16	0.86	1.17	0.85	1.17	0.86	1.18	0.85	1.18	0.85	1.17	0.85	1979
1.15	0.87	1.16	0.86	1.16	0.86	1.17	0.86	1.19	0.84	1.20	0.84	1980
1.21	0.83	1.22	0.82	1.20	0.83	1.20	0.83	1.19	0.84	1.19	0.84	1981
1.27	0.79	1.25	0.80	1.23	0.81	1.23	0.81	1.23	0.82	1.24	0.81	1982
1.23	0.81	1.23	0.81	1.23	0.81	1.23	0.81	1.24	0.81	1.25	0.80	1983
1.32	0.76	1.30	0.77	1.31	0.76	1.32	0.76	1.32	0.76	1.32	0.76	1984
1.35	0.74	1.36	0.74	1.37	0.73	1.37	0.73	1.38	0.73	1.40	0.72	1985
1.38	0.72	1.39	0.72	1.39	0.72	1.39	0.72	1.39	0.72	1.38	0.72	1986
1.33	0.75	1.33	0.75	1.32	0.76	1.31	0.76	1.32	0.76	1.31	0.76	1987
1.21	0.83	1.22	0.82	1.23	0.82	1.21	0.83	1.22	0.82	1.20	0.84	1988
1.19	0.84	1.18	0.85	1.18	0.85	1.17	0.85	1.17	0.85	1.16	0.86	1989
1.16	0.86	1.14	0.87	1.16	0.86	1.16	0.86	1.16	0.86	1.16	0.86	1990
1.15	0.87	1.15	0.87	1.14	0.88	1.13	0.89	1.13	0.88	1.15	0.87	1991
1.19	0.84	1.19	0.84	1.22	0.82	1.25	0.80	1.27	0.79	1.27	0.79	1992
1.28	0.78	1.31	0.76	1.32	0.76	1.33	0.75	1.32	0.76	1.33	0.75	1993
1.38	0.72	1.38	0.73	1.35	0.74	1.35	0.74	1.36	0.73	1.39	0.72	1994
1.36	0.73	1.36	0.74	1.35	0.74	1.35	0.74	1.35	0.74	1.37	0.73	1995
1.37	0.73	1.37	0.73	1.37	0.73	1.35	0.74	1.34	0.75	1.36	0.73	1996
1.38	0.73	1.39	0.72	1.39	0.72	1.39	0.72	1.41	0.71	1.43	0.70	1997
1.49	0.67	1.53	0.65	1.52	0.66	1.55	0.65	1.54	0.65	1.54	0.65	1998
1.49	0.67	1.49	0.67	1.48	0.68	1.48	0.68	1.47	0.68	1.47	0.68	1999
1.48	0.68	1.48	0.67	1.49	0.67	1.51	0.66	1.54	0.65	1.52	0.66	2000
1.53	0.65	1.54	0.65	1.57	0.64	1.57	0.64	1.59	0.63	1.58	0.63	2001
1.55	0.65	1.57	0.64	1.58	0.63	1.58	0.63	1.57	0.64	1.56	0.64	2002
1.38	0.72	1.40	0.72	1.36	0.73	1.32	0.76	1.31	0.76	1.31	0.76	2003
1.32	0.76	1.31	0.76	1.29	0.78	1.25	0.80	1.20	0.84	1.22	0.82	2004
1.22	0.82	1.20	0.83	1.18	0.85	1.18	0.85	1.18	0.85	1.16	0.86	2005
1.13	0.89	1.12	0.89	1.12	0.90	1.13	0.89	1.14	0.88	1.15	0.87	2006
1.05	0.95	1.06	0.95	1.03	0.97	0.98	1.03	0.97	1.03	1.00	1.00	2007
1.01	0.99	1.05	0.95	1.06	0.95	1.18	0.84	1.22	0.82	1.23	0.81	2008
1.12	0.89	1.09	0.92	1.08	0.92	1.05	0.95	1.06	0.94	1.05	0.95	2009
1.04	0.96	1.04	0.96	1.03	0.97	1.02	0.98	1.01	0.99	1.01	0.99	2010
0.96	1.05	0.98	1.02	1.00	1.00	1.02	0.98	1.02	0.98	1.02	0.98	2011
1.01	0.99	0.99	1.01	.098	1.02	0.99	1.01	1.00	1.00	0.99	1.01	2012
1.04	0.96	1.04	0.96	1.03	0.97	1.04	0.96	1.05	0.95	1.06	0.94	2013
1.07	0.93	1.09	0.92	1.10	0.91	1.12	0.89	1.13	0.88	1.15	0.87	2014
1.29	0.78	1.31	0.76	1.33	0.75	1.31	0.76	1.33	0.75	1.37	0.73	2015
1.31	0.77	1.30	0.77	1.31	0.76	1.33	0.75	1.34	0.74	1.33	0.75	2016
1.25	0.80	1.25	0.80	1.25	0.80	1.29	0.78	1.29	0.78	1.25	0.80	2017
1.31	0.76	1.30	0.77	1.30	0.77	1.30	0.77	1.32	0.76	1.34	0.74	2018
1.31	0.76	1.33	0.75	1.32	0.76	1.32	0.76	1.32	0.76	1.32	0.76	2019

U.S. DOLLAR vs EURO
MONTHLY AVG. VALUES

	JAN		FEB		MAR		APR		MAY		JUN	
	EUR / US	US / EUR	EUR / US	US / EUR	EUR / US	US / EUR	EUR / US	US / EUR	EUR / US	US / EUR	EUR / US	US / EUR
1999	1.16	0.86	1.12	0.89	1.09	0.92	1.07	0.93	1.06	0.94	1.04	0.96
2000	1.01	0.99	0.98	1.02	0.96	1.04	0.94	1.06	0.91	1.10	0.95	1.05
2001	0.94	1.07	0.92	1.09	0.91	1.10	0.89	1.12	0.88	1.14	0.85	1.17
2002	0.88	1.13	0.87	1.15	0.88	1.14	0.89	1.13	0.92	1.09	0.96	1.05
2003	1.06	0.94	1.08	0.93	1.08	0.93	1.09	0.92	1.16	0.87	1.17	0.86
2004	1.26	0.79	1.26	0.79	1.23	0.82	1.20	0.83	1.20	0.83	1.21	0.82
2005	1.31	0.76	1.30	0.77	1.32	0.76	1.29	0.77	1.27	0.79	1.22	0.82
2006	1.21	0.82	1.19	0.84	1.20	0.83	1.23	0.81	1.28	0.78	1.27	0.79
2007	1.30	0.77	1.31	0.76	1.32	0.75	1.35	0.74	1.35	0.74	1.34	0.75
2008	1.47	0.68	1.48	0.68	1.55	0.64	1.58	0.63	1.56	0.64	1.56	0.64
2009	1.32	0.76	1.28	0.78	1.31	0.77	1.32	0.76	1.36	0.73	1.40	0.71
2010	1.43	0.70	1.37	0.73	1.36	0.74	1.34	0.75	1.26	0.80	1.22	0.82
2011	1.34	0.75	1.37	0.73	1.40	0.71	1.45	0.69	1.43	0.70	1.44	0.69
2012	1.29	0.77	1.32	0.76	1.32	0.76	1.32	0.76	1.28	0.78	1.25	0.80
2013	1.33	0.75	1.33	0.75	1.30	0.77	1.30	0.77	1.30	0.77	1.32	0.76
2014	1.36	0.73	1.37	0.73	1.38	0.72	1.38	0.72	1.37	0.73	1.36	0.74
2015	1.16	0.86	1.14	0.88	1.08	0.92	1.08	0.92	1.12	0.90	1.12	0.89
2016	1.09	0.92	1.11	0.90	1.11	0.90	1.13	0.88	1.13	0.88	1.12	0.89
2017	1.06	0.94	1.07	0.94	1.07	0.94	1.07	0.93	1.11	0.90	1.12	0.89
2018	1.22	0.82	1.23	0.81	1.23	0.81	1.23	0.81	1.18	0.85	1.17	0.86
2019	1.14	0.88	1.13	0.88	1.13	0.89	1.12	0.89	1.12	0.89	1.13	0.89

Source: Federal Reserve: Avg of daily rates, noon buying rates in New York City for cable transfers payable in foreign currencies

US DOLLAR vs EURO
MONTHLY AVG. VALUES

JUL		AUG		SEP		OCT		NOV		DEC		
EUR / US	US / EUR	EUR / US	US / EUR	EUR / US	US / EUR	EUR / US	US / EUR	EUR / US	US / EUR	EUR / US	US / EUR	
1.04	0.96	1.06	0.94	1.05	0.95	1.07	0.93	1.03	0.97	1.01	0.99	1999
0.94	1.07	0.90	1.11	0.87	1.15	0.85	1.17	0.86	1.17	0.90	1.11	2000
0.86	1.16	0.90	1.11	0.91	1.10	0.91	1.10	0.89	1.13	0.89	1.12	2001
0.99	1.01	0.98	1.02	0.98	1.02	0.98	1.02	1.00	1.00	1.02	0.98	2002
1.14	0.88	1.12	0.90	1.13	0.89	1.17	0.85	1.17	0.85	1.23	0.81	2003
1.23	0.82	1.22	0.82	1.22	0.82	1.25	0.80	1.30	0.77	1.34	0.75	2004
1.20	0.83	1.23	0.81	1.22	0.82	1.20	0.83	1.18	0.85	1.19	0.84	2005
1.27	0.79	1.28	0.78	1.27	0.79	1.26	0.79	1.29	0.78	1.32	0.76	2006
1.37	0.73	1.36	0.73	1.39	0.72	1.42	0.70	1.47	0.68	1.46	0.69	2007
1.58	0.63	1.50	0.67	1.43	0.70	1.33	0.75	1.27	0.78	1.35	0.74	2008
1.41	0.71	1.43	0.70	1.46	0.69	1.48	0.67	1.49	0.67	1.46	0.69	2009
1.28	0.78	1.29	0.78	1.31	0.76	1.39	0.72	1.37	0.73	1.32	0.76	2010
1.43	0.70	1.43	0.70	1.37	0.73	1.37	0.73	1.36	0.74	1.32	0.76	2011
1.23	0.81	1.24	0.81	1.29	0.78	1.30	0.77	1.28	0.78	1.31	0.76	2012
1.31	0.76	1.33	0.75	1.34	0.75	1.36	0.73	1.35	0.74	1.37	0.73	2013
1.35	0.74	1.33	0.75	1.29	0.78	1.27	0.79	1.25	0.80	1.23	0.81	2014
1.10	0.91	1.11	0.90	1.12	0.89	1.12	0.89	1.07	0.93	1.09	0.92	2015
1.11	0.90	1.12	0.89	1.12	0.89	1.10	0.91	1.08	0.93	1.05	0.95	2016
1.15	0.87	1.18	0.85	1.19	0.84	1.18	0.85	1.17	0.85	1.18	0.84	2017
1.17	0.86	1.15	0.87	1.17	0.86	1.15	0.87	1.14	0.88	1.14	0.88	2018
1.12	0.89	1.11	0.90	1.10	0.91	1.11	0.90	1.11	0.90	1.11	0.90	2019